Max Brooks
story & script

Raulo Caceres
pencils & inks

Digikore Studios
colors

Kurt Hathaway
letters

William Christensen
editor-in-chief

Mark Seifert
creative director

Jim Kuhoric
managing editor

David Marks
director of events

Ariana Osborne
production assistant

The Extinction Parade Volume 1
March 2014. Published by Avatar Press, Inc.,
515 N. Century Blvd. Rantoul, IL 61866. ©2014 Avatar Press,
Inc. The Extinction Parade and all related properties TM &
©2014 Max Brooks. All characters as depicted in this story
are over the age of 18. The stories, characters, and institutions
mentioned in this magazine are entirely fictional.
Printed in Canada.

AVATAR

w w w . a v a t a r p r e s s . c o m
www.twitter.com/avatarpress
www.facebook.com/avatarpresscomics

Chapter 1

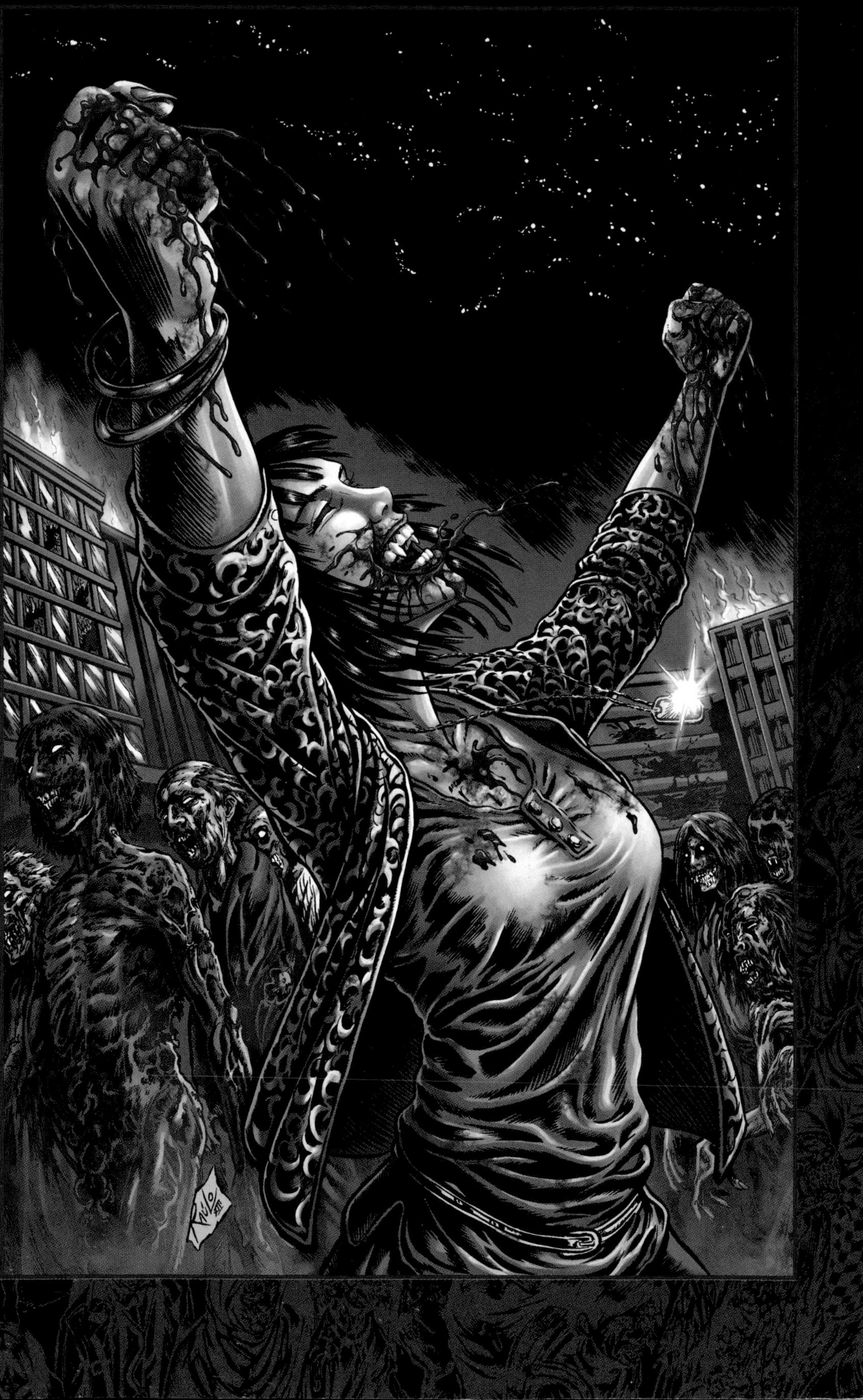

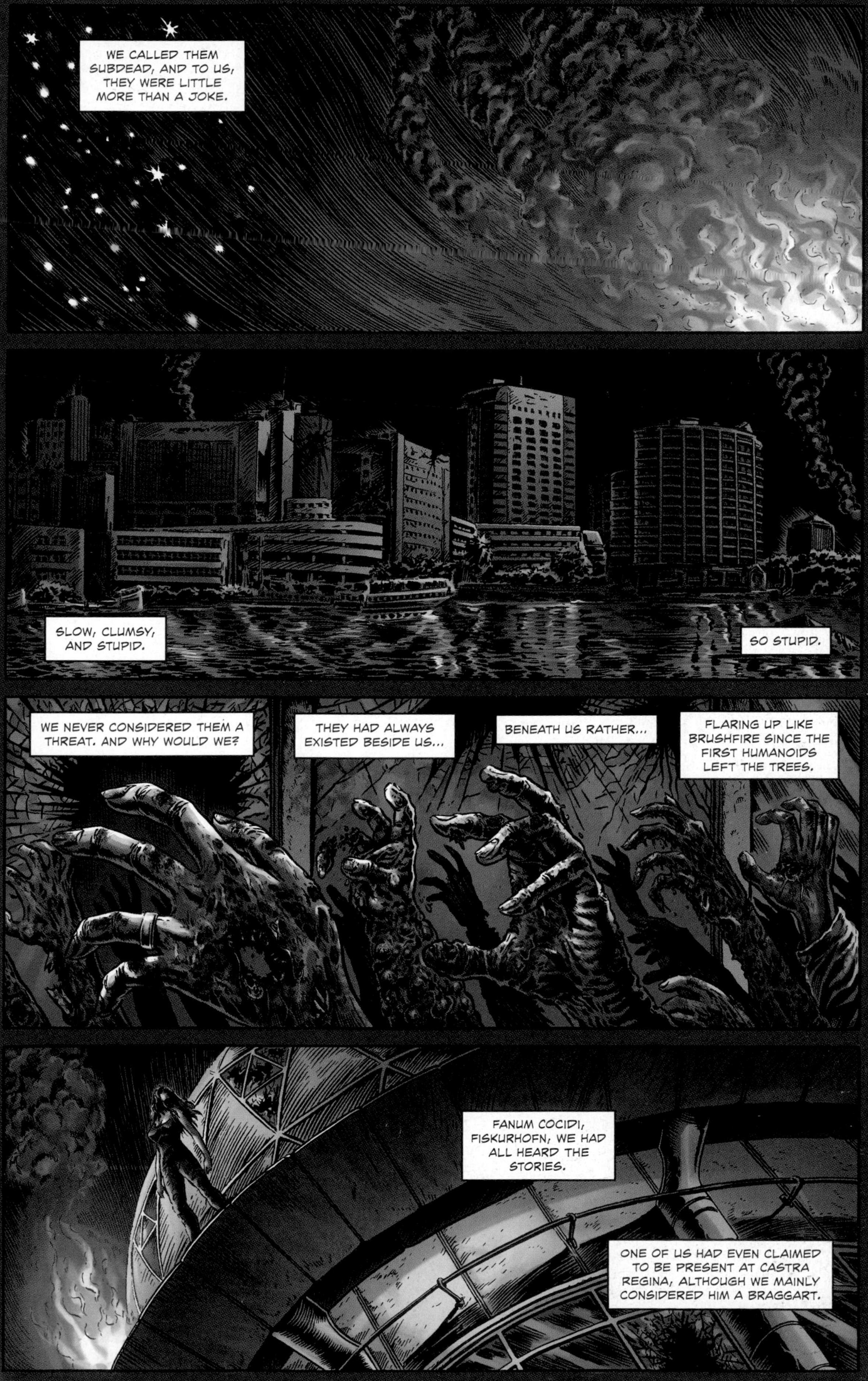
WE CALLED THEM SUBDEAD, AND TO US, THEY WERE LITTLE MORE THAN A JOKE.
SLOW, CLUMSY, AND STUPID.
SO STUPID.
WE NEVER CONSIDERED THEM A THREAT. AND WHY WOULD WE?
THEY HAD ALWAYS EXISTED BESIDE US...
BENEATH US RATHER...
FLARING UP LIKE BRUSHFIRE SINCE THE FIRST HUMANOIDS LEFT THE TREES.
FANUM COCIDI, FISKURHOFN, WE HAD ALL HEARD THE STORIES.
ONE OF US HAD EVEN CLAIMED TO BE PRESENT AT CASTRA REGINA, ALTHOUGH WE MAINLY CONSIDERED HIM A BRAGGART.

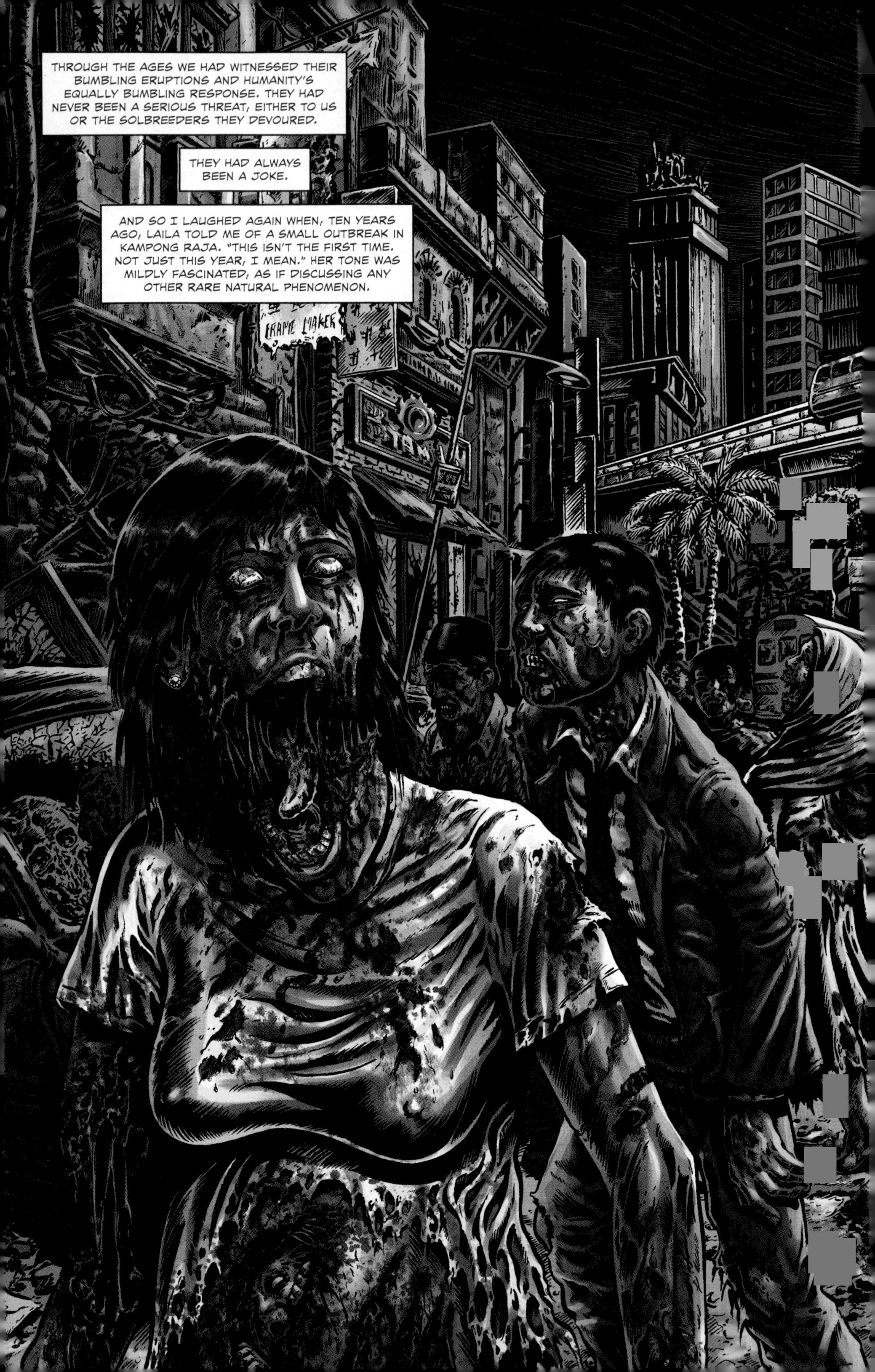
THROUGH THE AGES WE HAD WITNESSED THEIR BUMBLING ERUPTIONS AND HUMANITY'S EQUALLY BUMBLING RESPONSE. THEY HAD NEVER BEEN A SERIOUS THREAT, EITHER TO US OR THE SOLBREEDERS THEY DEVOURED.
THEY HAD ALWAYS BEEN A JOKE.
AND SO I LAUGHED AGAIN WHEN, TEN YEARS AGO, LAILA TOLD ME OF A SMALL OUTBREAK IN KAMPONG RAJA. "THIS ISN'T THE FIRST TIME. NOT JUST THIS YEAR, I MEAN." HER TONE WAS MILDLY FASCINATED, AS IF DISCUSSING ANY OTHER RARE NATURAL PHENOMENON.
FRAME MAKER

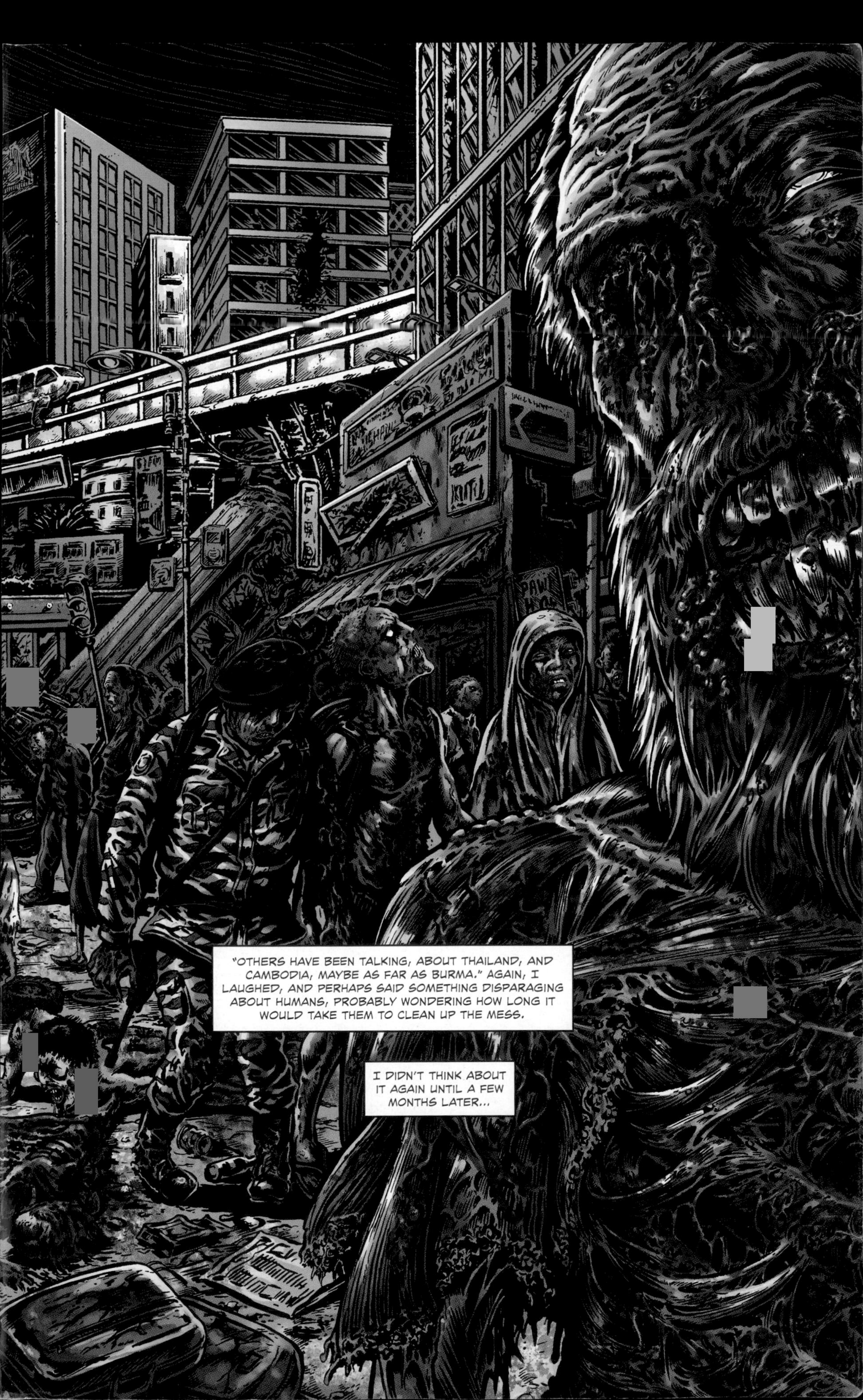
"OTHERS HAVE BEEN TALKING, ABOUT THAILAND, AND CAMBODIA, MAYBE AS FAR AS BURMA." AGAIN, I LAUGHED, AND PERHAPS SAID SOMETHING DISPARAGING ABOUT HUMANS, PROBABLY WONDERING HOW LONG IT WOULD TAKE THEM TO CLEAN UP THE MESS.
I DIDN'T THINK ABOUT IT AGAIN UNTIL A FEW MONTHS LATER...

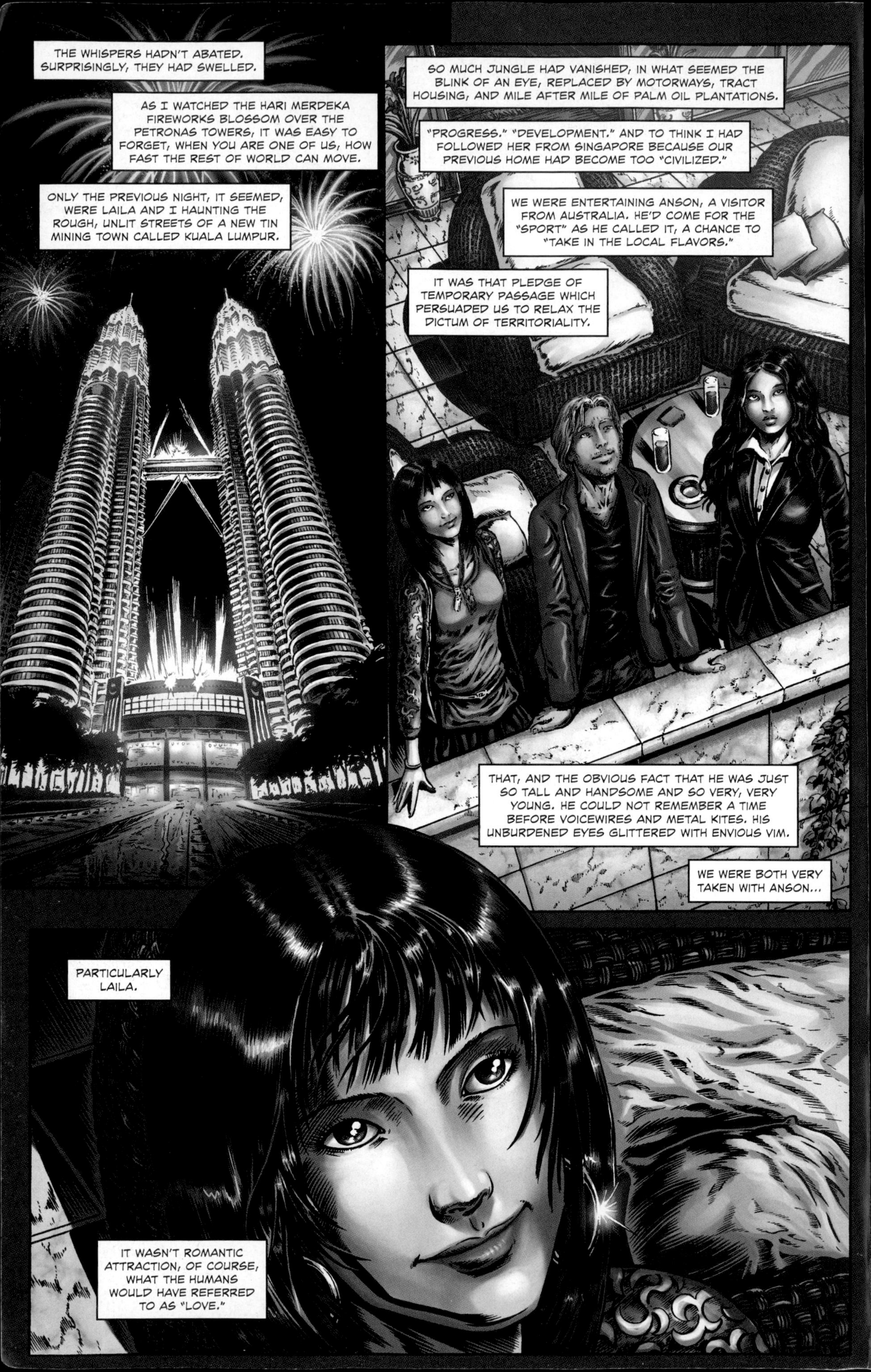
THE WHISPERS HADN'T ABATED. SURPRISINGLY, THEY HAD SWELLED.
AS I WATCHED THE HARI MERDEKA FIREWORKS BLOSSOM OVER THE PETRONAS TOWERS, IT WAS EASY TO FORGET, WHEN YOU ARE ONE OF US, HOW FAST THE REST OF WORLD CAN MOVE.
ONLY THE PREVIOUS NIGHT, IT SEEMED, WERE LAILA AND I HAUNTING THE ROUGH, UNLIT STREETS OF A NEW TIN MINING TOWN CALLED KUALA LUMPUR.
SO MUCH JUNGLE HAD VANISHED, IN WHAT SEEMED THE BLINK OF AN EYE, REPLACED BY MOTORWAYS, TRACT HOUSING, AND MILE AFTER MILE OF PALM OIL PLANTATIONS.
"PROGRESS." "DEVELOPMENT." AND TO THINK I HAD FOLLOWED HER FROM SINGAPORE BECAUSE OUR PREVIOUS HOME HAD BECOME TOO "CIVILIZED."
WE WERE ENTERTAINING ANSON, A VISITOR FROM AUSTRALIA. HE'D COME FOR THE "SPORT" AS HE CALLED IT, A CHANCE TO "TAKE IN THE LOCAL FLAVORS."
IT WAS THAT PLEDGE OF TEMPORARY PASSAGE WHICH PERSUADED US TO RELAX THE DICTUM OF TERRITORIALITY.
THAT, AND THE OBVIOUS FACT THAT HE WAS JUST SO TALL AND HANDSOME AND SO VERY, VERY YOUNG. HE COULD NOT REMEMBER A TIME BEFORE VOICEWIRES AND METAL KITES. HIS UNBURDENED EYES GLITTERED WITH ENVIOUS VIM.
WE WERE BOTH VERY TAKEN WITH ANSON...
PARTICULARLY LAILA.
IT WASN'T ROMANTIC ATTRACTION, OF COURSE, WHAT THE HUMANS WOULD HAVE REFERRED TO AS "LOVE."

AFTER ALL, WHAT WAS HUMAN "LOVE..."

...BUT AN APOLOGETIC PERFUME...

...FOR THE STENCH OF HUMAN LUST?

BECAUSE OUR BIOLOGY WAS SO MERCIFULLY DIFFERENT THAN THE "SOLBREEDER" RACE BELOW US, BECAUSE OUR METHOD OF REPRODUCTION WAS RARE, VOLUNTARY AND COMPLETELY DEVOID OF GENITAL CONTACT, OUR BODIES WERE AS FREE FROM THE EMBARRASSMENT OF LIBIDINOUS DESIRES AS OUR MINDS... OUR "HEARTS" WERE, OF THE PSYCHO-EMOTIONAL NEED TO JUSTIFY THEM.

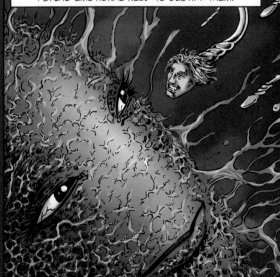

AND YET...

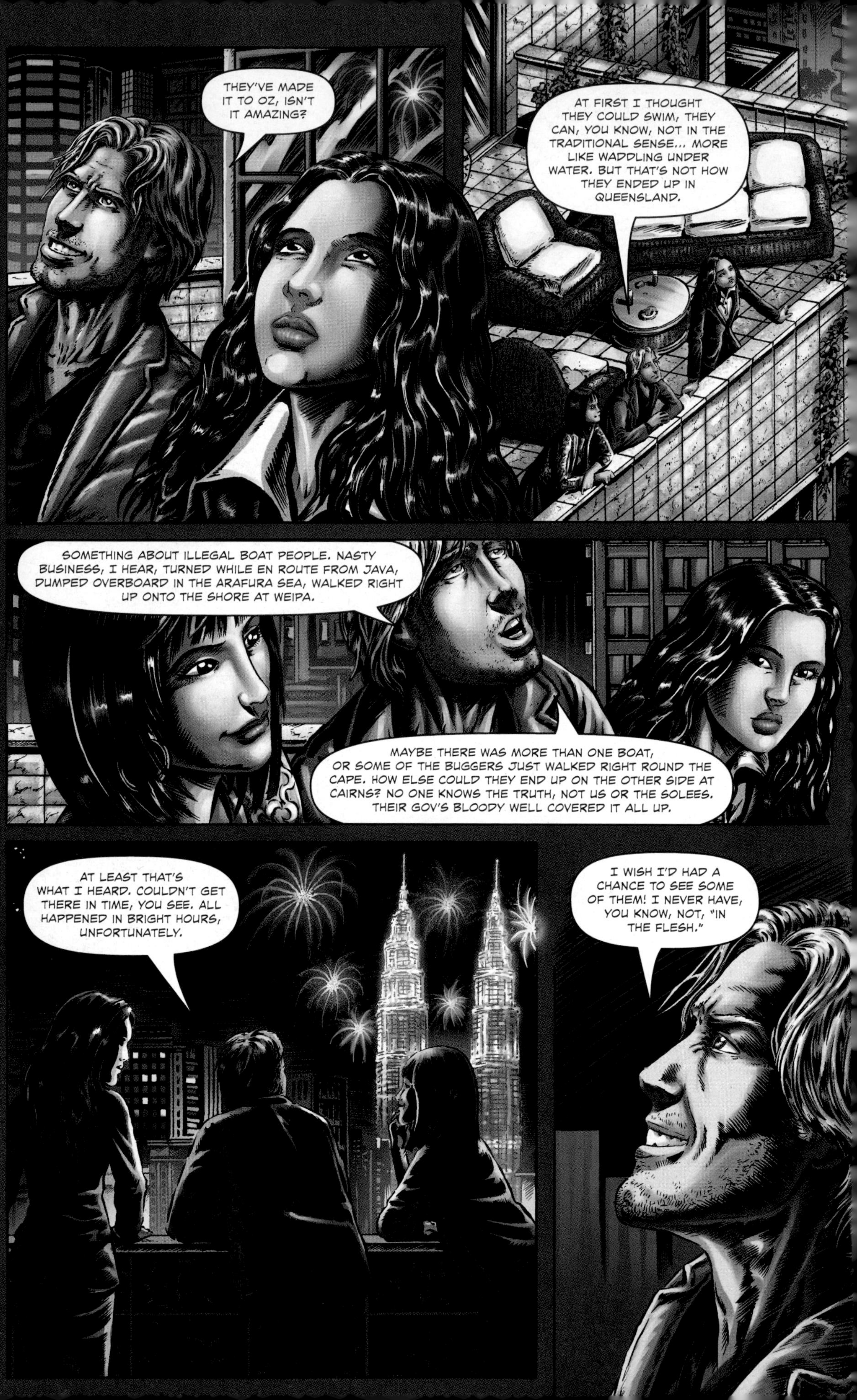
THEY'VE MADE IT TO OZ, ISN'T IT AMAZING?
AT FIRST I THOUGHT THEY COULD SWIM, THEY CAN, YOU KNOW, NOT IN THE TRADITIONAL SENSE... MORE LIKE WADDLING UNDER WATER. BUT THAT'S NOT HOW THEY ENDED UP IN QUEENSLAND.
SOMETHING ABOUT ILLEGAL BOAT PEOPLE. NASTY BUSINESS, I HEAR, TURNED WHILE EN ROUTE FROM JAVA, DUMPED OVERBOARD IN THE ARAFURA SEA, WALKED RIGHT UP ONTO THE SHORE AT WEIPA.
MAYBE THERE WAS MORE THAN ONE BOAT, OR SOME OF THE BUGGERS JUST WALKED RIGHT ROUND THE CAPE. HOW ELSE COULD THEY END UP ON THE OTHER SIDE AT CAIRNS? NO ONE KNOWS THE TRUTH, NOT US OR THE SOLEES. THEIR GOV'S BLOODY WELL COVERED IT ALL UP.
AT LEAST THAT'S WHAT I HEARD. COULDN'T GET THERE IN TIME, YOU SEE. ALL HAPPENED IN BRIGHT HOURS, UNFORTUNATELY.
I WISH I'D HAD A CHANCE TO SEE SOME OF THEM! I NEVER HAVE, YOU KNOW, NOT, "IN THE FLESH."

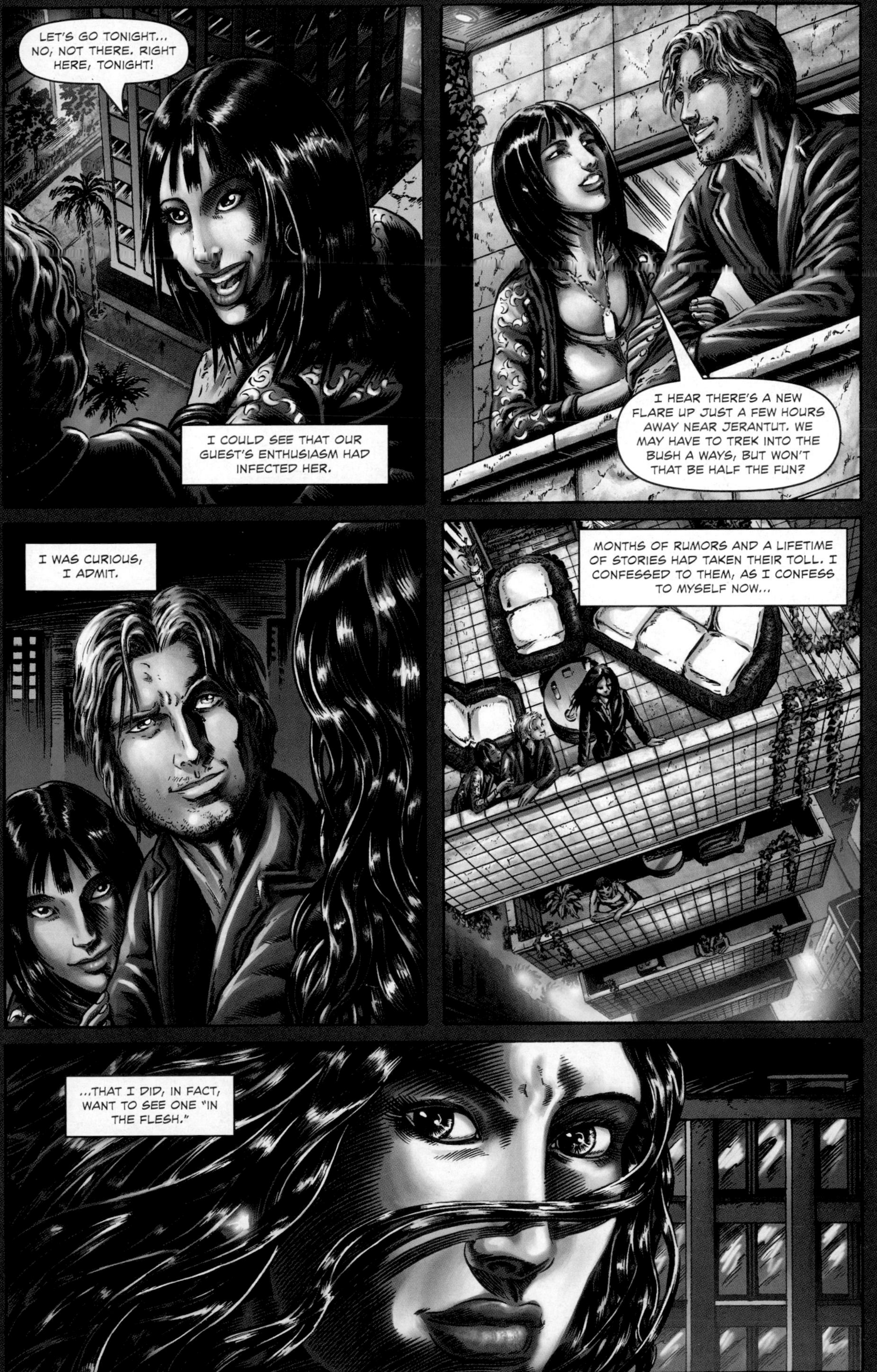
LET'S GO TONIGHT... NO, NOT THERE. RIGHT HERE, TONIGHT!
I COULD SEE THAT OUR GUEST'S ENTHUSIASM HAD INFECTED HER.
I HEAR THERE'S A NEW FLARE UP JUST A FEW HOURS AWAY NEAR JERANTUT. WE MAY HAVE TO TREK INTO THE BUSH A WAYS, BUT WON'T THAT BE HALF THE FUN?
I WAS CURIOUS, I ADMIT.
MONTHS OF RUMORS AND A LIFETIME OF STORIES HAD TAKEN THEIR TOLL. I CONFESSED TO THEM, AS I CONFESS TO MYSELF NOW...
...THAT I DID, IN FACT, WANT TO SEE ONE "IN THE FLESH."

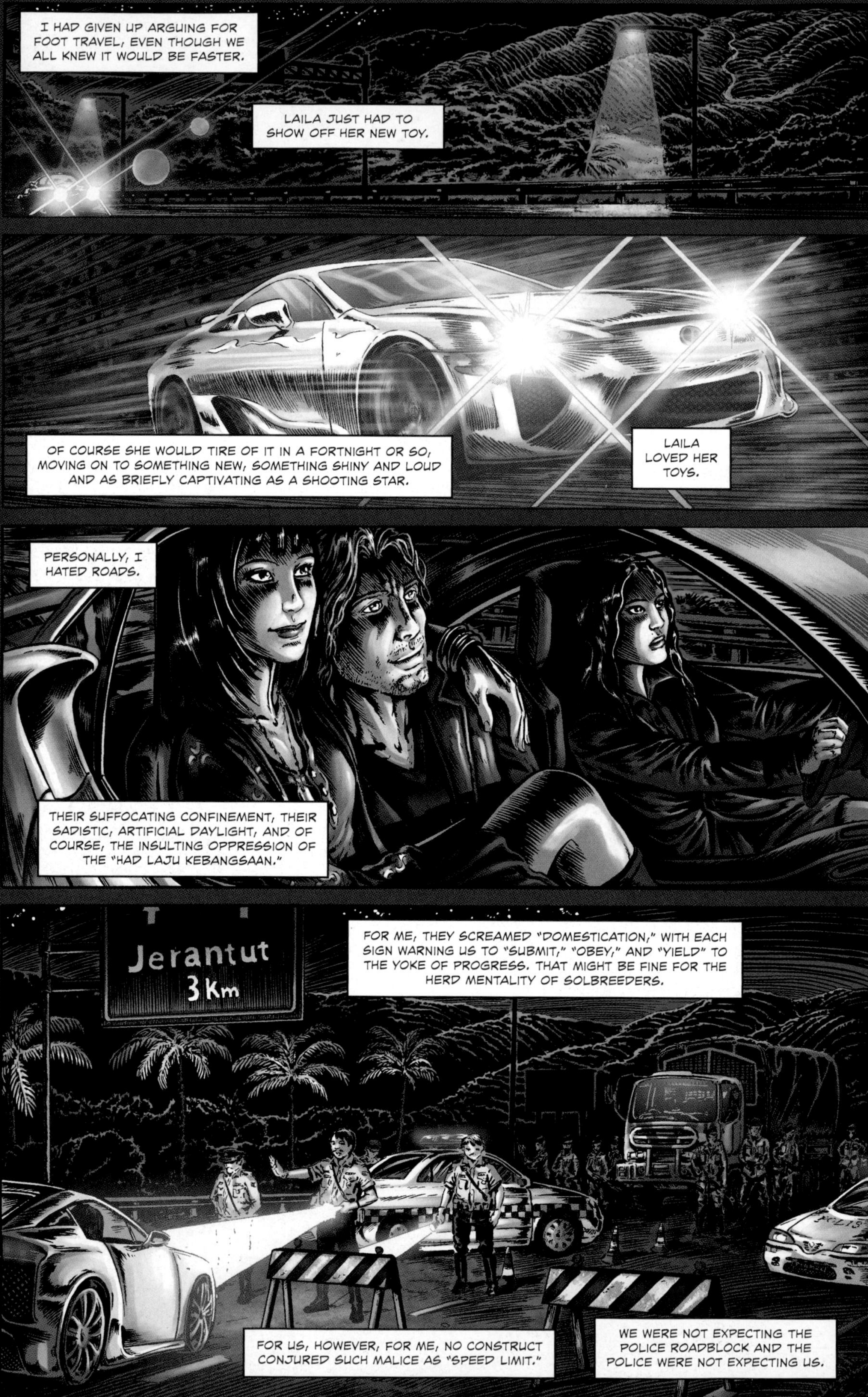
I HAD GIVEN UP ARGUING FOR FOOT TRAVEL, EVEN THOUGH WE ALL KNEW IT WOULD BE FASTER.
LAILA JUST HAD TO SHOW OFF HER NEW TOY.
OF COURSE SHE WOULD TIRE OF IT IN A FORTNIGHT OR SO, MOVING ON TO SOMETHING NEW, SOMETHING SHINY AND LOUD AND AS BRIEFLY CAPTIVATING AS A SHOOTING STAR.
LAILA LOVED HER TOYS.
PERSONALLY, I HATED ROADS.
THEIR SUFFOCATING CONFINEMENT, THEIR SADISTIC, ARTIFICIAL DAYLIGHT, AND OF COURSE, THE INSULTING OPPRESSION OF THE "HAD LAJU KEBANGSAAN."
Jerantut
3 Km
FOR ME, THEY SCREAMED "DOMESTICATION," WITH EACH SIGN WARNING US TO "SUBMIT," "OBEY," AND "YIELD" TO THE YOKE OF PROGRESS. THAT MIGHT BE FINE FOR THE HERD MENTALITY OF SOLBREEDERS.
FOR US, HOWEVER, FOR ME, NO CONSTRUCT CONJURED SUCH MALICE AS "SPEED LIMIT."
WE WERE NOT EXPECTING THE POLICE ROADBLOCK AND THE POLICE WERE NOT EXPECTING US.

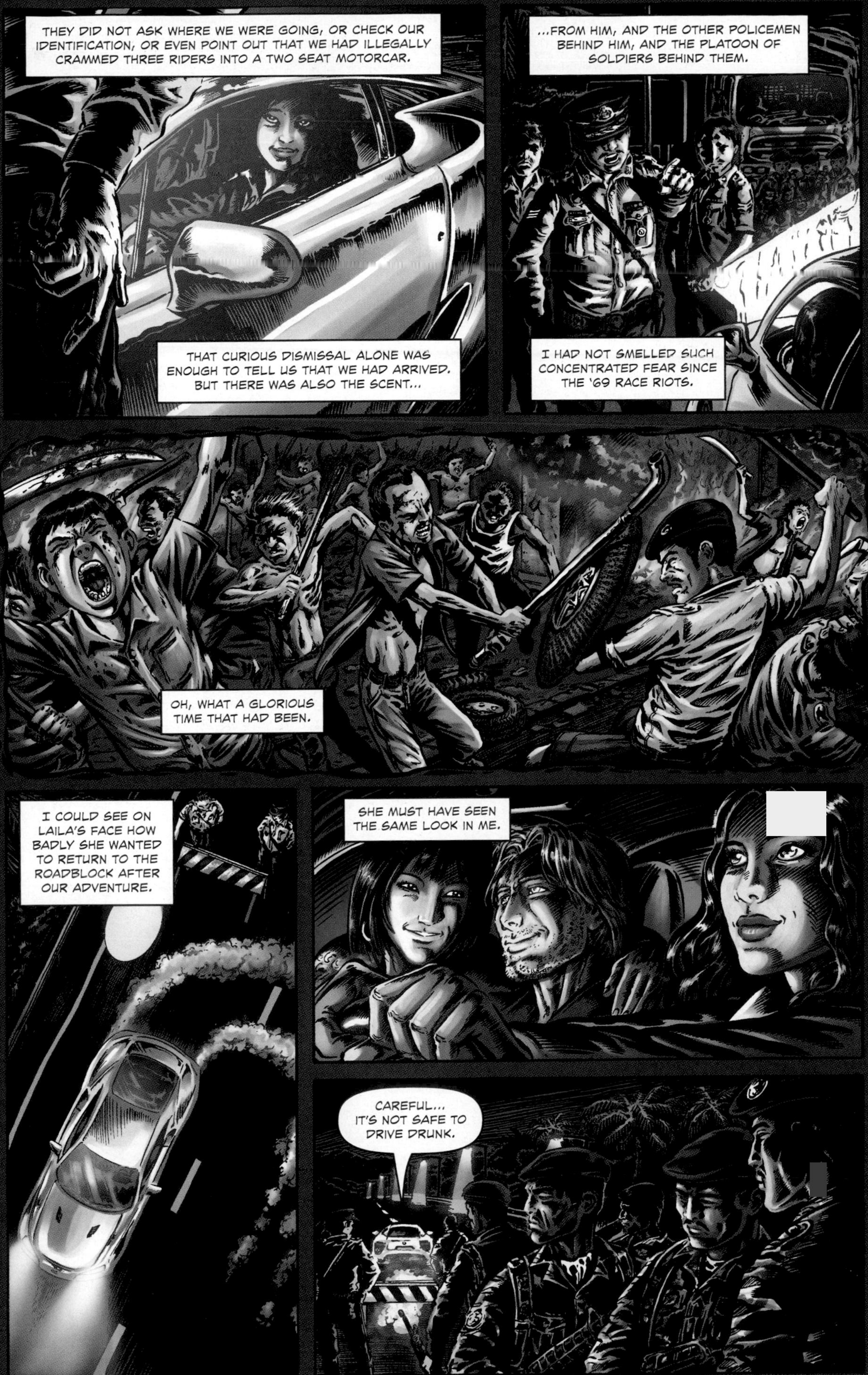
THEY DID NOT ASK WHERE WE WERE GOING, OR CHECK OUR IDENTIFICATION, OR EVEN POINT OUT THAT WE HAD ILLEGALLY CRAMMED THREE RIDERS INTO A TWO SEAT MOTORCAR.
THAT CURIOUS DISMISSAL ALONE WAS ENOUGH TO TELL US THAT WE HAD ARRIVED. BUT THERE WAS ALSO THE SCENT...
...FROM HIM, AND THE OTHER POLICEMEN BEHIND HIM, AND THE PLATOON OF SOLDIERS BEHIND THEM.
I HAD NOT SMELLED SUCH CONCENTRATED FEAR SINCE THE '69 RACE RIOTS.
OH, WHAT A GLORIOUS TIME THAT HAD BEEN.
I COULD SEE ON LAILA'S FACE HOW BADLY SHE WANTED TO RETURN TO THE ROADBLOCK AFTER OUR ADVENTURE.
SHE MUST HAVE SEEN THE SAME LOOK IN ME.
CAREFUL... IT'S NOT SAFE TO DRIVE DRUNK.

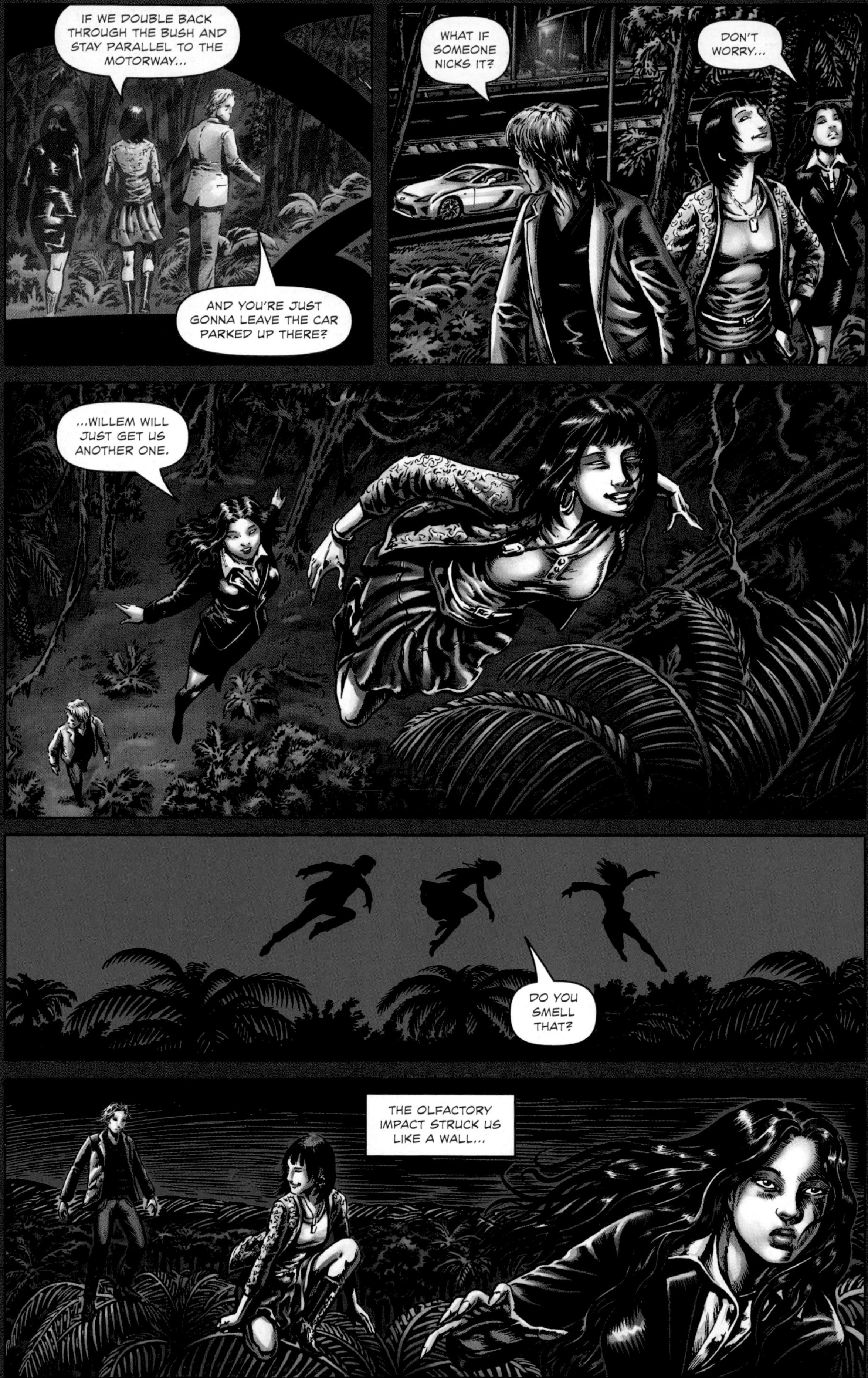
IF WE DOUBLE BACK THROUGH THE BUSH AND STAY PARALLEL TO THE MOTORWAY...
AND YOU'RE JUST GONNA LEAVE THE CAR PARKED UP THERE?
WHAT IF SOMEONE NICKS IT?
DON'T WORRY...
...WILLEM WILL JUST GET US ANOTHER ONE.
DO YOU SMELL THAT?
THE OLFACTORY IMPACT STRUCK US LIKE A WALL...

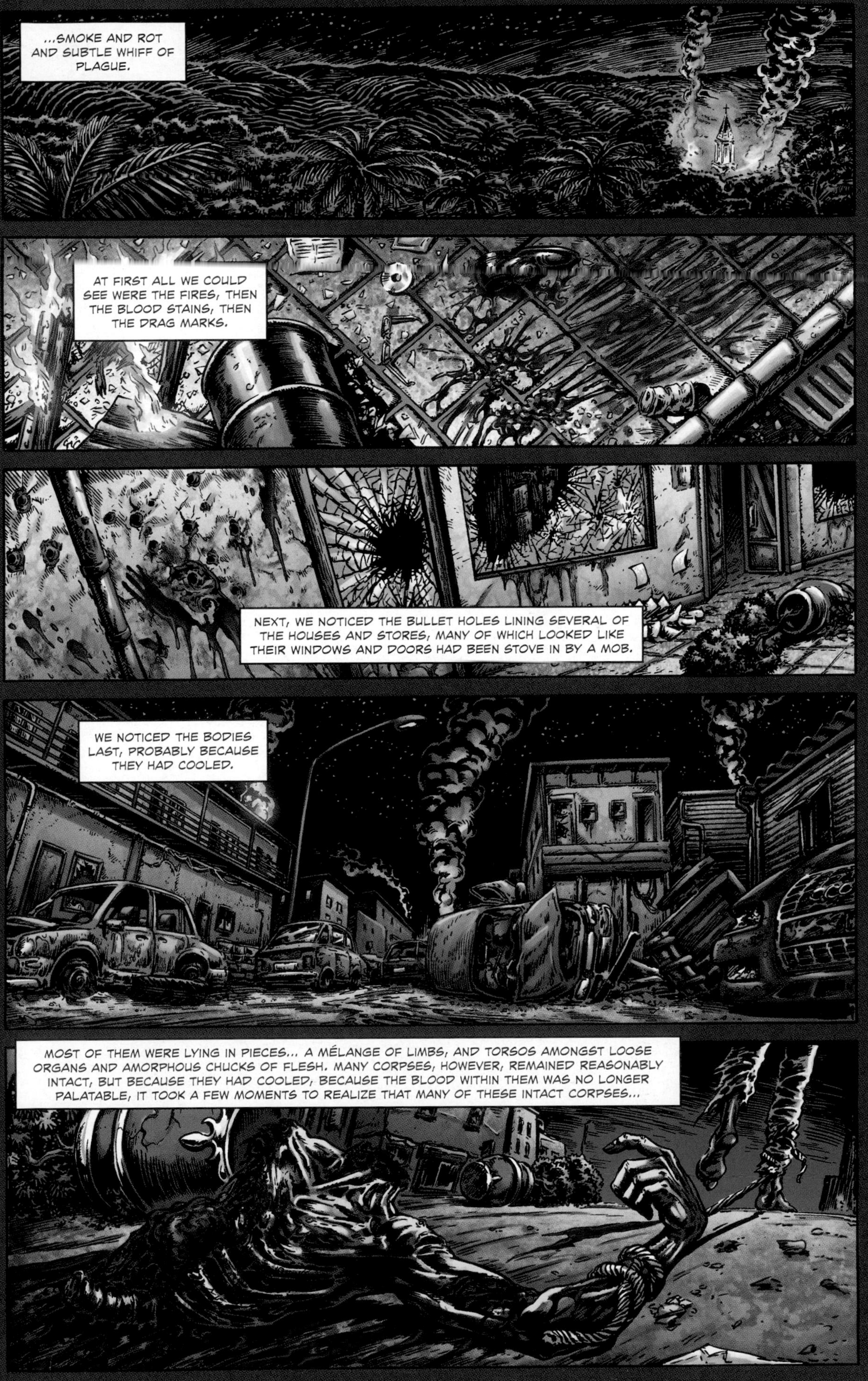
...SMOKE AND ROT AND SUBTLE WHIFF OF PLAGUE.
AT FIRST ALL WE COULD SEE WERE THE FIRES, THEN THE BLOOD STAINS, THEN THE DRAG MARKS.
NEXT, WE NOTICED THE BULLET HOLES LINING SEVERAL OF THE HOUSES AND STORES, MANY OF WHICH LOOKED LIKE THEIR WINDOWS AND DOORS HAD BEEN STOVE IN BY A MOB.
WE NOTICED THE BODIES LAST, PROBABLY BECAUSE THEY HAD COOLED.
MOST OF THEM WERE LYING IN PIECES... A MÉLANGE OF LIMBS, AND TORSOS AMONGST LOOSE ORGANS AND AMORPHOUS CHUCKS OF FLESH. MANY CORPSES, HOWEVER, REMAINED REASONABLY INTACT, BUT BECAUSE THEY HAD COOLED, BECAUSE THE BLOOD WITHIN THEM WAS NO LONGER PALATABLE, IT TOOK A FEW MOMENTS TO REALIZE THAT MANY OF THESE INTACT CORPSES...

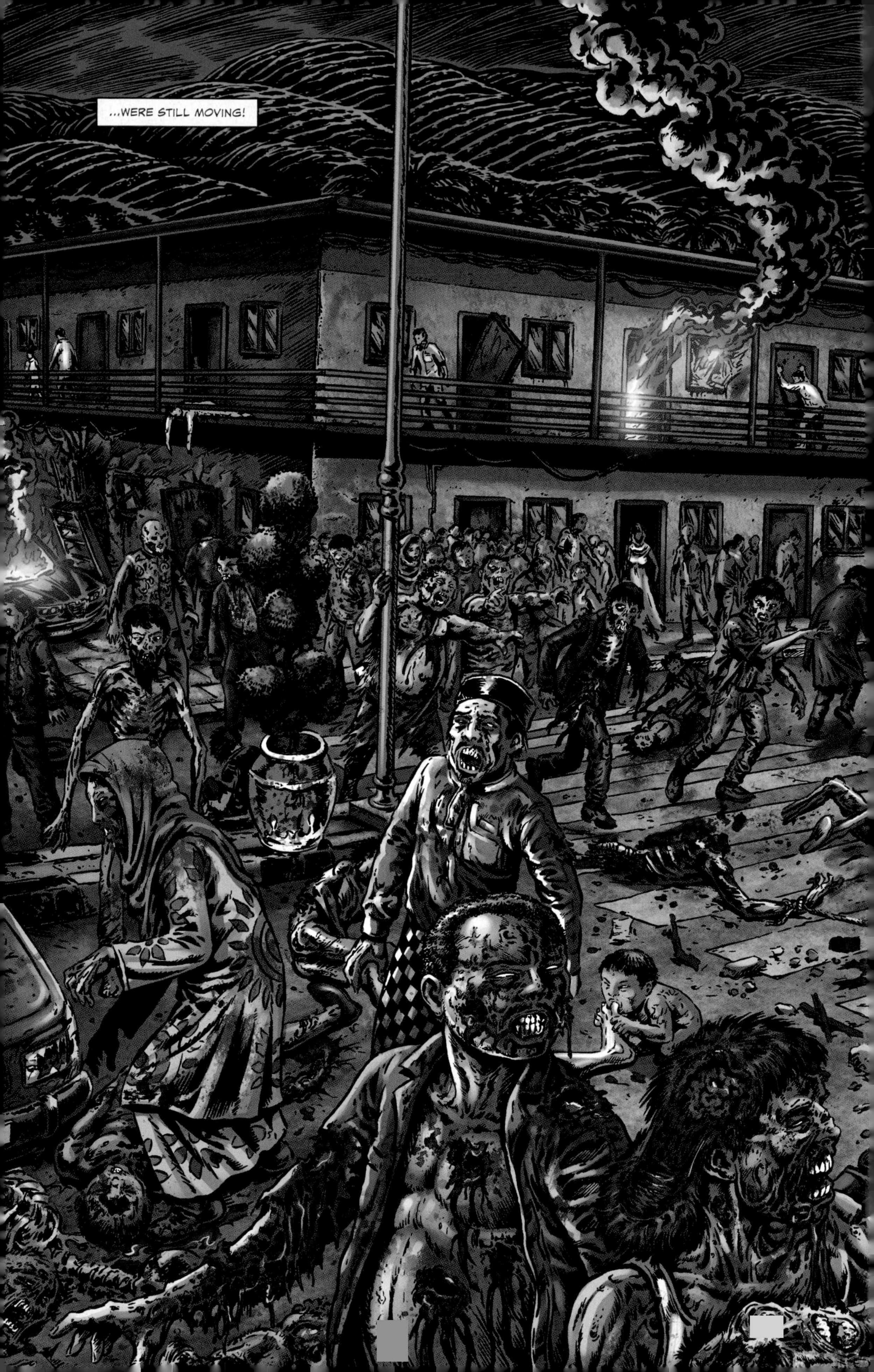
...WERE STILL MOVING!

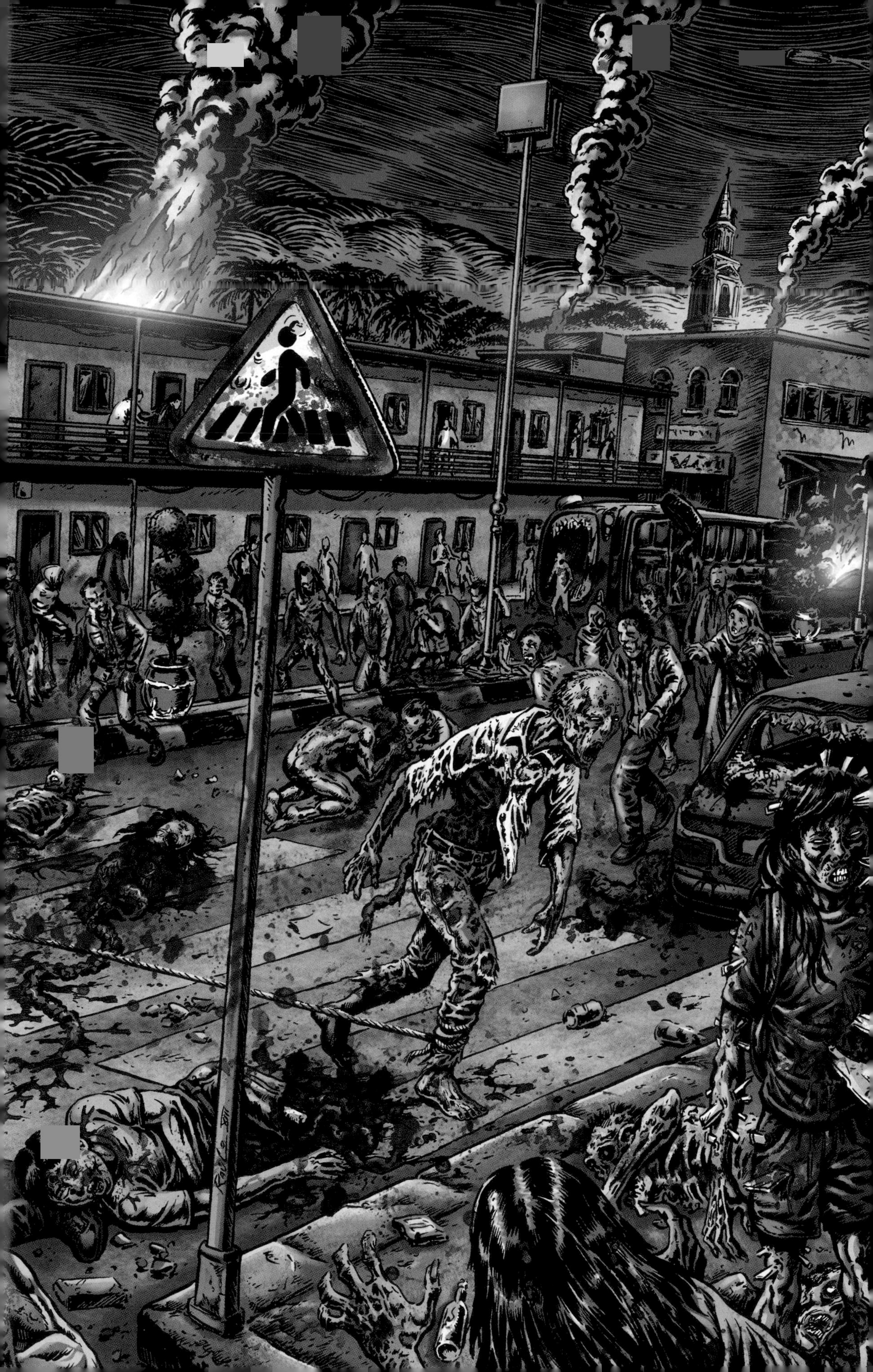

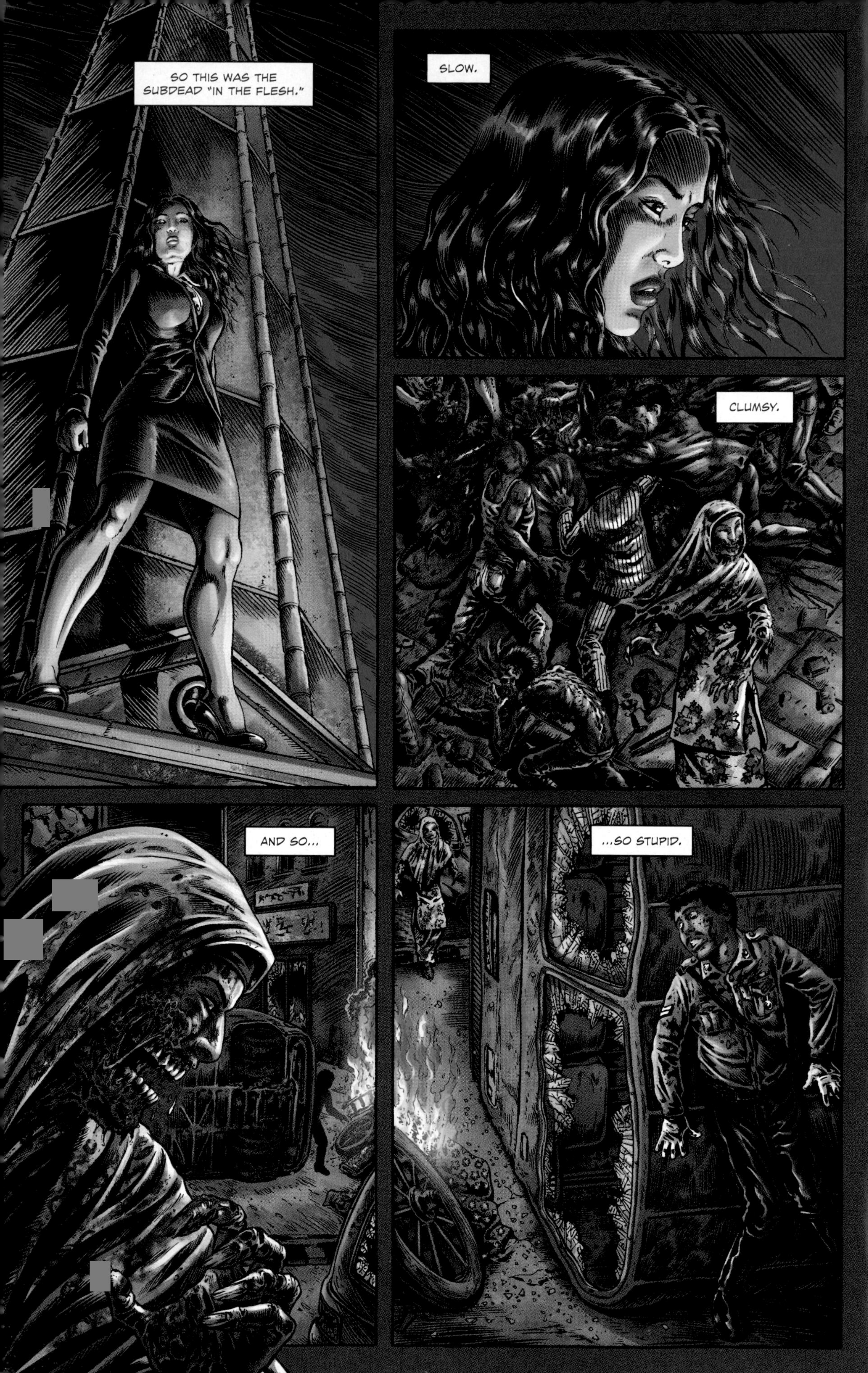
SO THIS WAS THE SUBDEAD "IN THE FLESH."
SLOW.
CLUMSY.
AND SO...
...SO STUPID.

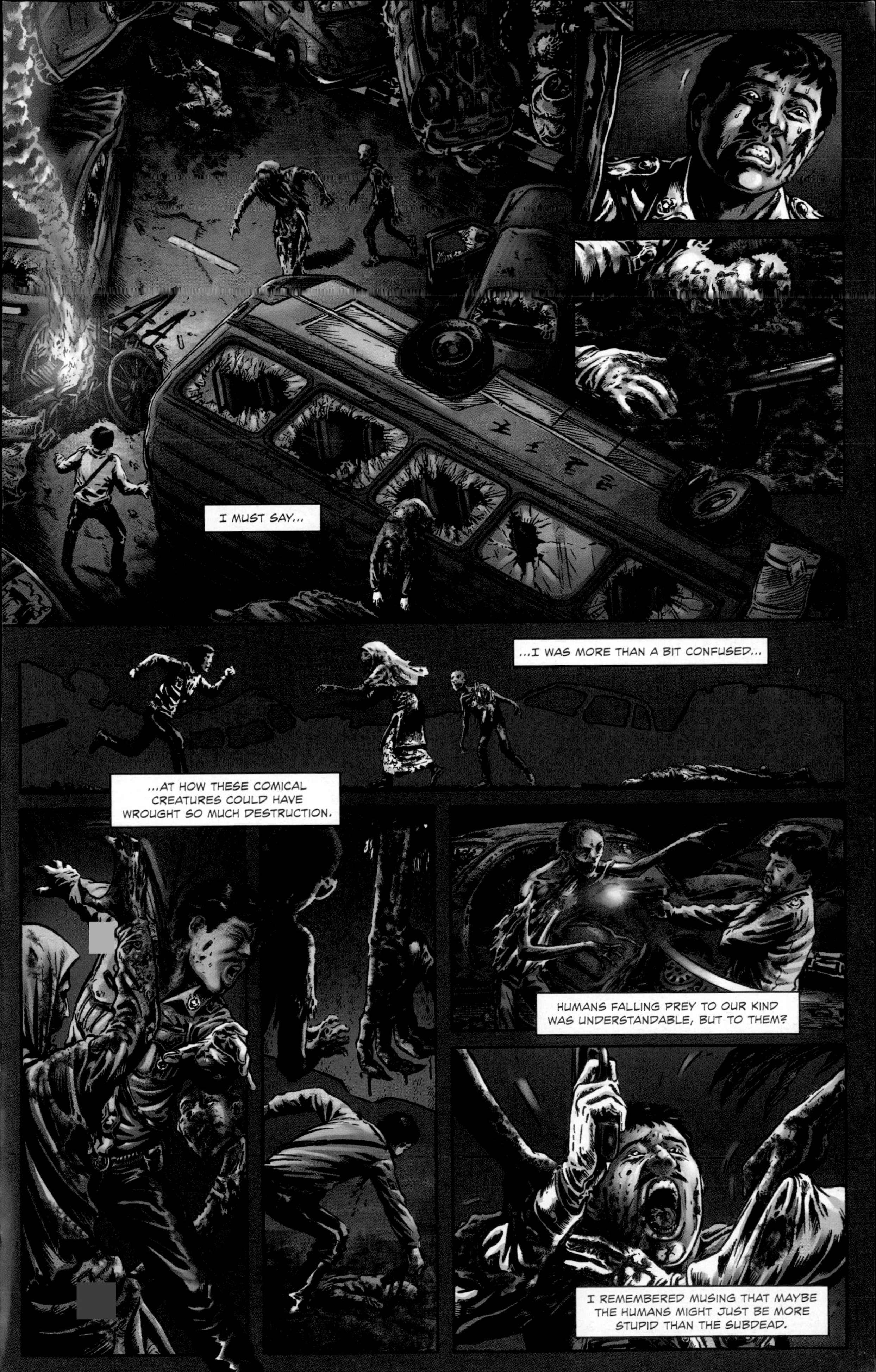
I MUST SAY...
...I WAS MORE THAN A BIT CONFUSED...
...AT HOW THESE COMICAL CREATURES COULD HAVE WROUGHT SO MUCH DESTRUCTION.
HUMANS FALLING PREY TO OUR KIND WAS UNDERSTANDABLE, BUT TO THEM?
I REMEMBERED MUSING THAT MAYBE THE HUMANS MIGHT JUST BE MORE STUPID THAN THE SUBDEAD.

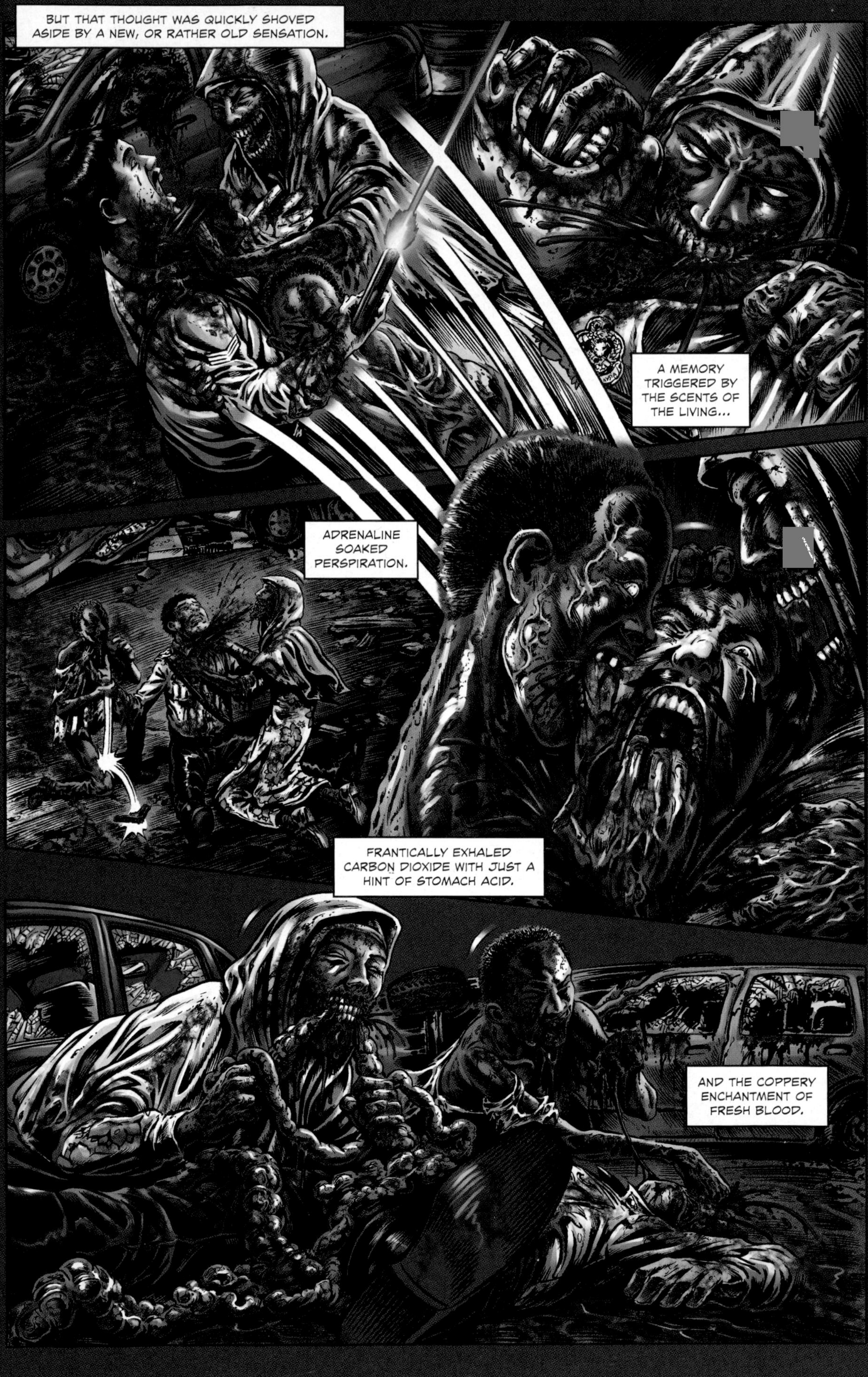
BUT THAT THOUGHT WAS QUICKLY SHOVED ASIDE BY A NEW, OR RATHER OLD SENSATION.
A MEMORY TRIGGERED BY THE SCENTS OF THE LIVING...
ADRENALINE SOAKED PERSPIRATION.
FRANTICALLY EXHALED CARBON DIOXIDE WITH JUST A HINT OF STOMACH ACID.
AND THE COPPERY ENCHANTMENT OF FRESH BLOOD.

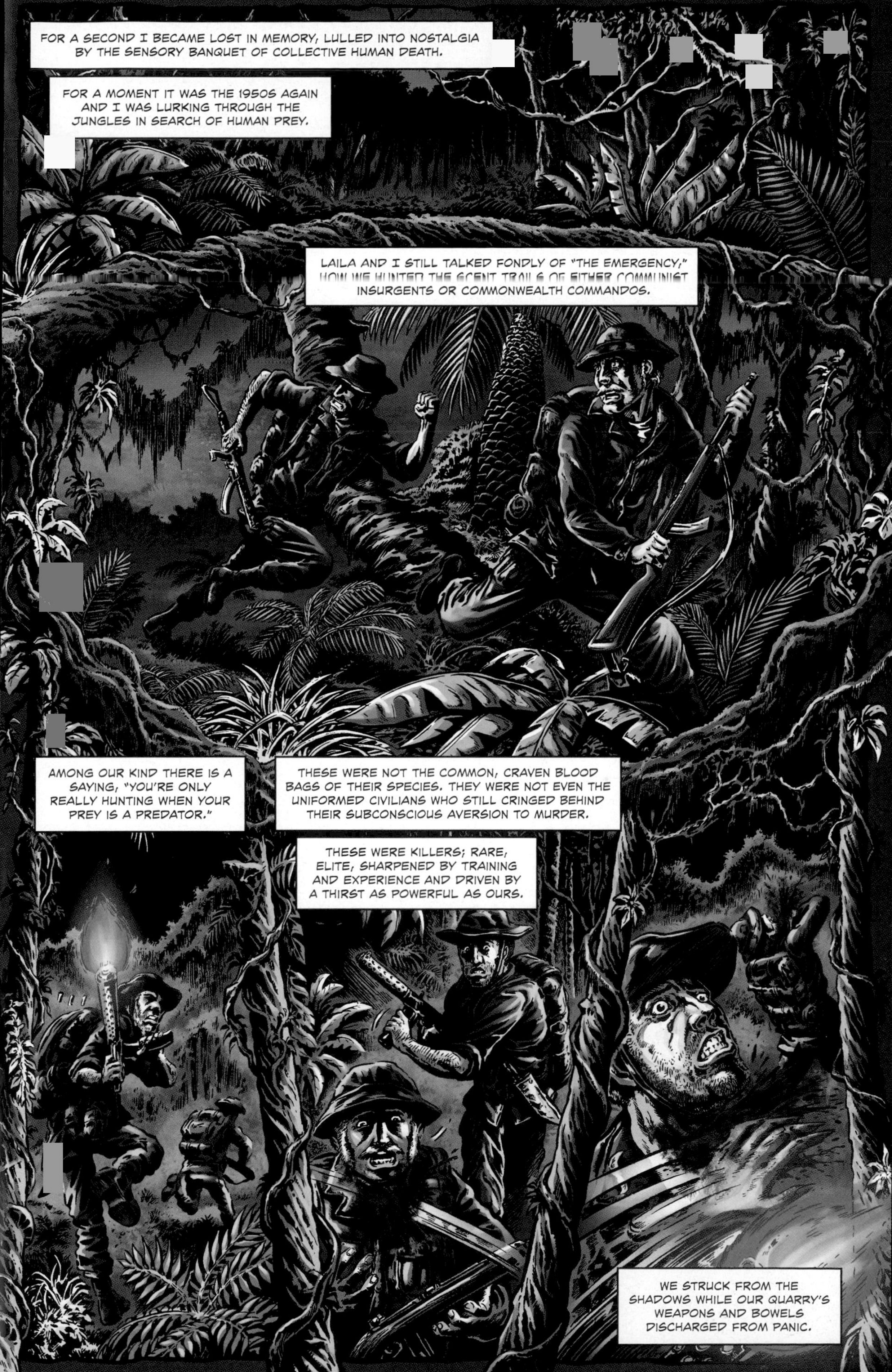
FOR A SECOND I BECAME LOST IN MEMORY, LULLED INTO NOSTALGIA BY THE SENSORY BANQUET OF COLLECTIVE HUMAN DEATH.
FOR A MOMENT IT WAS THE 1950S AGAIN AND I WAS LURKING THROUGH THE JUNGLES IN SEARCH OF HUMAN PREY.
LAILA AND I STILL TALKED FONDLY OF "THE EMERGENCY," HOW WE HUNTED THE SCENT TRAILS OF EITHER COMMUNIST INSURGENTS OR COMMONWEALTH COMMANDOS.
AMONG OUR KIND THERE IS A SAYING, "YOU'RE ONLY REALLY HUNTING WHEN YOUR PREY IS A PREDATOR."
THESE WERE NOT THE COMMON, CRAVEN BLOOD BAGS OF THEIR SPECIES. THEY WERE NOT EVEN THE UNIFORMED CIVILIANS WHO STILL CRINGED BEHIND THEIR SUBCONSCIOUS AVERSION TO MURDER.
THESE WERE KILLERS; RARE, ELITE, SHARPENED BY TRAINING AND EXPERIENCE AND DRIVEN BY A THIRST AS POWERFUL AS OURS.
WE STRUCK FROM THE SHADOWS WHILE OUR QUARRY'S WEAPONS AND BOWELS DISCHARGED FROM PANIC.

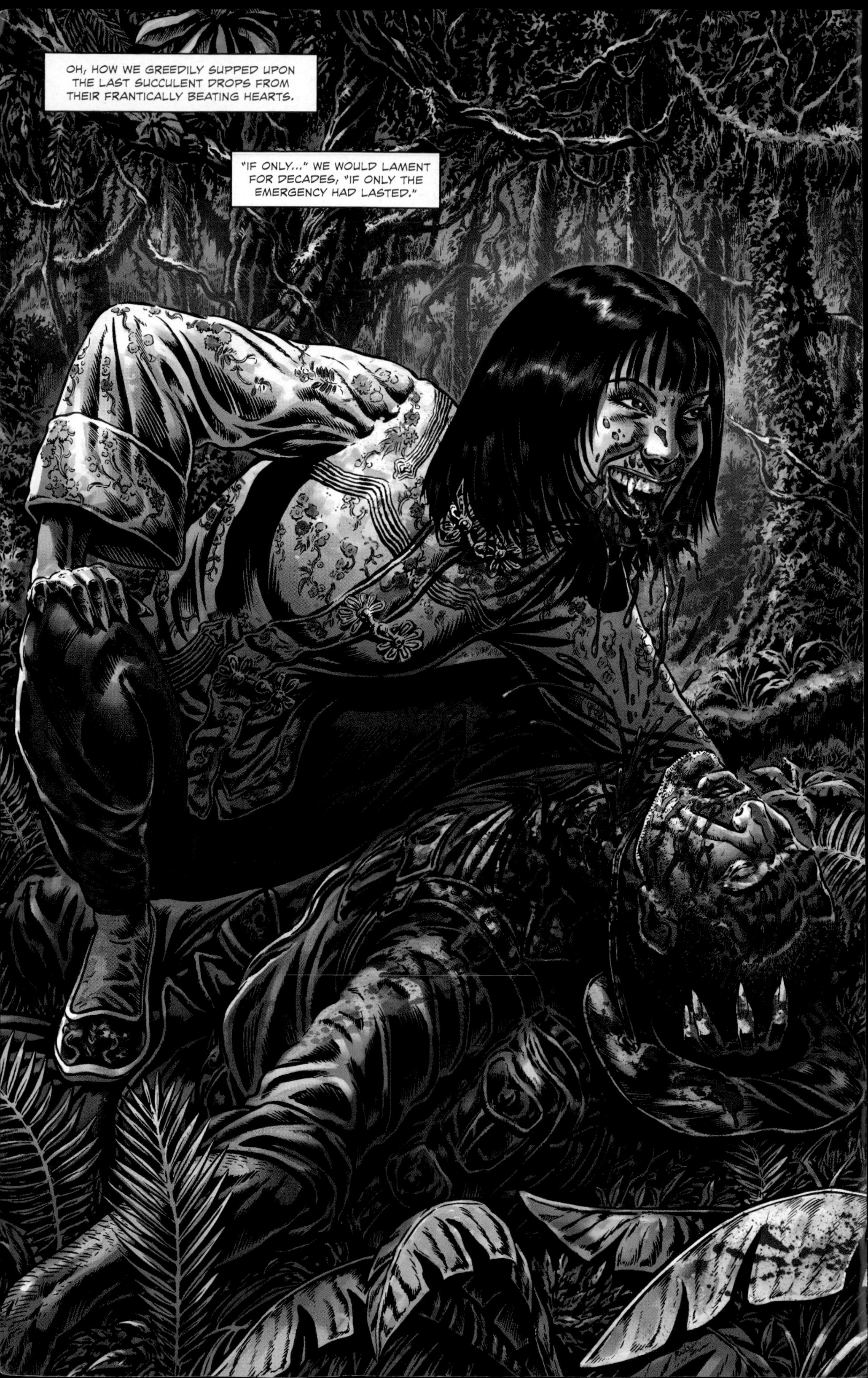
OH, HOW WE GREEDILY SUPPED UPON THE LAST SUCCULENT DROPS FROM THEIR FRANTICALLY BEATING HEARTS.
"IF ONLY..." WE WOULD LAMENT FOR DECADES, "IF ONLY THE EMERGENCY HAD LASTED."

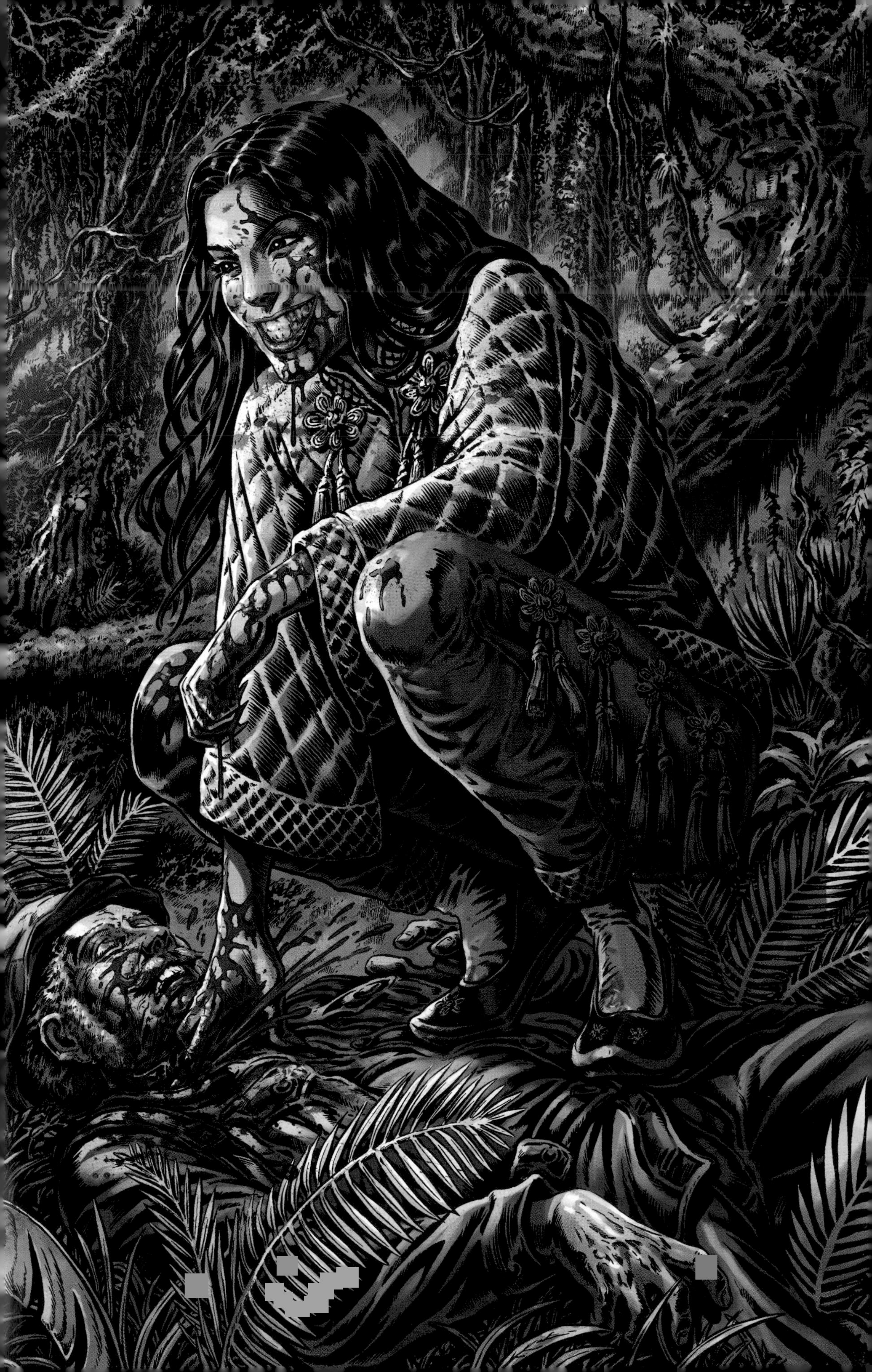

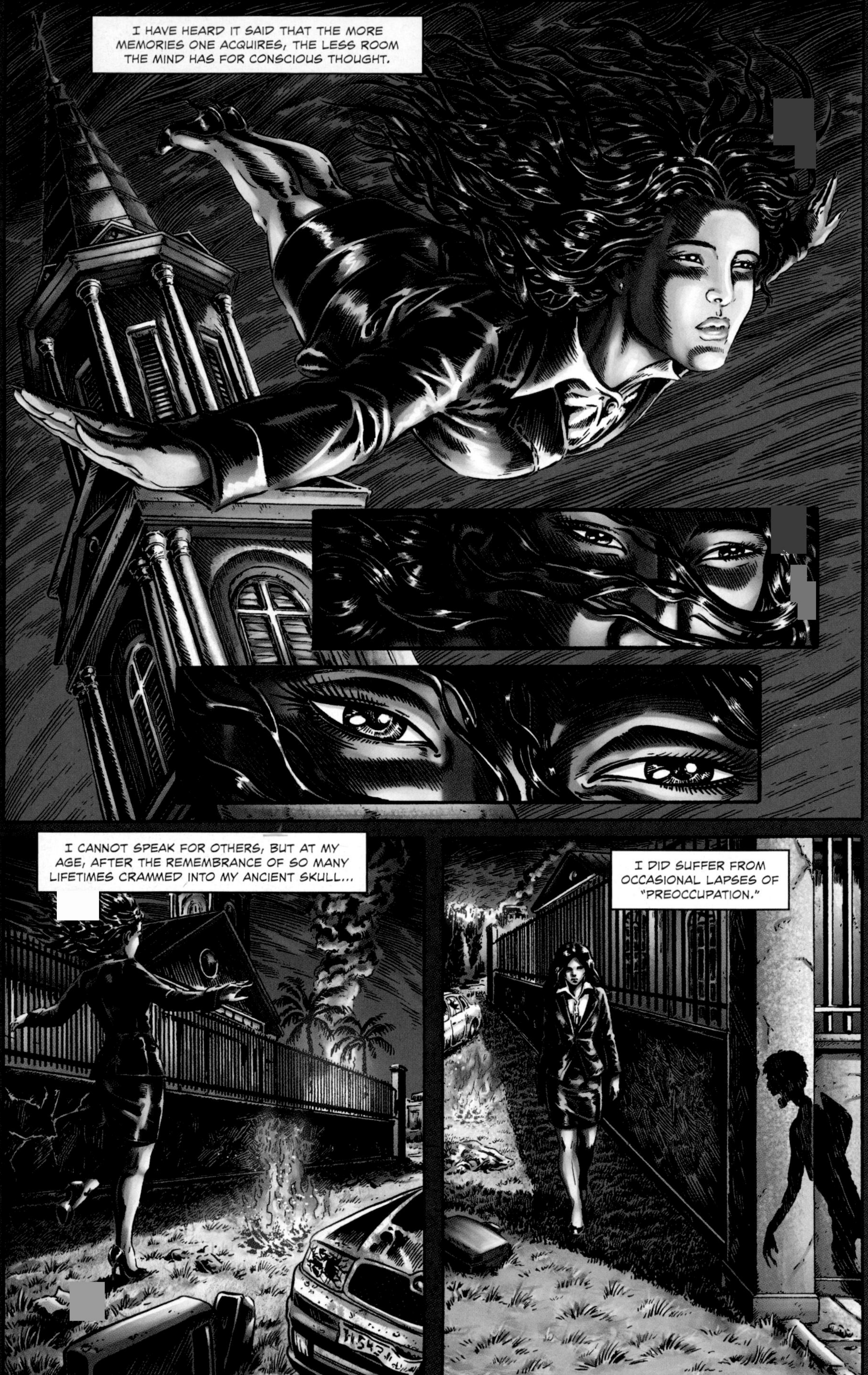
I HAVE HEARD IT SAID THAT THE MORE MEMORIES ONE ACQUIRES, THE LESS ROOM THE MIND HAS FOR CONSCIOUS THOUGHT.
I CANNOT SPEAK FOR OTHERS, BUT AT MY AGE, AFTER THE REMEMBRANCE OF SO MANY LIFETIMES CRAMMED INTO MY ANCIENT SKULL...
I DID SUFFER FROM OCCASIONAL LAPSES OF "PREOCCUPATION."

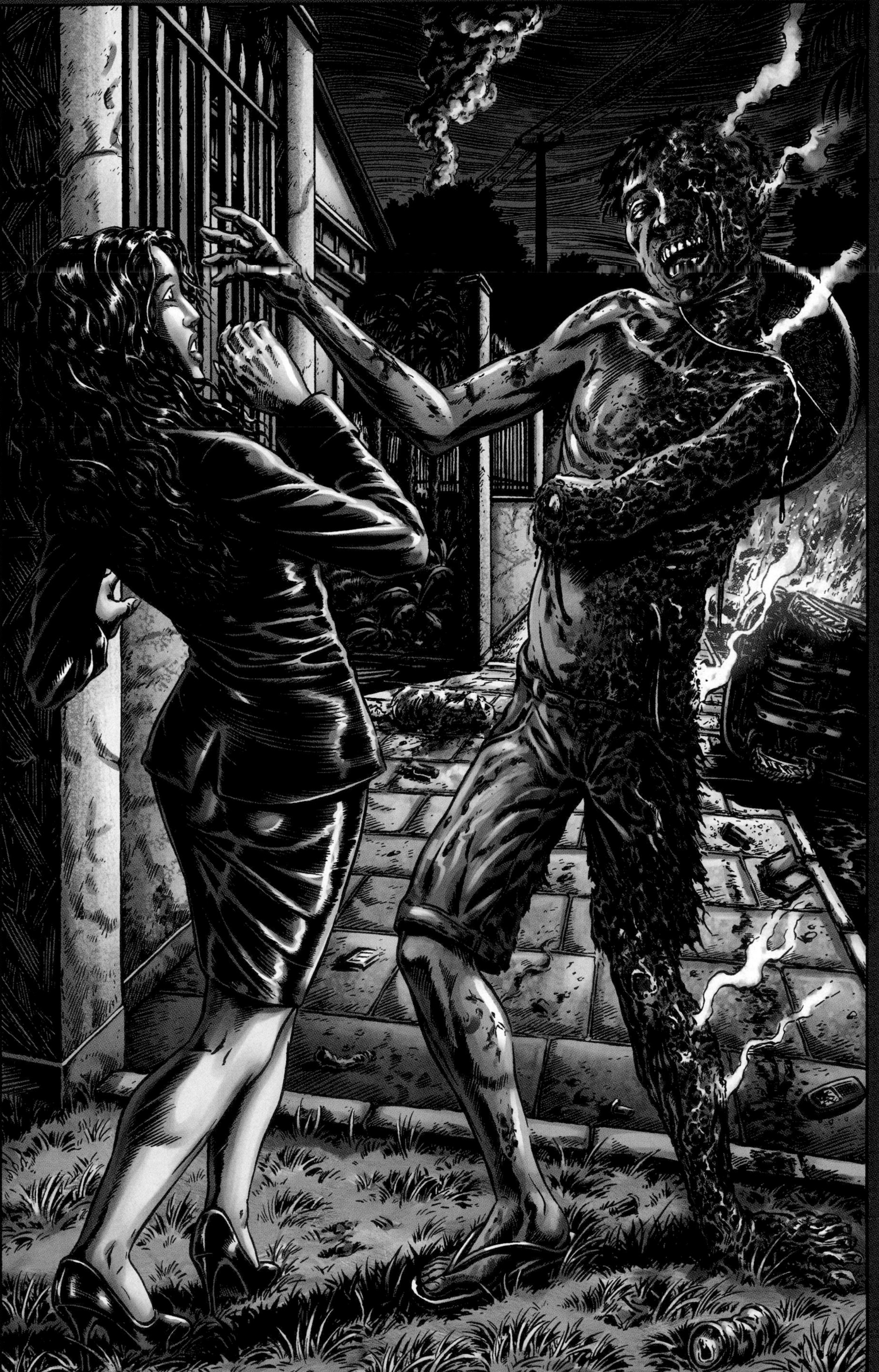

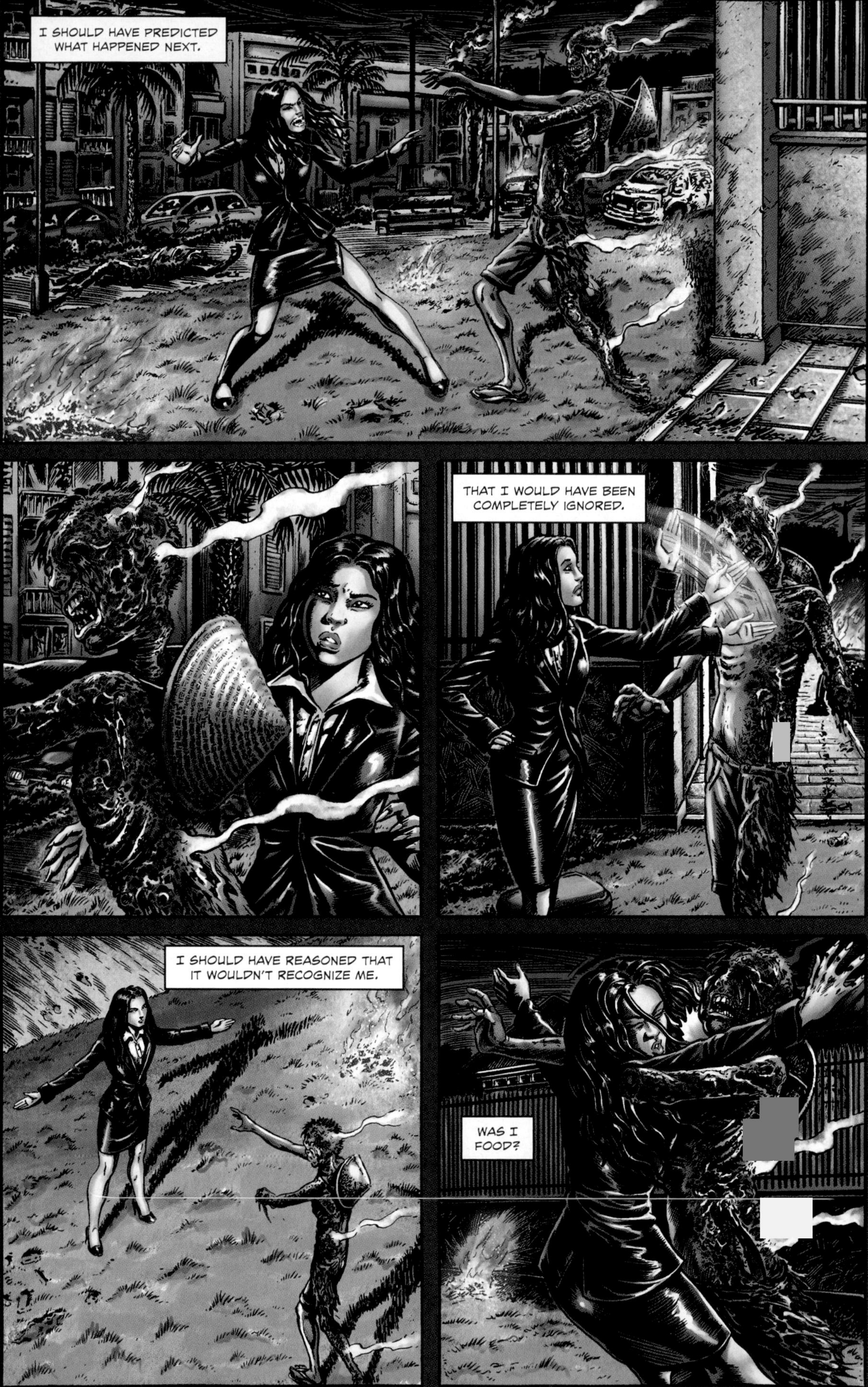
I SHOULD HAVE PREDICTED WHAT HAPPENED NEXT.
THAT I WOULD HAVE BEEN COMPLETELY IGNORED.
I SHOULD HAVE REASONED THAT IT WOULDN'T RECOGNIZE ME.
WAS I FOOD?

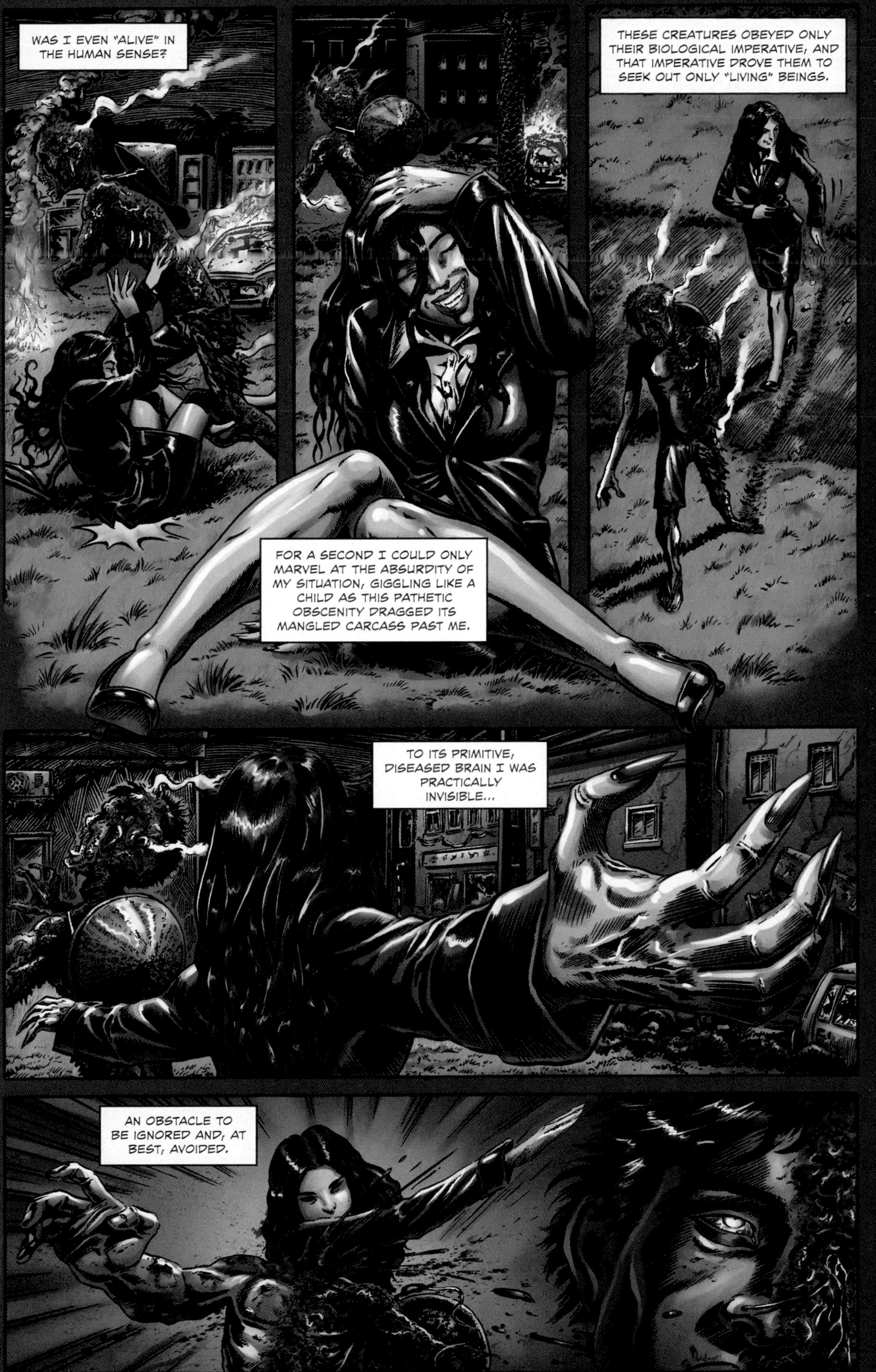
WAS I EVEN "ALIVE" IN THE HUMAN SENSE?
THESE CREATURES OBEYED ONLY THEIR BIOLOGICAL IMPERATIVE, AND THAT IMPERATIVE DROVE THEM TO SEEK OUT ONLY "LIVING" BEINGS.
FOR A SECOND I COULD ONLY MARVEL AT THE ABSURDITY OF MY SITUATION, GIGGLING LIKE A CHILD AS THIS PATHETIC OBSCENITY DRAGGED ITS MANGLED CARCASS PAST ME.
TO ITS PRIMITIVE, DISEASED BRAIN I WAS PRACTICALLY INVISIBLE...
AN OBSTACLE TO BE IGNORED AND, AT BEST, AVOIDED.

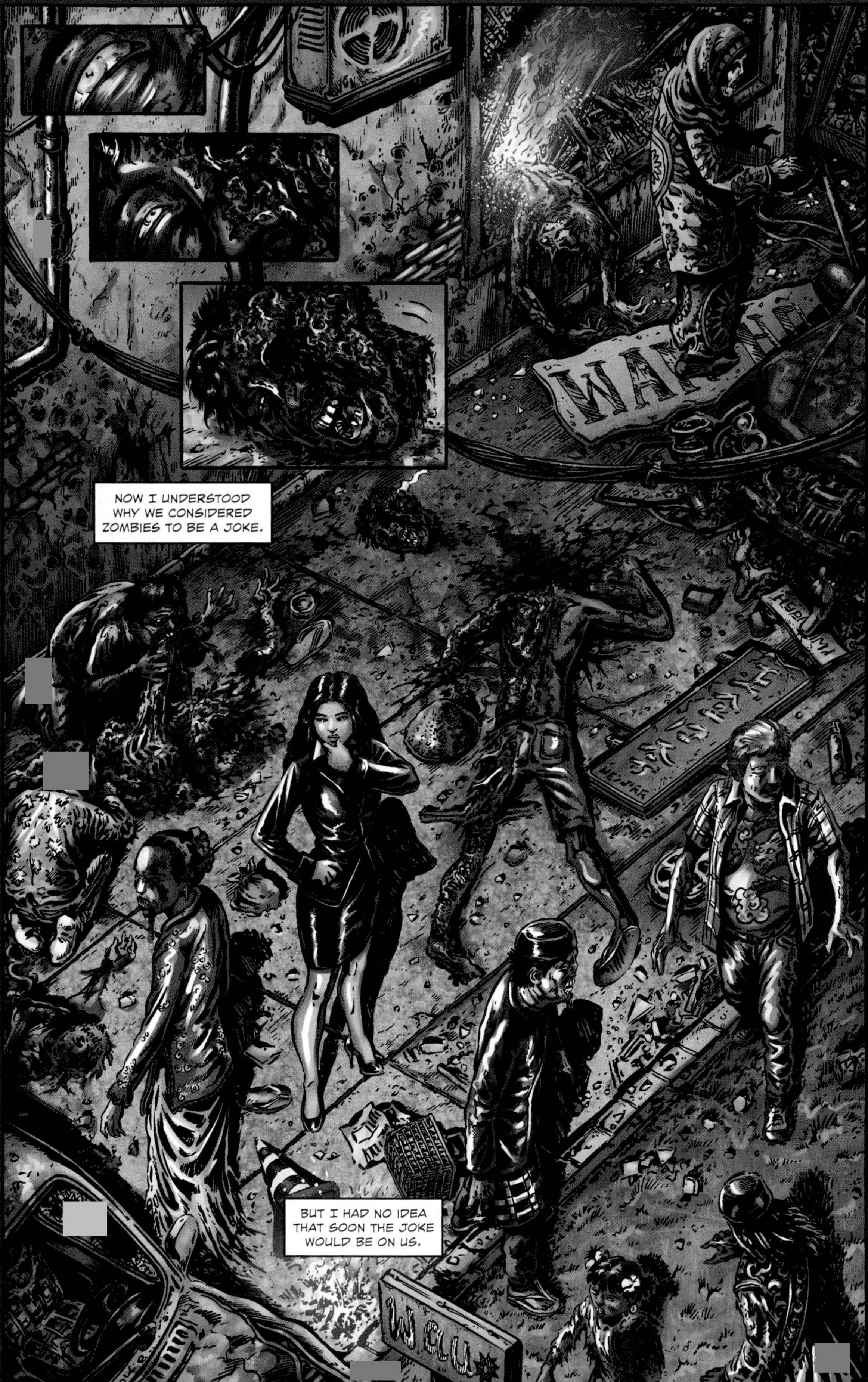
NOW I UNDERSTOOD WHY WE CONSIDERED ZOMBIES TO BE A JOKE.
BUT I HAD NO IDEA THAT SOON THE JOKE WOULD BE ON US.

Chapter 2

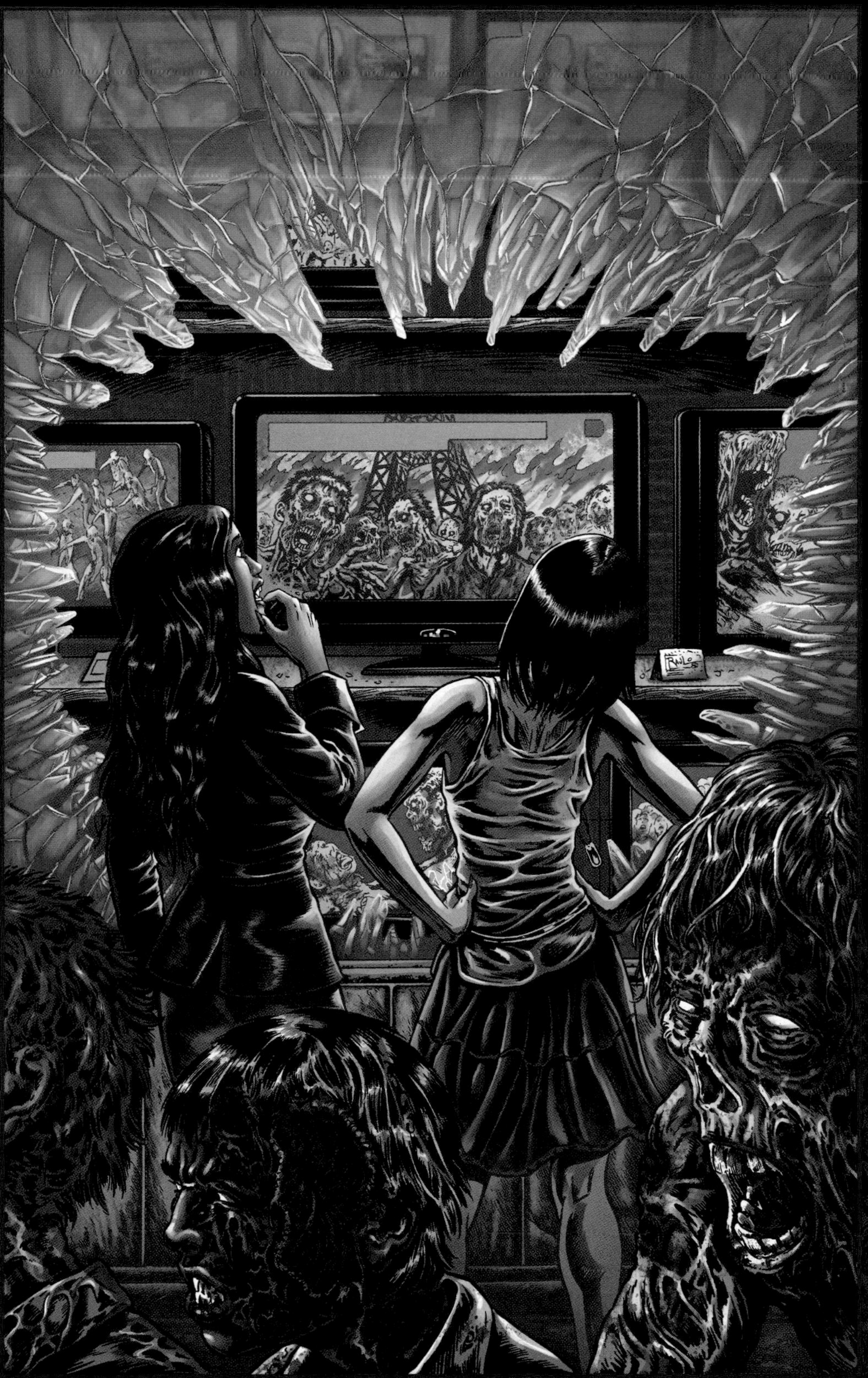

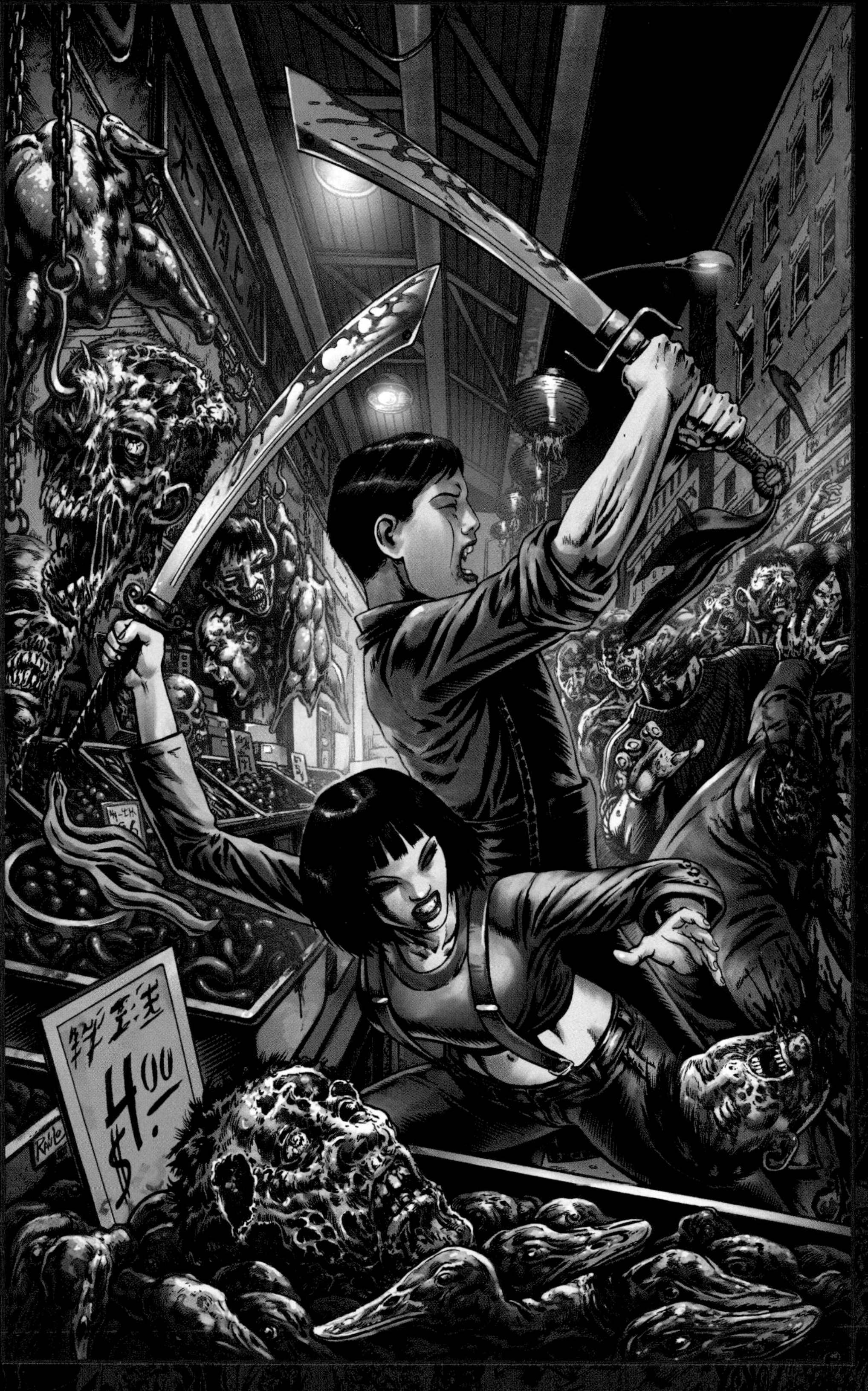
$4.00

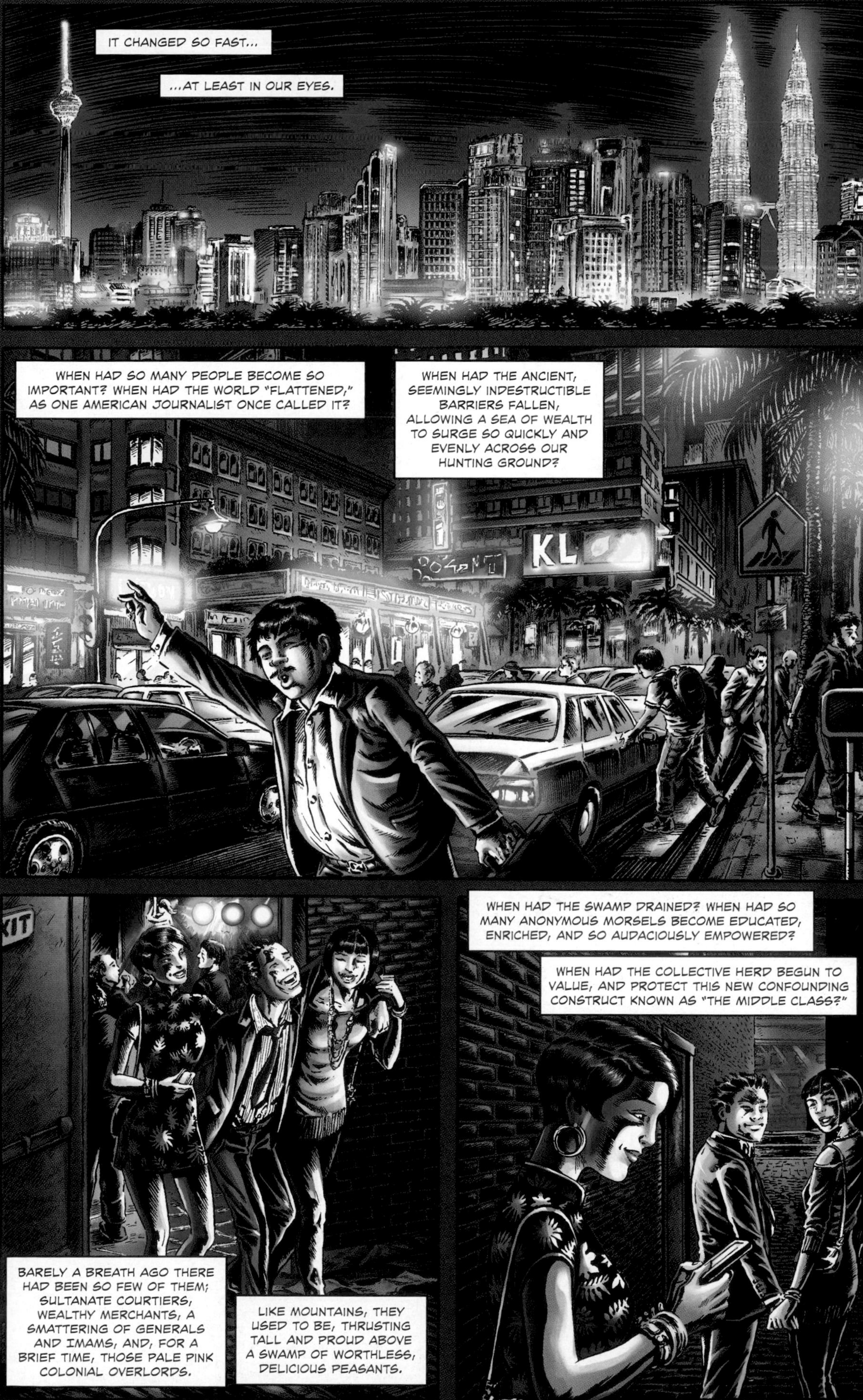
IT CHANGED SO FAST...
...AT LEAST IN OUR EYES.
WHEN HAD SO MANY PEOPLE BECOME SO IMPORTANT? WHEN HAD THE WORLD "FLATTENED," AS ONE AMERICAN JOURNALIST ONCE CALLED IT?
WHEN HAD THE ANCIENT, SEEMINGLY INDESTRUCTIBLE BARRIERS FALLEN, ALLOWING A SEA OF WEALTH TO SURGE SO QUICKLY AND EVENLY ACROSS OUR HUNTING GROUND?
KL
EXIT
BARELY A BREATH AGO THERE HAD BEEN SO FEW OF THEM; SULTANATE COURTIERS, WEALTHY MERCHANTS, A SMATTERING OF GENERALS AND IMAMS, AND, FOR A BRIEF TIME, THOSE PALE PINK COLONIAL OVERLORDS.
LIKE MOUNTAINS, THEY USED TO BE, THRUSTING TALL AND PROUD ABOVE A SWAMP OF WORTHLESS, DELICIOUS PEASANTS.
WHEN HAD THE SWAMP DRAINED? WHEN HAD SO MANY ANONYMOUS MORSELS BECOME EDUCATED, ENRICHED, AND SO AUDACIOUSLY EMPOWERED?
WHEN HAD THE COLLECTIVE HERD BEGUN TO VALUE, AND PROTECT THIS NEW CONFOUNDING CONSTRUCT KNOWN AS "THE MIDDLE CLASS?"

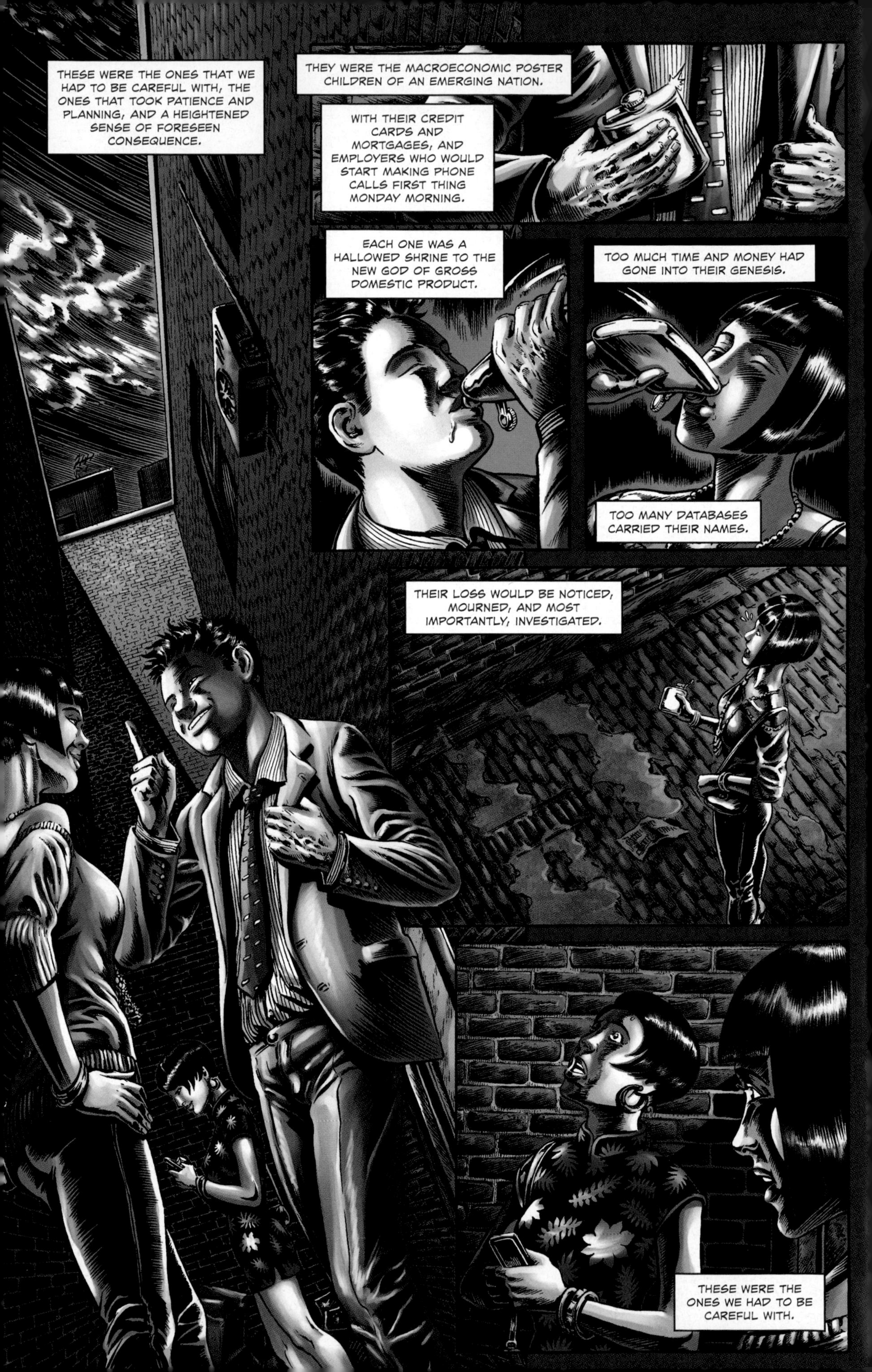
THESE WERE THE ONES THAT WE HAD TO BE CAREFUL WITH, THE ONES THAT TOOK PATIENCE AND PLANNING, AND A HEIGHTENED SENSE OF FORESEEN CONSEQUENCE.
THEY WERE THE MACROECONOMIC POSTER CHILDREN OF AN EMERGING NATION.
WITH THEIR CREDIT CARDS AND MORTGAGES, AND EMPLOYERS WHO WOULD START MAKING PHONE CALLS FIRST THING MONDAY MORNING.
EACH ONE WAS A HALLOWED SHRINE TO THE NEW GOD OF GROSS DOMESTIC PRODUCT.
TOO MUCH TIME AND MONEY HAD GONE INTO THEIR GENESIS.
TOO MANY DATABASES CARRIED THEIR NAMES.
THEIR LOSS WOULD BE NOTICED, MOURNED, AND MOST IMPORTANTLY, INVESTIGATED.
THESE WERE THE ONES WE HAD TO BE CAREFUL WITH.

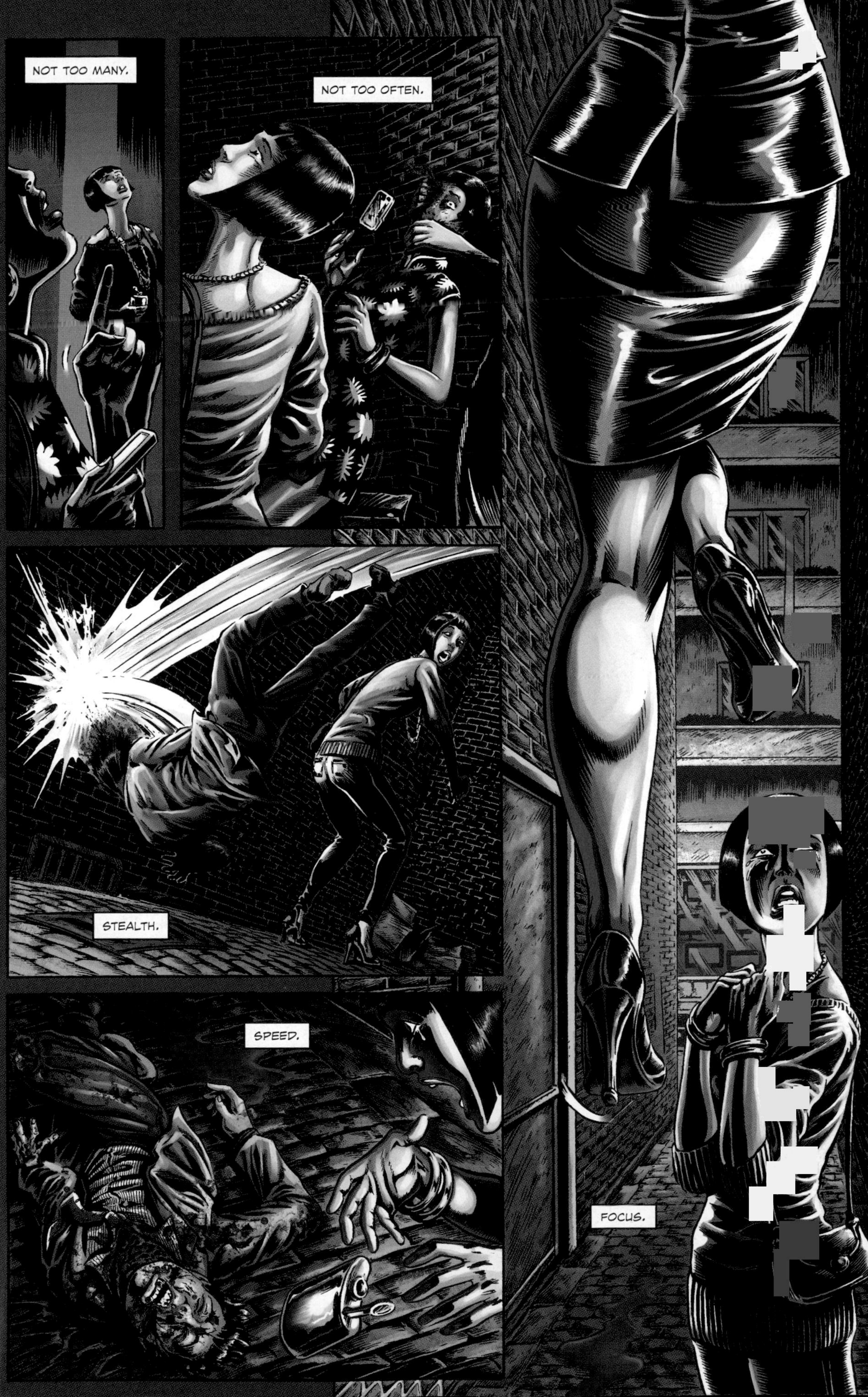
NOT TOO MANY.
NOT TOO OFTEN.
STEALTH.
SPEED.
FOCUS.

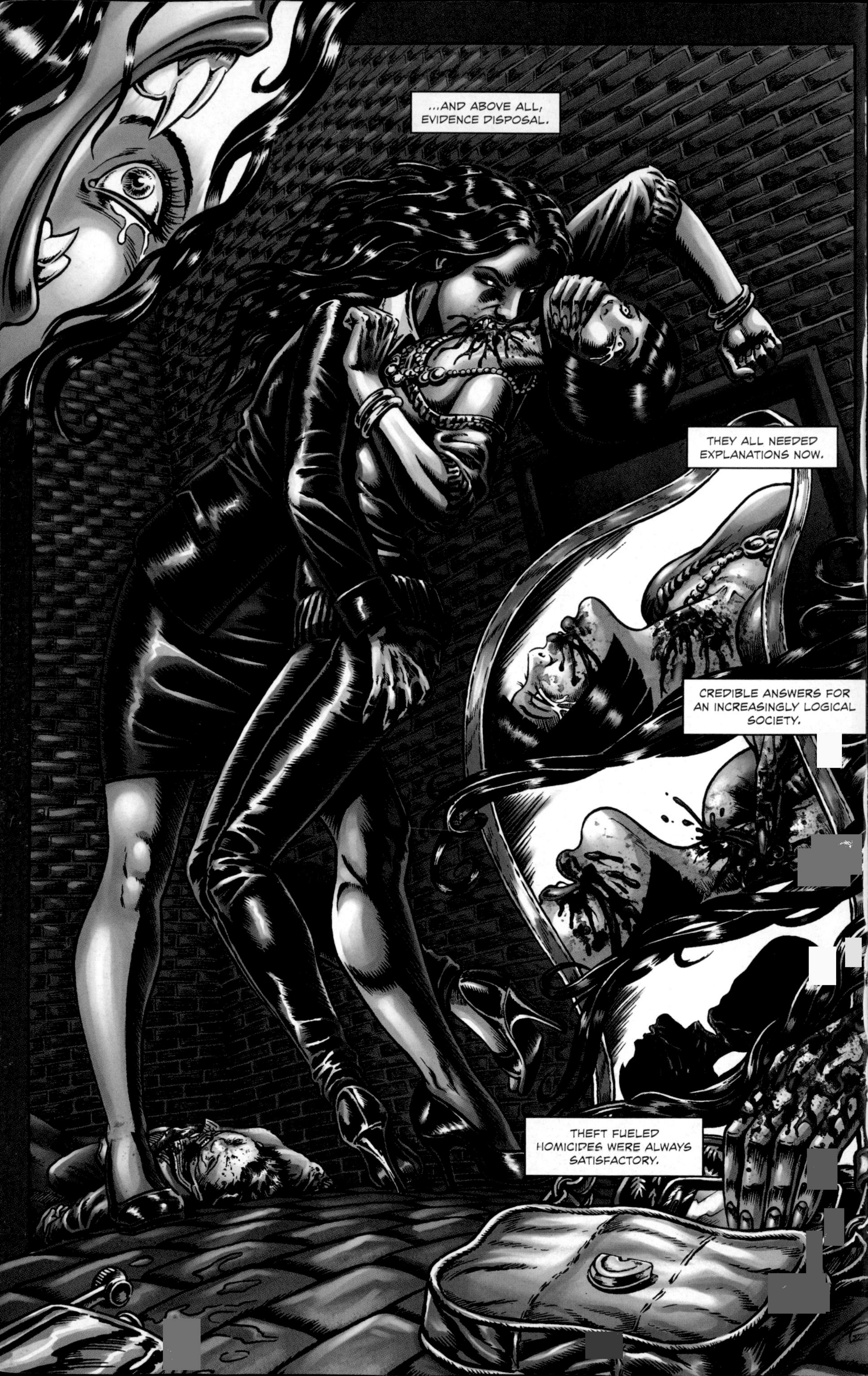
...AND ABOVE ALL, EVIDENCE DISPOSAL.
THEY ALL NEEDED EXPLANATIONS NOW.
CREDIBLE ANSWERS FOR AN INCREASINGLY LOGICAL SOCIETY.
THEFT FUELED HOMICIDES WERE ALWAYS SATISFACTORY.

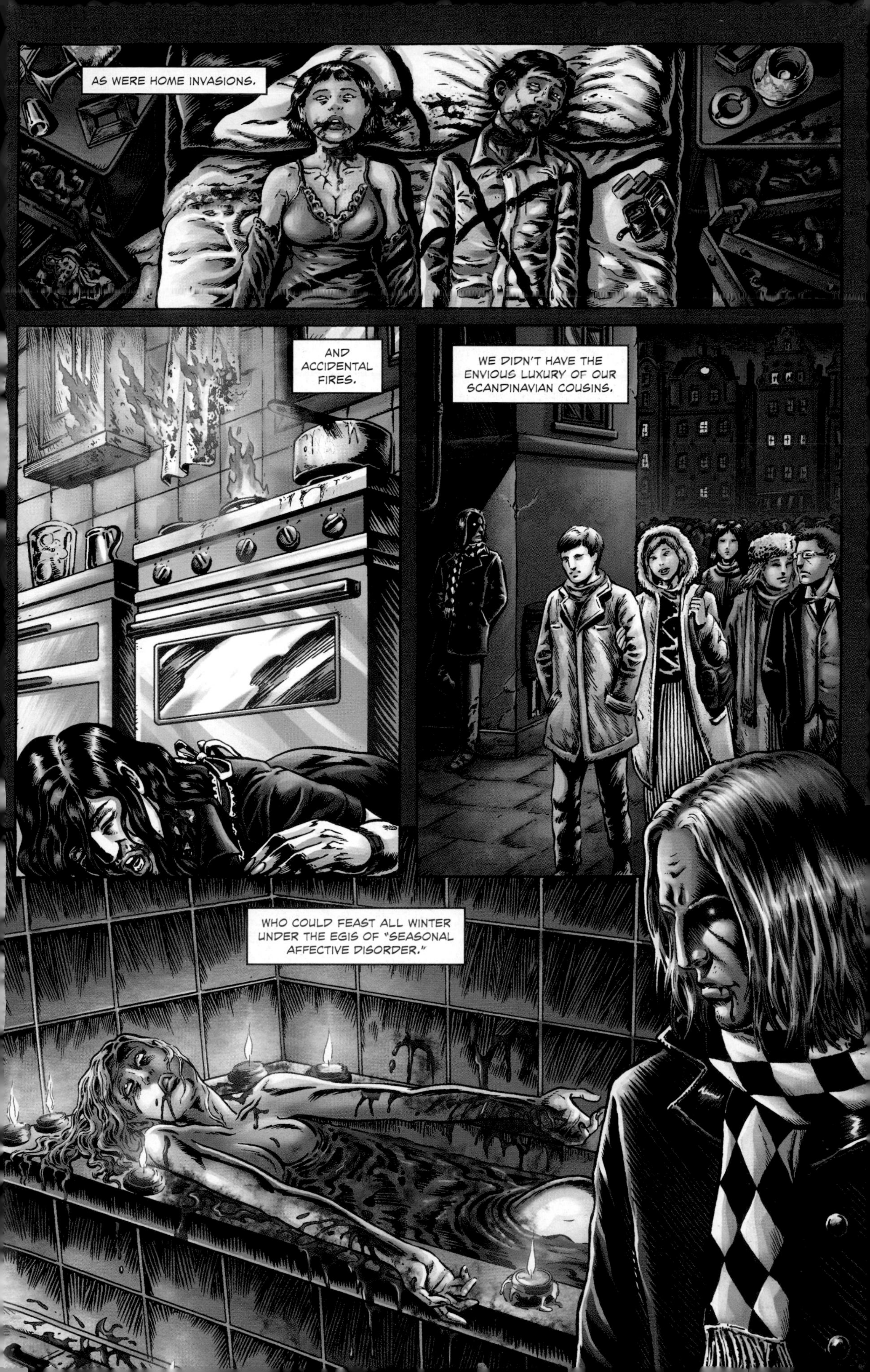
AS WERE HOME INVASIONS.
AND ACCIDENTAL FIRES.
WE DIDN'T HAVE THE ENVIOUS LUXURY OF OUR SCANDINAVIAN COUSINS.
WHO COULD FEAST ALL WINTER UNDER THE EGIS OF "SEASONAL AFFECTIVE DISORDER."

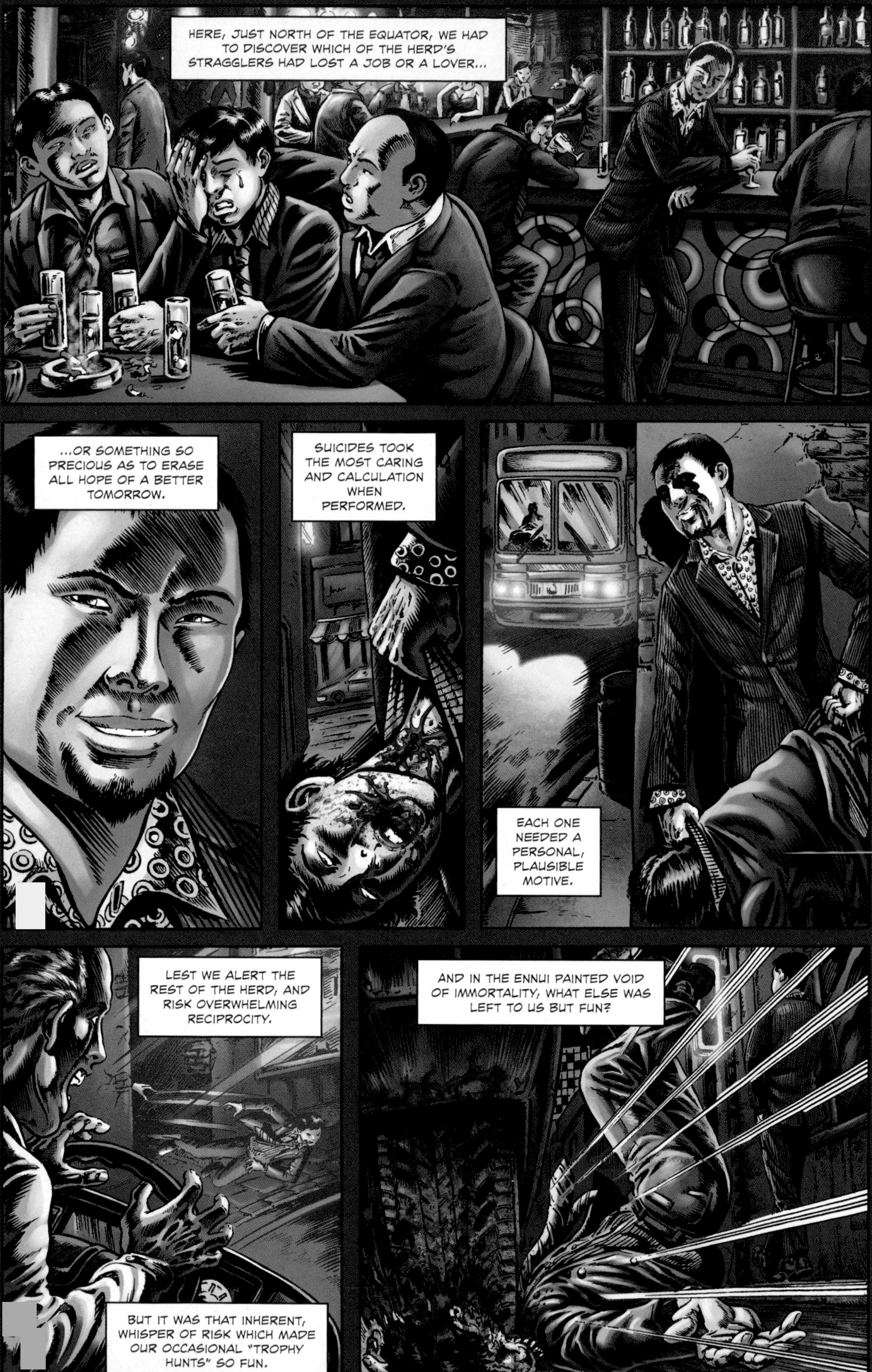
HERE, JUST NORTH OF THE EQUATOR, WE HAD TO DISCOVER WHICH OF THE HERD'S STRAGGLERS HAD LOST A JOB OR A LOVER...
...OR SOMETHING SO PRECIOUS AS TO ERASE ALL HOPE OF A BETTER TOMORROW.
SUICIDES TOOK THE MOST CARING AND CALCULATION WHEN PERFORMED.
EACH ONE NEEDED A PERSONAL, PLAUSIBLE MOTIVE.
LEST WE ALERT THE REST OF THE HERD, AND RISK OVERWHELMING RECIPROCITY.
BUT IT WAS THAT INHERENT, WHISPER OF RISK WHICH MADE OUR OCCASIONAL "TROPHY HUNTS" SO FUN.
AND IN THE ENNUI PAINTED VOID OF IMMORTALITY, WHAT ELSE WAS LEFT TO US BUT FUN?

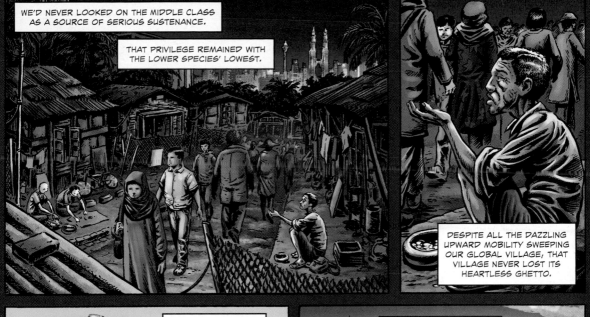

WE'D NEVER LOOKED ON THE MIDDLE CLASS AS A SOURCE OF SERIOUS SUSTENANCE.

THAT PRIVILEGE REMAINED WITH THE LOWER SPECIES' LOWEST.

DESPITE ALL THE DAZZLING UPWARD MOBILITY SWEEPING OUR GLOBAL VILLAGE, THAT VILLAGE NEVER LOST ITS HEARTLESS GHETTO.

RIPE, SAFE HUNTING PRESERVES STILL FESTERED...

...IN THE DEVELOPING, DYNAMIC POWERS OF ASIA...

...OR IN LIBERAL, SOCIALIST, ENLIGHTENED EUROPE...

...OR EVEN ACROSS THE SHINING PACIFIC, IN THE "LAND OF OPPORTUNITY."

HOMELESS, VET ANYTHING YOU CAN SPARE. GOD BLESS YOU!

FOR ALL THEIR LATEST TECHNICAL AND ECONOMIC SORCERY, HUMANS NEVER LOST THEIR MASTERY OF IGNORANCE WHEN IT CAME TO THE SUFFERING OF OTHERS.

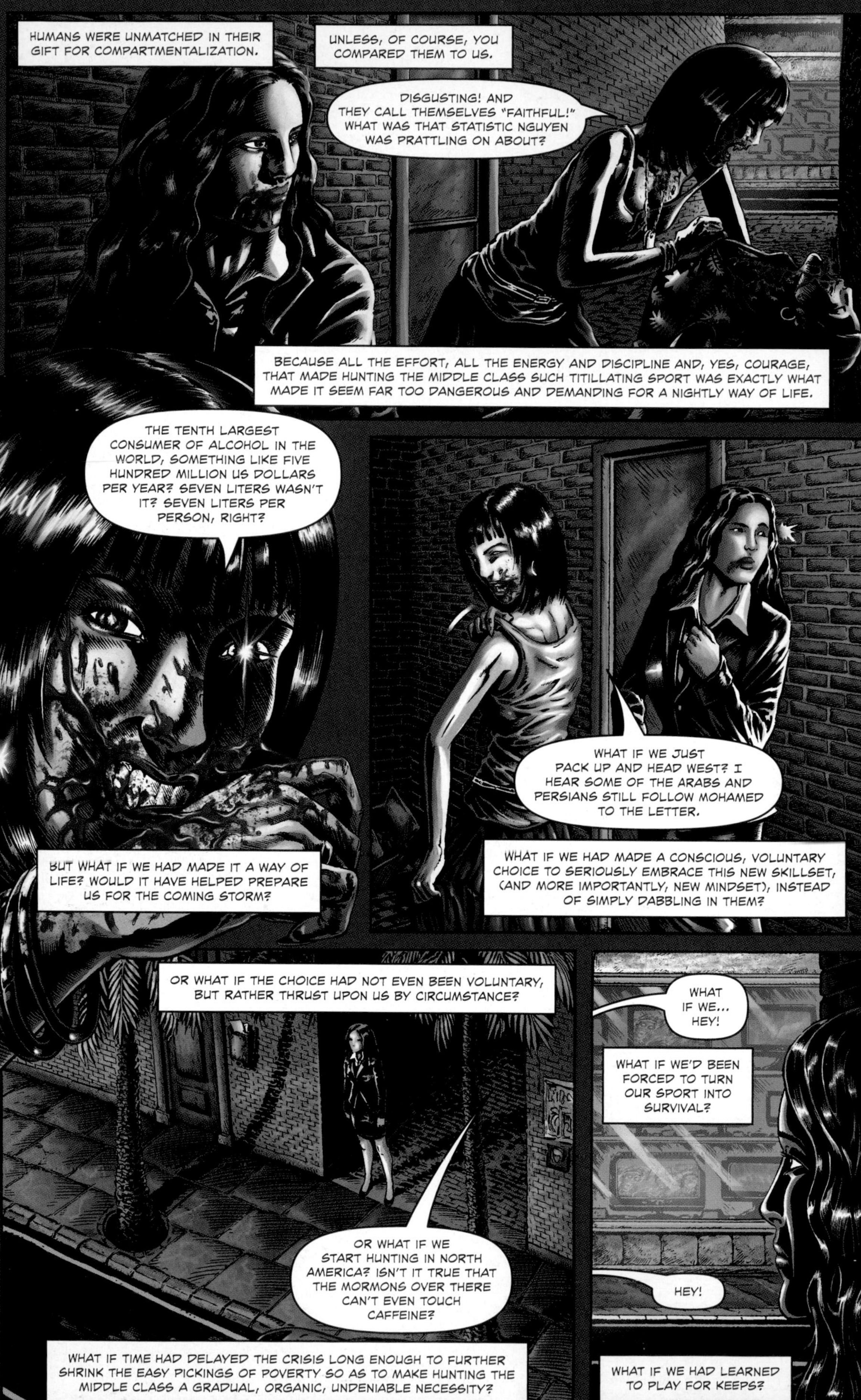
HUMANS WERE UNMATCHED IN THEIR GIFT FOR COMPARTMENTALIZATION.
UNLESS, OF COURSE, YOU COMPARED THEM TO US.
DISGUSTING! AND THEY CALL THEMSELVES "FAITHFUL!" WHAT WAS THAT STATISTIC NGUYEN WAS PRATTLING ON ABOUT?
BECAUSE ALL THE EFFORT, ALL THE ENERGY AND DISCIPLINE AND, YES, COURAGE, THAT MADE HUNTING THE MIDDLE CLASS SUCH TITILLATING SPORT WAS EXACTLY WHAT MADE IT SEEM FAR TOO DANGEROUS AND DEMANDING FOR A NIGHTLY WAY OF LIFE.
THE TENTH LARGEST CONSUMER OF ALCOHOL IN THE WORLD, SOMETHING LIKE FIVE HUNDRED MILLION US DOLLARS PER YEAR? SEVEN LITERS WASN'T IT? SEVEN LITERS PER PERSON, RIGHT?
BUT WHAT IF WE HAD MADE IT A WAY OF LIFE? WOULD IT HAVE HELPED PREPARE US FOR THE COMING STORM?
WHAT IF WE JUST PACK UP AND HEAD WEST? I HEAR SOME OF THE ARABS AND PERSIANS STILL FOLLOW MOHAMED TO THE LETTER.
WHAT IF WE HAD MADE A CONSCIOUS, VOLUNTARY CHOICE TO SERIOUSLY EMBRACE THIS NEW SKILLSET, (AND MORE IMPORTANTLY, NEW MINDSET), INSTEAD OF SIMPLY DABBLING IN THEM?
OR WHAT IF THE CHOICE HAD NOT EVEN BEEN VOLUNTARY, BUT RATHER THRUST UPON US BY CIRCUMSTANCE?
OR WHAT IF WE START HUNTING IN NORTH AMERICA? ISN'T IT TRUE THAT THE MORMONS OVER THERE CAN'T EVEN TOUCH CAFFEINE?
WHAT IF TIME HAD DELAYED THE CRISIS LONG ENOUGH TO FURTHER SHRINK THE EASY PICKINGS OF POVERTY SO AS TO MAKE HUNTING THE MIDDLE CLASS A GRADUAL, ORGANIC, UNDENIABLE NECESSITY?
WHAT IF WE... HEY!
WHAT IF WE'D BEEN FORCED TO TURN OUR SPORT INTO SURVIVAL?
HEY!
WHAT IF WE HAD LEARNED TO PLAY FOR KEEPS?

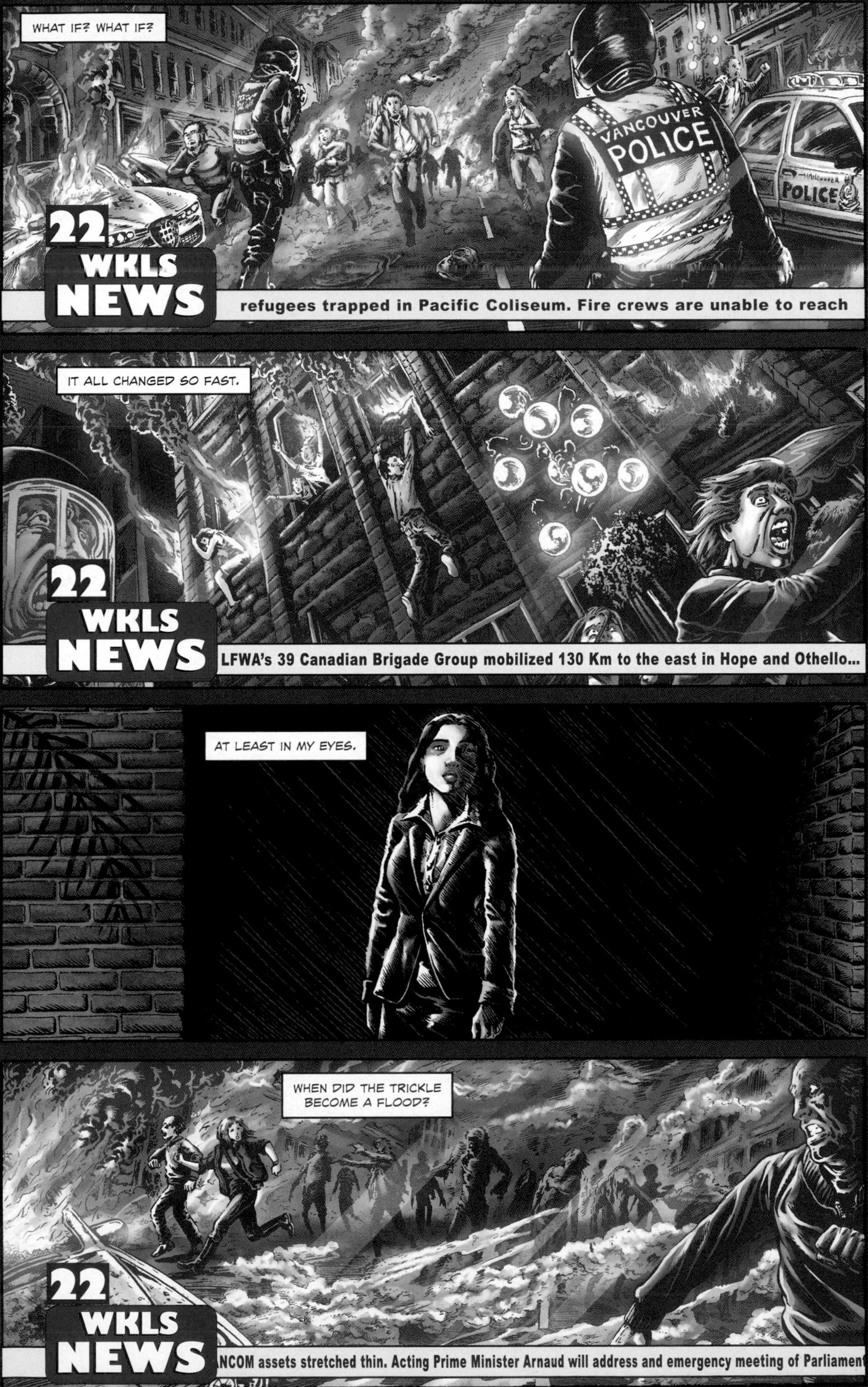
WHAT IF? WHAT IF?
VANCOUVER POLICE
POLICE
22
WKLS NEWS
refugees trapped in Pacific Coliseum. Fire crews are unable to reach
IT ALL CHANGED SO FAST.
22
WKLS NEWS
LFWA's 39 Canadian Brigade Group mobilized 130 Km to the east in Hope and Othello...
AT LEAST IN MY EYES.
WHEN DID THE TRICKLE BECOME A FLOOD?
22
WKLS NEWS
ANCOM assets stretched thin. Acting Prime Minister Arnaud will address and emergency meeting of Parliament

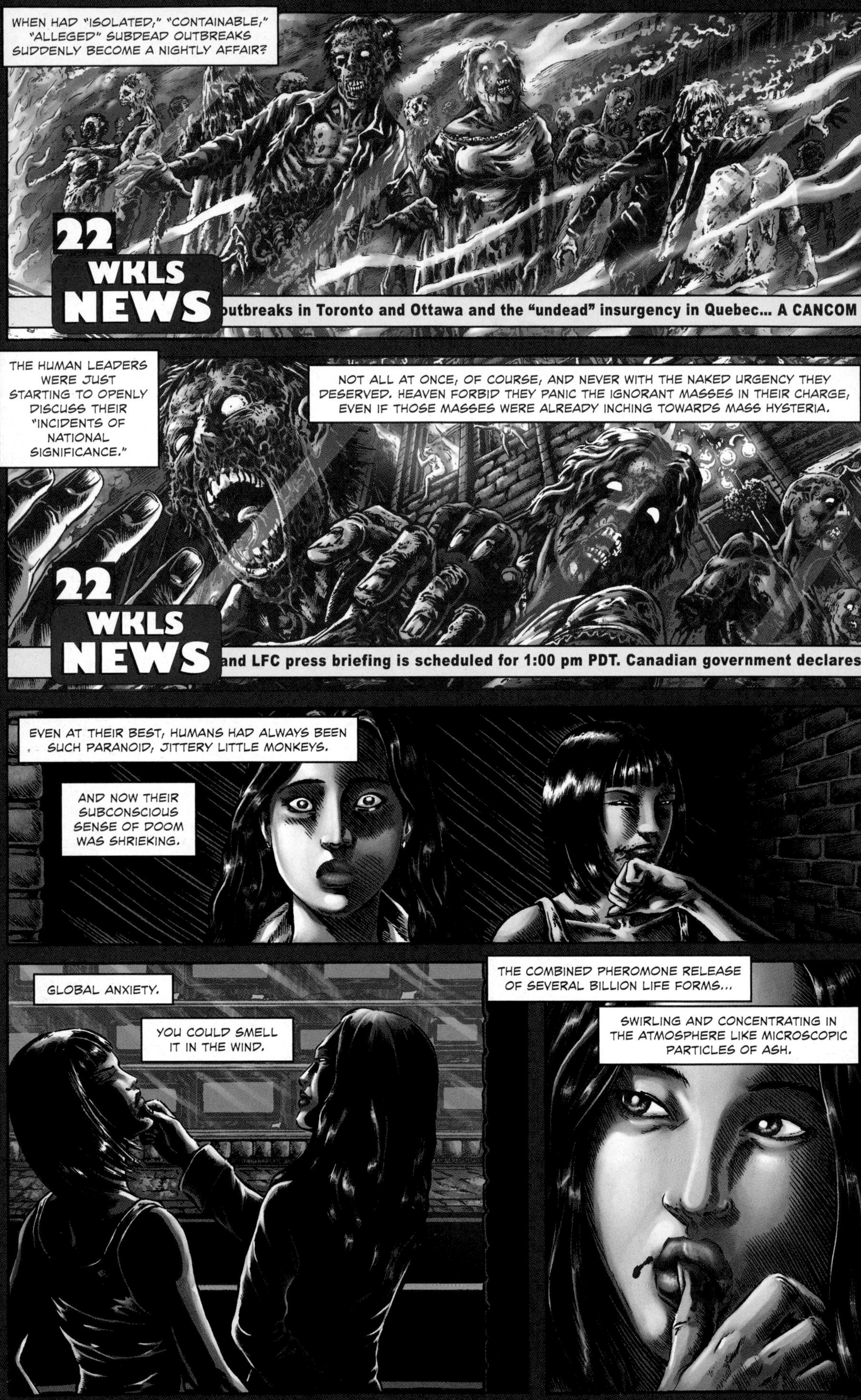
WHEN HAD "ISOLATED," "CONTAINABLE," "ALLEGED" SUBDEAD OUTBREAKS SUDDENLY BECOME A NIGHTLY AFFAIR?
22 WKLS NEWS
outbreaks in Toronto and Ottawa and the "undead" insurgency in Quebec... A CANCOM
THE HUMAN LEADERS WERE JUST STARTING TO OPENLY DISCUSS THEIR "INCIDENTS OF NATIONAL SIGNIFICANCE."
NOT ALL AT ONCE, OF COURSE, AND NEVER WITH THE NAKED URGENCY THEY DESERVED. HEAVEN FORBID THEY PANIC THE IGNORANT MASSES IN THEIR CHARGE, EVEN IF THOSE MASSES WERE ALREADY INCHING TOWARDS MASS HYSTERIA.
22 WKLS NEWS
and LFC press briefing is scheduled for 1:00 pm PDT. Canadian government declares
EVEN AT THEIR BEST, HUMANS HAD ALWAYS BEEN SUCH PARANOID, JITTERY LITTLE MONKEYS.
AND NOW THEIR SUBCONSCIOUS SENSE OF DOOM WAS SHRIEKING.
GLOBAL ANXIETY.
YOU COULD SMELL IT IN THE WIND.
THE COMBINED PHEROMONE RELEASE OF SEVERAL BILLION LIFE FORMS...
SWIRLING AND CONCENTRATING IN THE ATMOSPHERE LIKE MICROSCOPIC PARTICLES OF ASH.

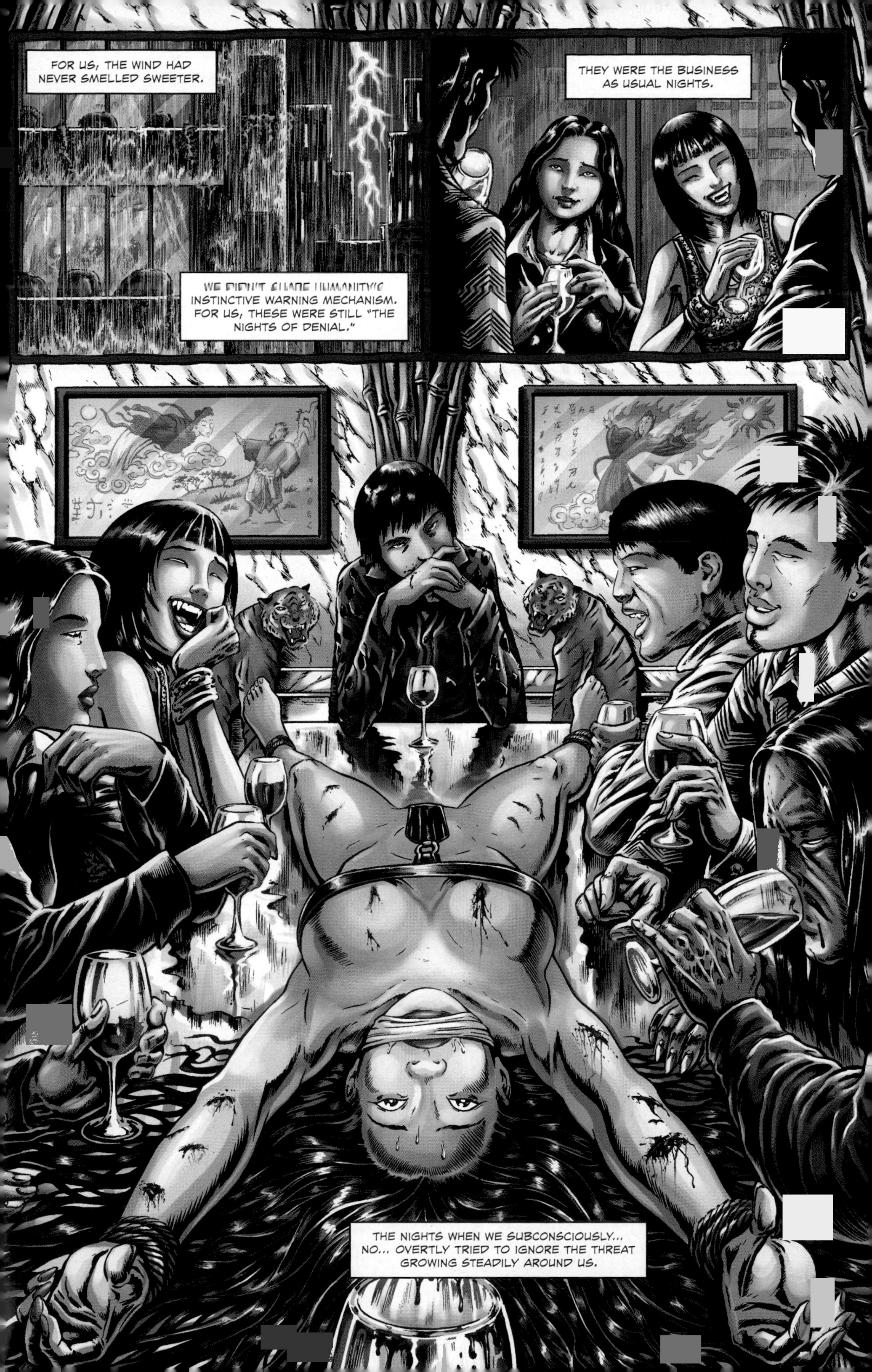
FOR US, THE WIND HAD NEVER SMELLED SWEETER.
WE DIDN'T SHARE HUMANITY'S INSTINCTIVE WARNING MECHANISM. FOR US, THESE WERE STILL "THE NIGHTS OF DENIAL."
THEY WERE THE BUSINESS AS USUAL NIGHTS.
THE NIGHTS WHEN WE SUBCONSCIOUSLY... NO... OVERTLY TRIED TO IGNORE THE THREAT GROWING STEADILY AROUND US.

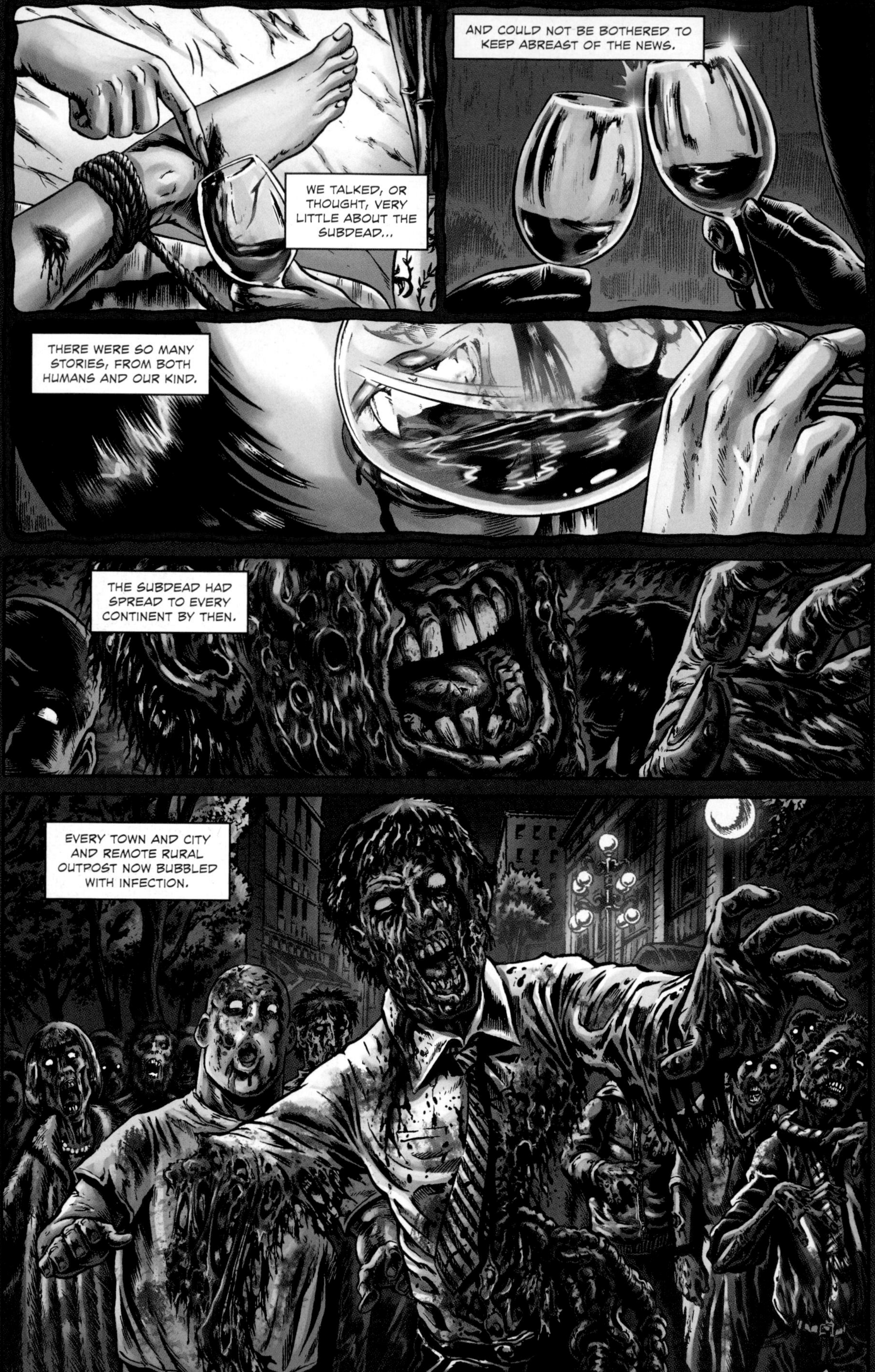
WE TALKED, OR THOUGHT, VERY LITTLE ABOUT THE SUBDEAD...
AND COULD NOT BE BOTHERED TO KEEP ABREAST OF THE NEWS.
THERE WERE SO MANY STORIES, FROM BOTH HUMANS AND OUR KIND.
THE SUBDEAD HAD SPREAD TO EVERY CONTINENT BY THEN.
EVERY TOWN AND CITY AND REMOTE RURAL OUTPOST NOW BUBBLED WITH INFECTION.

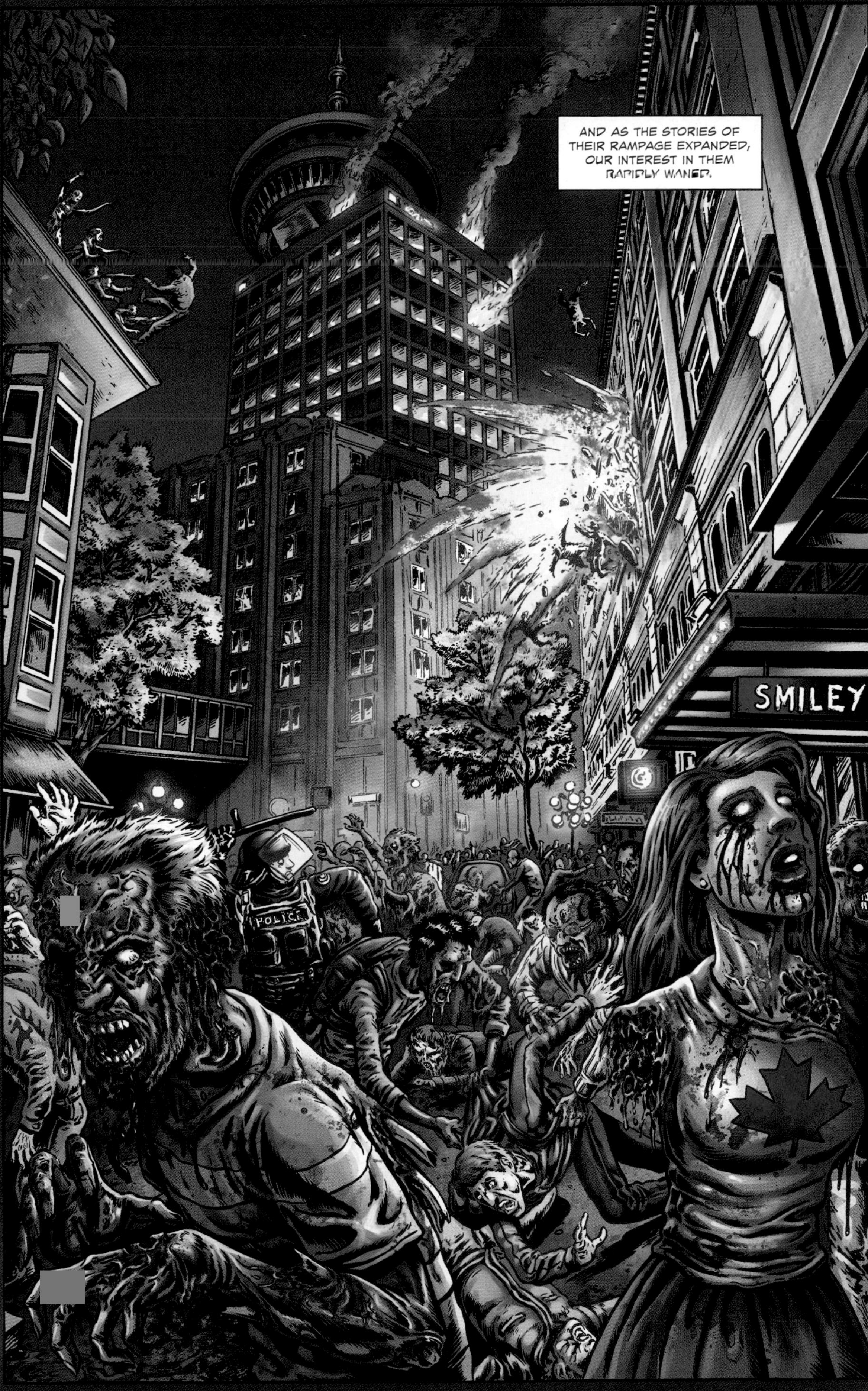
AND AS THE STORIES OF THEIR RAMPAGE EXPANDED, OUR INTEREST IN THEM RAPIDLY WANED.
SMILEY
POLICE

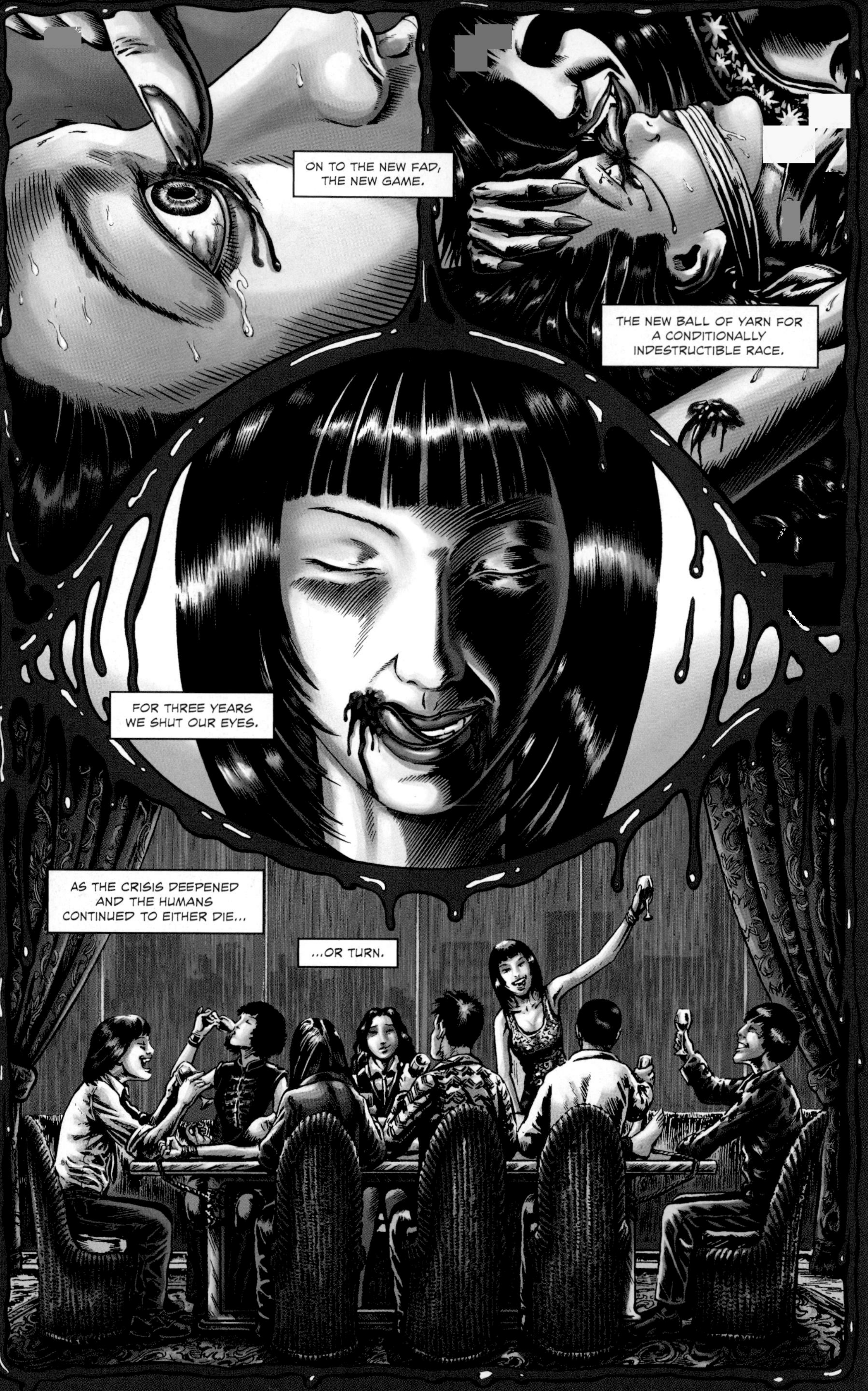
ON TO THE NEW FAD, THE NEW GAME.
THE NEW BALL OF YARN FOR A CONDITIONALLY INDESTRUCTIBLE RACE.
FOR THREE YEARS WE SHUT OUR EYES.
AS THE CRISIS DEEPENED AND THE HUMANS CONTINUED TO EITHER DIE...
...OR TURN.

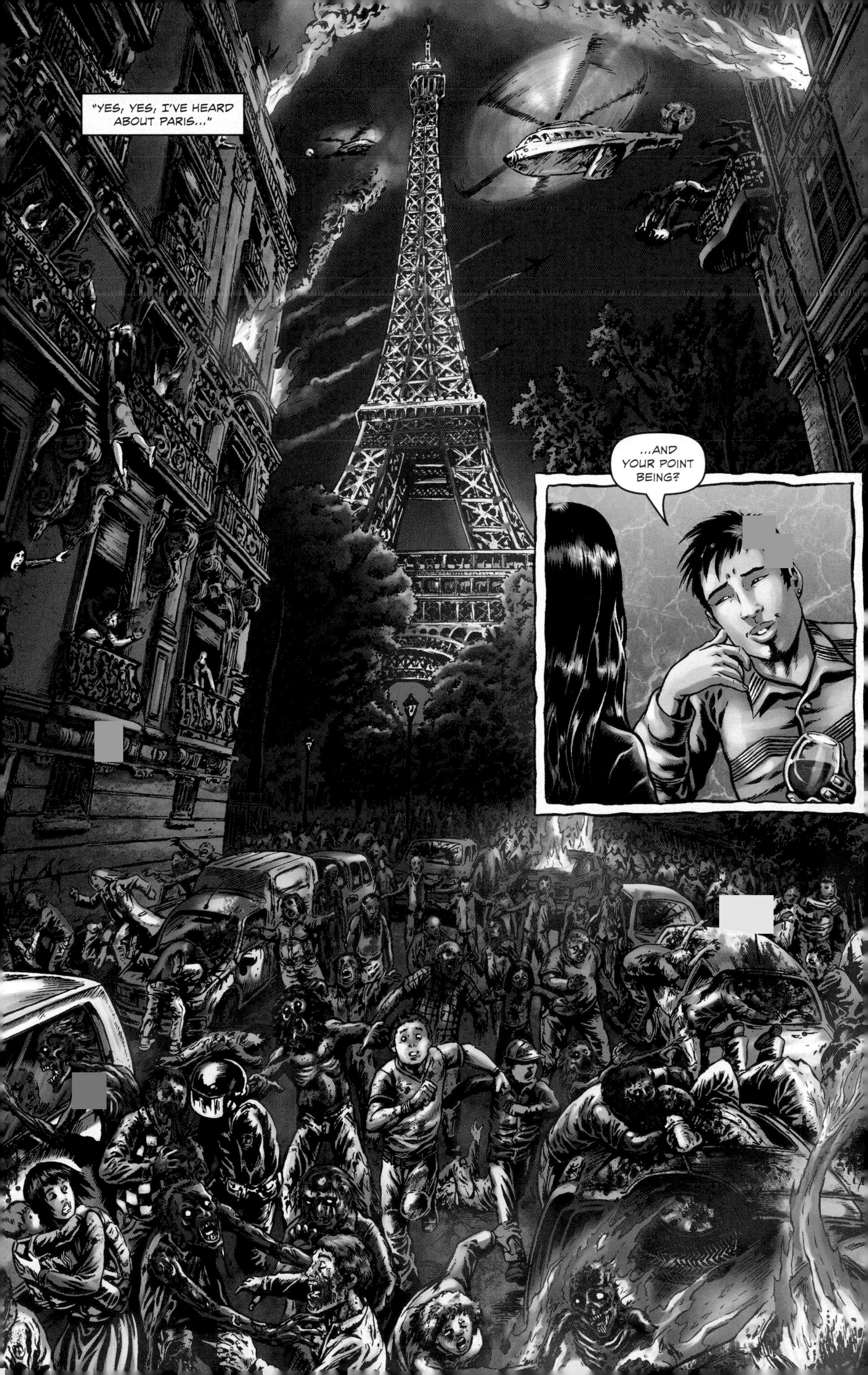
"YES, YES, I'VE HEARD ABOUT PARIS..."
...AND YOUR POINT BEING?

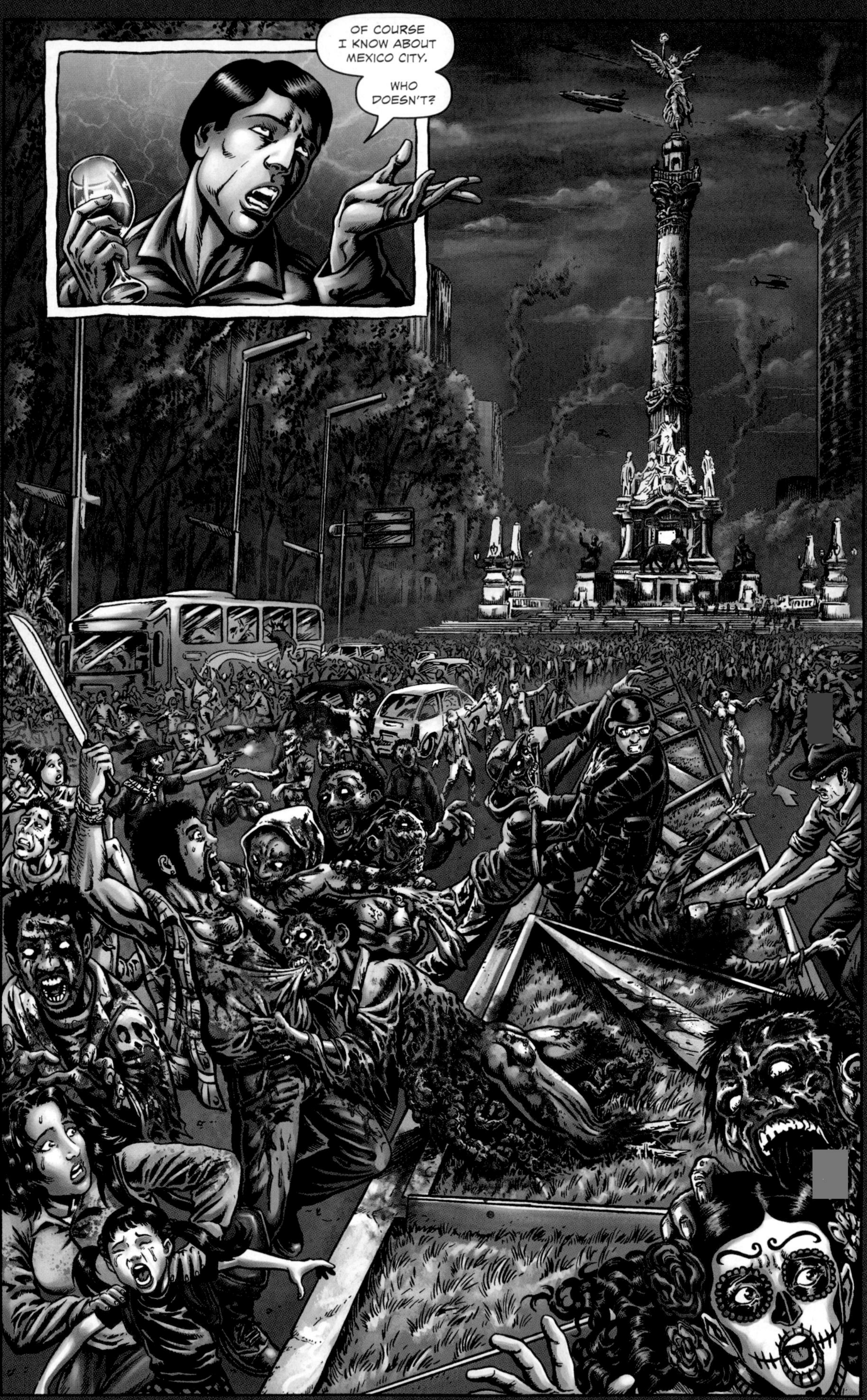
OF COURSE I KNOW ABOUT MEXICO CITY.
WHO DOESN'T?

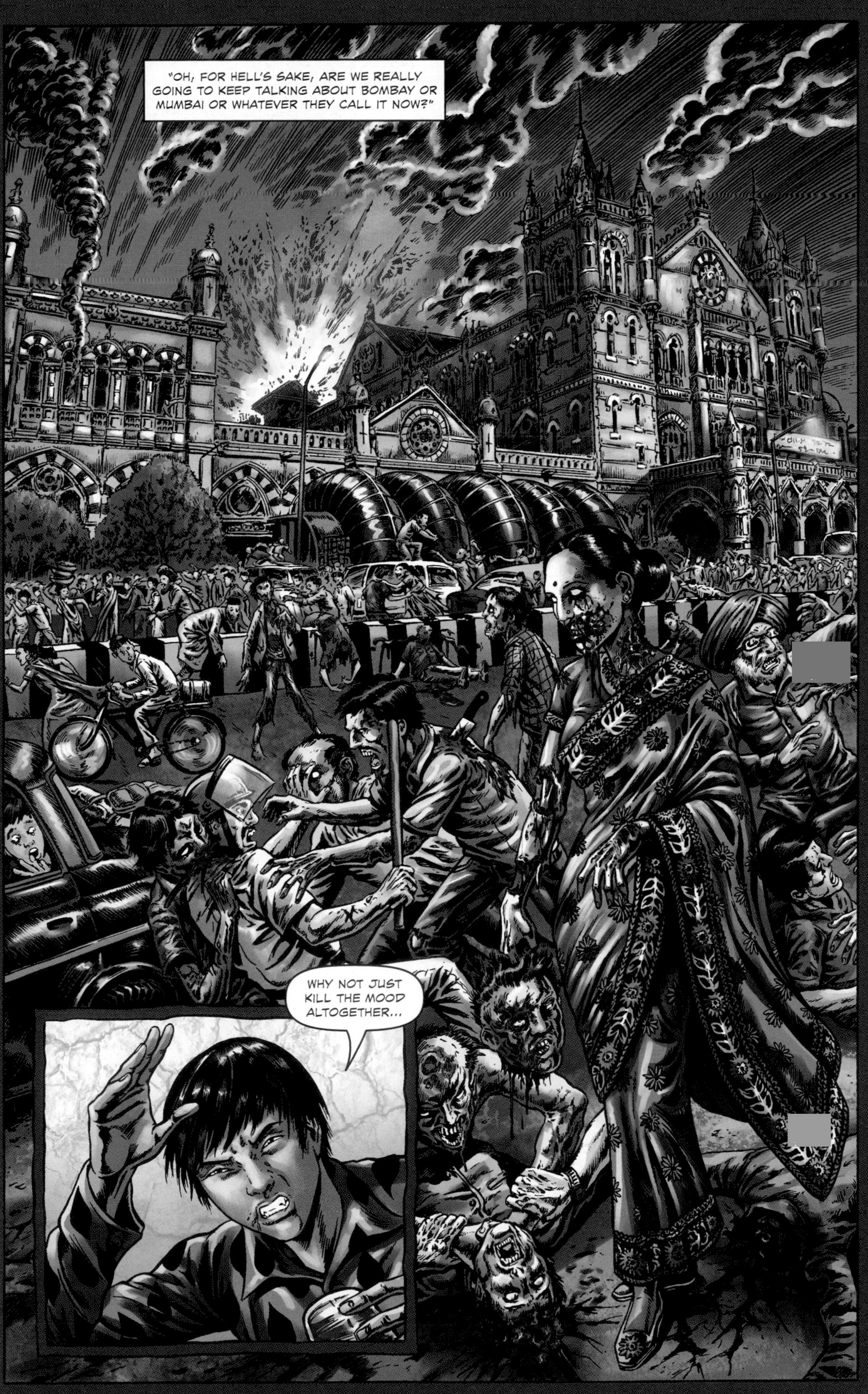
"OH, FOR HELL'S SAKE, ARE WE REALLY GOING TO KEEP TALKING ABOUT BOMBAY OR MUMBAI OR WHATEVER THEY CALL IT NOW?"
WHY NOT JUST KILL THE MOOD ALTOGETHER...

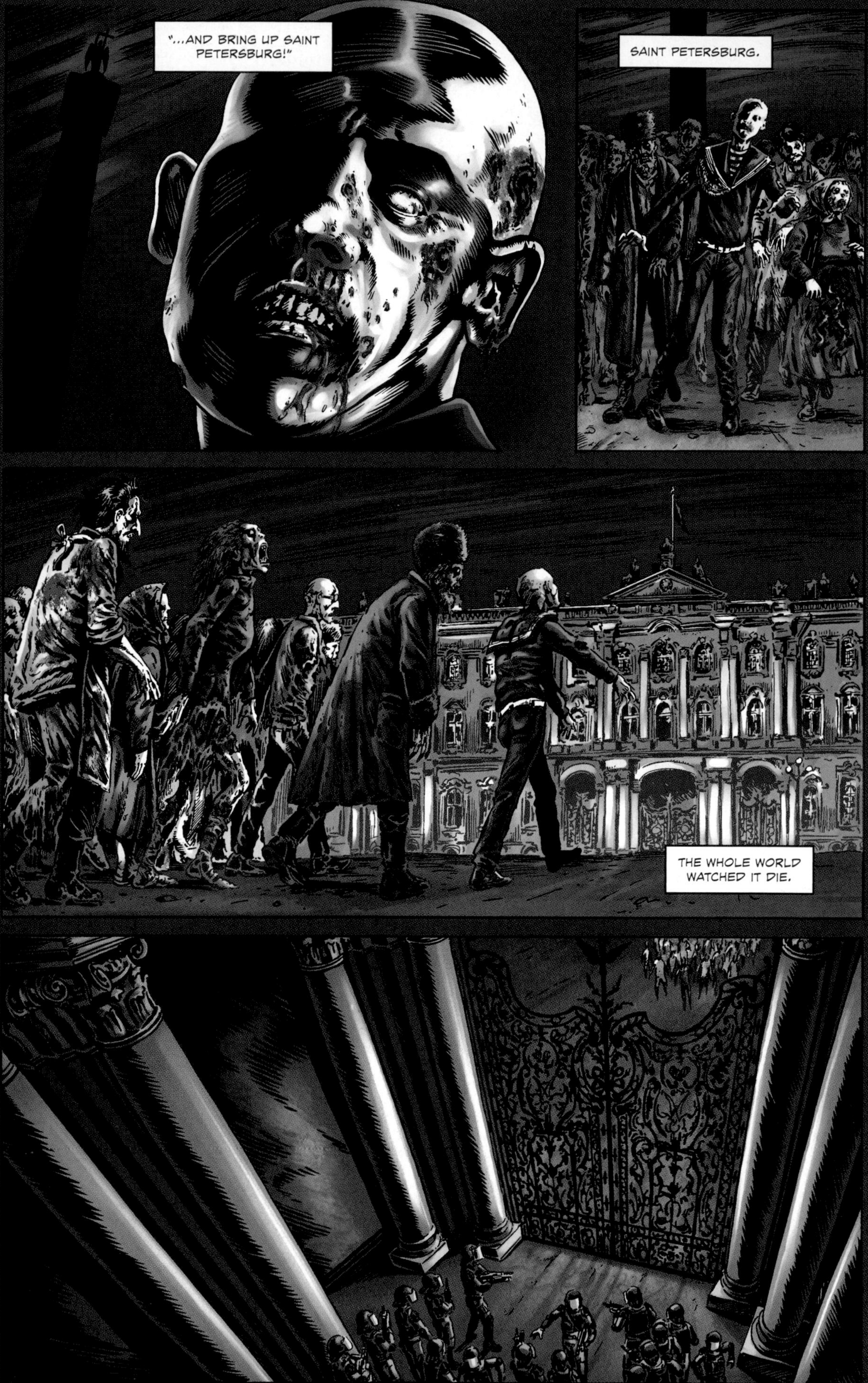
"...AND BRING UP SAINT PETERSBURG!"
SAINT PETERSBURG.
THE WHOLE WORLD WATCHED IT DIE.

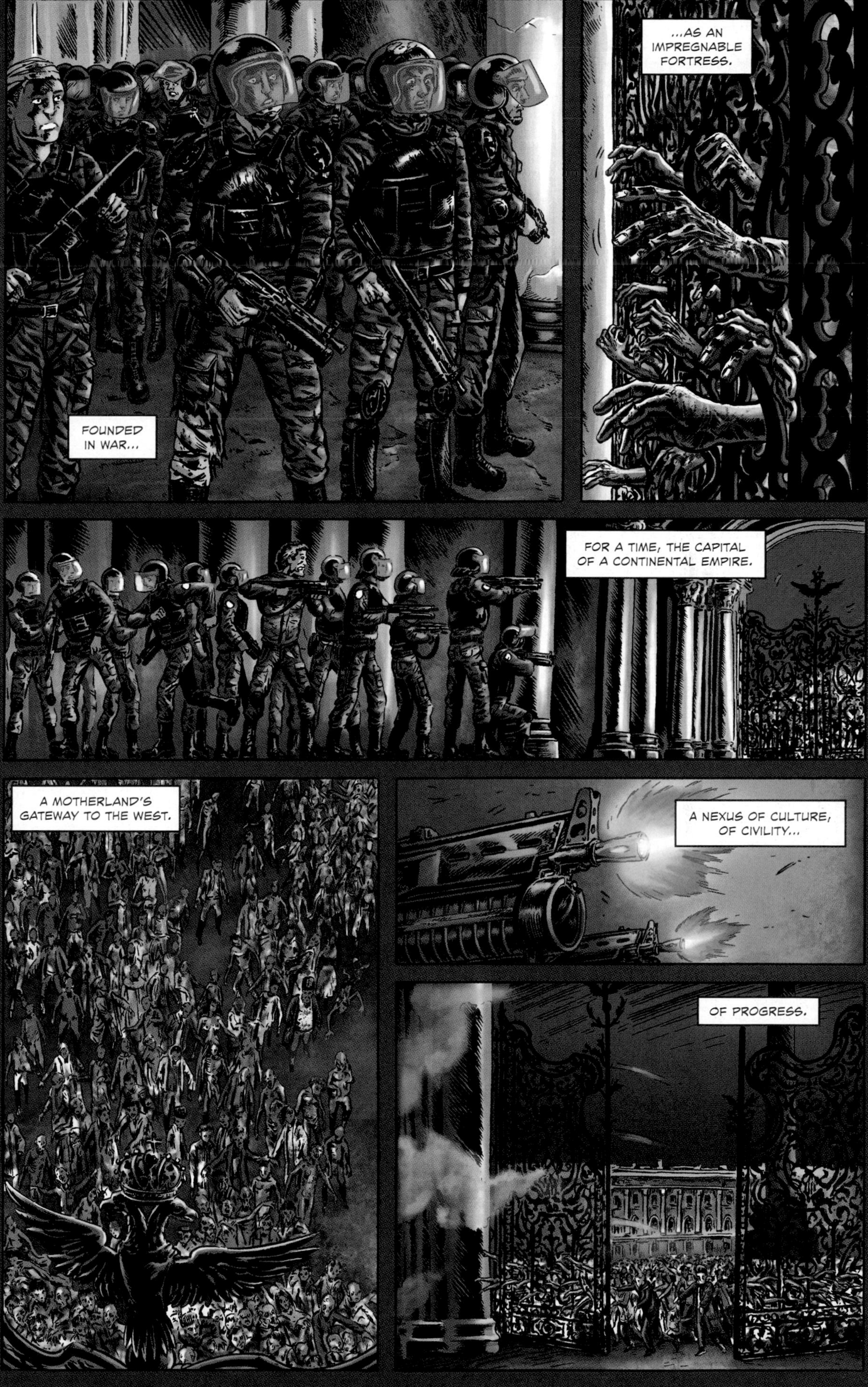
FOUNDED IN WAR...
...AS AN IMPREGNABLE FORTRESS.
FOR A TIME, THE CAPITAL OF A CONTINENTAL EMPIRE.
A MOTHERLAND'S GATEWAY TO THE WEST.
A NEXUS OF CULTURE, OF CIVILITY...
OF PROGRESS.

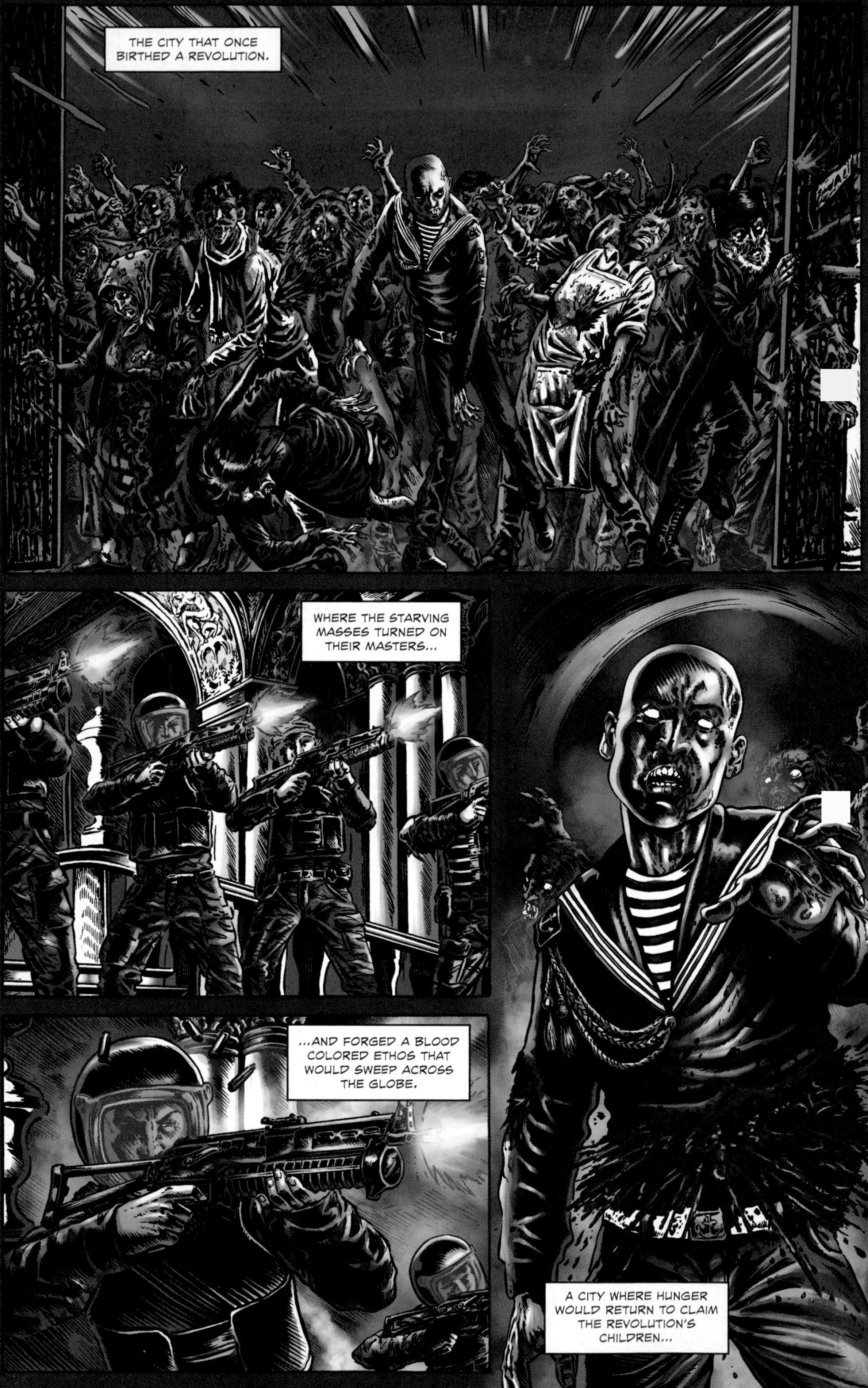
THE CITY THAT ONCE BIRTHED A REVOLUTION.
WHERE THE STARVING MASSES TURNED ON THEIR MASTERS...
...AND FORGED A BLOOD COLORED ETHOS THAT WOULD SWEEP ACROSS THE GLOBE.
A CITY WHERE HUNGER WOULD RETURN TO CLAIM THE REVOLUTION'S CHILDREN...

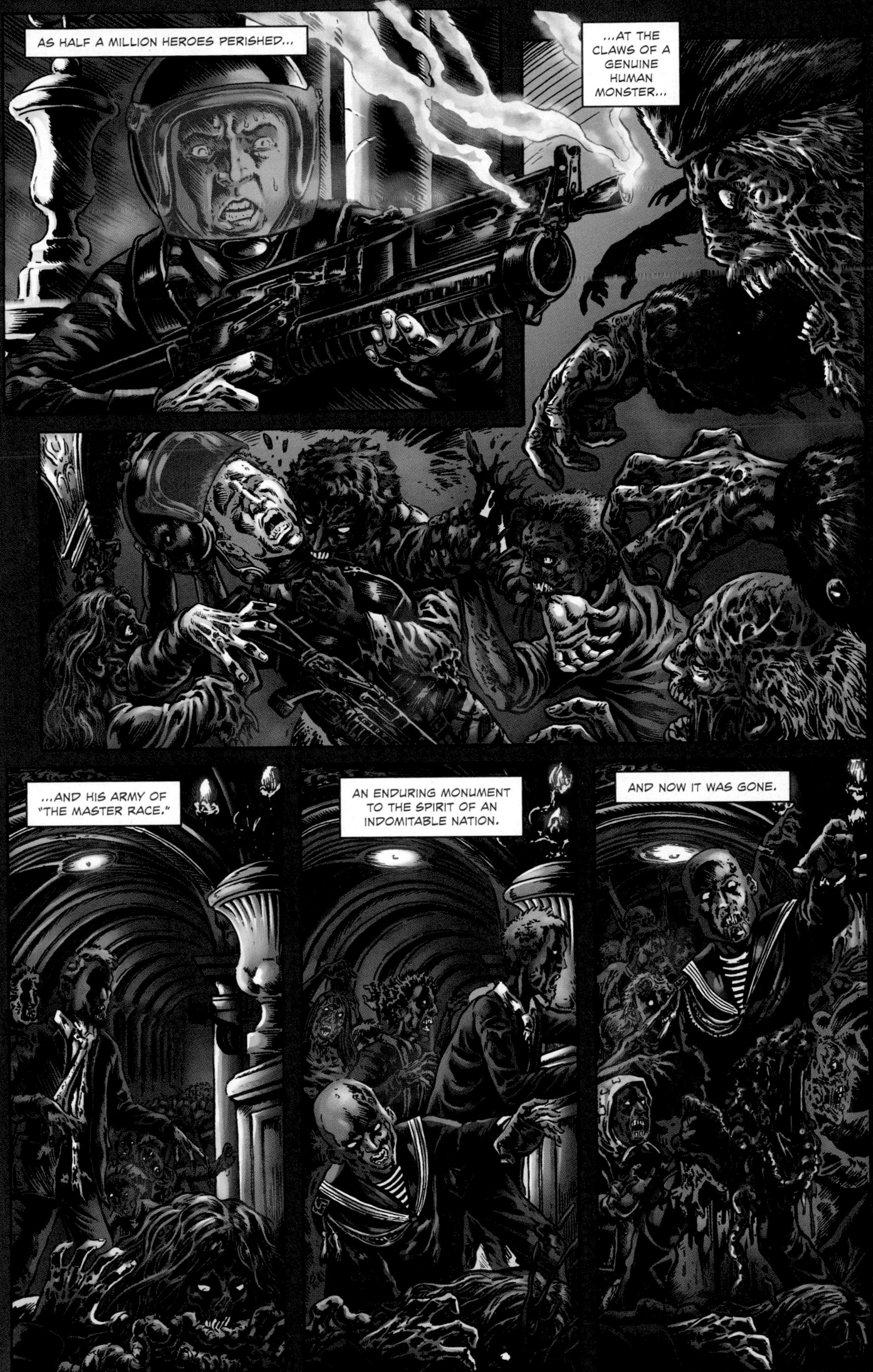
AS HALF A MILLION HEROES PERISHED...
...AT THE CLAWS OF A GENUINE HUMAN MONSTER...
...AND HIS ARMY OF "THE MASTER RACE."
AN ENDURING MONUMENT TO THE SPIRIT OF AN INDOMITABLE NATION.
AND NOW IT WAS GONE.

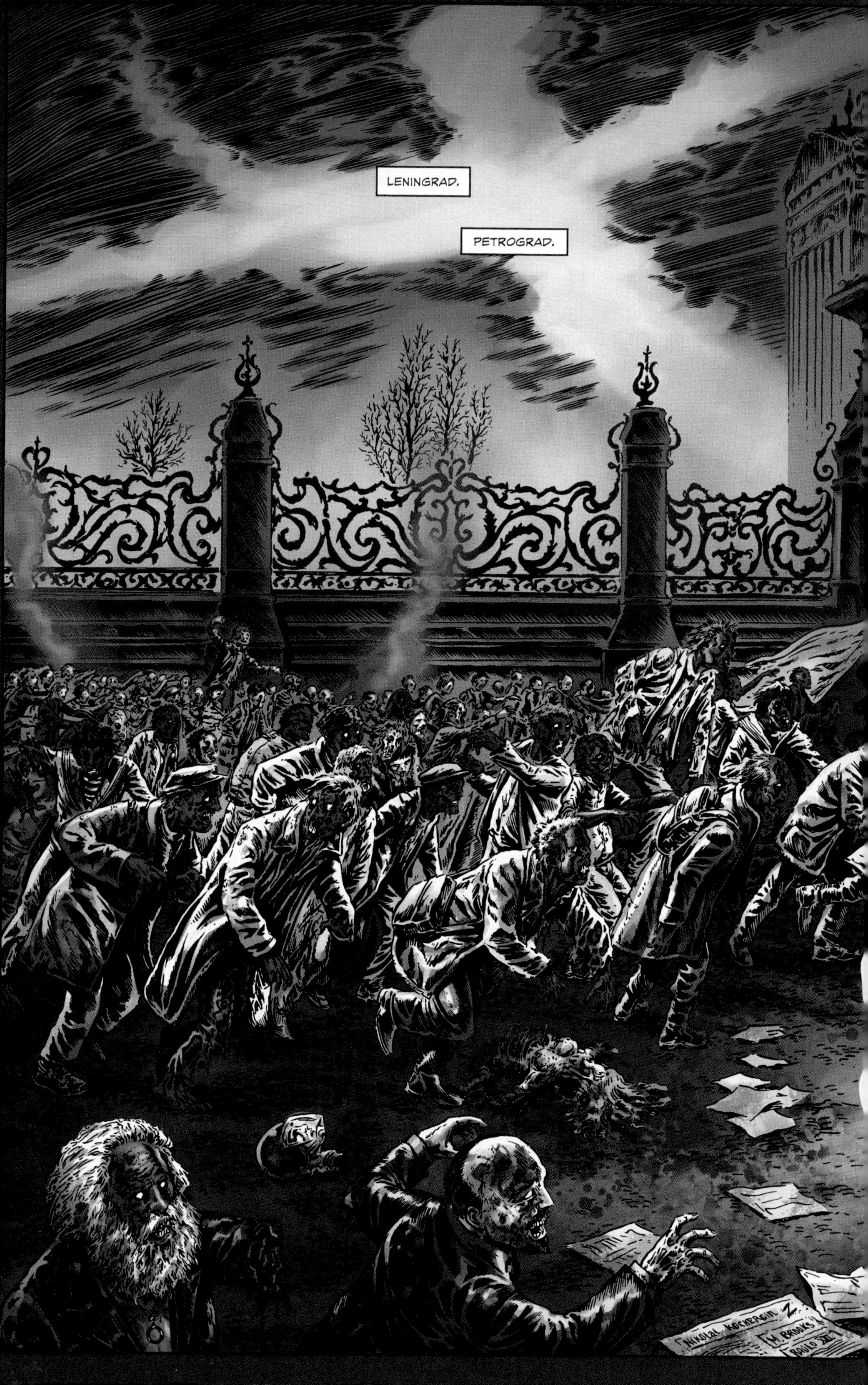
LENINGRAD.
PETROGRAD.
NIKOLAI KOCHERGIN
Z
M. BROOKS

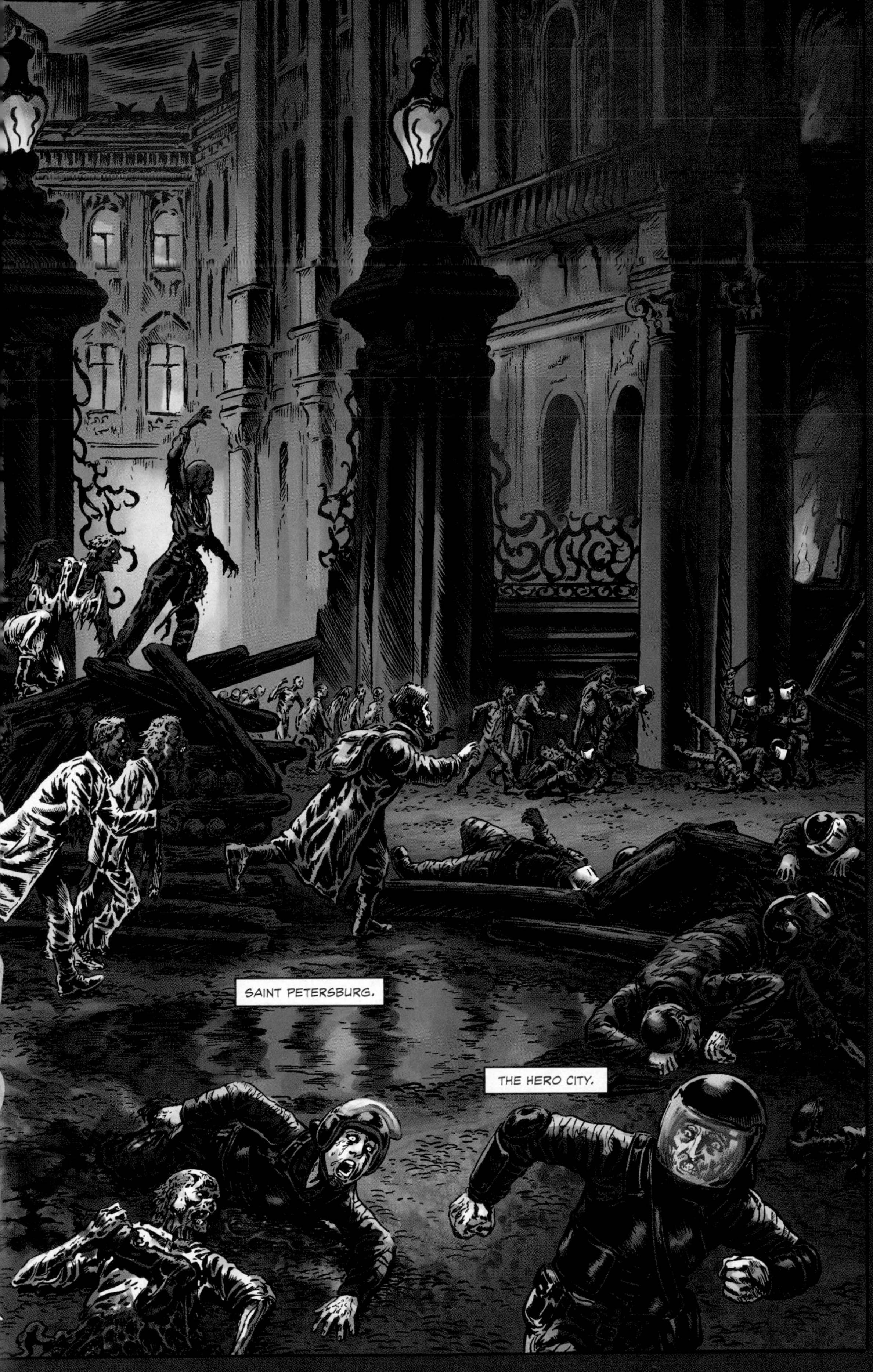
SAINT PETERSBURG.
THE HERO CITY.

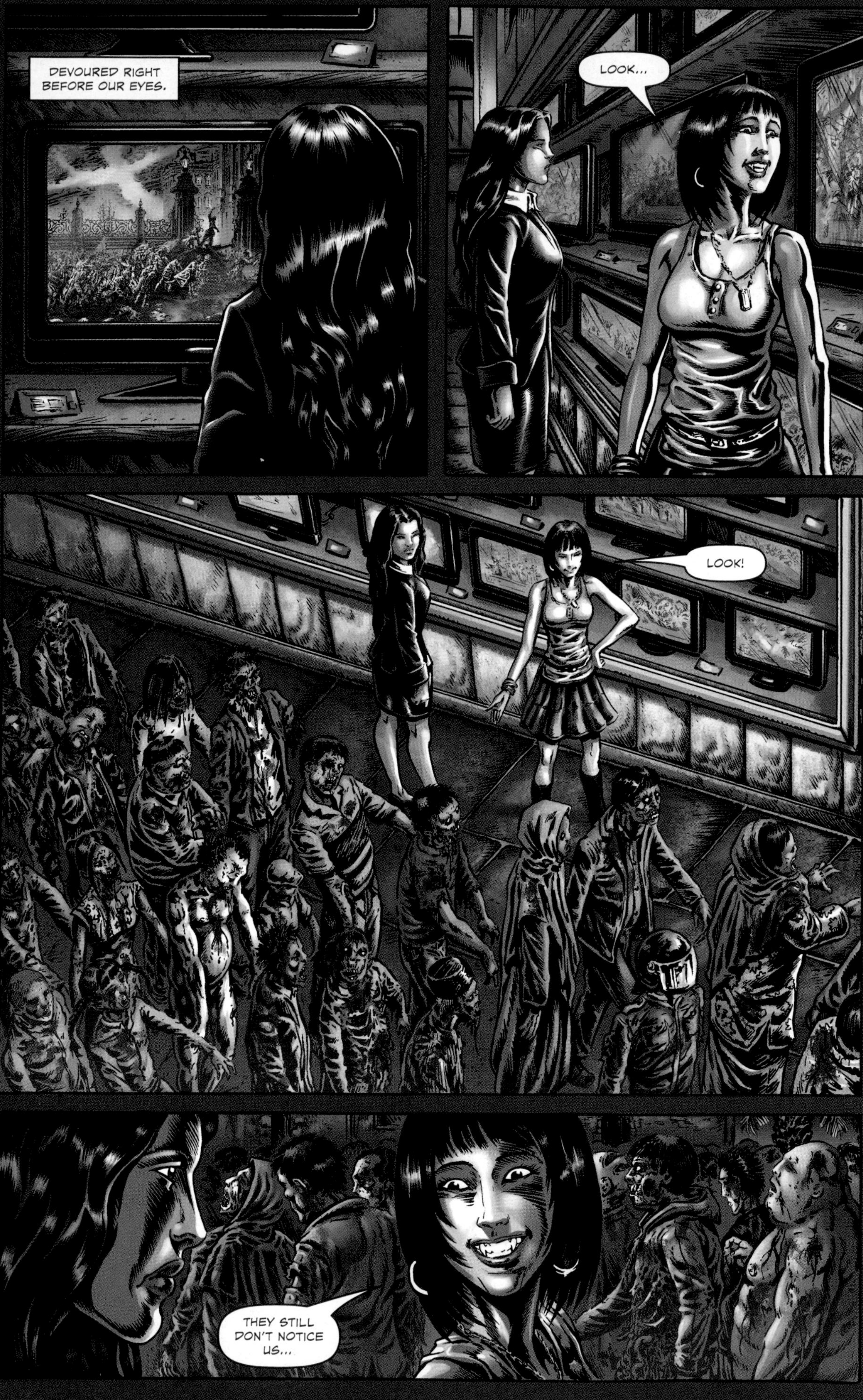
DEVOURED RIGHT BEFORE OUR EYES.
LOOK...
LOOK!
THEY STILL DON'T NOTICE US...

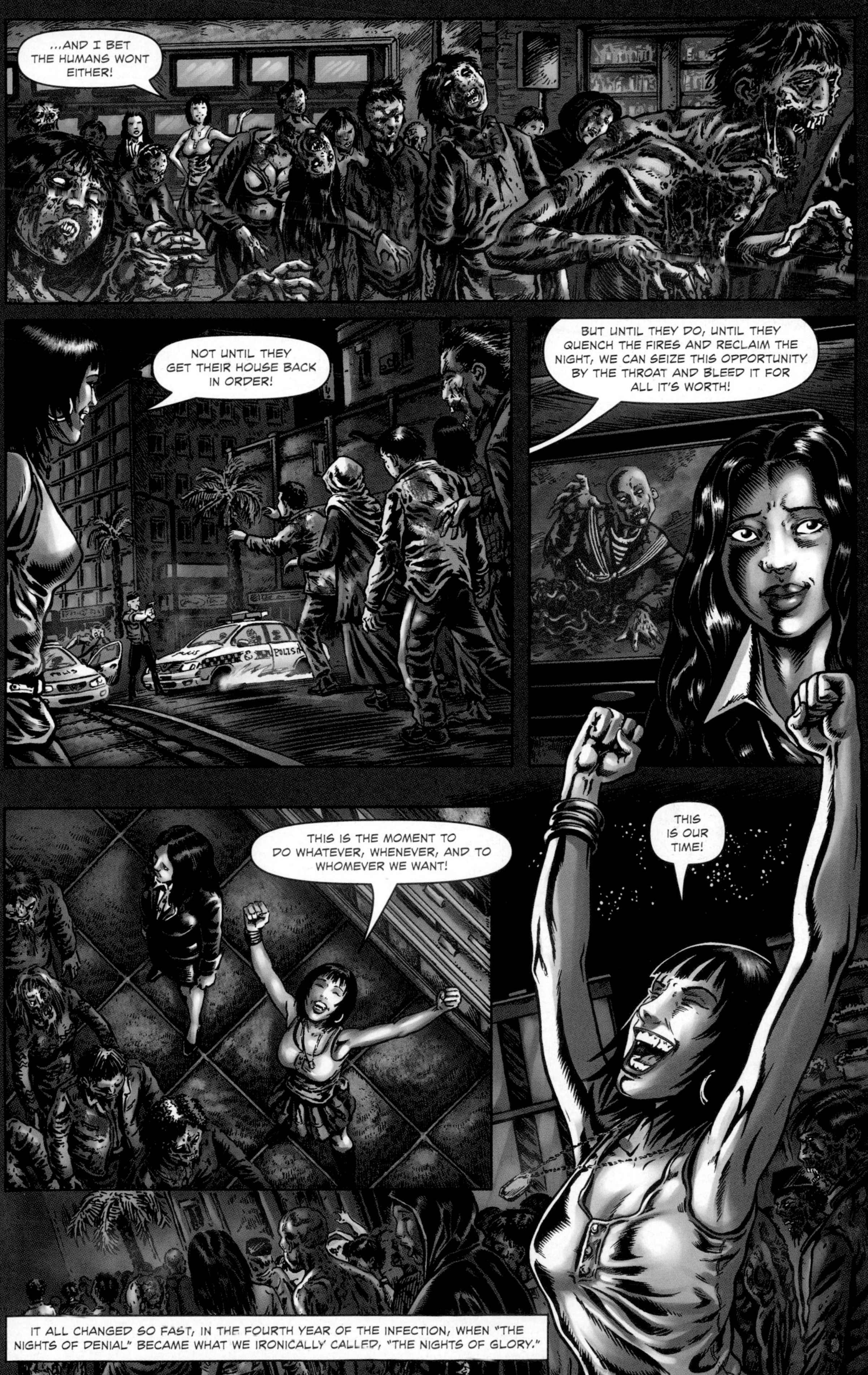
...AND I BET THE HUMANS WONT EITHER!
NOT UNTIL THEY GET THEIR HOUSE BACK IN ORDER!
BUT UNTIL THEY DO, UNTIL THEY QUENCH THE FIRES AND RECLAIM THE NIGHT, WE CAN SEIZE THIS OPPORTUNITY BY THE THROAT AND BLEED IT FOR ALL IT'S WORTH!
THIS IS THE MOMENT TO DO WHATEVER, WHENEVER, AND TO WHOMEVER WE WANT!
THIS IS OUR TIME!
IT ALL CHANGED SO FAST, IN THE FOURTH YEAR OF THE INFECTION, WHEN "THE NIGHTS OF DENIAL" BECAME WHAT WE IRONICALLY CALLED, "THE NIGHTS OF GLORY."

Chapter 3

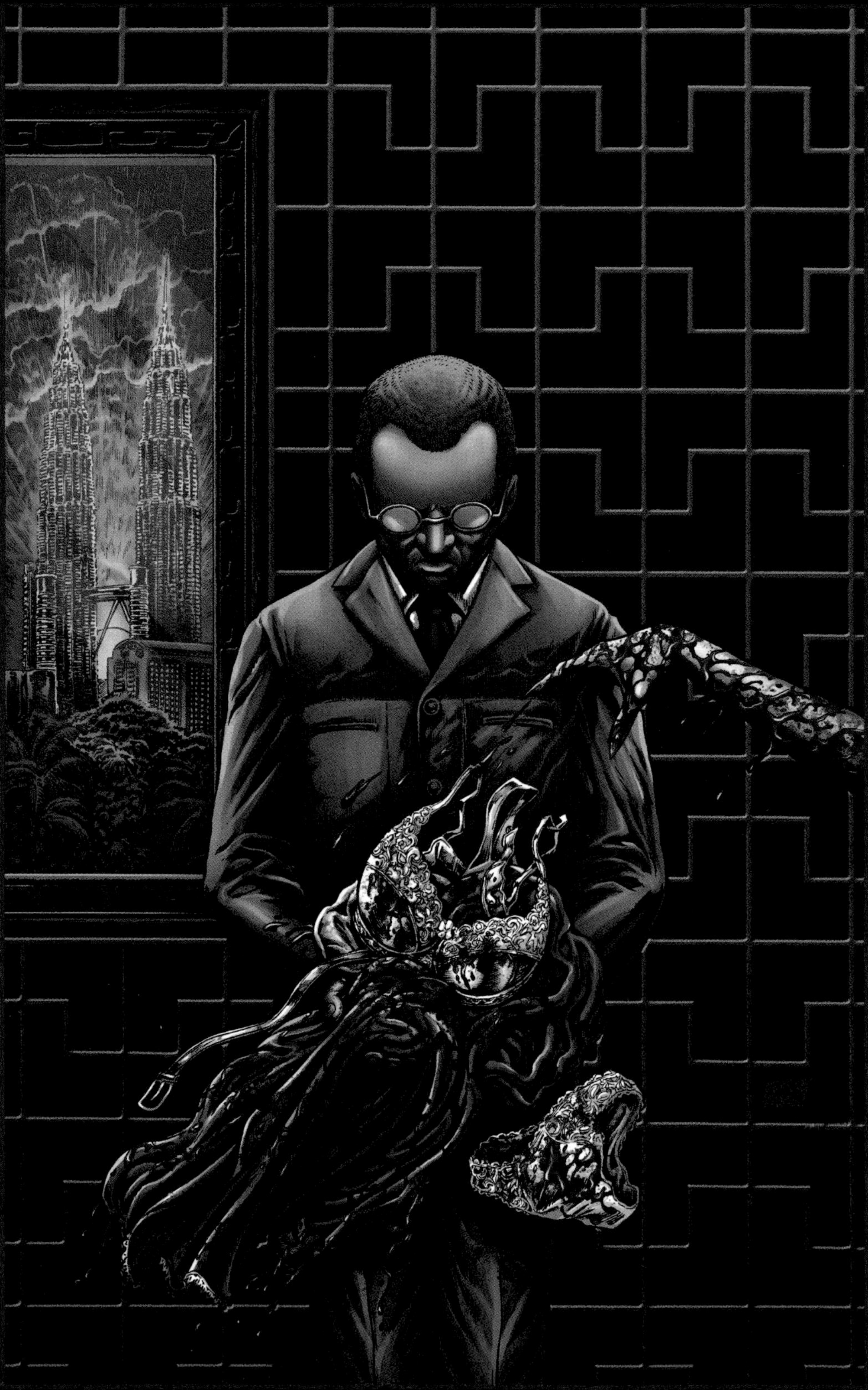

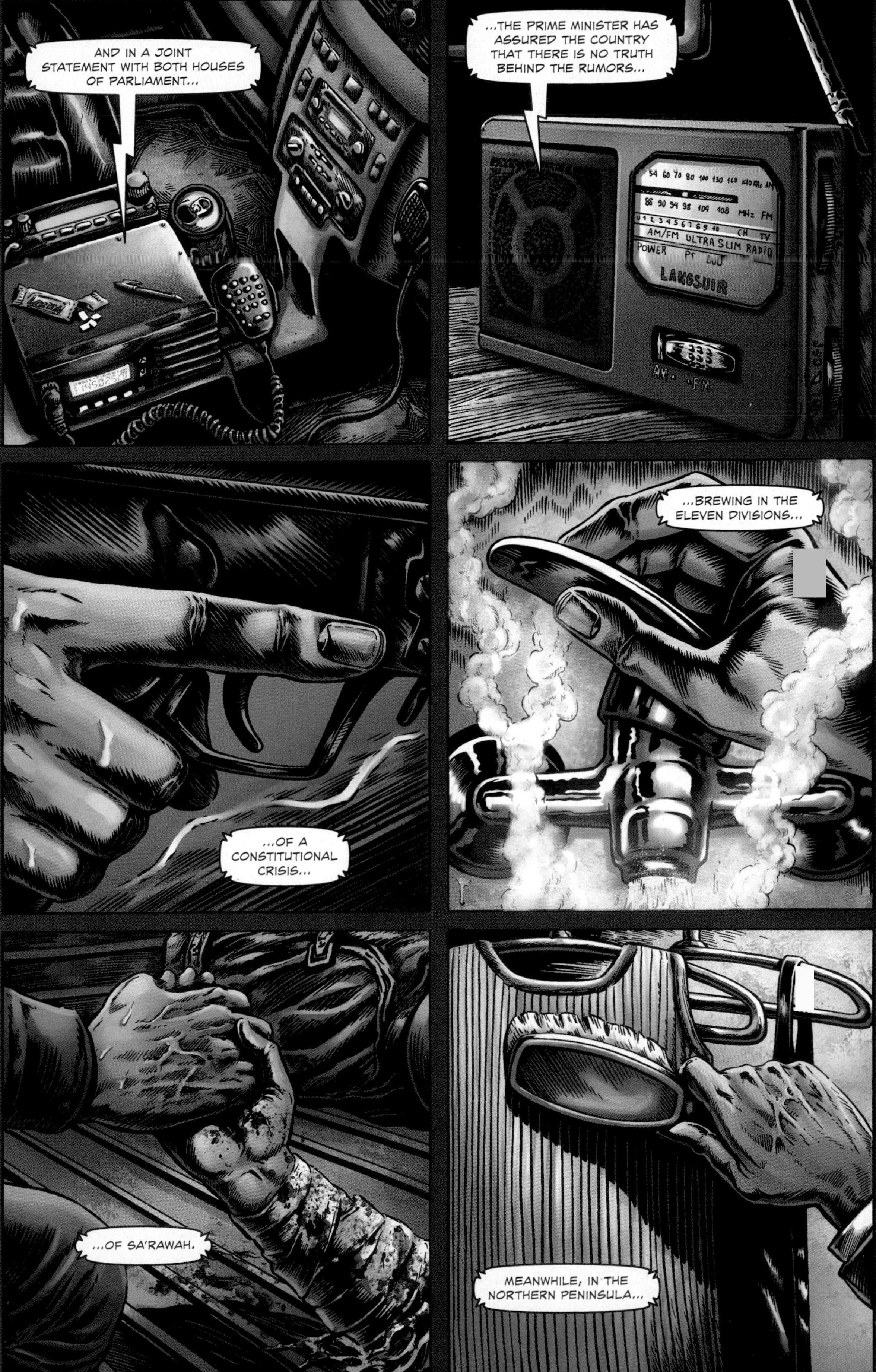
AND IN A JOINT STATEMENT WITH BOTH HOUSES OF PARLIAMENT...
...THE PRIME MINISTER HAS ASSURED THE COUNTRY THAT THERE IS NO TRUTH BEHIND THE RUMORS...
AM/FM ULTRA SLIM RADIO
LANGSUIR
...OF A CONSTITUTIONAL CRISIS...
...BREWING IN THE ELEVEN DIVISIONS...
...OF SA'RAWAH.
MEANWHILE, IN THE NORTHERN PENINSULA...

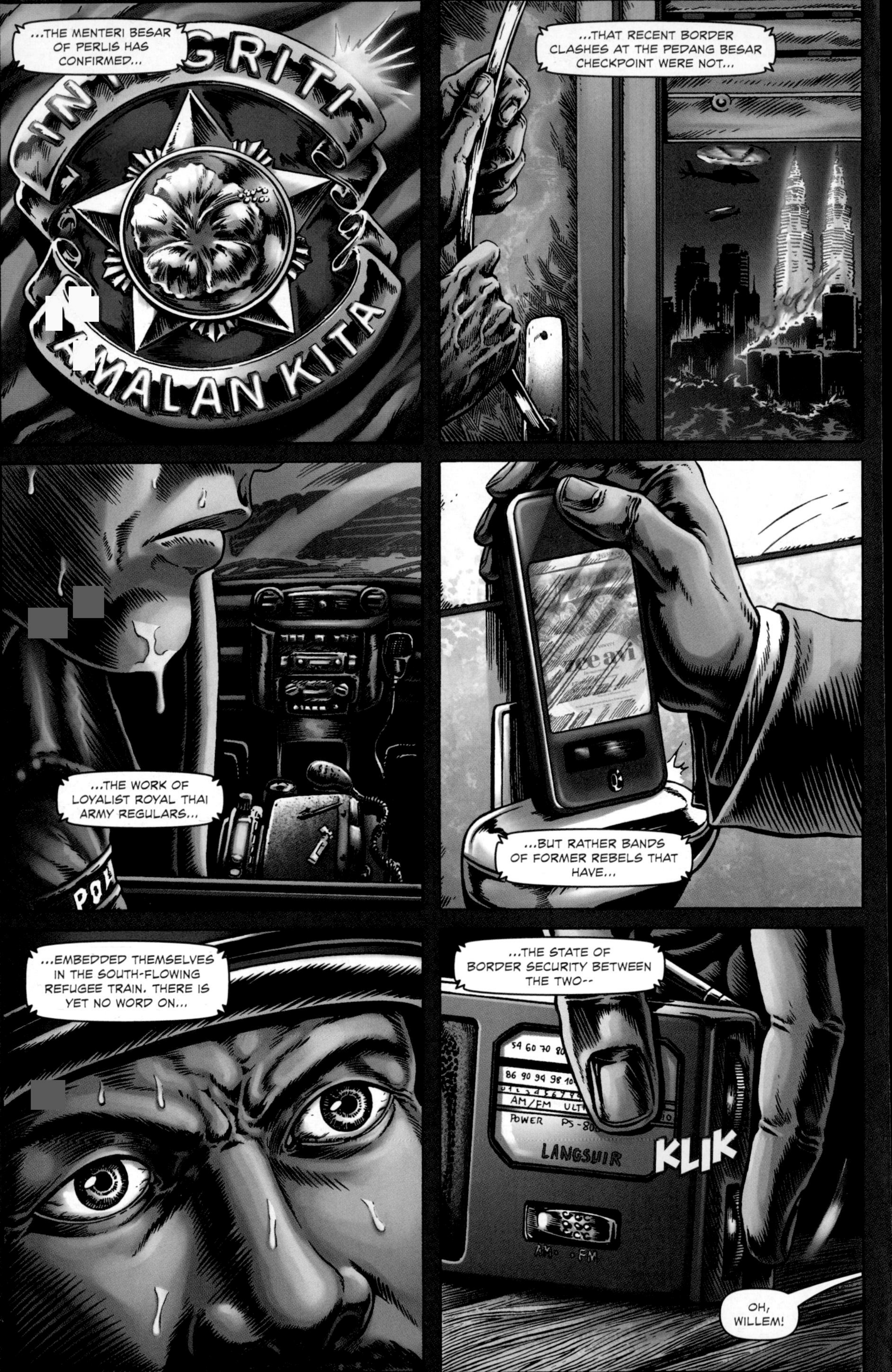
...THE MENTERI BESAR OF PERLIS HAS CONFIRMED...
...THAT RECENT BORDER CLASHES AT THE PEDANG BESAR CHECKPOINT WERE NOT...
...THE WORK OF LOYALIST ROYAL THAI ARMY REGULARS...
...BUT RATHER BANDS OF FORMER REBELS THAT HAVE...
...EMBEDDED THEMSELVES IN THE SOUTH-FLOWING REFUGEE TRAIN. THERE IS YET NO WORD ON...
...THE STATE OF BORDER SECURITY BETWEEN THE TWO--
LANGSUIR
KLIK
OH, WILLEM!

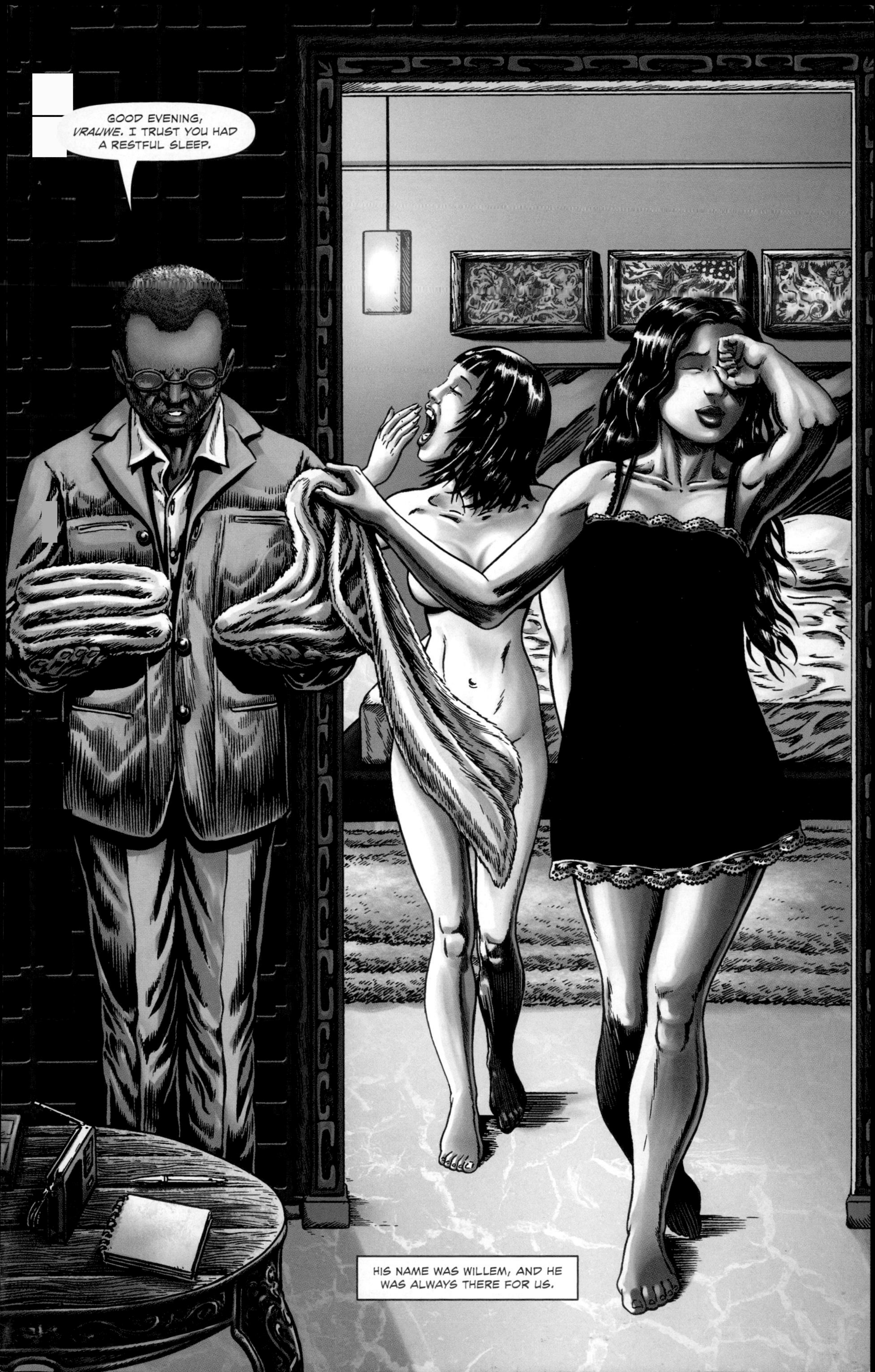
GOOD EVENING, *VRAUWE*. I TRUST YOU HAD A RESTFUL SLEEP.
HIS NAME WAS WILLEM, AND HE WAS ALWAYS THERE FOR US.

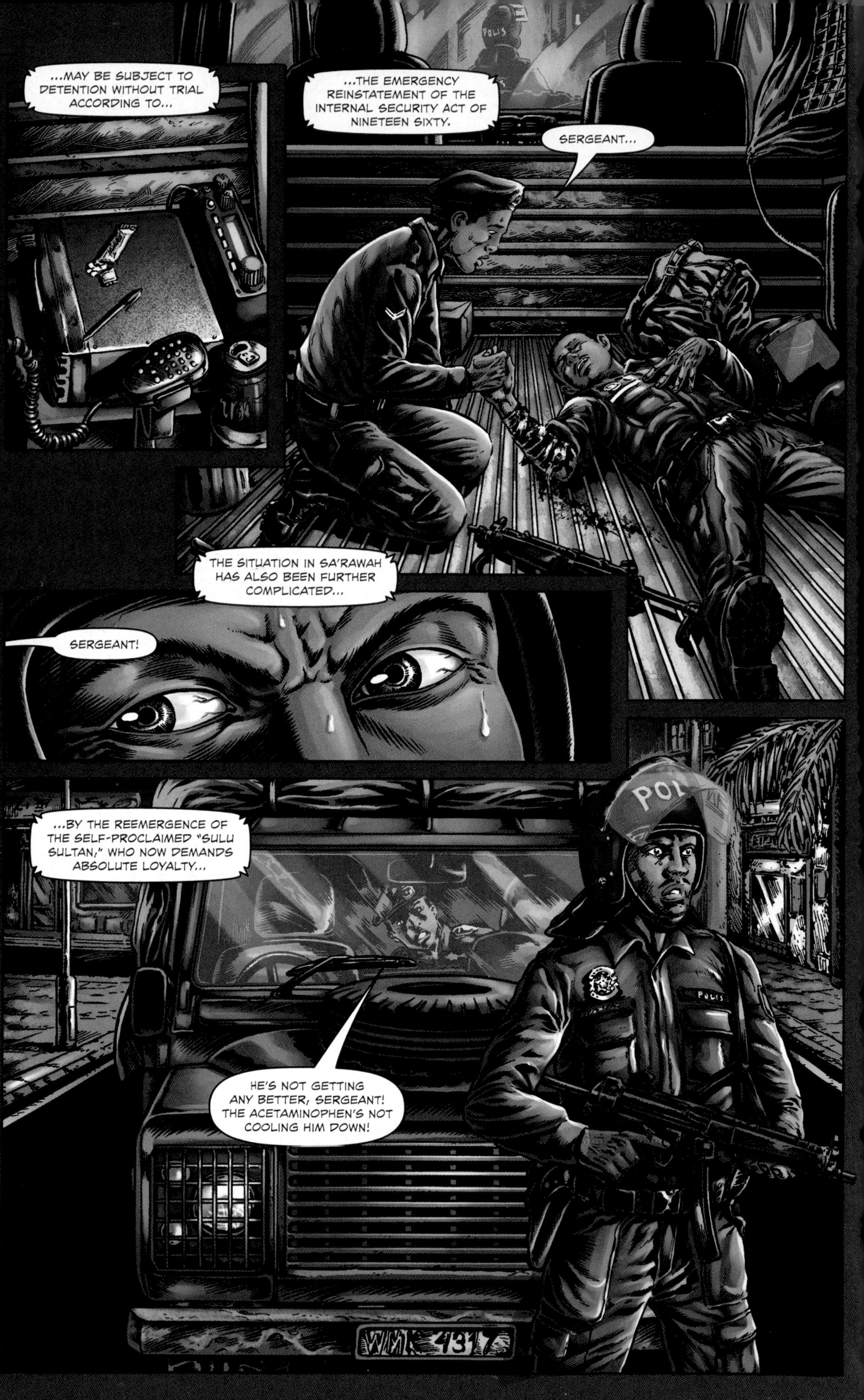
...MAY BE SUBJECT TO DETENTION WITHOUT TRIAL ACCORDING TO...
...THE EMERGENCY REINSTATEMENT OF THE INTERNAL SECURITY ACT OF NINETEEN SIXTY.
SERGEANT...
THE SITUATION IN SA'RAWAH HAS ALSO BEEN FURTHER COMPLICATED...
SERGEANT!
...BY THE REEMERGENCE OF THE SELF-PROCLAIMED "SULU SULTAN," WHO NOW DEMANDS ABSOLUTE LOYALTY...
HE'S NOT GETTING ANY BETTER, SERGEANT! THE ACETAMINOPHEN'S NOT COOLING HIM DOWN!

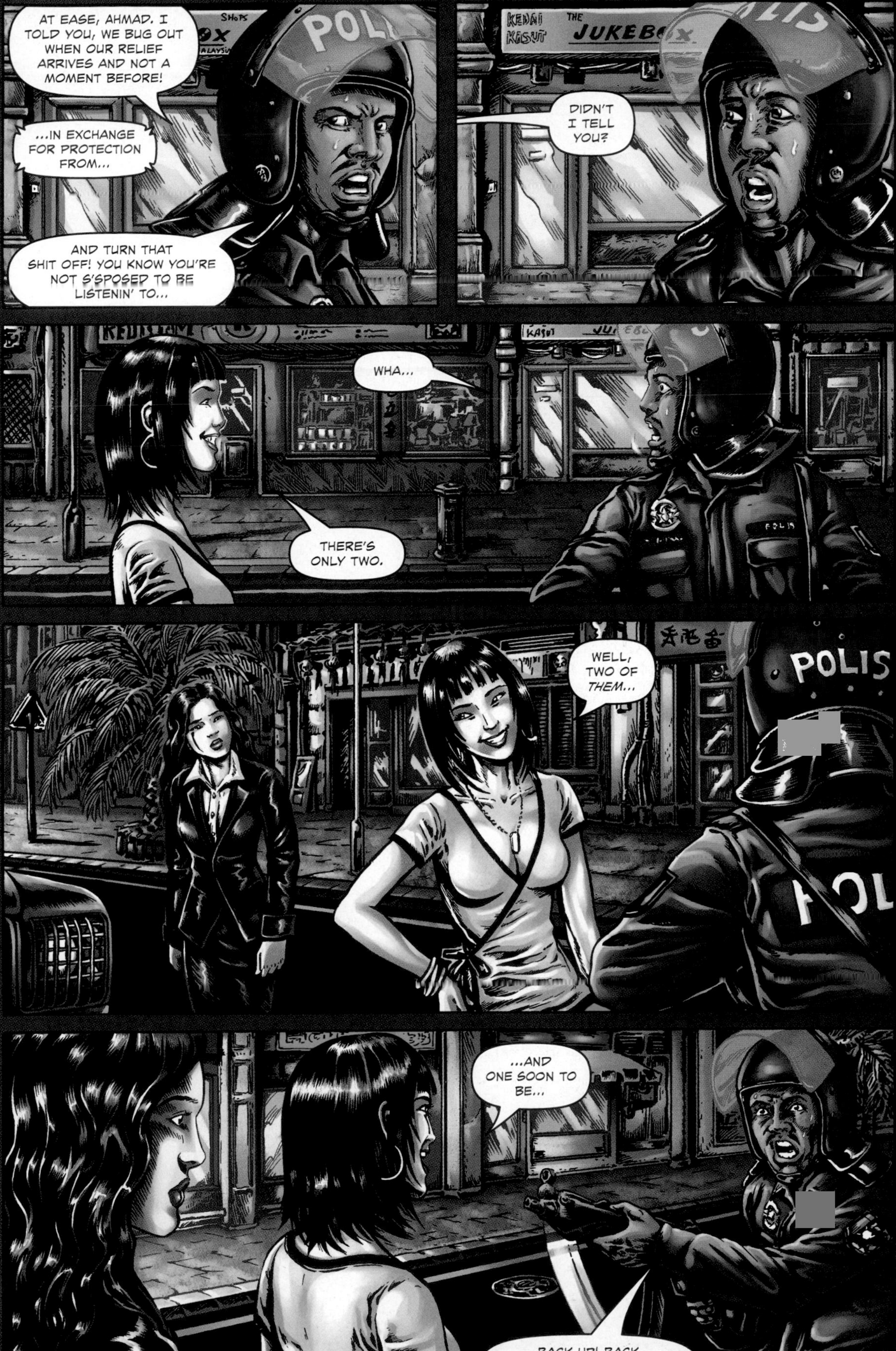

AT EASE, AHMAD. I TOLD YOU, WE BUG OUT WHEN OUR RELIEF ARRIVES AND NOT A MOMENT BEFORE!
...IN EXCHANGE FOR PROTECTION FROM...
AND TURN THAT SHIT OFF! YOU KNOW YOU'RE NOT S'SPOSED TO BE LISTENIN' TO...
KEDAI KASUT
THE JUKEBOX
DIDN'T I TELL YOU?
WHA...
THERE'S ONLY TWO.
POLIS
WELL, TWO OF *THEM*...
...AND ONE SOON TO BE...
BACK UP! BACK IT UP! HANDS WHERE I CAN SEE THEM! ***NOW!***

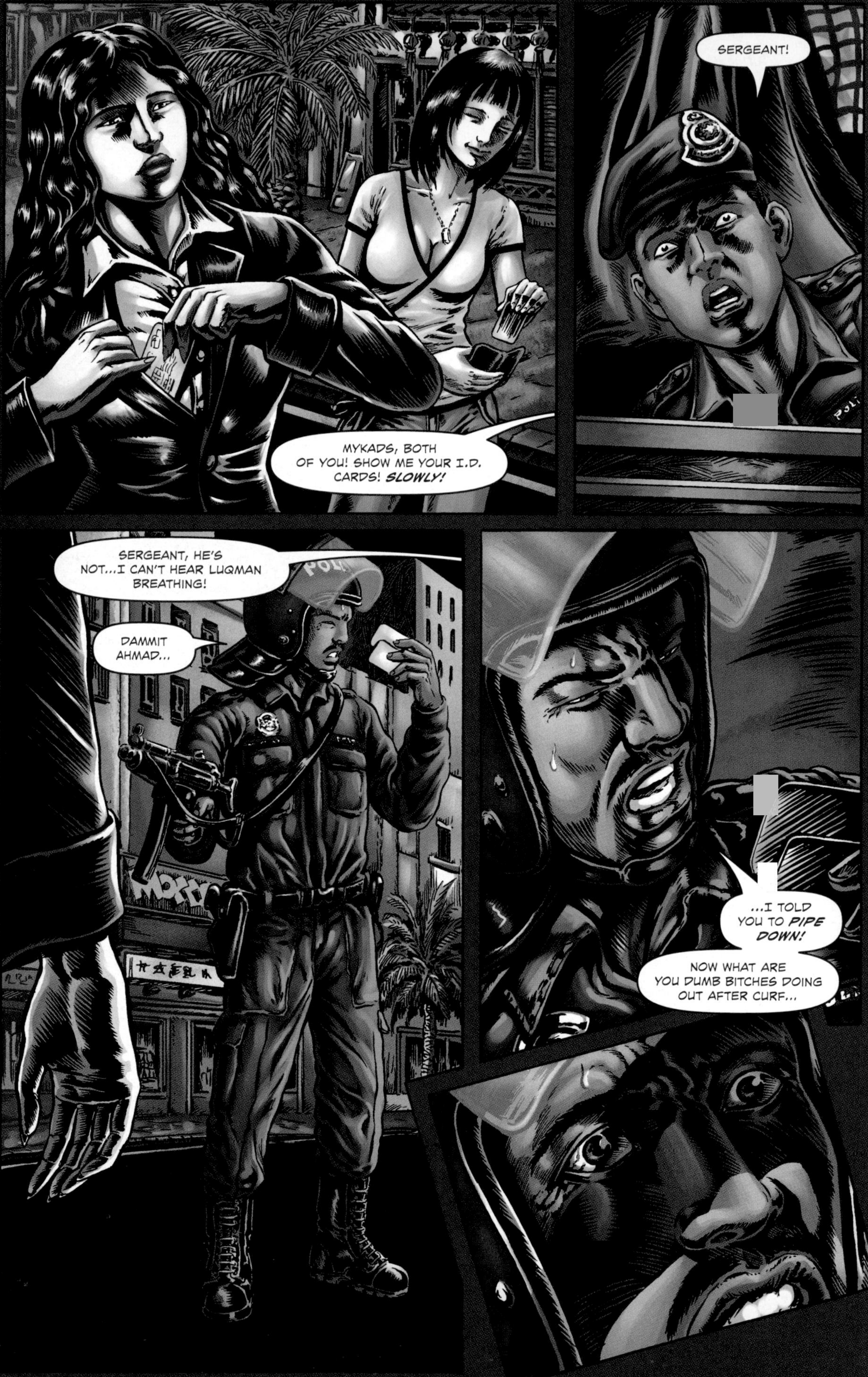
MYKADS, BOTH OF YOU! SHOW ME YOUR I.D. CARDS! *SLOWLY!*
SERGEANT!
SERGEANT, HE'S NOT...I CAN'T HEAR LUQMAN BREATHING!
DAMMIT AHMAD...
...I TOLD YOU TO *PIPE DOWN!*
NOW WHAT ARE YOU DUMB BITCHES DOING OUT AFTER CURF...

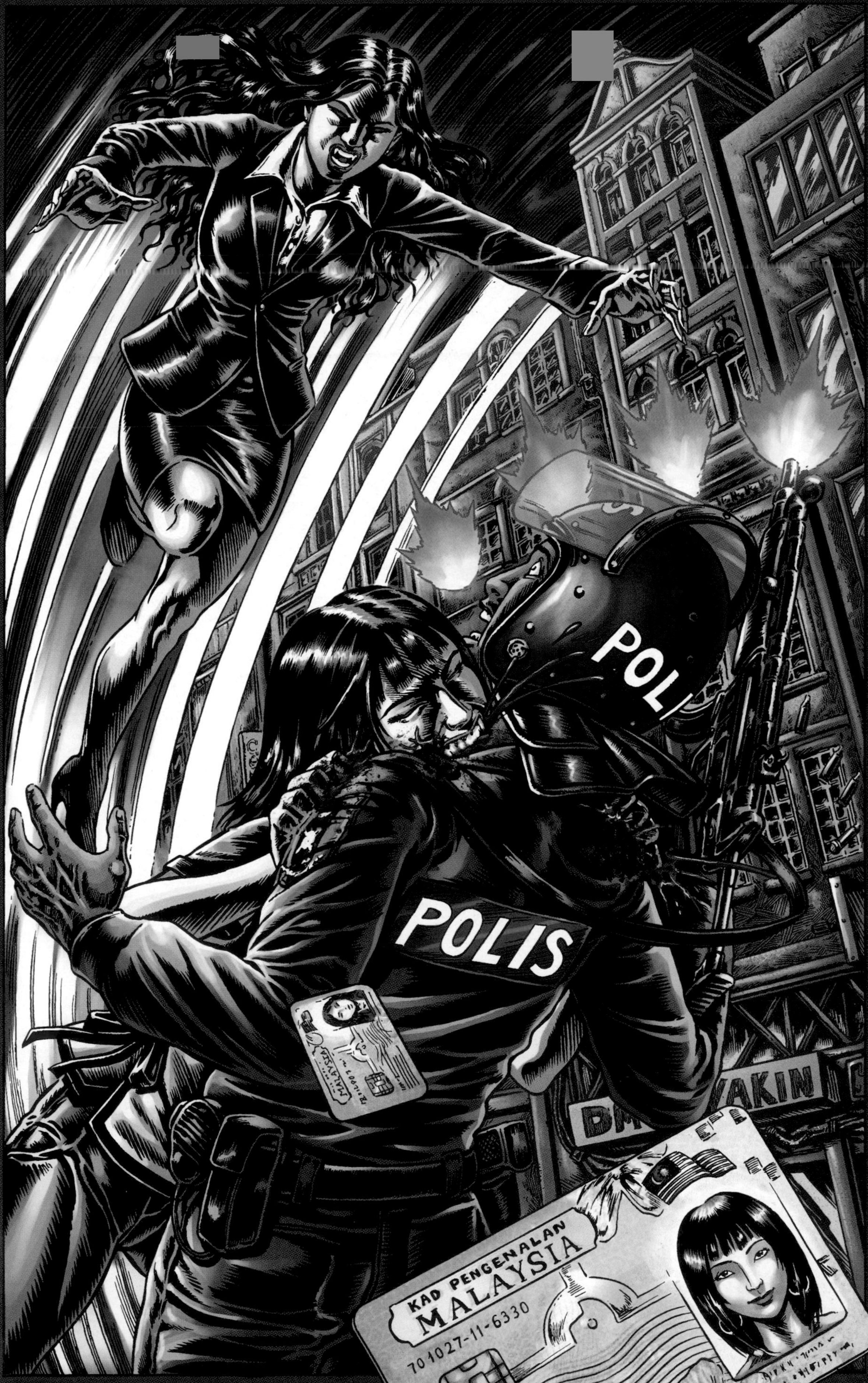
POLIS
KAD PENGENALAN
MALAYSIA
701027-11-6330

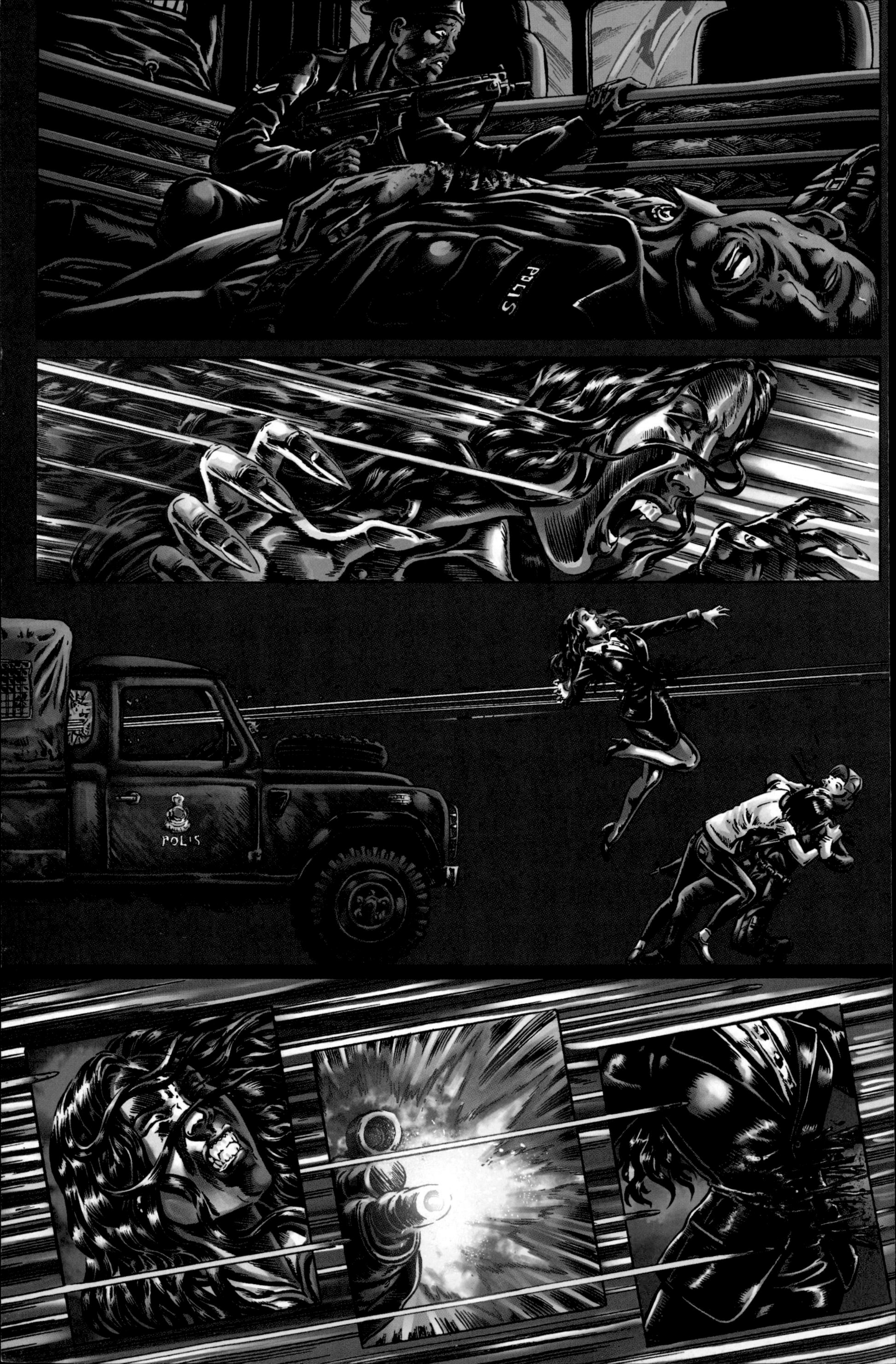
POLIS
POLIS

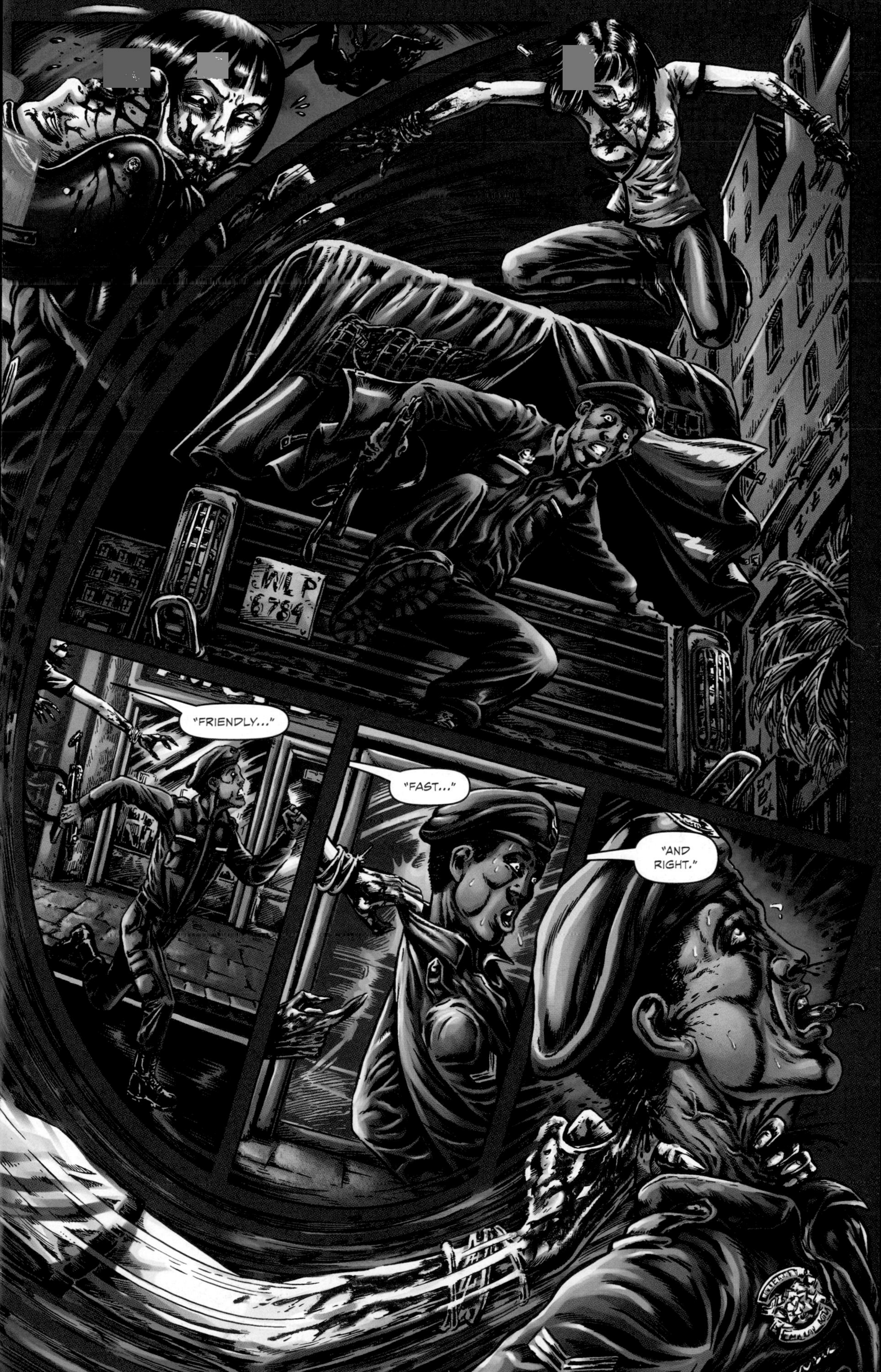
WLP 6784
"FRIENDLY..."
"FAST..."
"AND RIGHT."

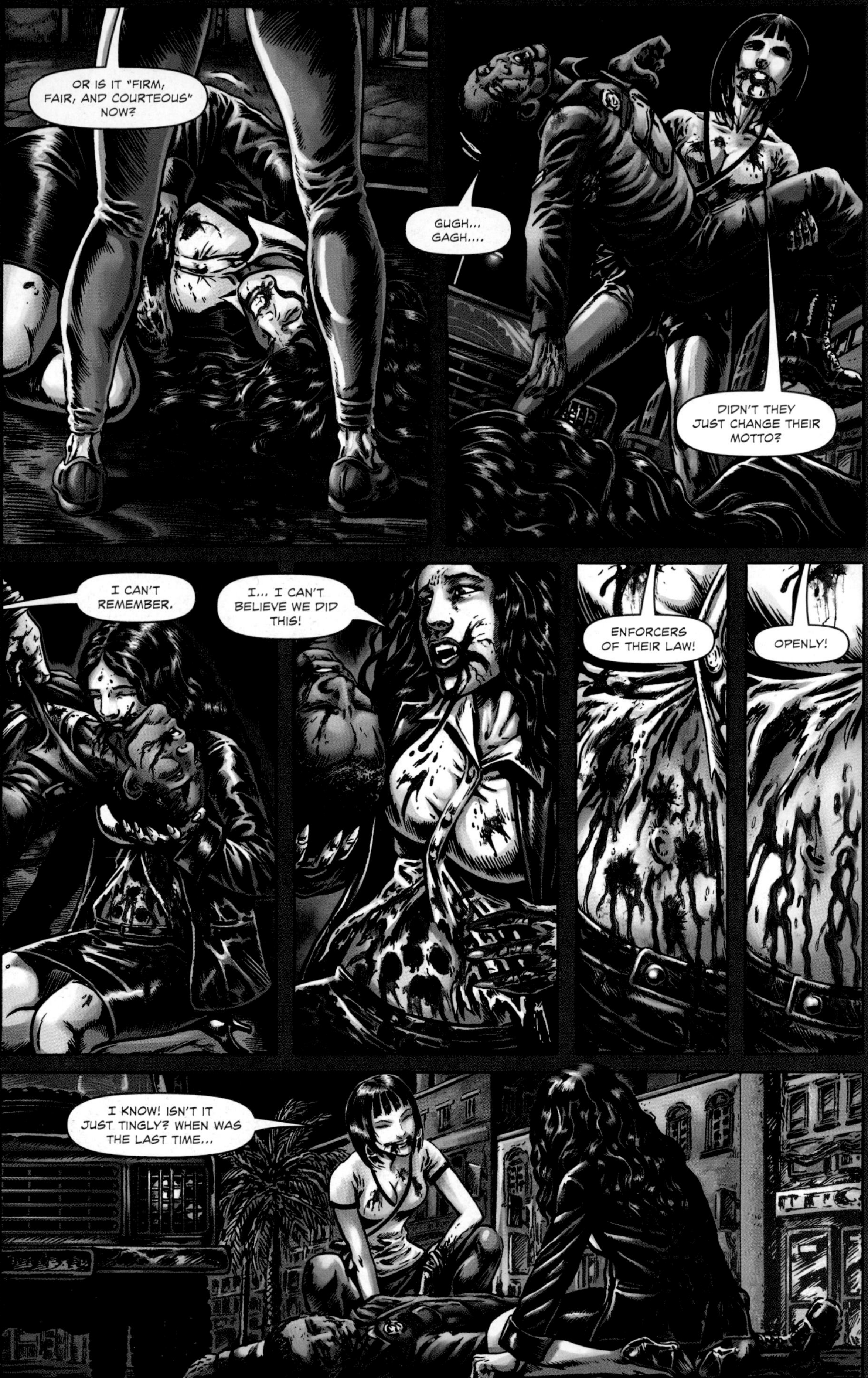
OR IS IT "FIRM, FAIR, AND COURTEOUS" NOW?
GUGH... GAGH....
DIDN'T THEY JUST CHANGE THEIR MOTTO?
I CAN'T REMEMBER.
I... I CAN'T BELIEVE WE DID THIS!
ENFORCERS OF THEIR LAW!
OPENLY!
I KNOW! ISN'T IT JUST TINGLY? WHEN WAS THE LAST TIME...

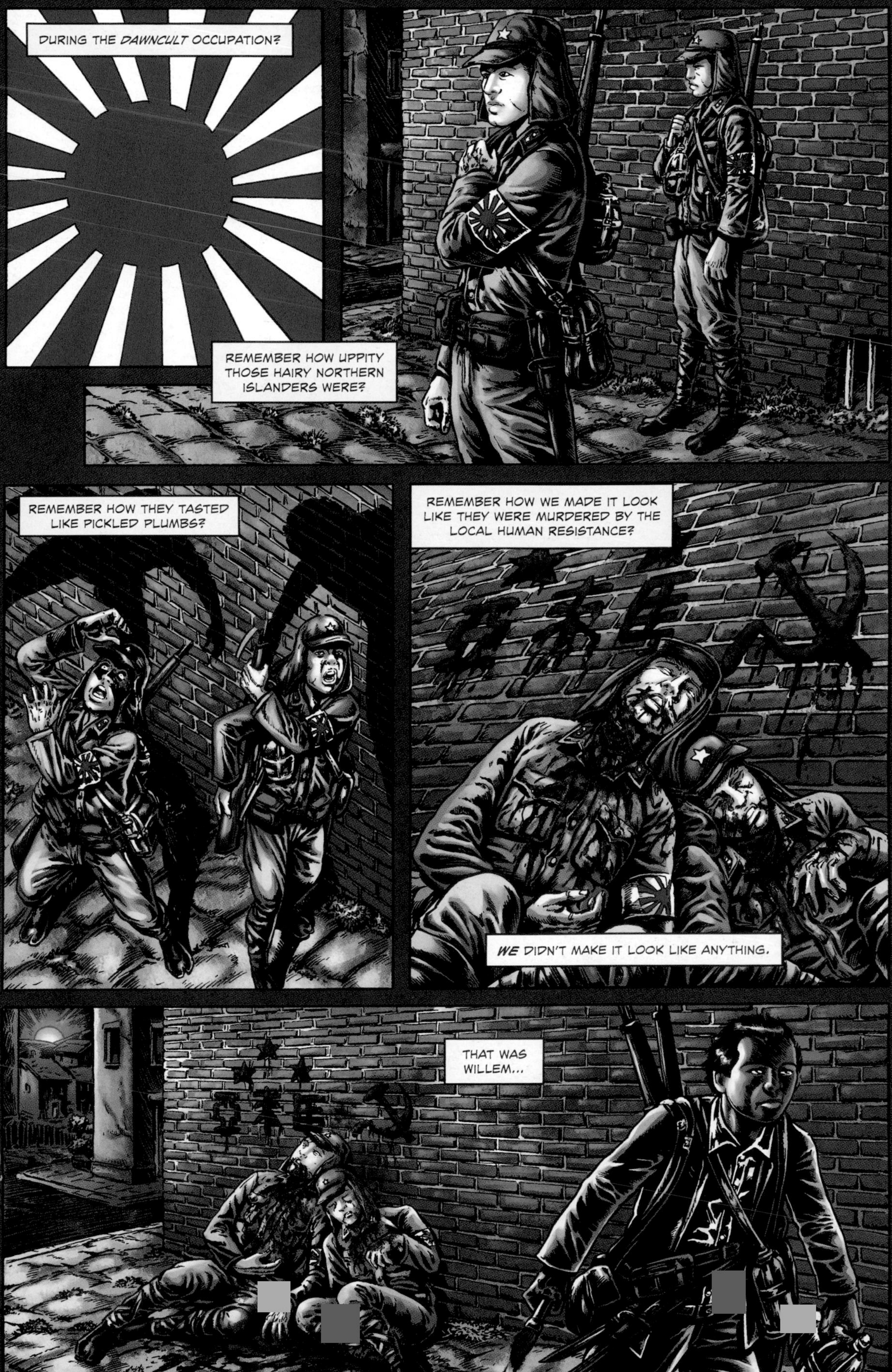
DURING THE *DAWNCULT* OCCUPATION?
REMEMBER HOW UPPITY THOSE HAIRY NORTHERN ISLANDERS WERE?
REMEMBER HOW THEY TASTED LIKE PICKLED PLUMBS?
REMEMBER HOW WE MADE IT LOOK LIKE THEY WERE MURDERED BY THE LOCAL HUMAN RESISTANCE?
WE DIDN'T MAKE IT LOOK LIKE ANYTHING.
THAT WAS WILLEM...

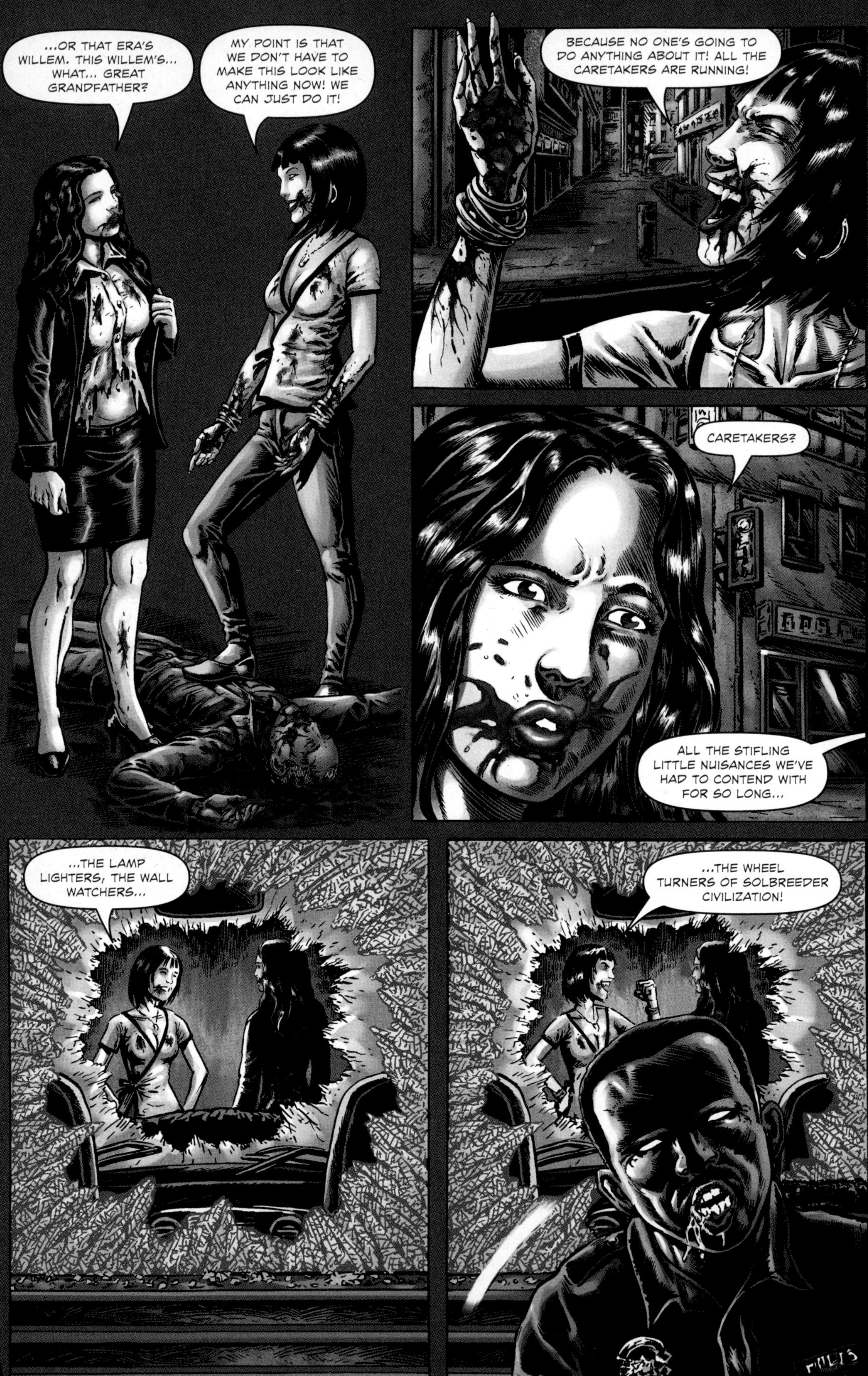
...OR THAT ERA'S WILLEM. THIS WILLEM'S... WHAT... GREAT GRANDFATHER?
MY POINT IS THAT WE DON'T HAVE TO MAKE THIS LOOK LIKE ANYTHING NOW! WE CAN JUST DO IT!
BECAUSE NO ONE'S GOING TO DO ANYTHING ABOUT IT! ALL THE CARETAKERS ARE RUNNING!
CARETAKERS?
ALL THE STIFLING LITTLE NUISANCES WE'VE HAD TO CONTEND WITH FOR SO LONG...
...THE LAMP LIGHTERS, THE WALL WATCHERS...
...THE WHEEL TURNERS OF SOLBREEDER CIVILIZATION!

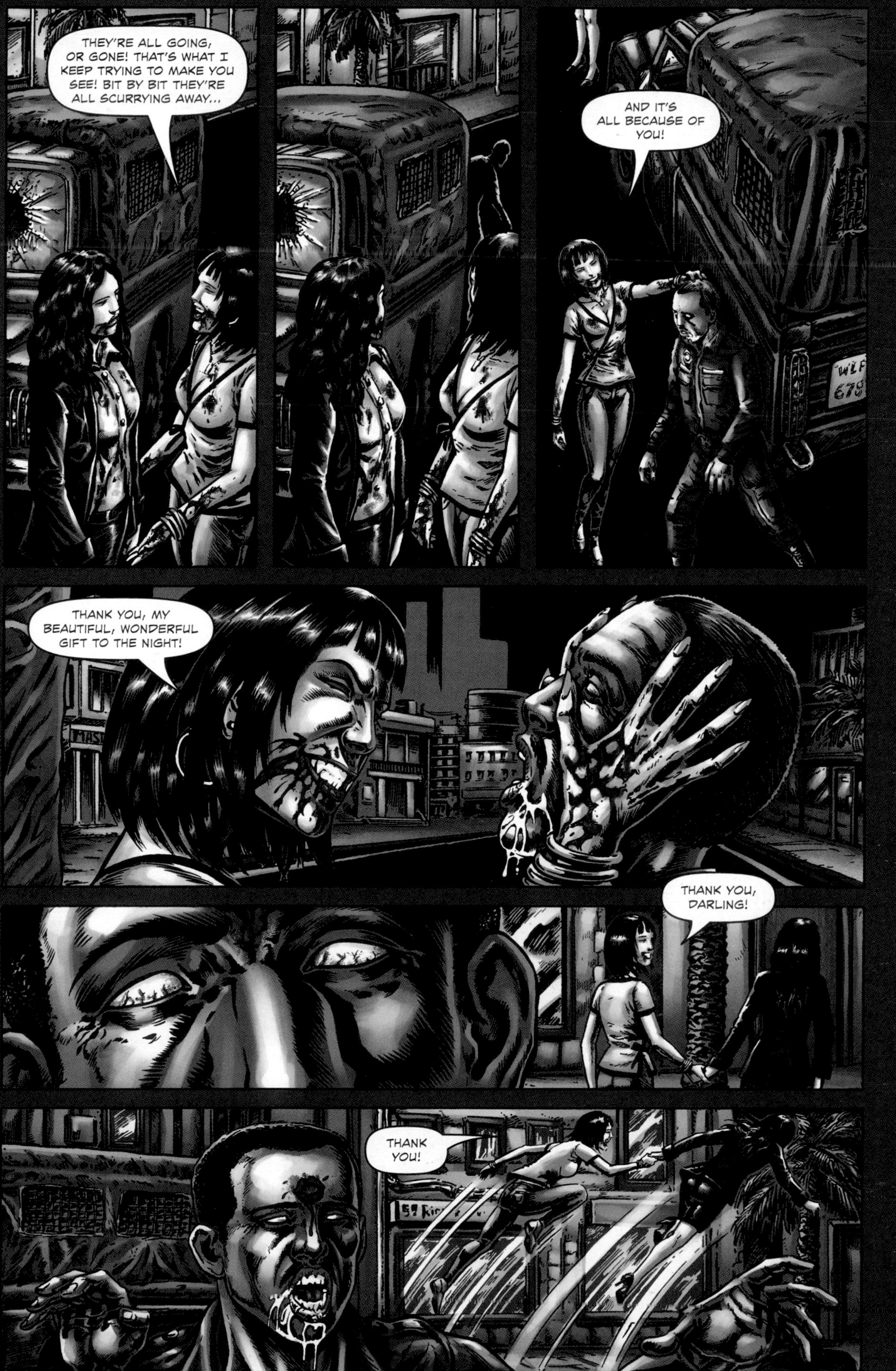
THEY'RE ALL GOING, OR GONE! THAT'S WHAT I KEEP TRYING TO MAKE YOU SEE! BIT BY BIT THEY'RE ALL SCURRYING AWAY...
AND IT'S ALL BECAUSE OF YOU!
WLF 678
THANK YOU, MY BEAUTIFUL, WONDERFUL GIFT TO THE NIGHT!
THANK YOU, DARLING!
THANK YOU!

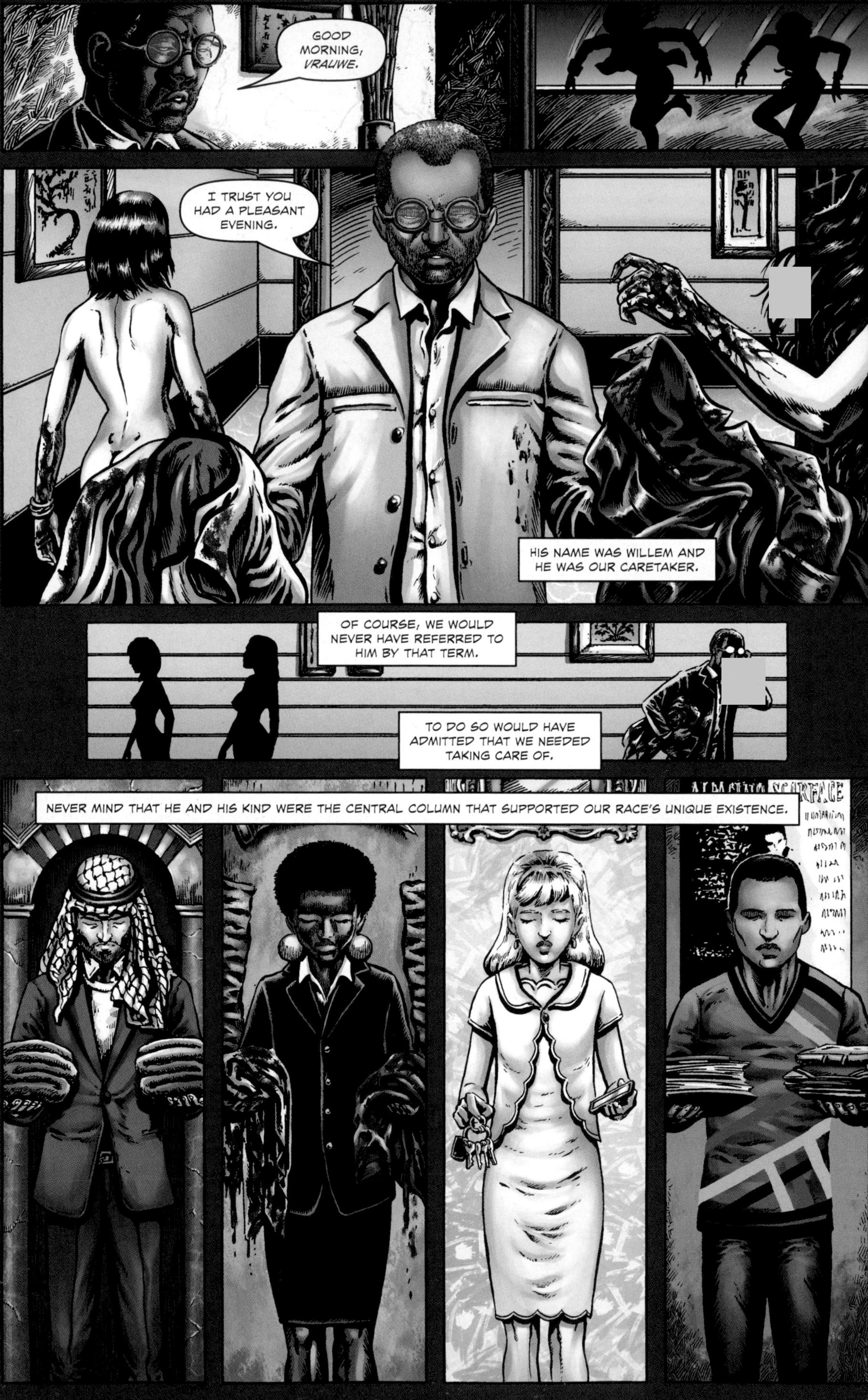
GOOD MORNING, *VRAUWE*.
I TRUST YOU HAD A PLEASANT EVENING.
HIS NAME WAS WILLEM AND HE WAS OUR CARETAKER.
OF COURSE, WE WOULD NEVER HAVE REFERRED TO HIM BY THAT TERM.
TO DO SO WOULD HAVE ADMITTED THAT WE NEEDED TAKING CARE OF.
NEVER MIND THAT HE AND HIS KIND WERE THE CENTRAL COLUMN THAT SUPPORTED OUR RACE'S UNIQUE EXISTENCE.

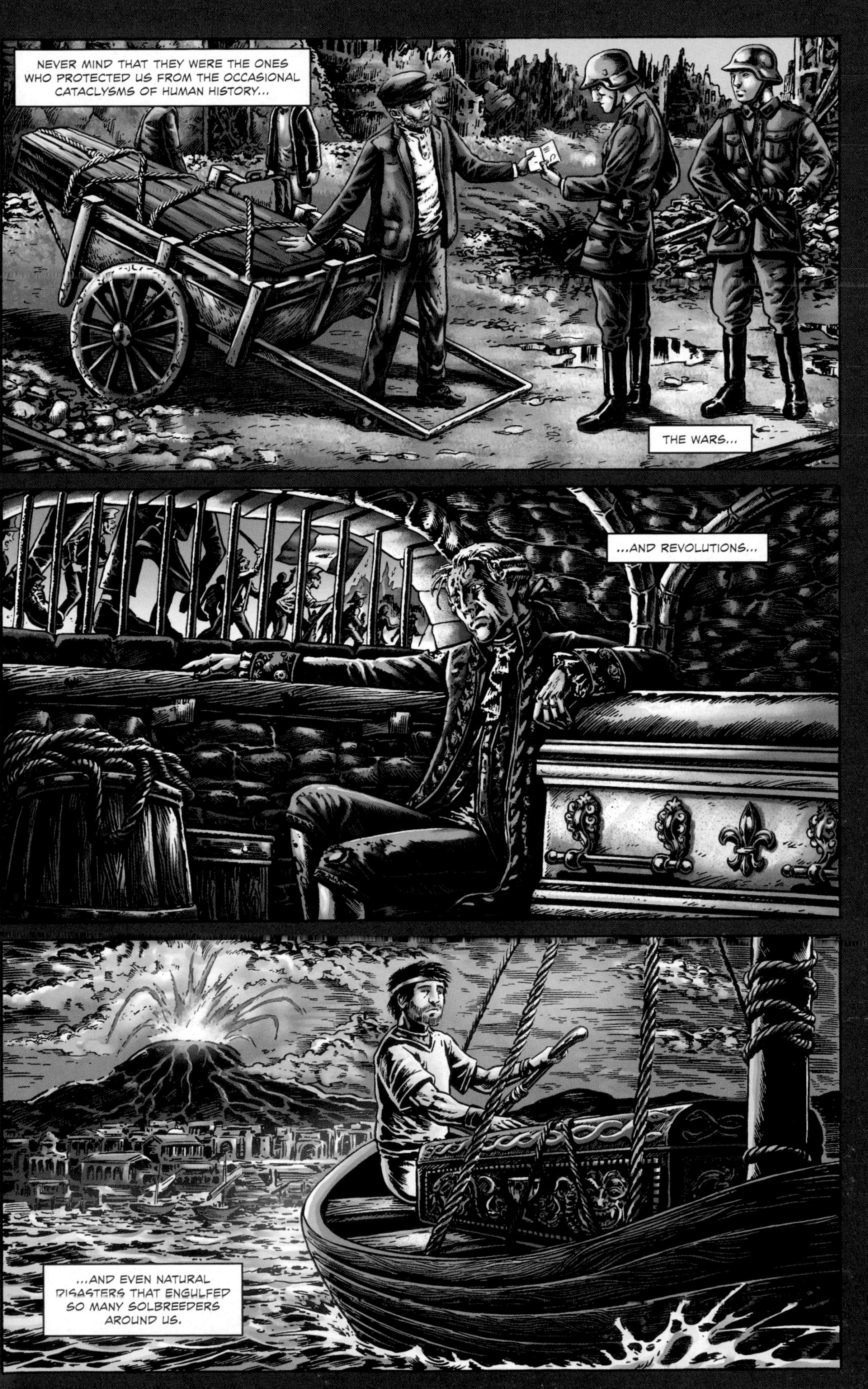
NEVER MIND THAT THEY WERE THE ONES WHO PROTECTED US FROM THE OCCASIONAL CATACLYSMS OF HUMAN HISTORY...
THE WARS...
...AND REVOLUTIONS...
...AND EVEN NATURAL DISASTERS THAT ENGULFED SO MANY SOLBREEDERS AROUND US.

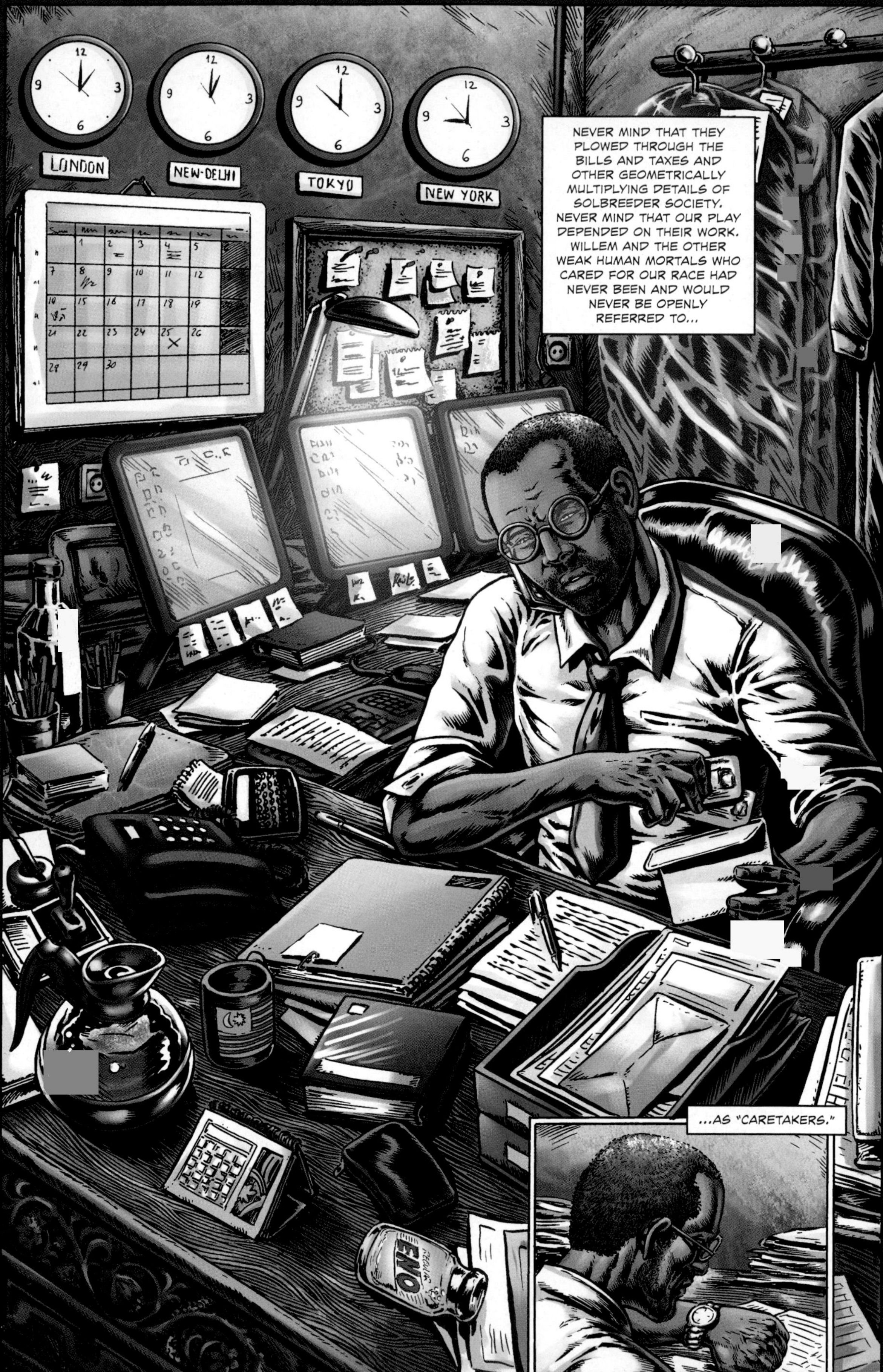
LONDON
NEW-DELHI
TOKYO
NEW YORK
NEVER MIND THAT THEY PLOWED THROUGH THE BILLS AND TAXES AND OTHER GEOMETRICALLY MULTIPLYING DETAILS OF SOLBREEDER SOCIETY. NEVER MIND THAT OUR PLAY DEPENDED ON THEIR WORK. WILLEM AND THE OTHER WEAK HUMAN MORTALS WHO CARED FOR OUR RACE HAD NEVER BEEN AND WOULD NEVER BE OPENLY REFERRED TO...
...AS "CARETAKERS."
ENO

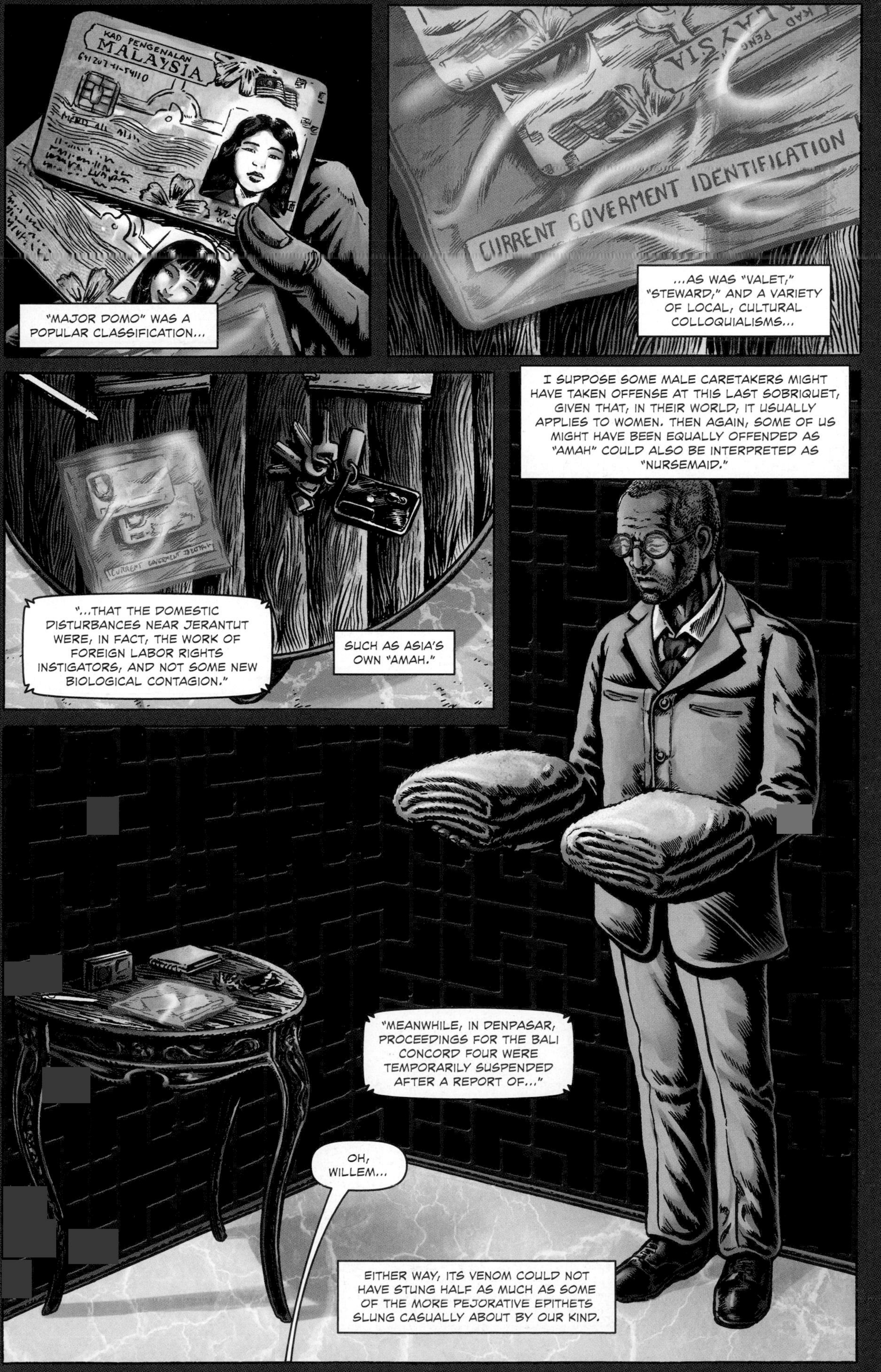
KAD PENGENALAN
MALAYSIA
"MAJOR DOMO" WAS A POPULAR CLASSIFICATION...
CURRENT GOVERMENT IDENTIFICATION
...AS WAS "VALET," "STEWARD," AND A VARIETY OF LOCAL, CULTURAL COLLOQUIALISMS...
"...THAT THE DOMESTIC DISTURBANCES NEAR JERANTUT WERE, IN FACT, THE WORK OF FOREIGN LABOR RIGHTS INSTIGATORS, AND NOT SOME NEW BIOLOGICAL CONTAGION."
SUCH AS ASIA'S OWN "AMAH."
I SUPPOSE SOME MALE CARETAKERS MIGHT HAVE TAKEN OFFENSE AT THIS LAST SOBRIQUET, GIVEN THAT, IN THEIR WORLD, IT USUALLY APPLIES TO WOMEN. THEN AGAIN, SOME OF US MIGHT HAVE BEEN EQUALLY OFFENDED AS "AMAH" COULD ALSO BE INTERPRETED AS "NURSEMAID."
"MEANWHILE, IN DENPASAR, PROCEEDINGS FOR THE BALI CONCORD FOUR WERE TEMPORARILY SUSPENDED AFTER A REPORT OF..."
OH, WILLEM...
EITHER WAY, ITS VENOM COULD NOT HAVE STUNG HALF AS MUCH AS SOME OF THE MORE PEJORATIVE EPITHETS SLUNG CASUALLY ABOUT BY OUR KIND.

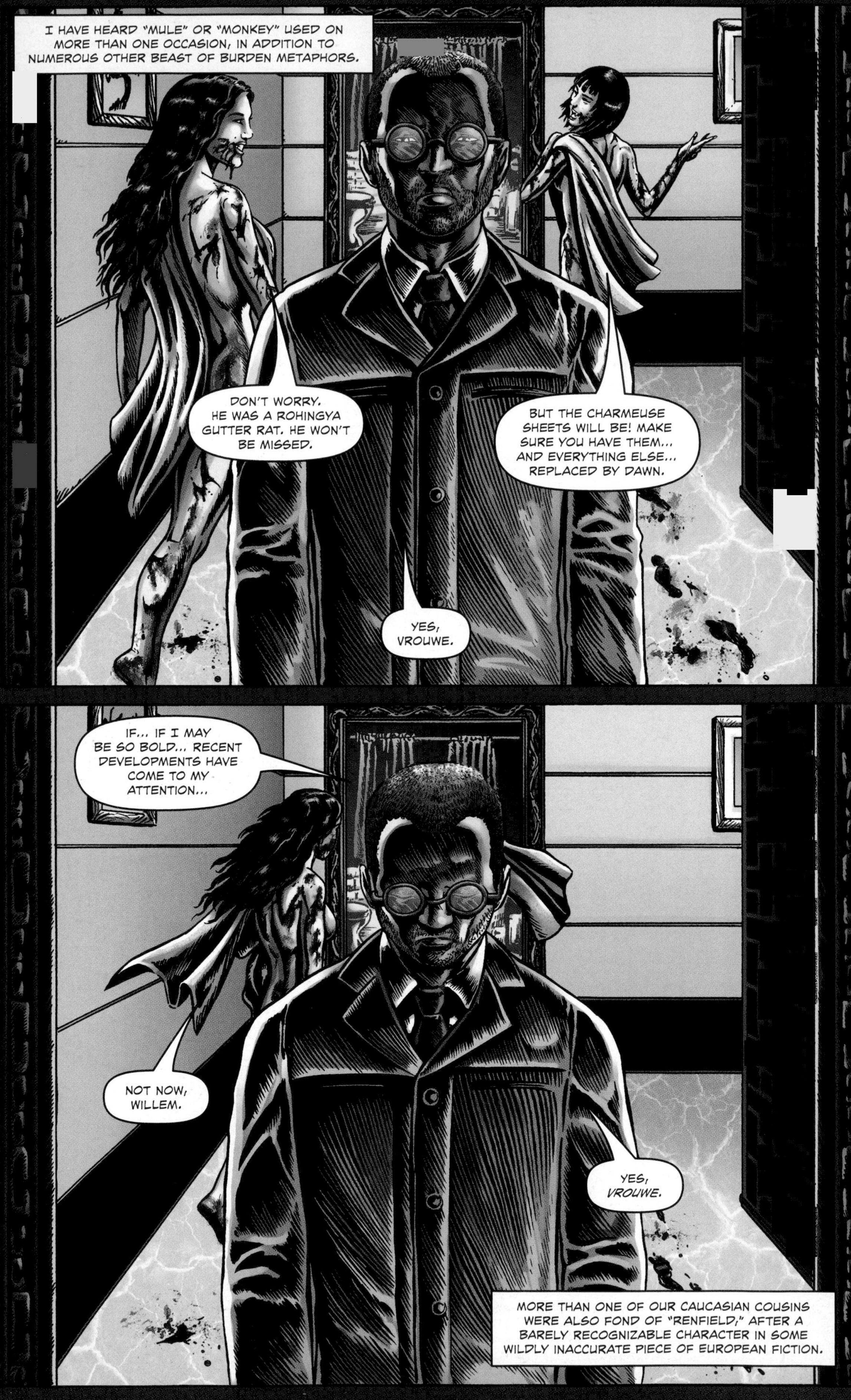
I HAVE HEARD "MULE" OR "MONKEY" USED ON MORE THAN ONE OCCASION, IN ADDITION TO NUMEROUS OTHER BEAST OF BURDEN METAPHORS.
DON'T WORRY. HE WAS A ROHINGYA GUTTER RAT. HE WON'T BE MISSED.
BUT THE CHARMEUSE SHEETS WILL BE! MAKE SURE YOU HAVE THEM... AND EVERYTHING ELSE... REPLACED BY DAWN.
YES, VROUWE.
IF... IF I MAY BE SO BOLD... RECENT DEVELOPMENTS HAVE COME TO MY ATTENTION...
NOT NOW, WILLEM.
YES, *VROUWE.*
MORE THAN ONE OF OUR CAUCASIAN COUSINS WERE ALSO FOND OF "RENFIELD," AFTER A BARELY RECOGNIZABLE CHARACTER IN SOME WILDLY INACCURATE PIECE OF EUROPEAN FICTION.

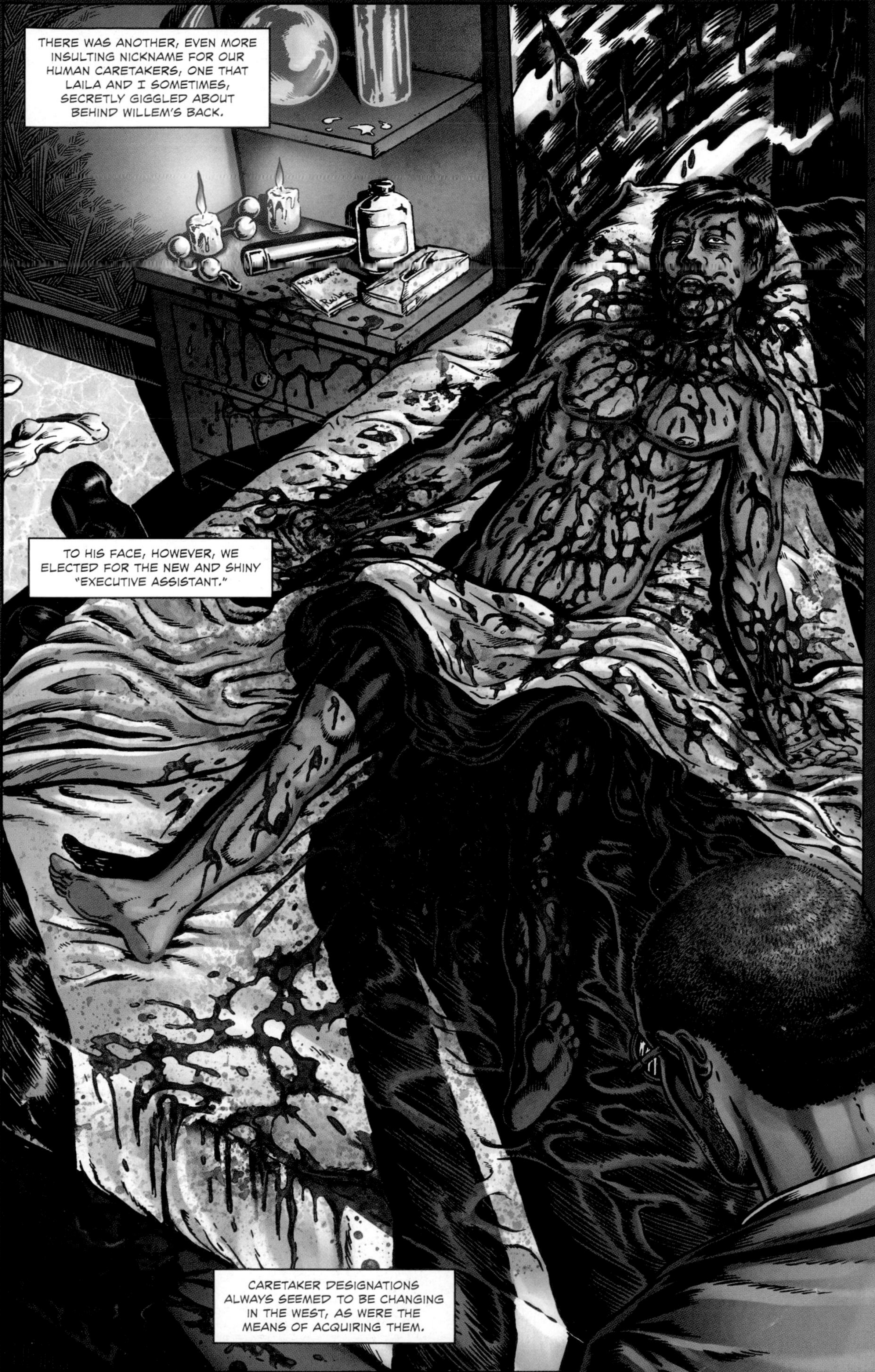
THERE WAS ANOTHER, EVEN MORE INSULTING NICKNAME FOR OUR HUMAN CARETAKERS, ONE THAT LAILA AND I SOMETIMES, SECRETLY GIGGLED ABOUT BEHIND WILLEM'S BACK.
TO HIS FACE, HOWEVER, WE ELECTED FOR THE NEW AND SHINY "EXECUTIVE ASSISTANT."
CARETAKER DESIGNATIONS ALWAYS SEEMED TO BE CHANGING IN THE WEST, AS WERE THE MEANS OF ACQUIRING THEM.

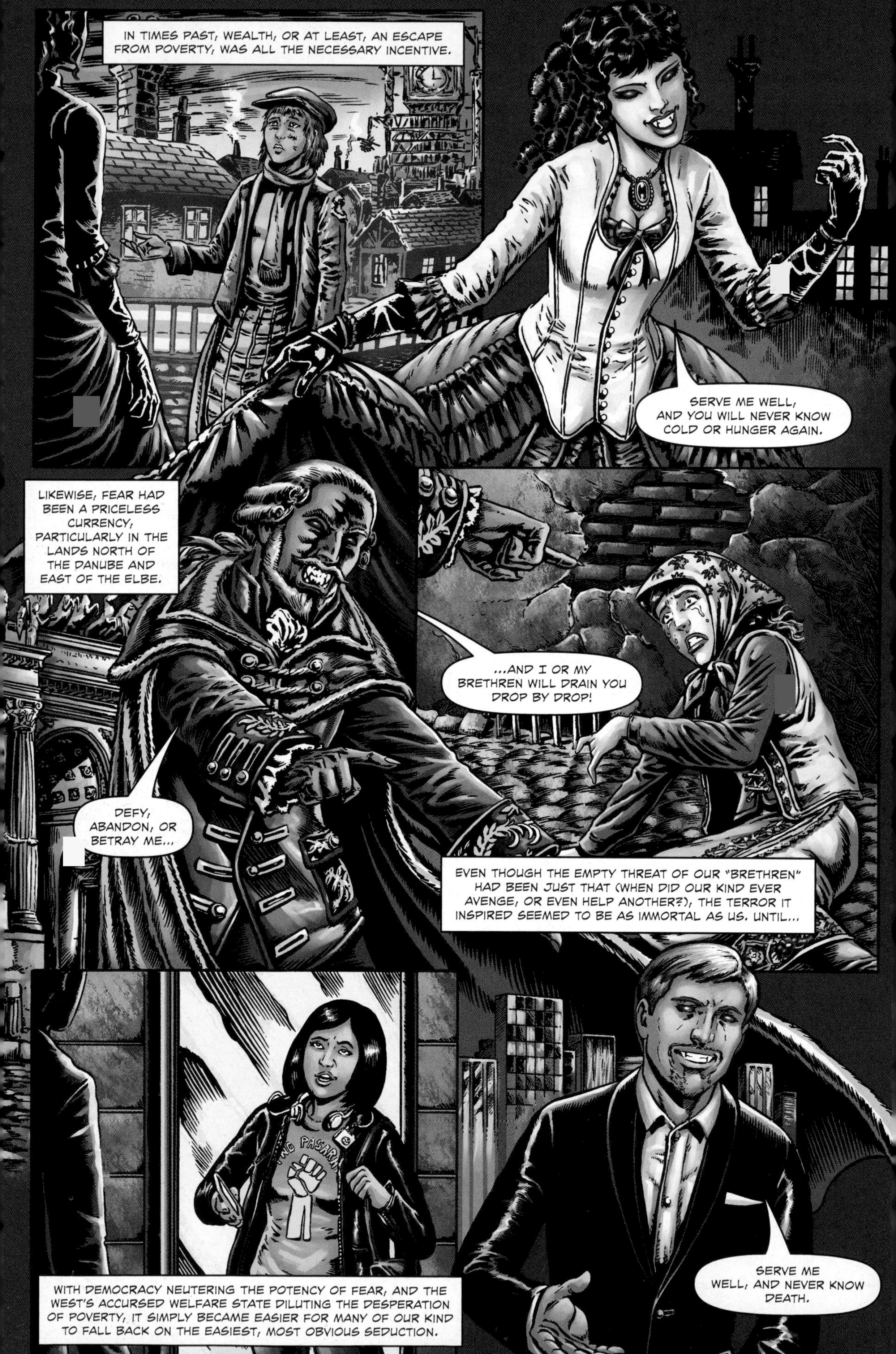
IN TIMES PAST, WEALTH, OR AT LEAST, AN ESCAPE FROM POVERTY, WAS ALL THE NECESSARY INCENTIVE.
SERVE ME WELL, AND YOU WILL NEVER KNOW COLD OR HUNGER AGAIN.
LIKEWISE, FEAR HAD BEEN A PRICELESS CURRENCY, PARTICULARLY IN THE LANDS NORTH OF THE DANUBE AND EAST OF THE ELBE.
DEFY, ABANDON, OR BETRAY ME...
...AND I OR MY BRETHREN WILL DRAIN YOU DROP BY DROP!
EVEN THOUGH THE EMPTY THREAT OF OUR "BRETHREN" HAD BEEN JUST THAT (WHEN DID OUR KIND EVER AVENGE, OR EVEN HELP ANOTHER?), THE TERROR IT INSPIRED SEEMED TO BE AS IMMORTAL AS US. UNTIL...
WITH DEMOCRACY NEUTERING THE POTENCY OF FEAR, AND THE WEST'S ACCURSED WELFARE STATE DILUTING THE DESPERATION OF POVERTY, IT SIMPLY BECAME EASIER FOR MANY OF OUR KIND TO FALL BACK ON THE EASIEST, MOST OBVIOUS SEDUCTION.
SERVE ME WELL, AND NEVER KNOW DEATH.

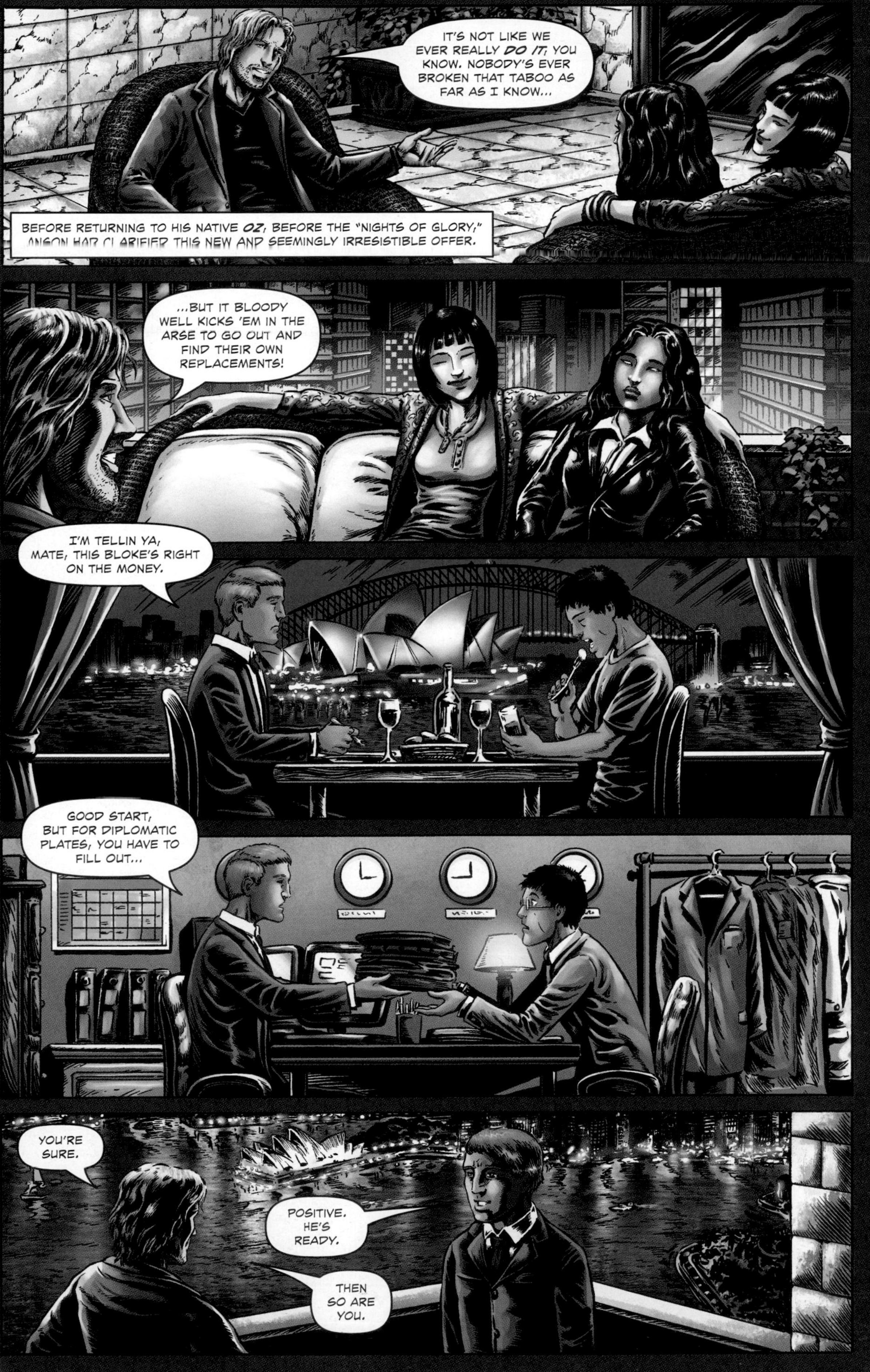

IT'S NOT LIKE WE EVER REALLY DO IT, YOU KNOW. NOBODY'S EVER BROKEN THAT TABOO AS FAR AS I KNOW...
BEFORE RETURNING TO HIS NATIVE OZ, BEFORE THE "NIGHTS OF GLORY," ANSON HAD CLARIFIED THIS NEW AND SEEMINGLY IRRESISTIBLE OFFER.
...BUT IT BLOODY WELL KICKS 'EM IN THE ARSE TO GO OUT AND FIND THEIR OWN REPLACEMENTS!
I'M TELLIN YA, MATE, THIS BLOKE'S RIGHT ON THE MONEY.
GOOD START, BUT FOR DIPLOMATIC PLATES, YOU HAVE TO FILL OUT...
YOU'RE SURE.
POSITIVE. HE'S READY.
THEN SO ARE YOU.

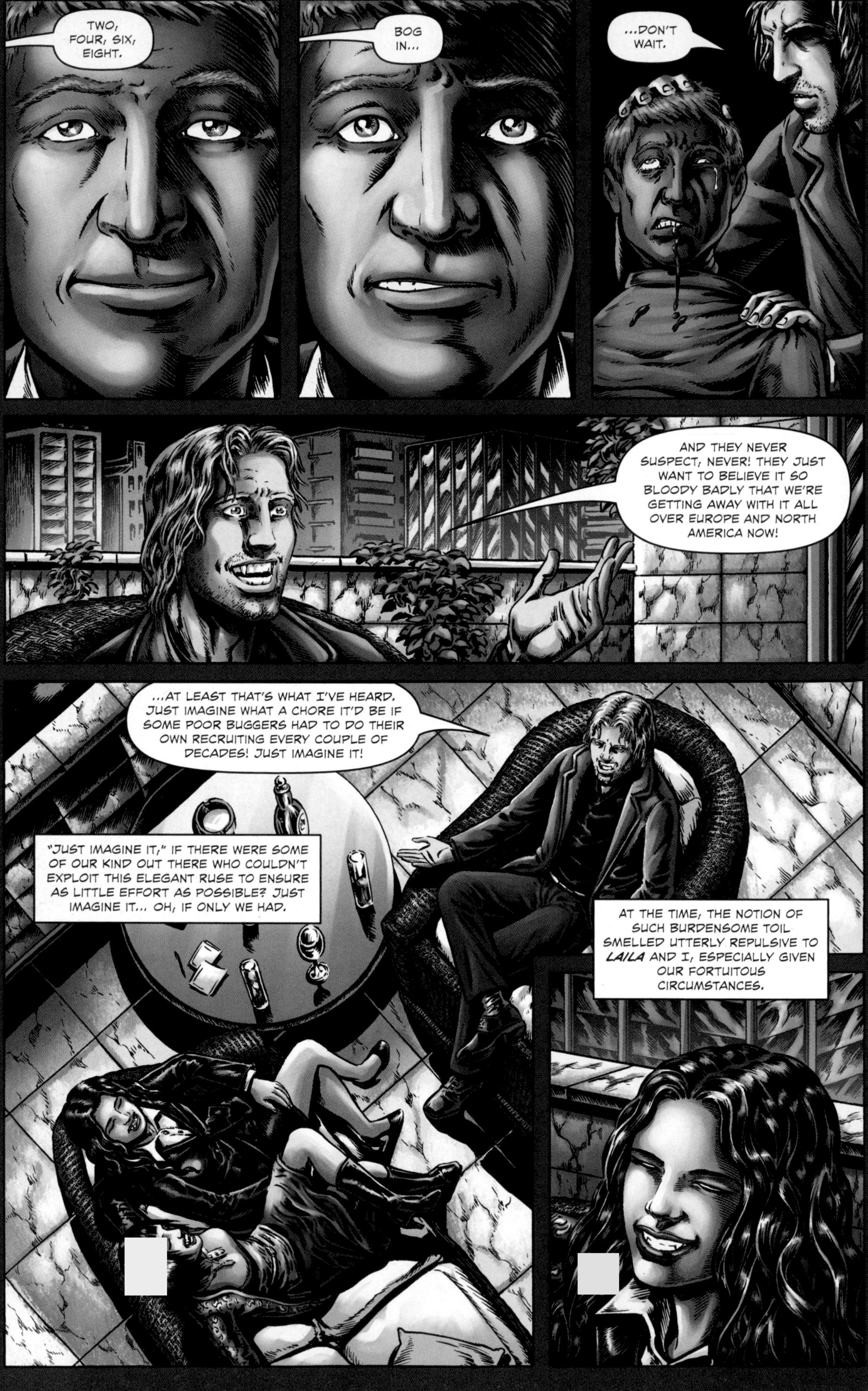
TWO, FOUR, SIX, EIGHT.
BOG IN...
...DON'T WAIT.
AND THEY NEVER SUSPECT, NEVER! THEY JUST WANT TO BELIEVE IT SO BLOODY BADLY THAT WE'RE GETTING AWAY WITH IT ALL OVER EUROPE AND NORTH AMERICA NOW!
...AT LEAST THAT'S WHAT I'VE HEARD. JUST IMAGINE WHAT A CHORE IT'D BE IF SOME POOR BUGGERS HAD TO DO THEIR OWN RECRUITING EVERY COUPLE OF DECADES! JUST IMAGINE IT!
"JUST IMAGINE IT," IF THERE WERE SOME OF OUR KIND OUT THERE WHO COULDN'T EXPLOIT THIS ELEGANT RUSE TO ENSURE AS LITTLE EFFORT AS POSSIBLE? JUST IMAGINE IT... OH, IF ONLY WE HAD.
AT THE TIME, THE NOTION OF SUCH BURDENSOME TOIL SMELLED UTTERLY REPULSIVE TO *LAILA* AND I, ESPECIALLY GIVEN OUR FORTUITOUS CIRCUMSTANCES.

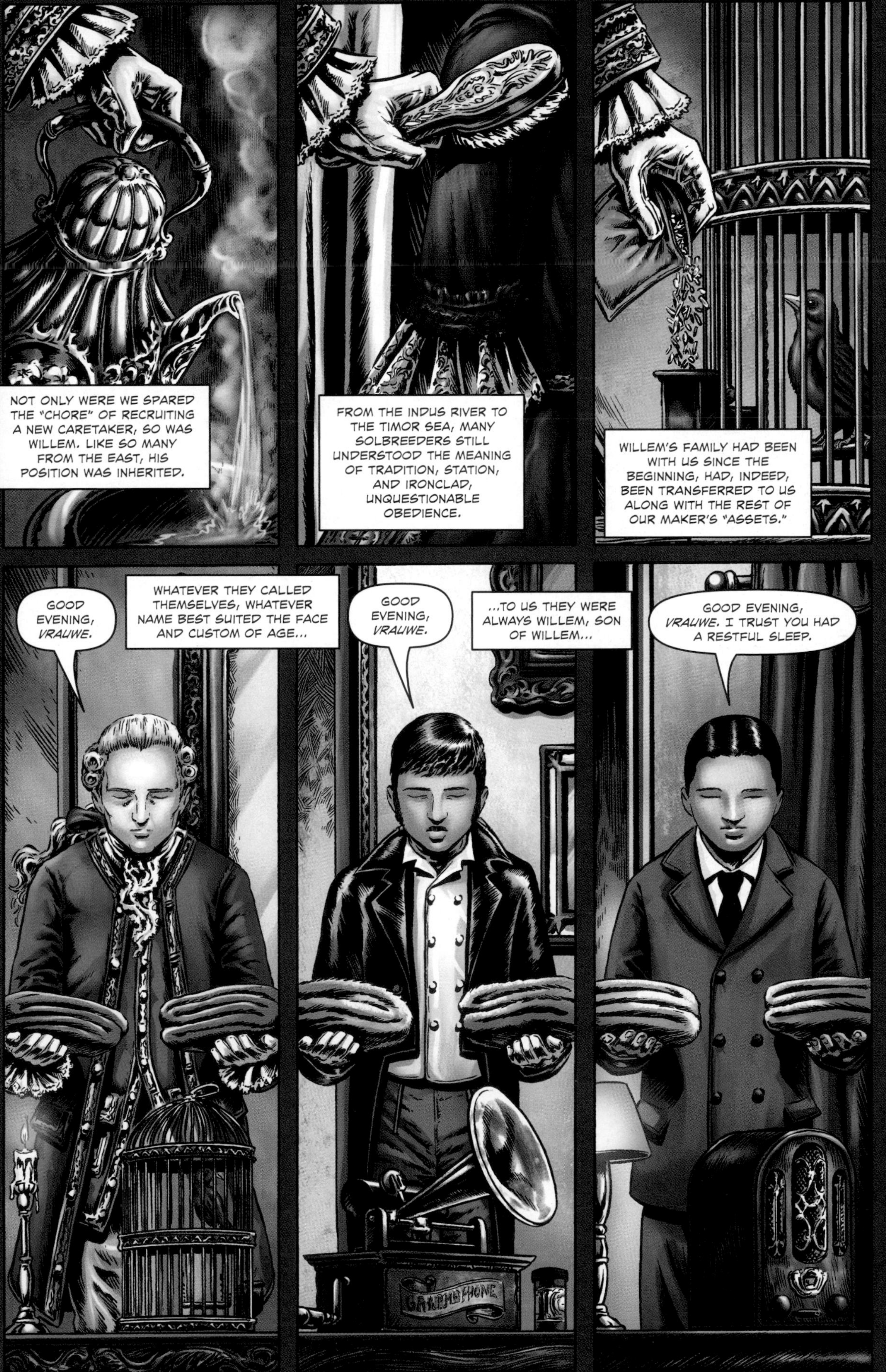
NOT ONLY WERE WE SPARED THE "CHORE" OF RECRUITING A NEW CARETAKER, SO WAS WILLEM. LIKE SO MANY FROM THE EAST, HIS POSITION WAS INHERITED.
FROM THE INDUS RIVER TO THE TIMOR SEA, MANY SOLBREEDERS STILL UNDERSTOOD THE MEANING OF TRADITION, STATION, AND IRONCLAD, UNQUESTIONABLE OBEDIENCE.
WILLEM'S FAMILY HAD BEEN WITH US SINCE THE BEGINNING, HAD, INDEED, BEEN TRANSFERRED TO US ALONG WITH THE REST OF OUR MAKER'S "ASSETS."
GOOD EVENING, *VRAUWE.*
WHATEVER THEY CALLED THEMSELVES, WHATEVER NAME BEST SUITED THE FACE AND CUSTOM OF AGE...
GOOD EVENING, *VRAUWE.*
...TO US THEY WERE ALWAYS WILLEM, SON OF WILLEM...
GOOD EVENING, *VRAUWE.* I TRUST YOU HAD A RESTFUL SLEEP.
GRAMOPHONE

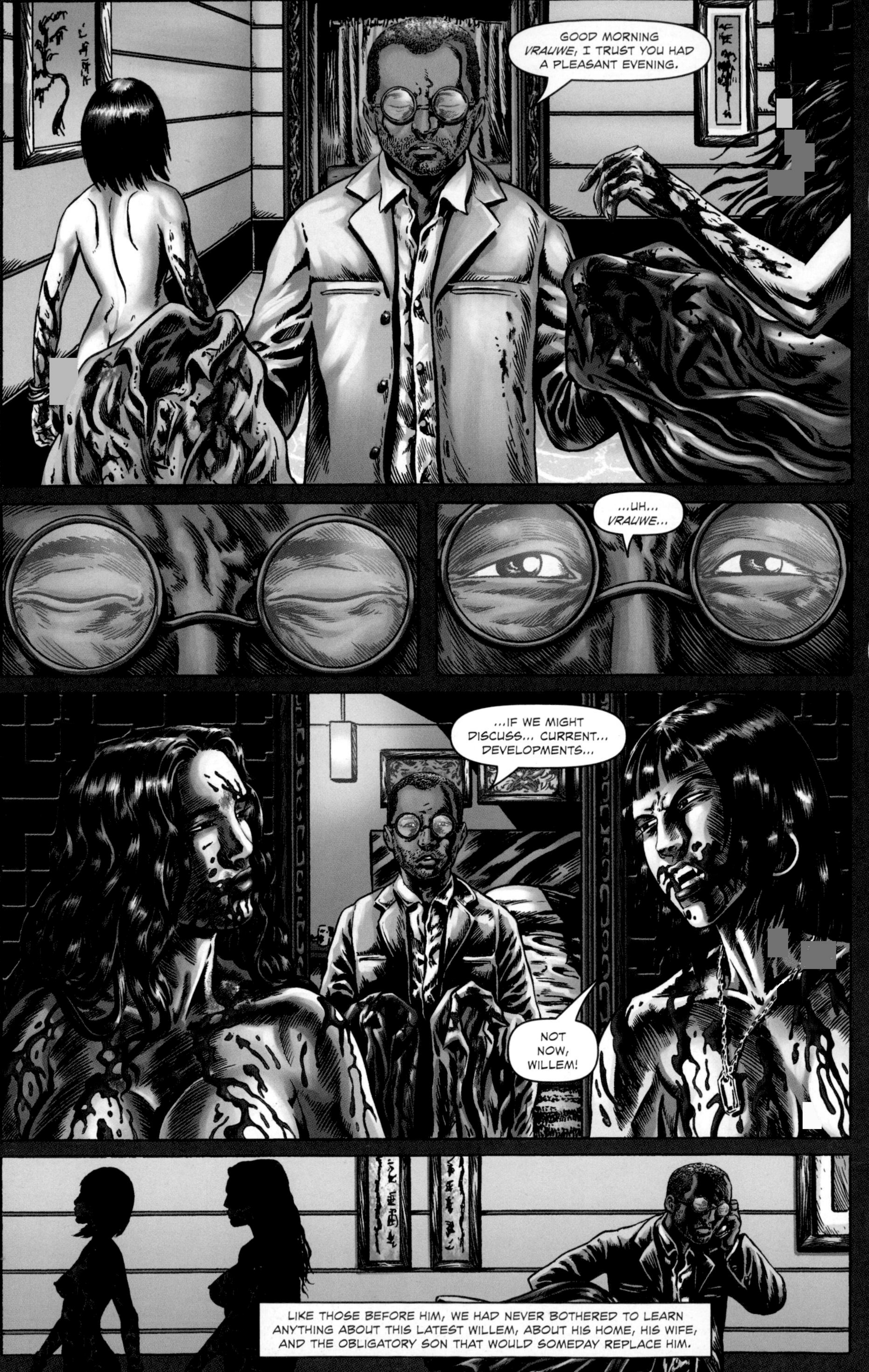
GOOD MORNING *VRAUWE*, I TRUST YOU HAD A PLEASANT EVENING.
...UH... *VRAUWE*...
...IF WE MIGHT DISCUSS... CURRENT... DEVELOPMENTS...
NOT NOW, WILLEM!
LIKE THOSE BEFORE HIM, WE HAD NEVER BOTHERED TO LEARN ANYTHING ABOUT THIS LATEST WILLEM, ABOUT HIS HOME, HIS WIFE, AND THE OBLIGATORY SON THAT WOULD SOMEDAY REPLACE HIM.

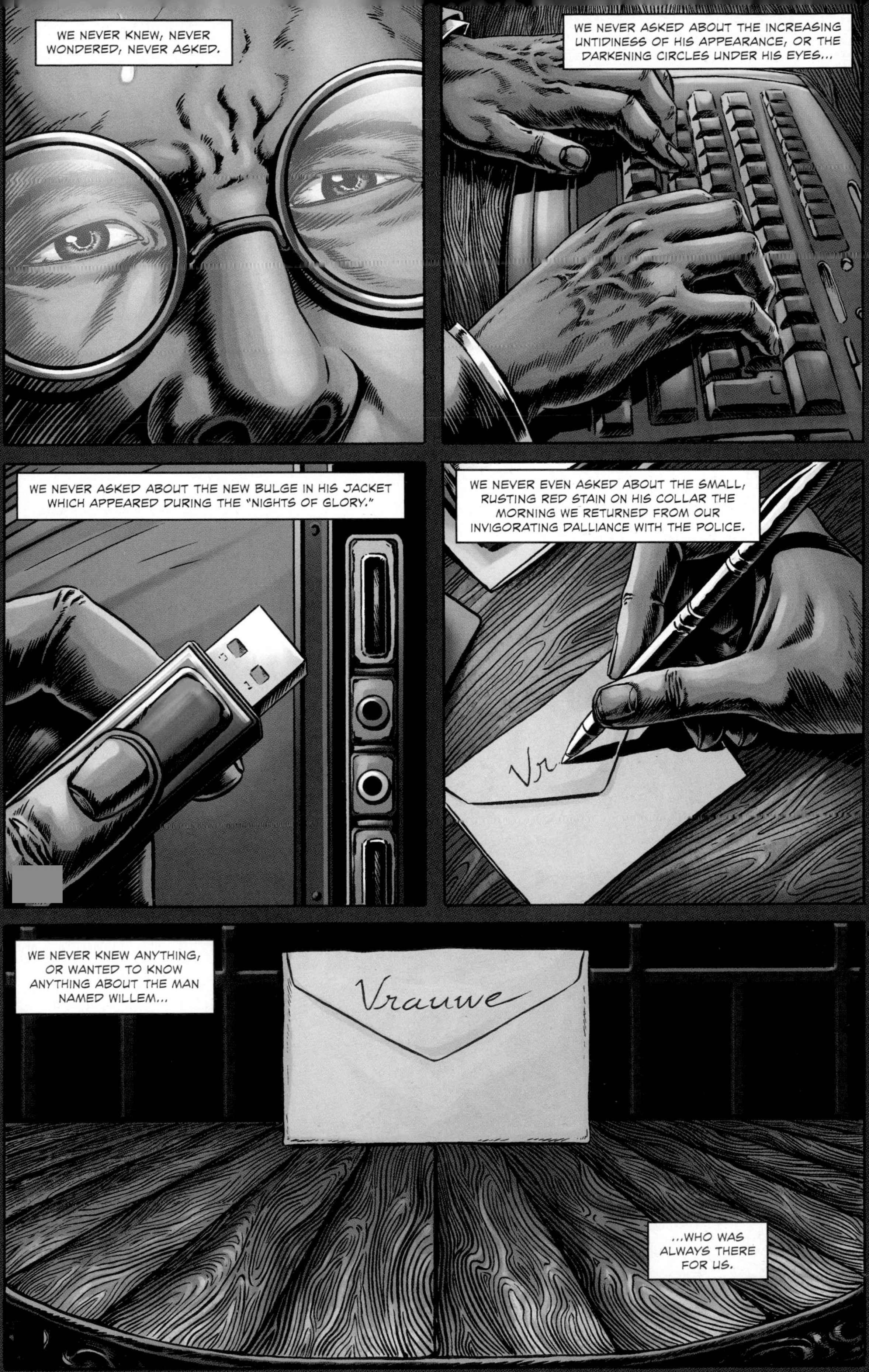
WE NEVER KNEW, NEVER WONDERED, NEVER ASKED.
WE NEVER ASKED ABOUT THE INCREASING UNTIDINESS OF HIS APPEARANCE, OR THE DARKENING CIRCLES UNDER HIS EYES...
WE NEVER ASKED ABOUT THE NEW BULGE IN HIS JACKET WHICH APPEARED DURING THE "NIGHTS OF GLORY."
WE NEVER EVEN ASKED ABOUT THE SMALL, RUSTING RED STAIN ON HIS COLLAR THE MORNING WE RETURNED FROM OUR INVIGORATING DALLIANCE WITH THE POLICE.
Vr
WE NEVER KNEW ANYTHING, OR WANTED TO KNOW ANYTHING ABOUT THE MAN NAMED WILLEM...
Vrauwe
...WHO WAS ALWAYS THERE FOR US.

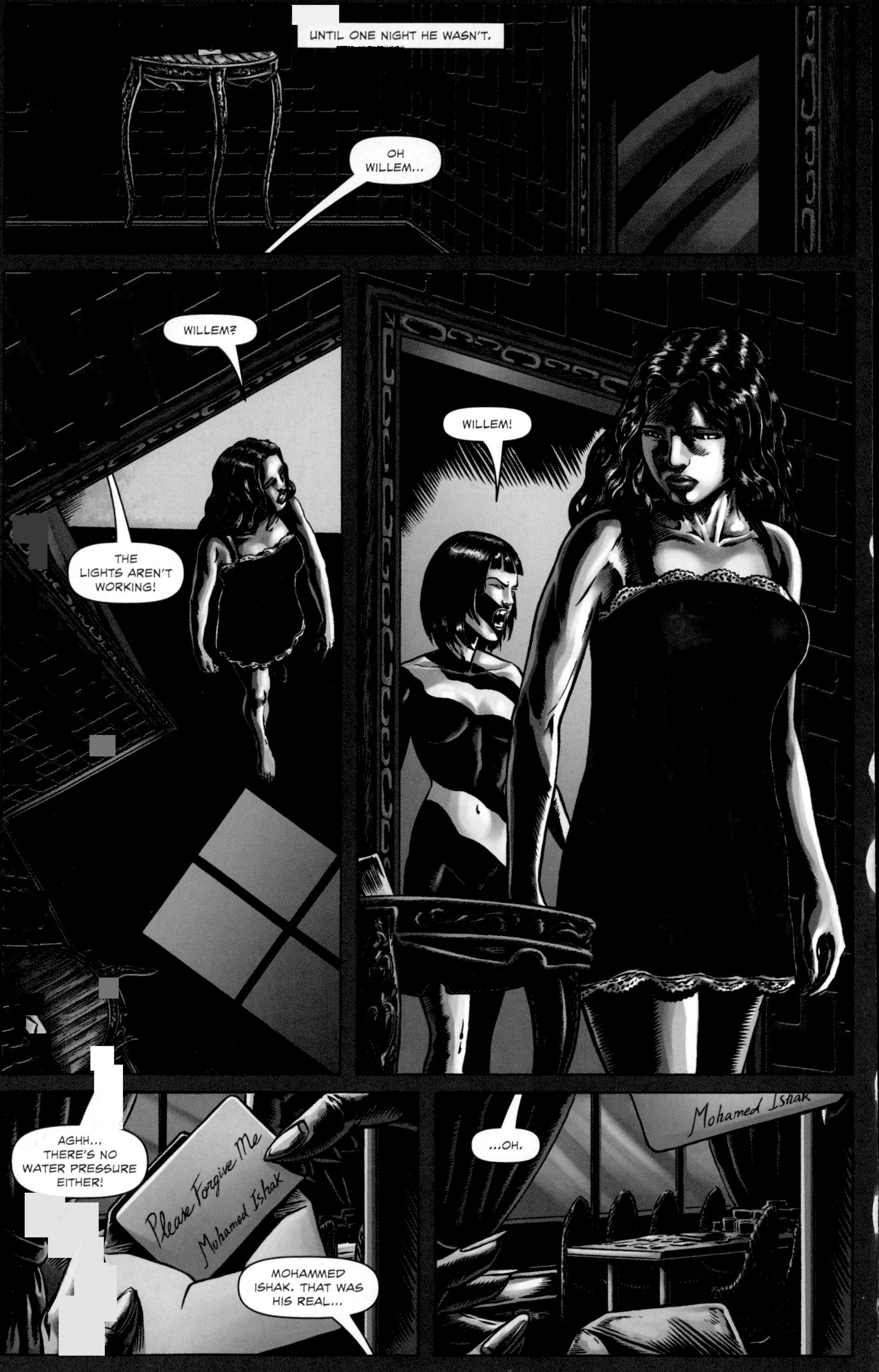
UNTIL ONE NIGHT HE WASN'T.
OH WILLEM...
WILLEM?
THE LIGHTS AREN'T WORKING!
WILLEM!
AGHH... THERE'S NO WATER PRESSURE EITHER!
Please Forgive Me
Mohamed Ishak
MOHAMMED ISHAK. THAT WAS HIS REAL...
...OH.
Mohamed Ishak

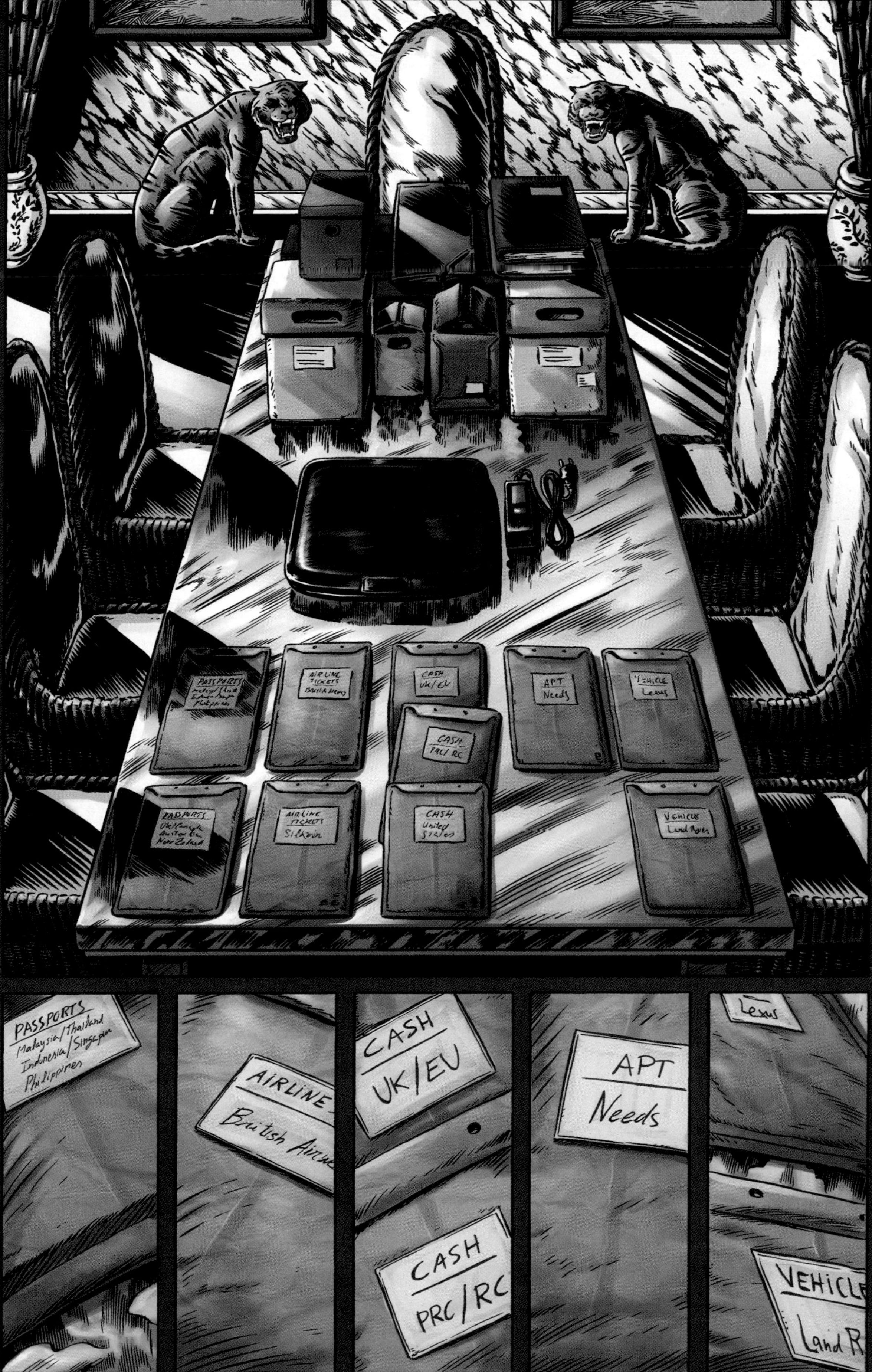
PASSPORTS
AIRLINE TICKETS
CASH UK/EU
APT Needs
VEHICLE Lexus
CASH PRC/RC
PASSPORTS
AIRLINE TICKETS Silkair
CASH United States
VEHICLE Land Rover
PASSPORTS Malaysia/Thailand Indonesia/Singapore Philippines
AIRLINE
CASH UK/EU
APT Needs
Lexus
CASH PRC/RC

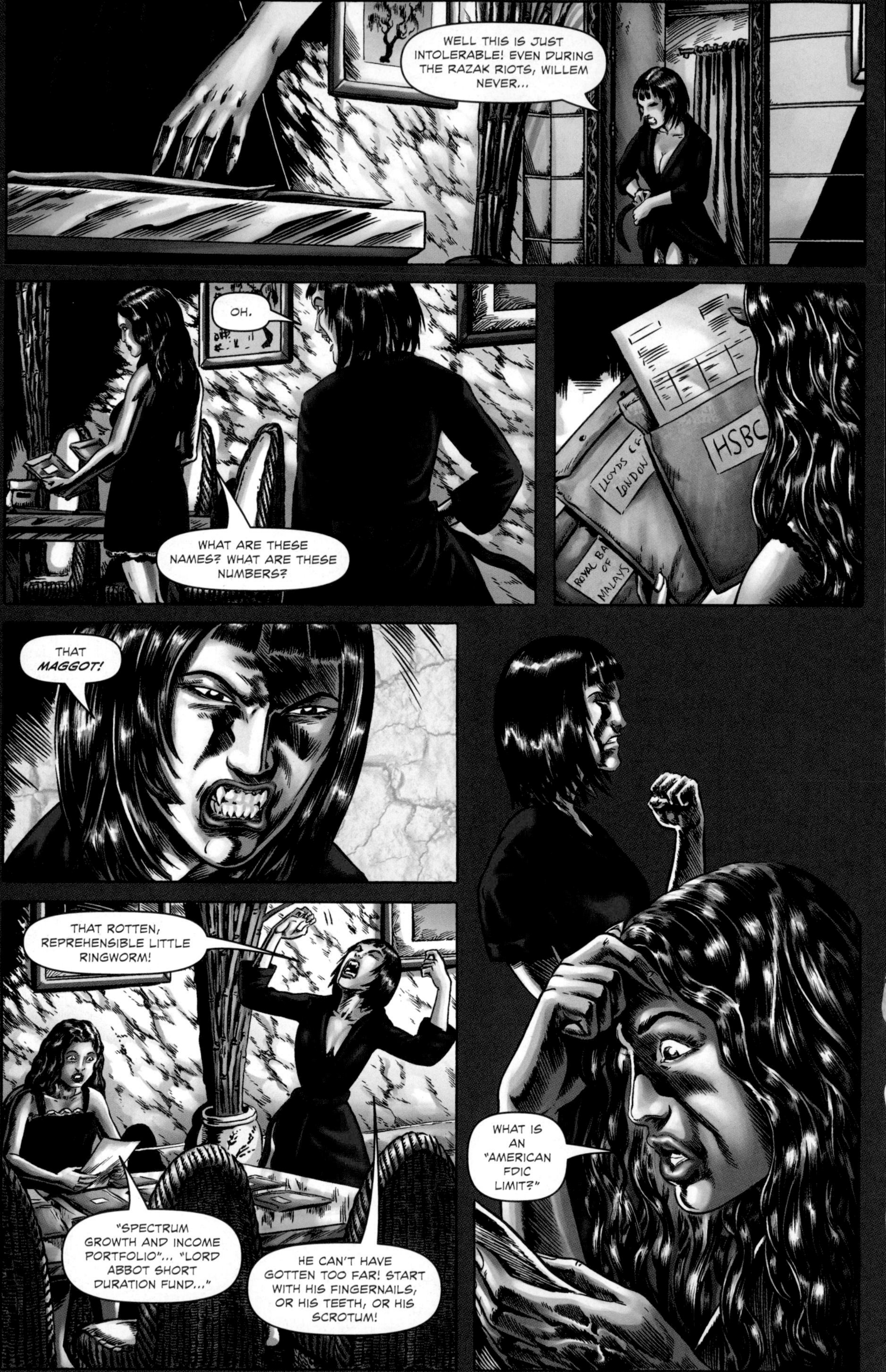
WELL THIS IS JUST INTOLERABLE! EVEN DURING THE RAZAK RIOTS, WILLEM NEVER...
OH.
WHAT ARE THESE NAMES? WHAT ARE THESE NUMBERS?
HSBC
LLOYDS OF LONDON
ROYAL BA... OF MALAYS...
THAT MAGGOT!
THAT ROTTEN, REPREHENSIBLE LITTLE RINGWORM!
"SPECTRUM GROWTH AND INCOME PORTFOLIO"... "LORD ABBOT SHORT DURATION FUND..."
HE CAN'T HAVE GOTTEN TOO FAR! START WITH HIS FINGERNAILS, OR HIS TEETH, OR HIS SCROTUM!
WHAT IS AN "AMERICAN FDIC LIMIT?"

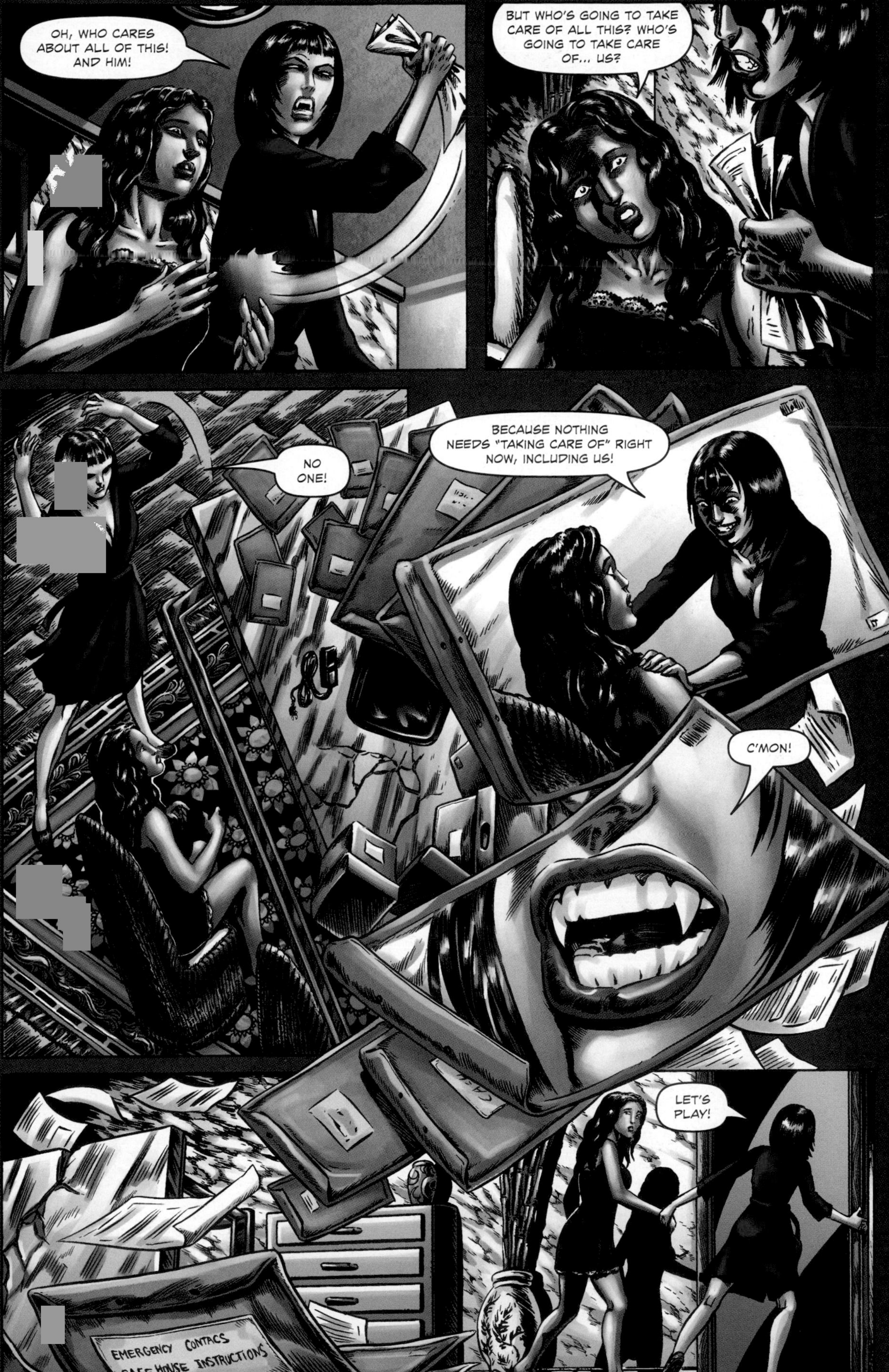
OH, WHO CARES ABOUT ALL OF THIS! AND HIM!
BUT WHO'S GOING TO TAKE CARE OF ALL THIS? WHO'S GOING TO TAKE CARE OF... US?
NO ONE!
BECAUSE NOTHING NEEDS "TAKING CARE OF" RIGHT NOW, INCLUDING US!
C'MON!
LET'S PLAY!
EMERGENCY CONTACS
SAFE HOUSE INSTRUCTIONS

Chapter 4

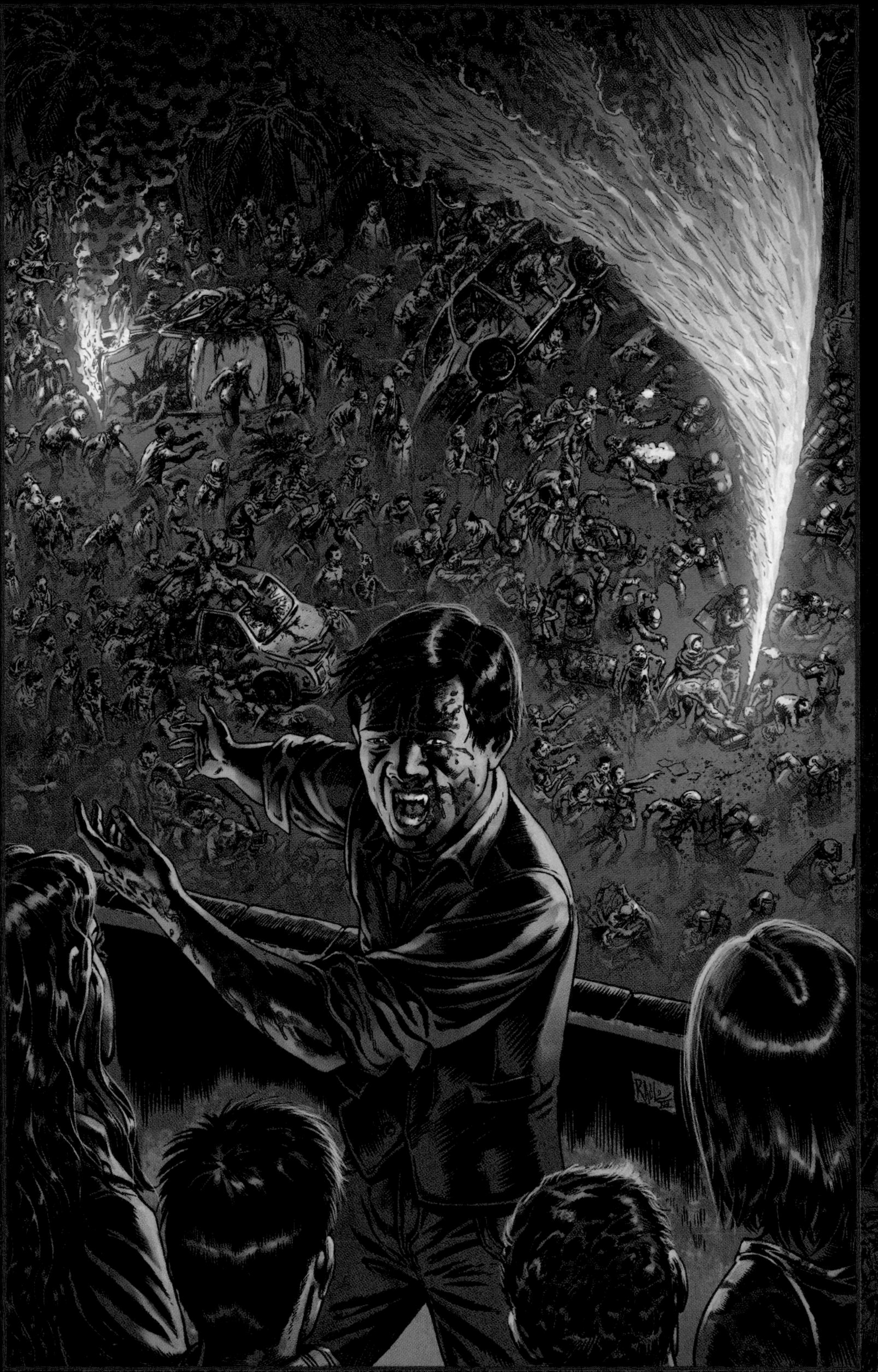

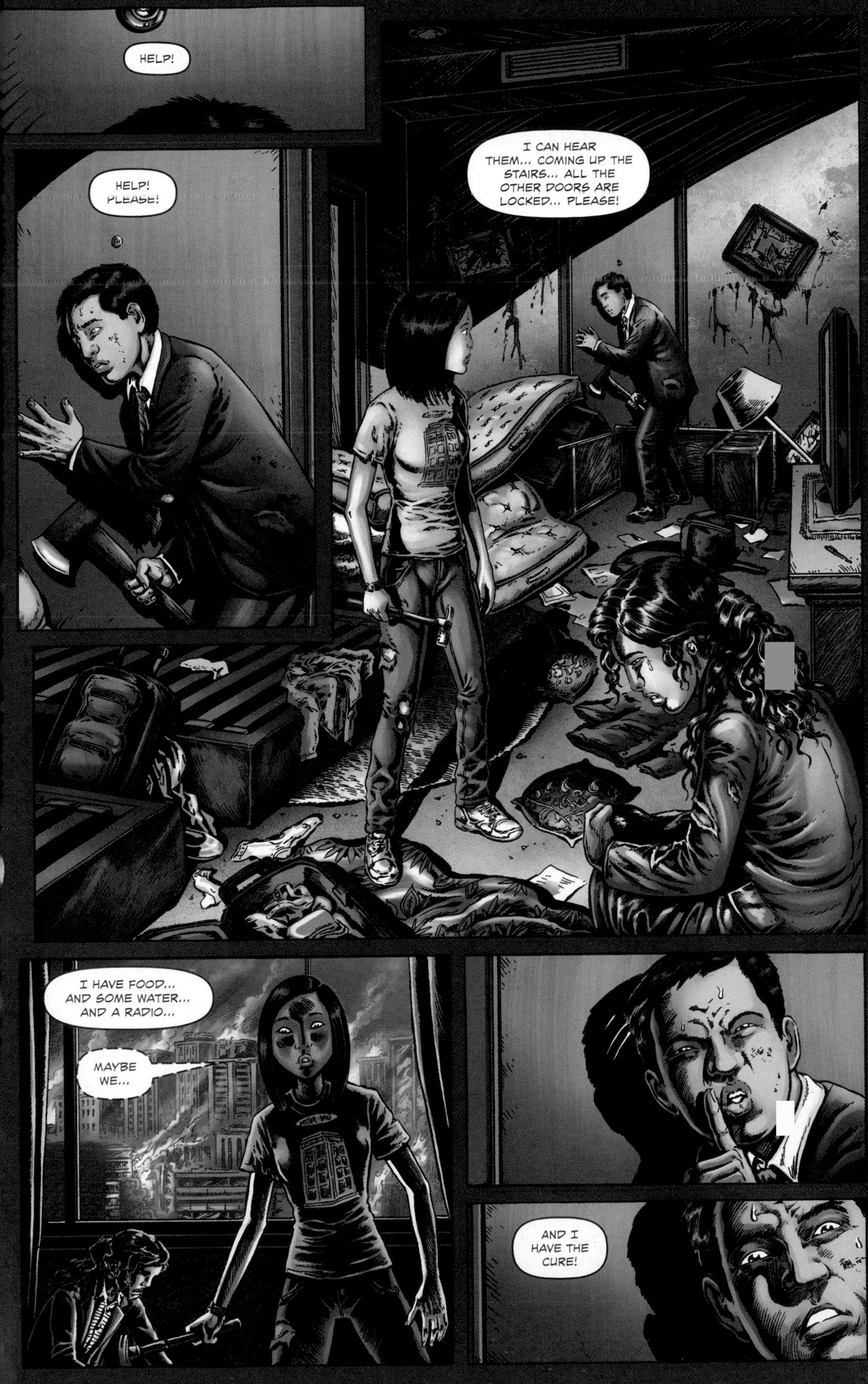

HELP!
HELP! PLEASE!
I CAN HEAR THEM... COMING UP THE STAIRS... ALL THE OTHER DOORS ARE LOCKED... PLEASE!
I HAVE FOOD... AND SOME WATER... AND A RADIO...
MAYBE WE...
AND I HAVE THE CURE!

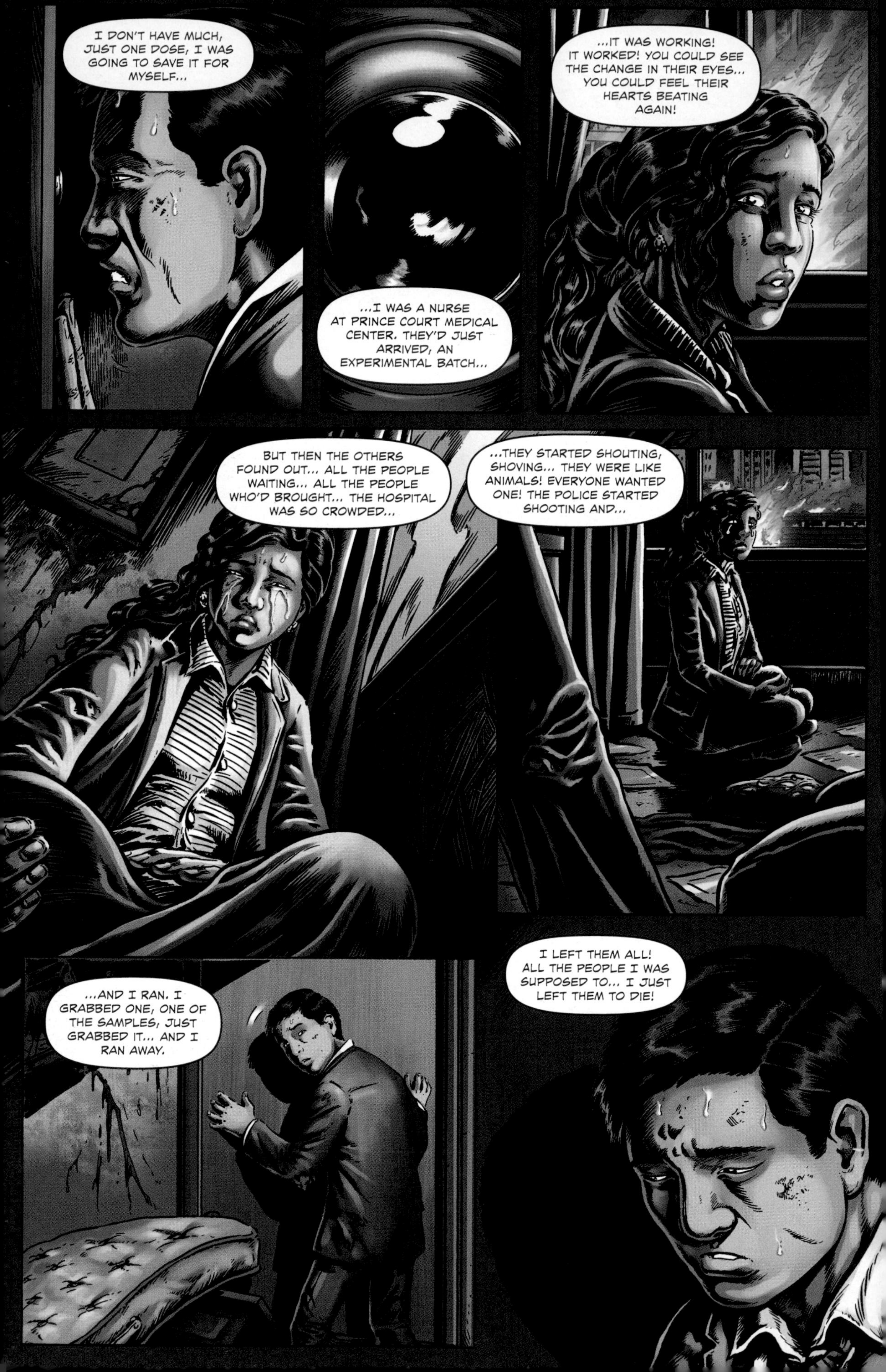
I DON'T HAVE MUCH, JUST ONE DOSE, I WAS GOING TO SAVE IT FOR MYSELF...
...I WAS A NURSE AT PRINCE COURT MEDICAL CENTER. THEY'D JUST ARRIVED, AN EXPERIMENTAL BATCH...
...IT WAS WORKING! IT WORKED! YOU COULD SEE THE CHANGE IN THEIR EYES... YOU COULD FEEL THEIR HEARTS BEATING AGAIN!
BUT THEN THE OTHERS FOUND OUT... ALL THE PEOPLE WAITING... ALL THE PEOPLE WHO'D BROUGHT... THE HOSPITAL WAS SO CROWDED...
...THEY STARTED SHOUTING, SHOVING... THEY WERE LIKE ANIMALS! EVERYONE WANTED ONE! THE POLICE STARTED SHOOTING AND...
...AND I RAN. I GRABBED ONE, ONE OF THE SAMPLES, JUST GRABBED IT... AND I RAN AWAY.
I LEFT THEM ALL! ALL THE PEOPLE I WAS SUPPOSED TO... I JUST LEFT THEM TO DIE!

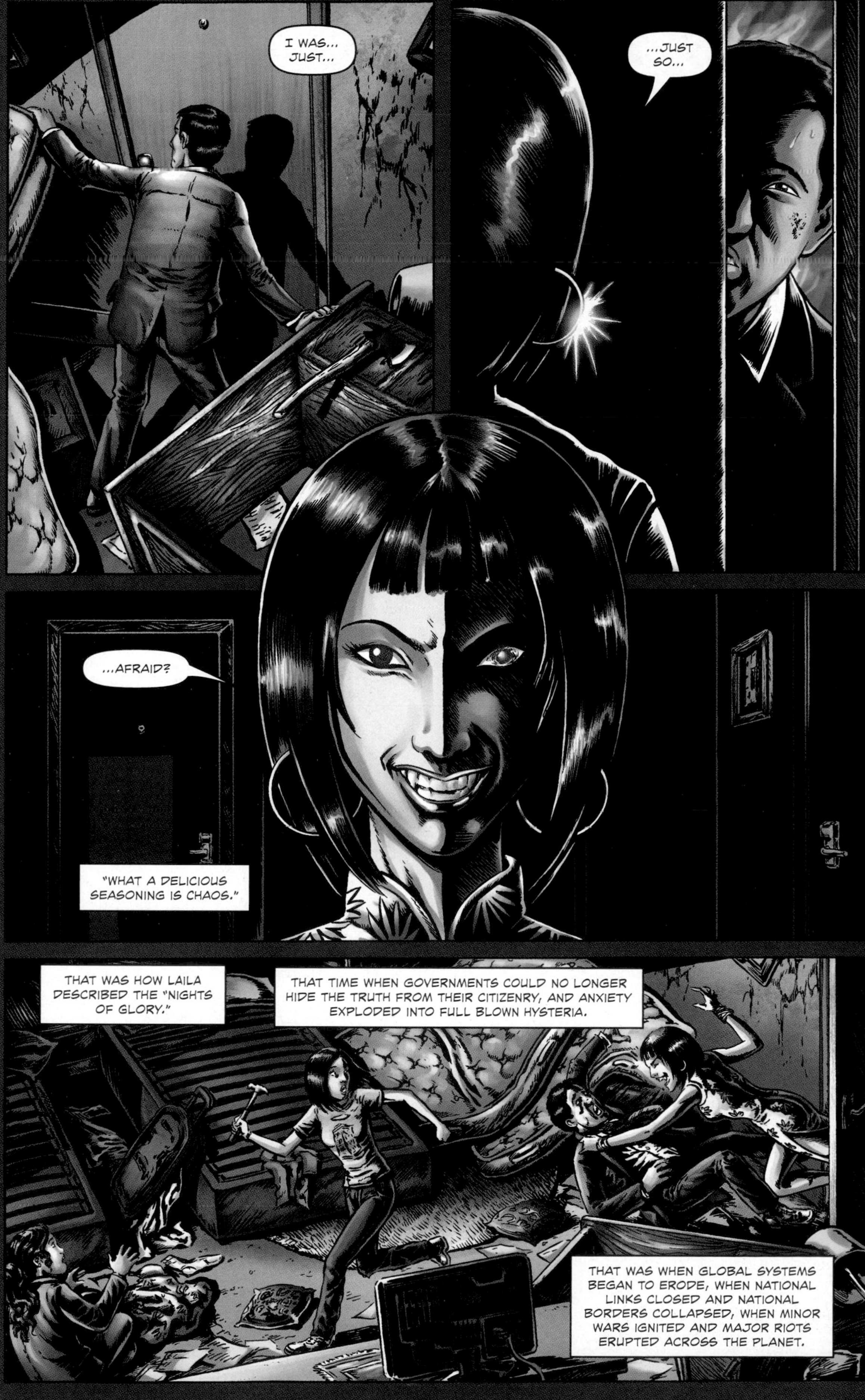
I WAS... JUST...
...JUST SO...
...AFRAID?
"WHAT A DELICIOUS SEASONING IS CHAOS."
THAT WAS HOW LAILA DESCRIBED THE "NIGHTS OF GLORY."
THAT TIME WHEN GOVERNMENTS COULD NO LONGER HIDE THE TRUTH FROM THEIR CITIZENRY, AND ANXIETY EXPLODED INTO FULL BLOWN HYSTERIA.
THAT WAS WHEN GLOBAL SYSTEMS BEGAN TO ERODE, WHEN NATIONAL LINKS CLOSED AND NATIONAL BORDERS COLLAPSED, WHEN MINOR WARS IGNITED AND MAJOR RIOTS ERUPTED ACROSS THE PLANET.

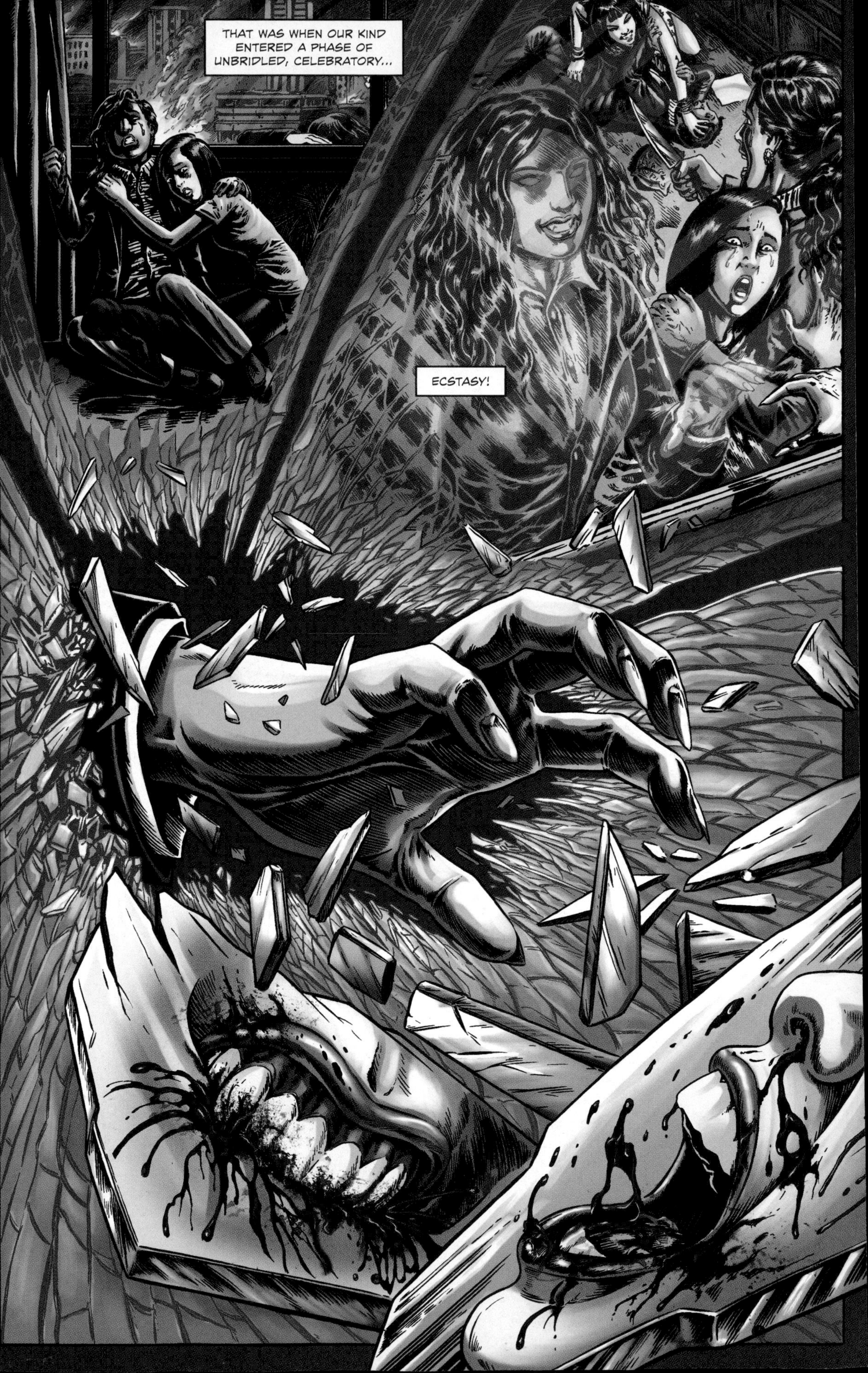
THAT WAS WHEN OUR KIND ENTERED A PHASE OF UNBRIDLED, CELEBRATORY...
ECSTASY!

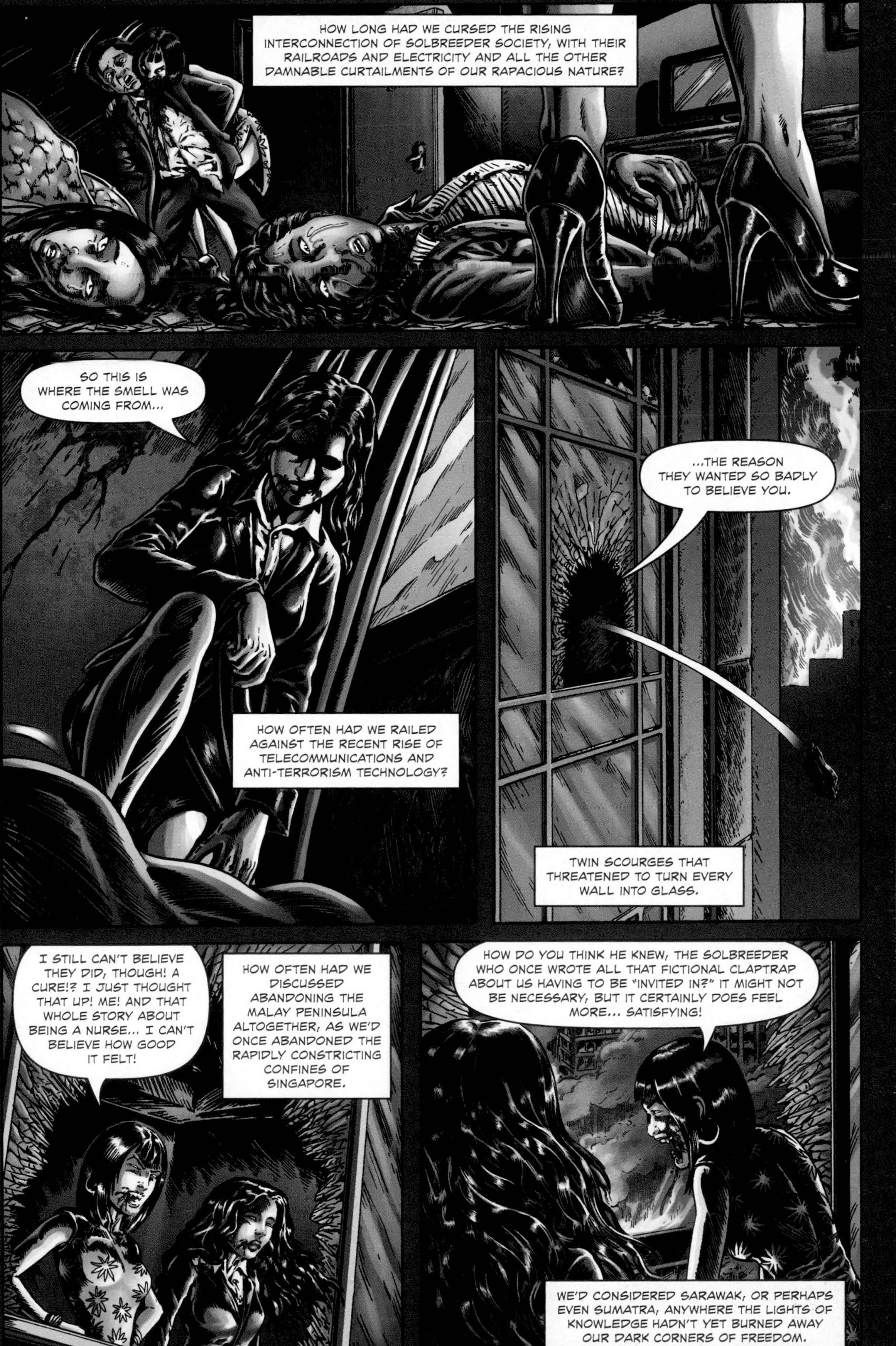
HOW LONG HAD WE CURSED THE RISING INTERCONNECTION OF SOLBREEDER SOCIETY, WITH THEIR RAILROADS AND ELECTRICITY AND ALL THE OTHER DAMNABLE CURTAILMENTS OF OUR RAPACIOUS NATURE?
SO THIS IS WHERE THE SMELL WAS COMING FROM...
HOW OFTEN HAD WE RAILED AGAINST THE RECENT RISE OF TELECOMMUNICATIONS AND ANTI-TERRORISM TECHNOLOGY?
...THE REASON THEY WANTED SO BADLY TO BELIEVE YOU.
TWIN SCOURGES THAT THREATENED TO TURN EVERY WALL INTO GLASS.
I STILL CAN'T BELIEVE THEY DID, THOUGH! A CURE!? I JUST THOUGHT THAT UP! ME! AND THAT WHOLE STORY ABOUT BEING A NURSE... I CAN'T BELIEVE HOW GOOD IT FELT!
HOW OFTEN HAD WE DISCUSSED ABANDONING THE MALAY PENINSULA ALTOGETHER, AS WE'D ONCE ABANDONED THE RAPIDLY CONSTRICTING CONFINES OF SINGAPORE.
HOW DO YOU THINK HE KNEW, THE SOLBREEDER WHO ONCE WROTE ALL THAT FICTIONAL CLAPTRAP ABOUT US HAVING TO BE "INVITED IN?" IT MIGHT NOT BE NECESSARY, BUT IT CERTAINLY DOES FEEL MORE... SATISFYING!
WE'D CONSIDERED SARAWAK, OR PERHAPS EVEN SUMATRA, ANYWHERE THE LIGHTS OF KNOWLEDGE HADN'T YET BURNED AWAY OUR DARK CORNERS OF FREEDOM.

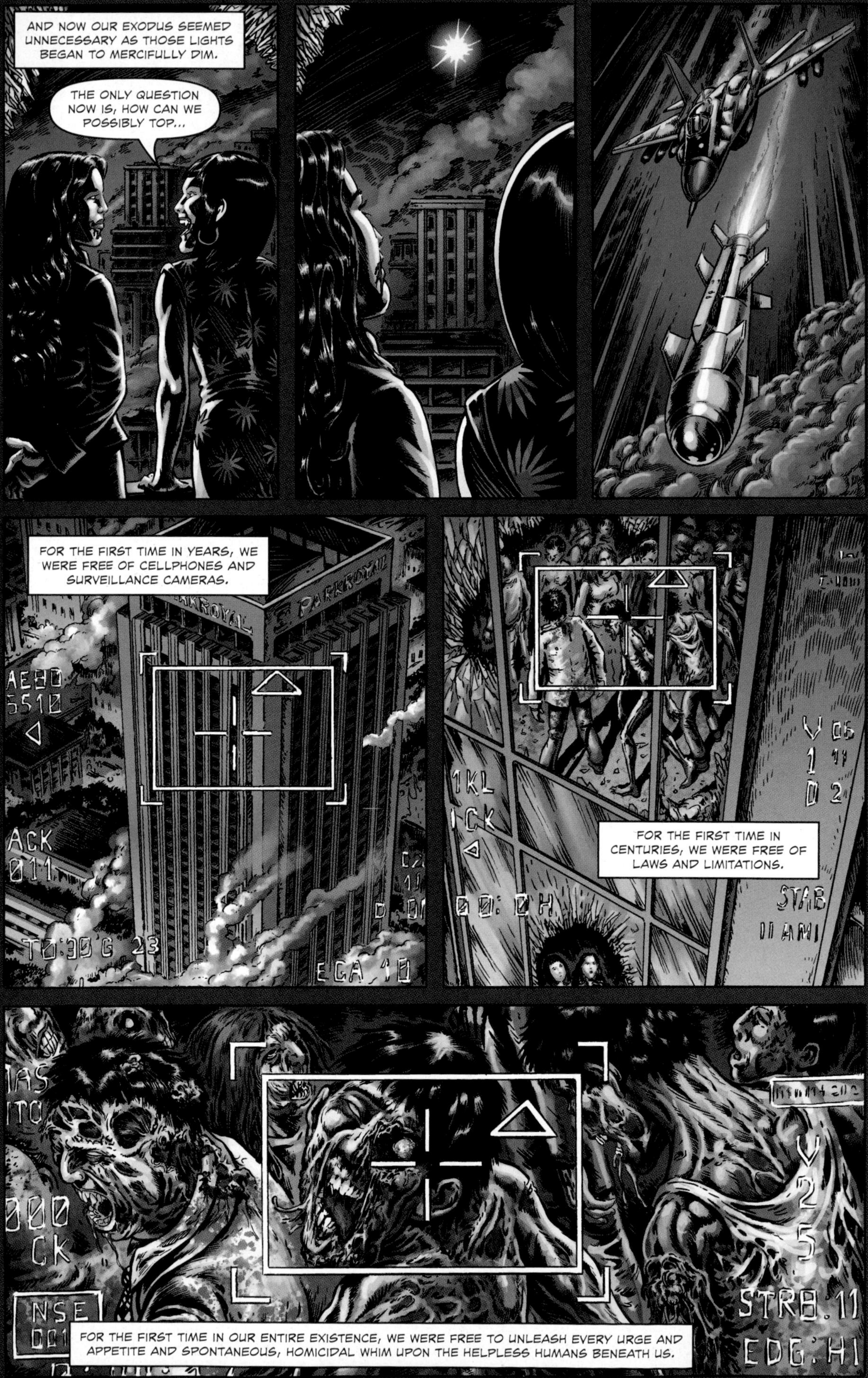
AND NOW OUR EXODUS SEEMED UNNECESSARY AS THOSE LIGHTS BEGAN TO MERCIFULLY DIM.
THE ONLY QUESTION NOW IS, HOW CAN WE POSSIBLY TOP...
FOR THE FIRST TIME IN YEARS, WE WERE FREE OF CELLPHONES AND SURVEILLANCE CAMERAS.
FOR THE FIRST TIME IN CENTURIES, WE WERE FREE OF LAWS AND LIMITATIONS.
FOR THE FIRST TIME IN OUR ENTIRE EXISTENCE, WE WERE FREE TO UNLEASH EVERY URGE AND APPETITE AND SPONTANEOUS, HOMICIDAL WHIM UPON THE HELPLESS HUMANS BENEATH US.

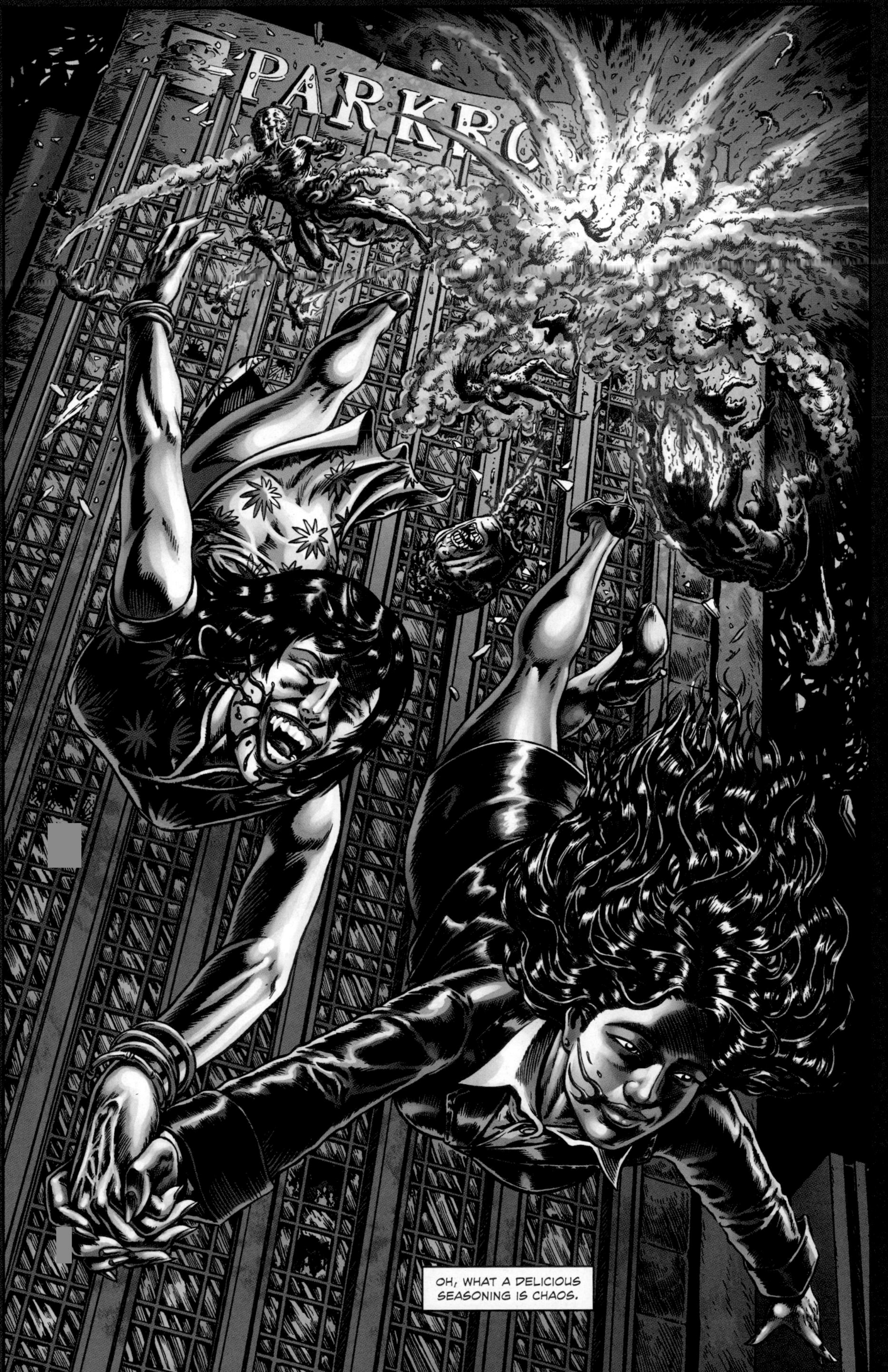
PARKRO
OH, WHAT A DELICIOUS SEASONING IS CHAOS.

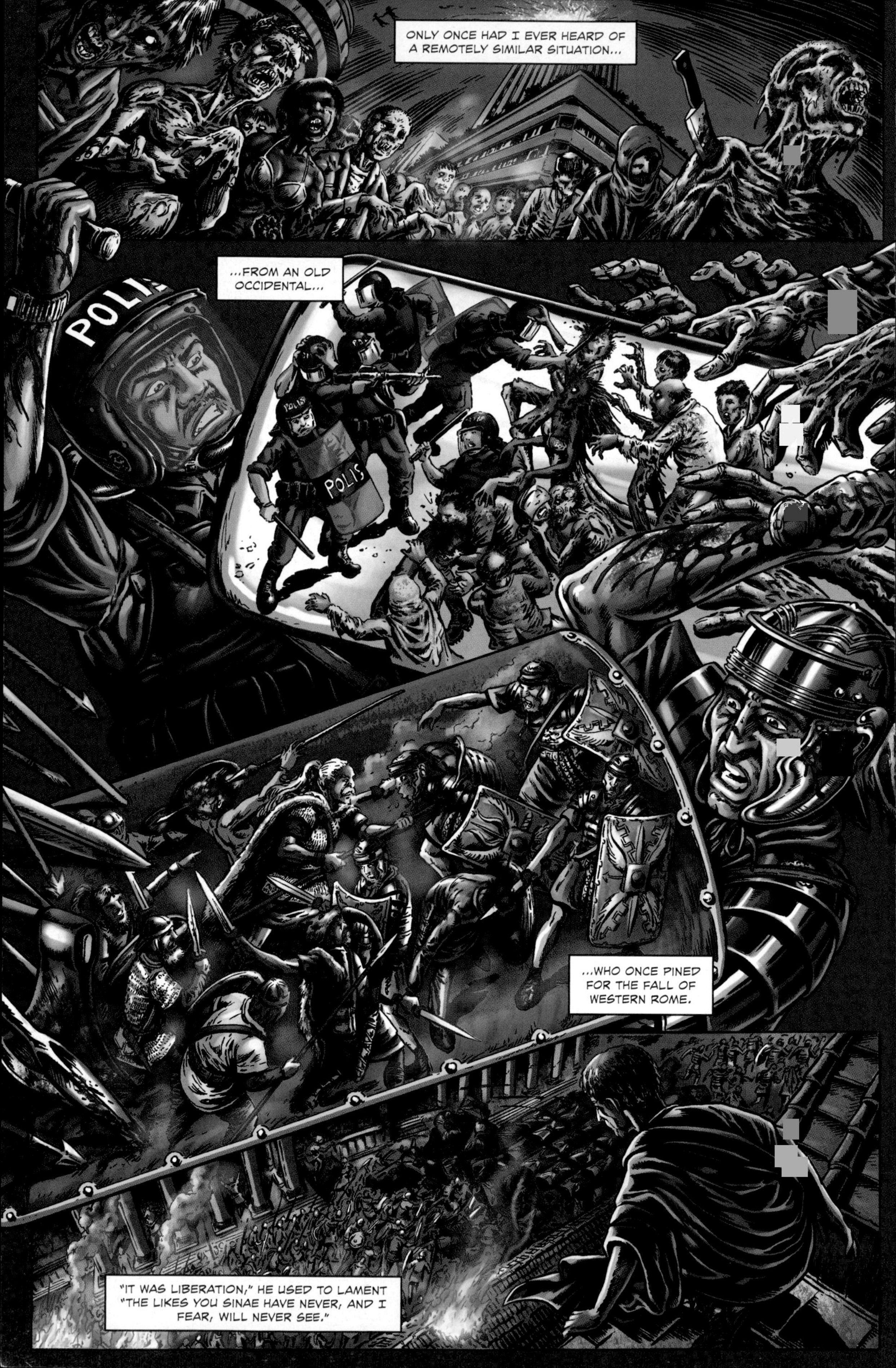
ONLY ONCE HAD I EVER HEARD OF A REMOTELY SIMILAR SITUATION...
...FROM AN OLD OCCIDENTAL...
POLIS
POLIS
POLIS
...WHO ONCE PINED FOR THE FALL OF WESTERN ROME.
"IT WAS LIBERATION," HE USED TO LAMENT "THE LIKES YOU SINAE HAVE NEVER, AND I FEAR, WILL NEVER SEE."

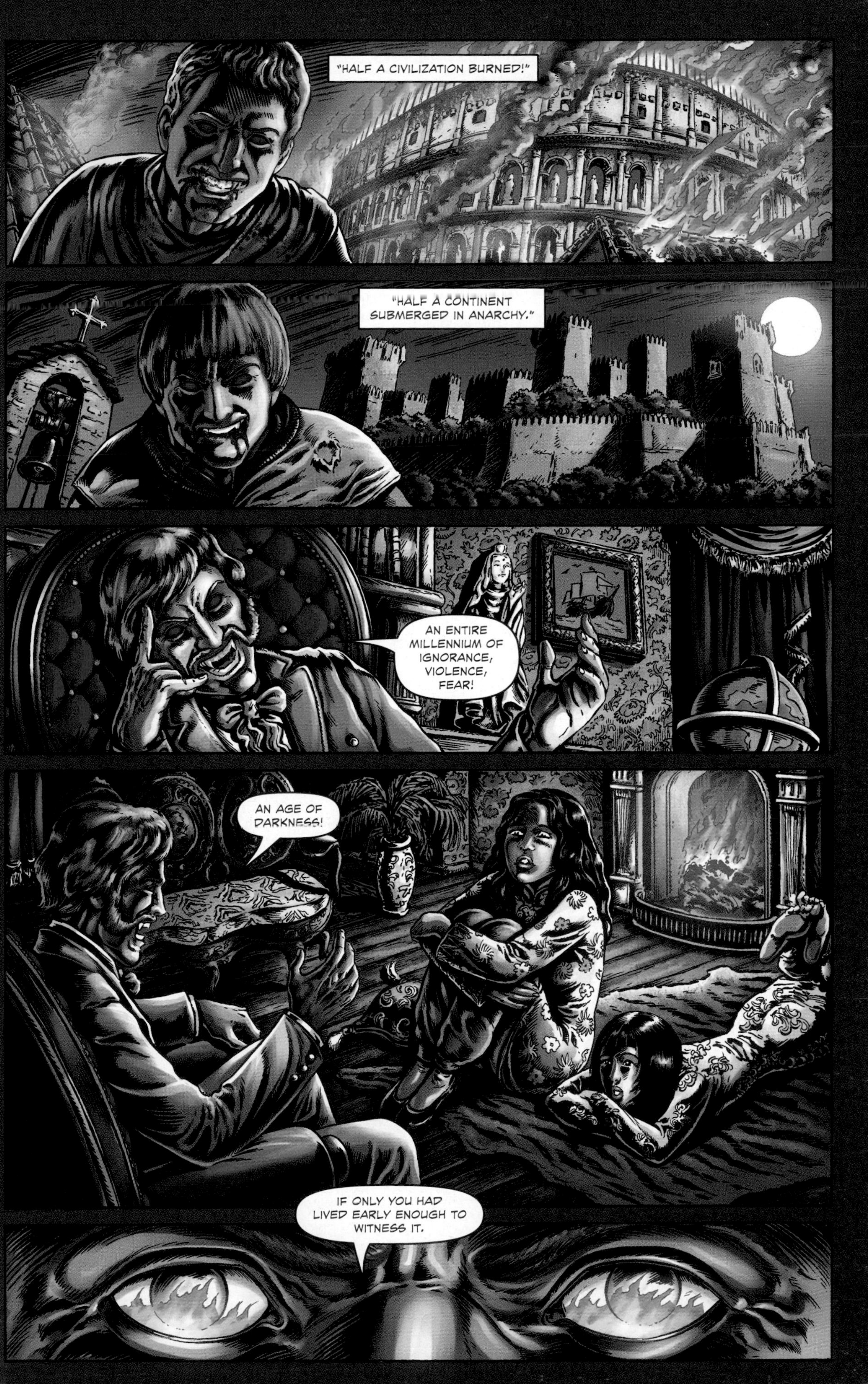
"HALF A CIVILIZATION BURNED!"
"HALF A CONTINENT SUBMERGED IN ANARCHY."
AN ENTIRE MILLENNIUM OF IGNORANCE, VIOLENCE, FEAR!
AN AGE OF DARKNESS!
IF ONLY YOU HAD LIVED EARLY ENOUGH TO WITNESS IT.

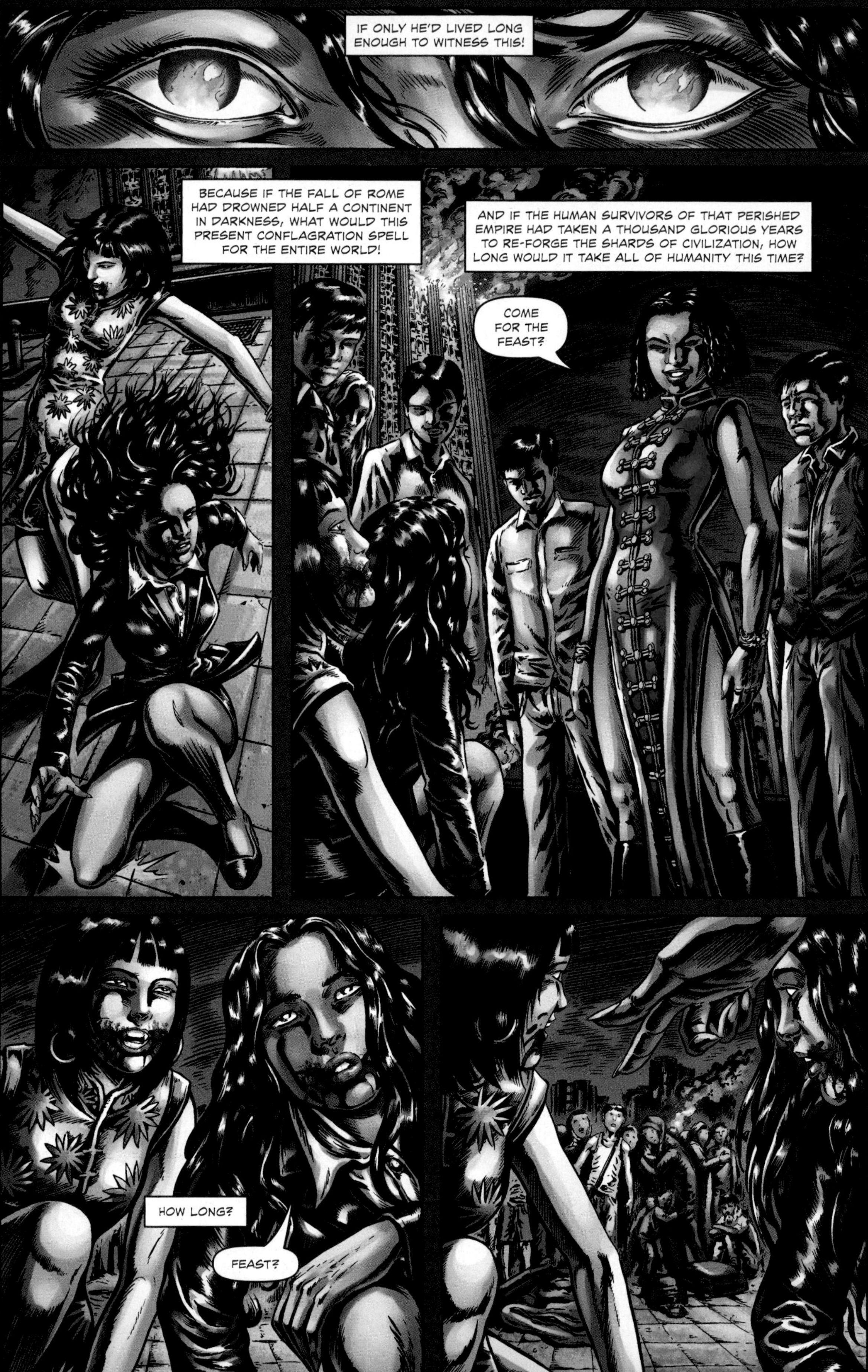
IF ONLY HE'D LIVED LONG ENOUGH TO WITNESS THIS!
BECAUSE IF THE FALL OF ROME HAD DROWNED HALF A CONTINENT IN DARKNESS, WHAT WOULD THIS PRESENT CONFLAGRATION SPELL FOR THE ENTIRE WORLD!
AND IF THE HUMAN SURVIVORS OF THAT PERISHED EMPIRE HAD TAKEN A THOUSAND GLORIOUS YEARS TO RE-FORGE THE SHARDS OF CIVILIZATION, HOW LONG WOULD IT TAKE ALL OF HUMANITY THIS TIME?
COME FOR THE FEAST?
HOW LONG?
FEAST?

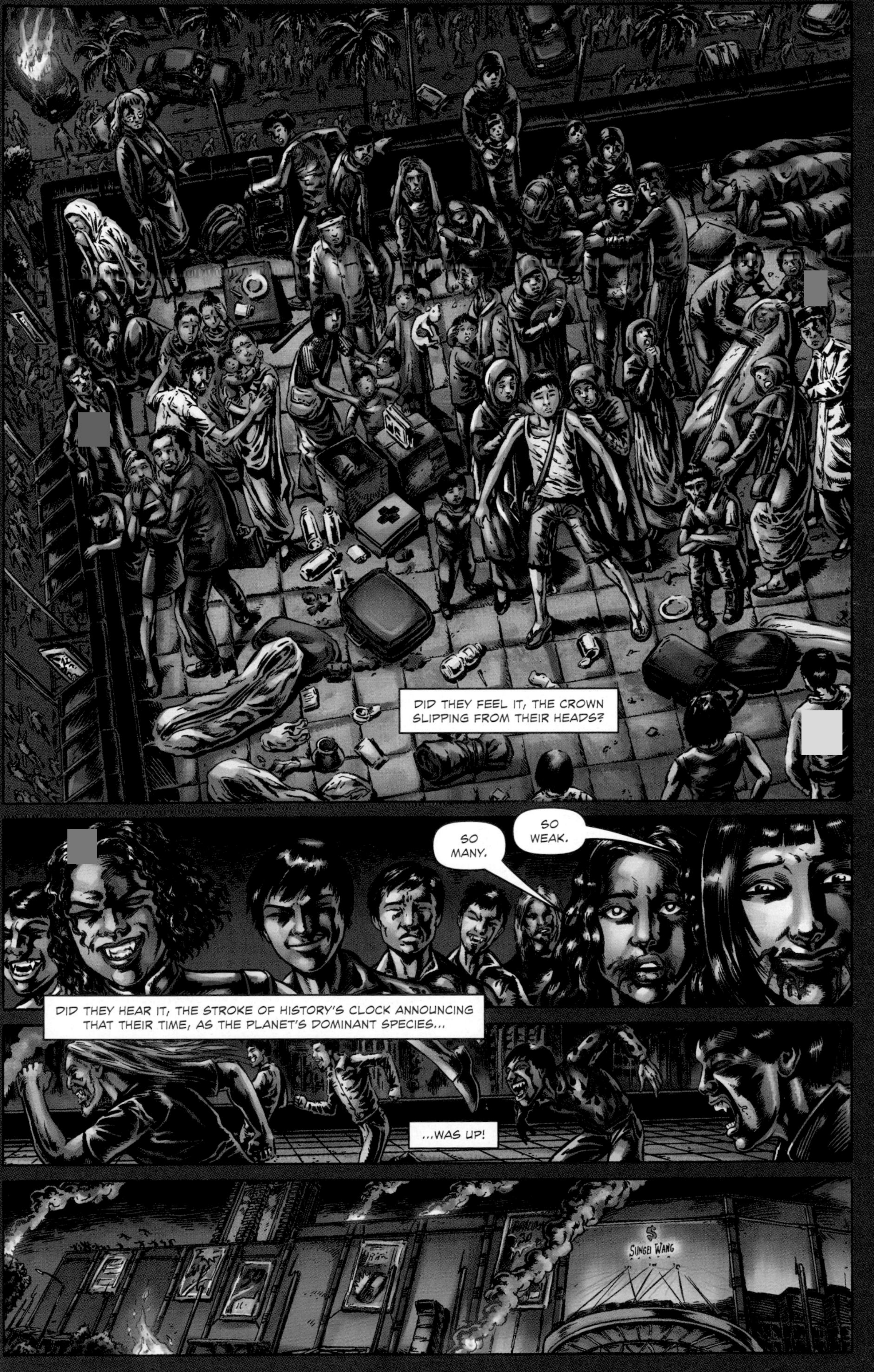
DID THEY FEEL IT, THE CROWN SLIPPING FROM THEIR HEADS?
SO MANY.
SO WEAK.
DID THEY HEAR IT, THE STROKE OF HISTORY'S CLOCK ANNOUNCING THAT THEIR TIME, AS THE PLANET'S DOMINANT SPECIES...
...WAS UP!
SUNGEI WANG

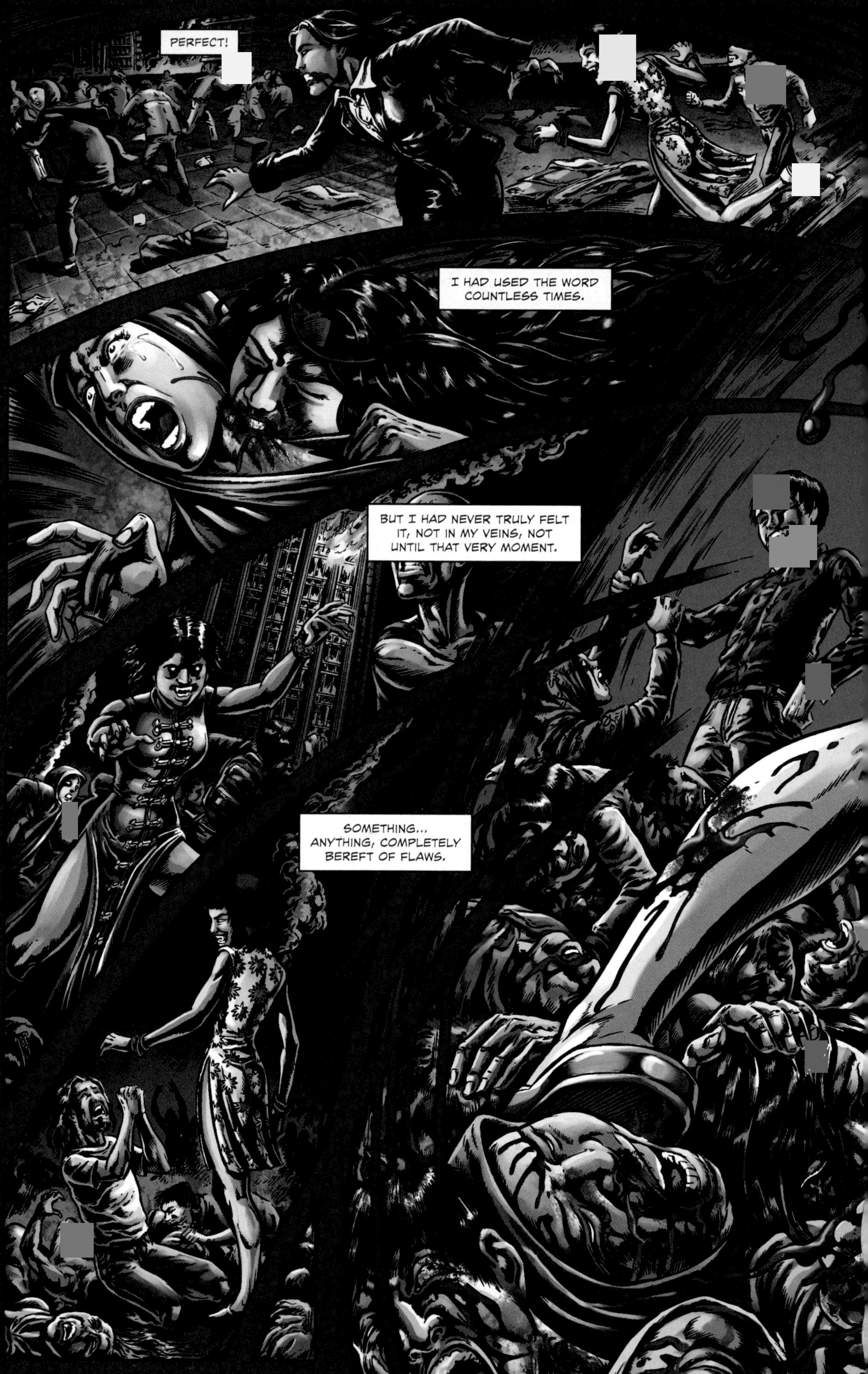
PERFECT!
I HAD USED THE WORD COUNTLESS TIMES.
BUT I HAD NEVER TRULY FELT IT, NOT IN MY VEINS, NOT UNTIL THAT VERY MOMENT.
SOMETHING... ANYTHING, COMPLETELY BEREFT OF FLAWS.

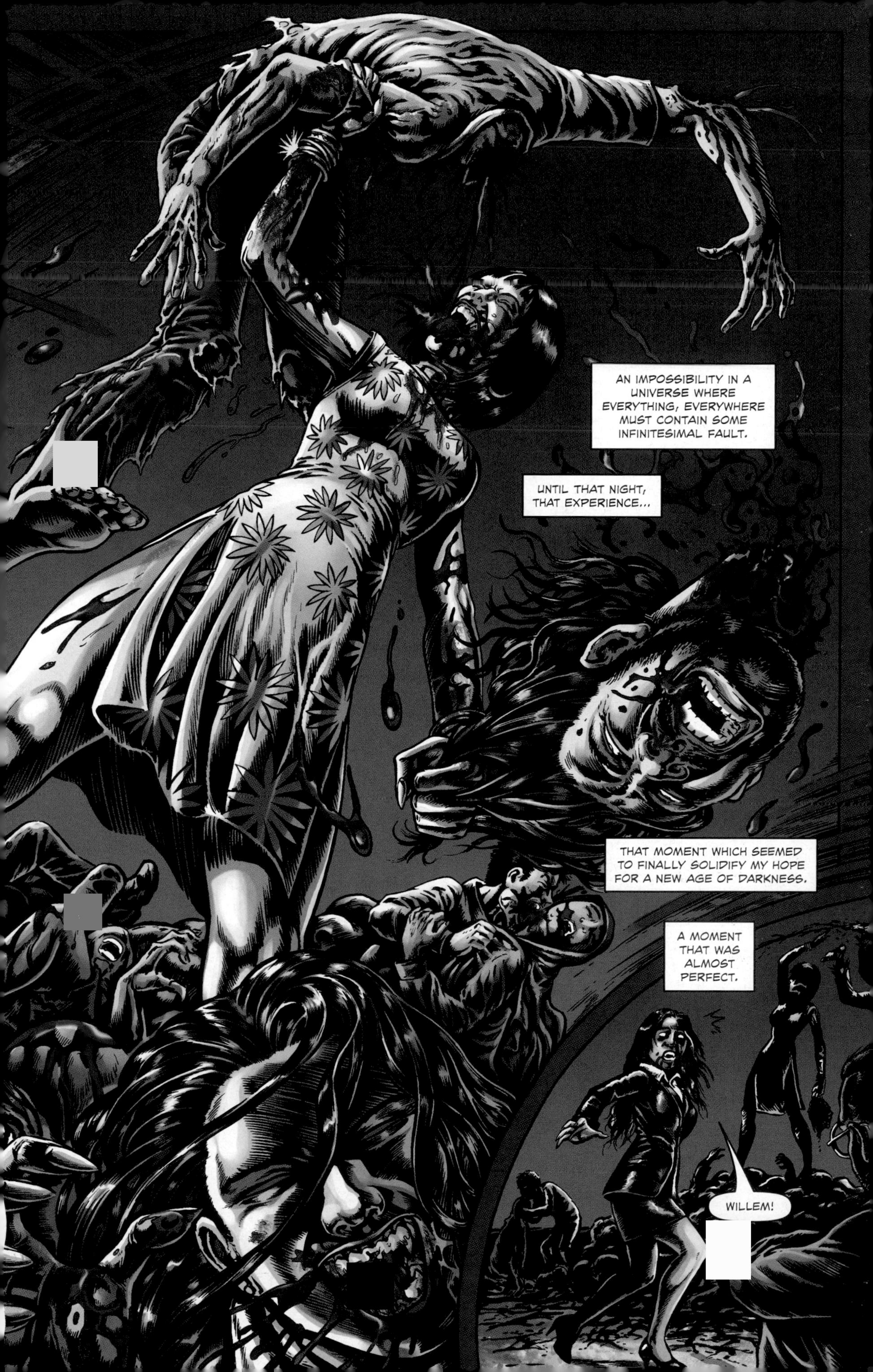
AN IMPOSSIBILITY IN A UNIVERSE WHERE EVERYTHING, EVERYWHERE MUST CONTAIN SOME INFINITESIMAL FAULT.
UNTIL THAT NIGHT, THAT EXPERIENCE...
THAT MOMENT WHICH SEEMED TO FINALLY SOLIDIFY MY HOPE FOR A NEW AGE OF DARKNESS.
A MOMENT THAT WAS ALMOST PERFECT.
WILLEM!

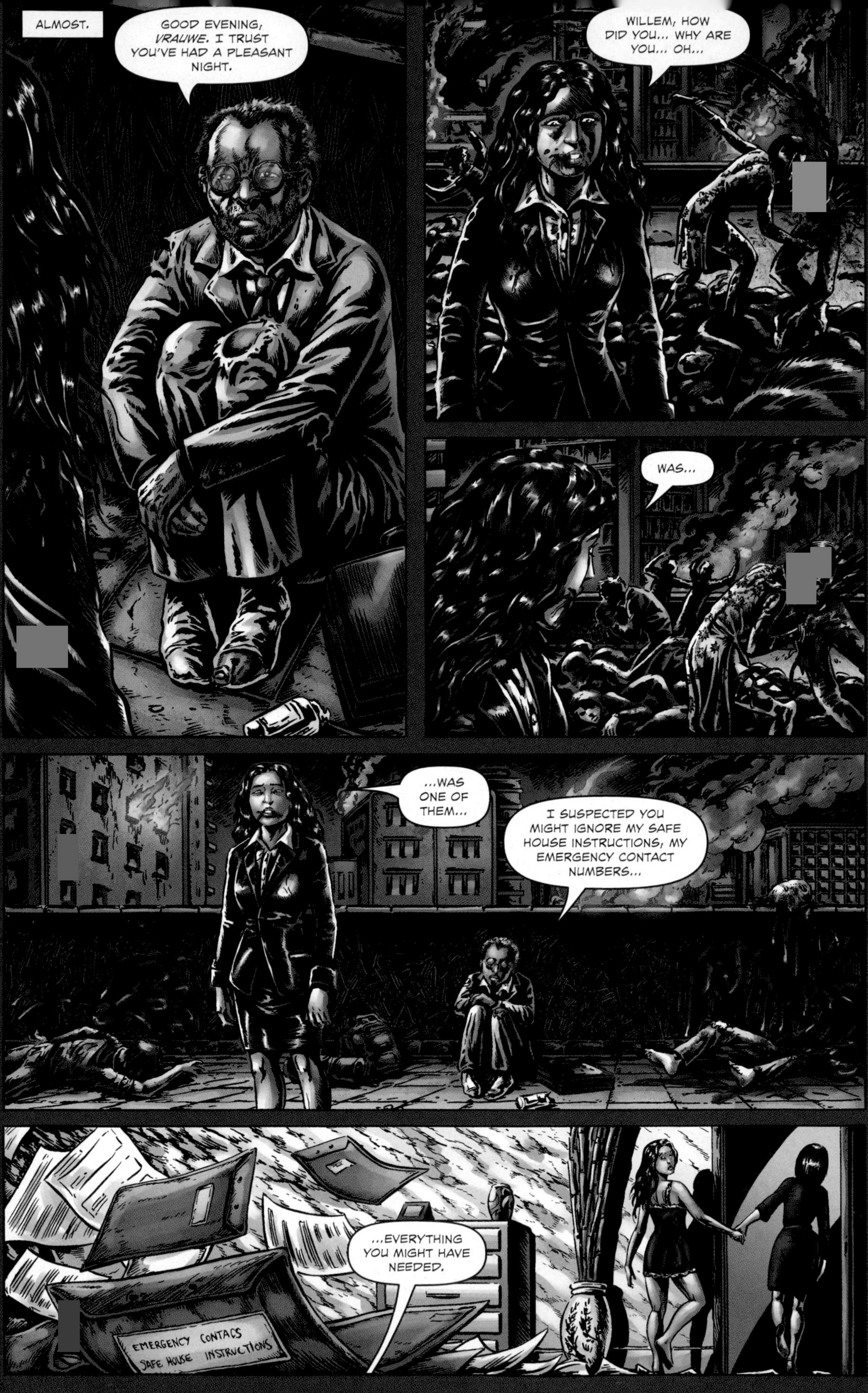
ALMOST.
GOOD EVENING, *VRAUWE*. I TRUST YOU'VE HAD A PLEASANT NIGHT.
WILLEM, HOW DID YOU... WHY ARE YOU... OH...
WAS...
...WAS ONE OF THEM...
I SUSPECTED YOU MIGHT IGNORE MY SAFE HOUSE INSTRUCTIONS, MY EMERGENCY CONTACT NUMBERS...
...EVERYTHING YOU MIGHT HAVE NEEDED.
EMERGENCY CONTACS
SAFE HOUSE INSTRUCTIONS

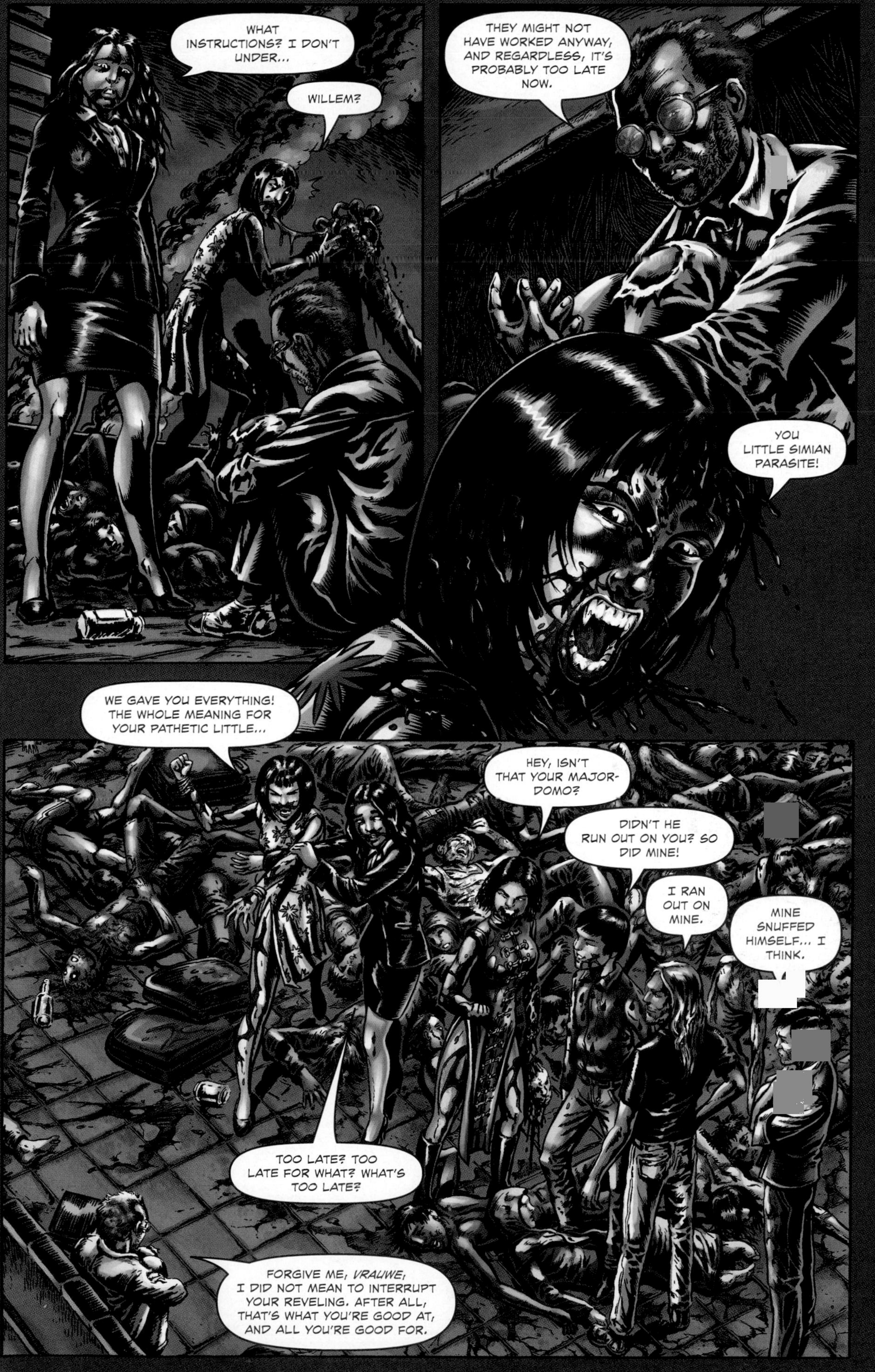
WHAT INSTRUCTIONS? I DON'T UNDER...
WILLEM?
THEY MIGHT NOT HAVE WORKED ANYWAY, AND REGARDLESS, IT'S PROBABLY TOO LATE NOW.
YOU LITTLE SIMIAN PARASITE!
WE GAVE YOU EVERYTHING! THE WHOLE MEANING FOR YOUR PATHETIC LITTLE...
HEY, ISN'T THAT YOUR MAJOR-DOMO?
DIDN'T HE RUN OUT ON YOU? SO DID MINE!
I RAN OUT ON MINE.
MINE SNUFFED HIMSELF... I THINK.
TOO LATE? TOO LATE FOR WHAT? WHAT'S TOO LATE?
FORGIVE ME, *VRAUWE*; I DID NOT MEAN TO INTERRUPT YOUR REVELING. AFTER ALL, THAT'S WHAT YOU'RE GOOD AT, AND ALL YOU'RE GOOD FOR.

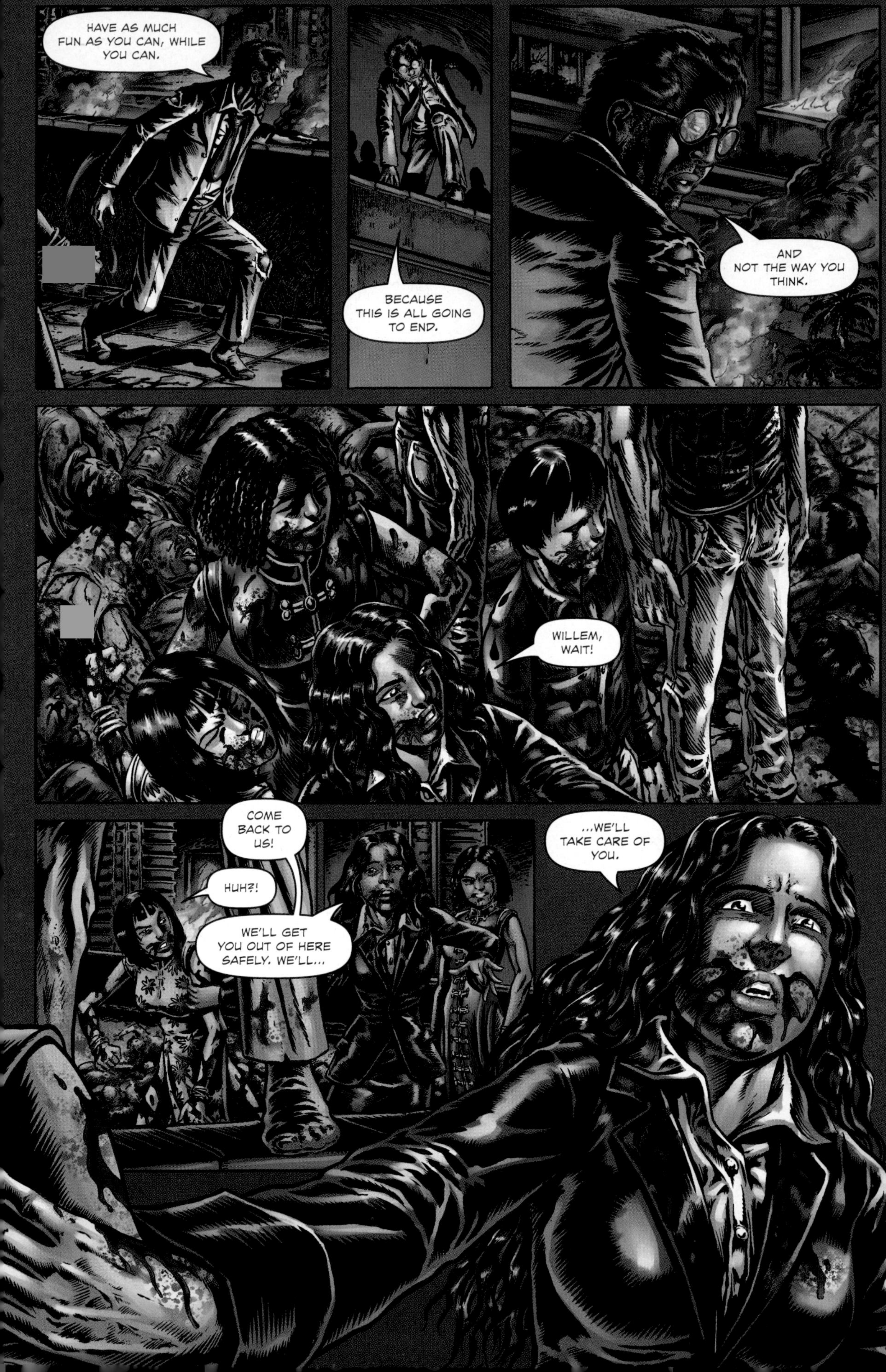
HAVE AS MUCH FUN AS YOU CAN, WHILE YOU CAN.
BECAUSE THIS IS ALL GOING TO END.
AND NOT THE WAY YOU THINK.
WILLEM, WAIT!
COME BACK TO US!
HUH?!
WE'LL GET YOU OUT OF HERE SAFELY. WE'LL...
...WE'LL TAKE CARE OF YOU.

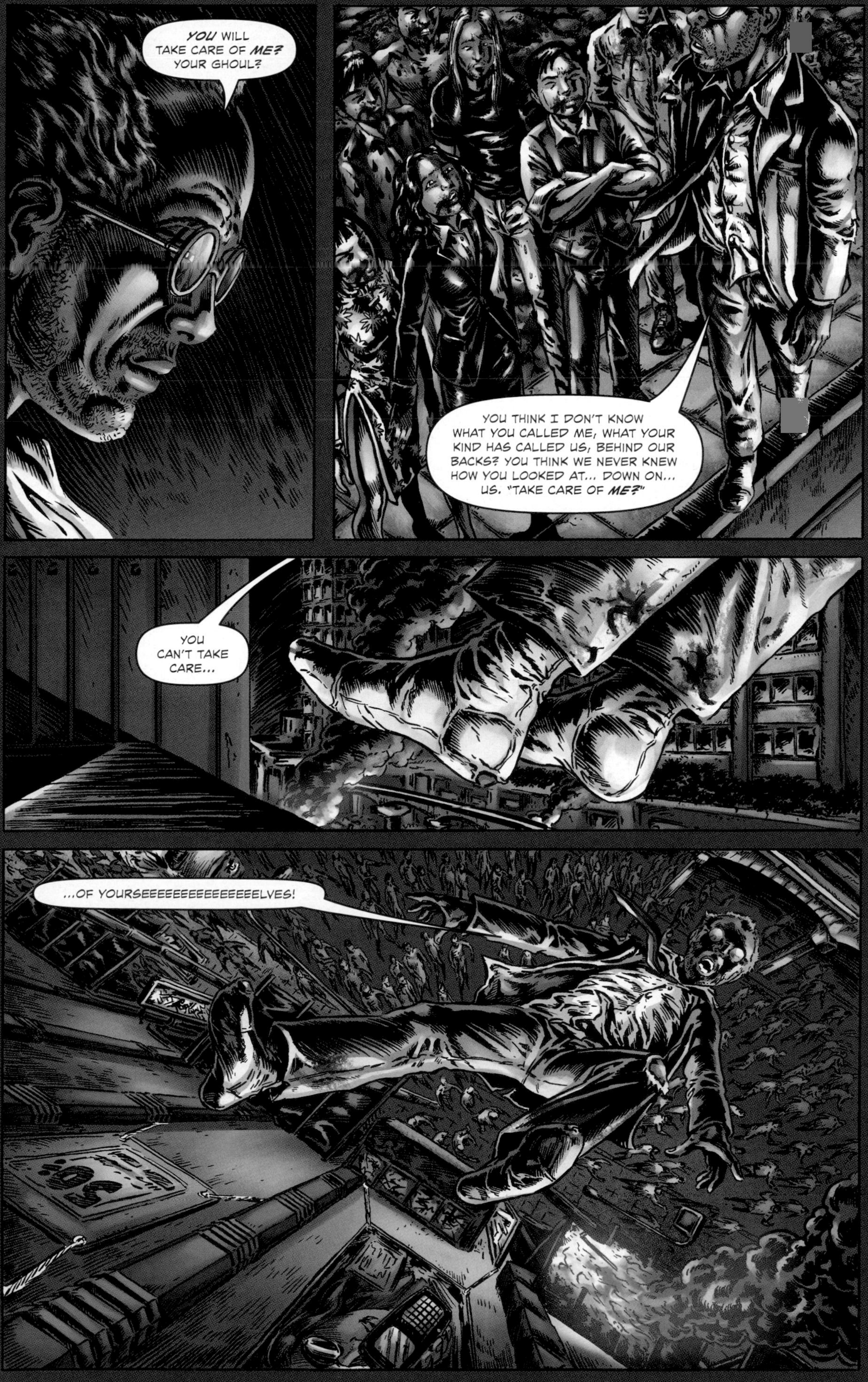
YOU WILL TAKE CARE OF ME? YOUR GHOUL?
YOU THINK I DON'T KNOW WHAT YOU CALLED ME, WHAT YOUR KIND HAS CALLED US, BEHIND OUR BACKS? YOU THINK WE NEVER KNEW HOW YOU LOOKED AT... DOWN ON... US. "TAKE CARE OF ME?"
YOU CAN'T TAKE CARE...
...OF YOURSEEEEEEEEEEEEEEELVES!

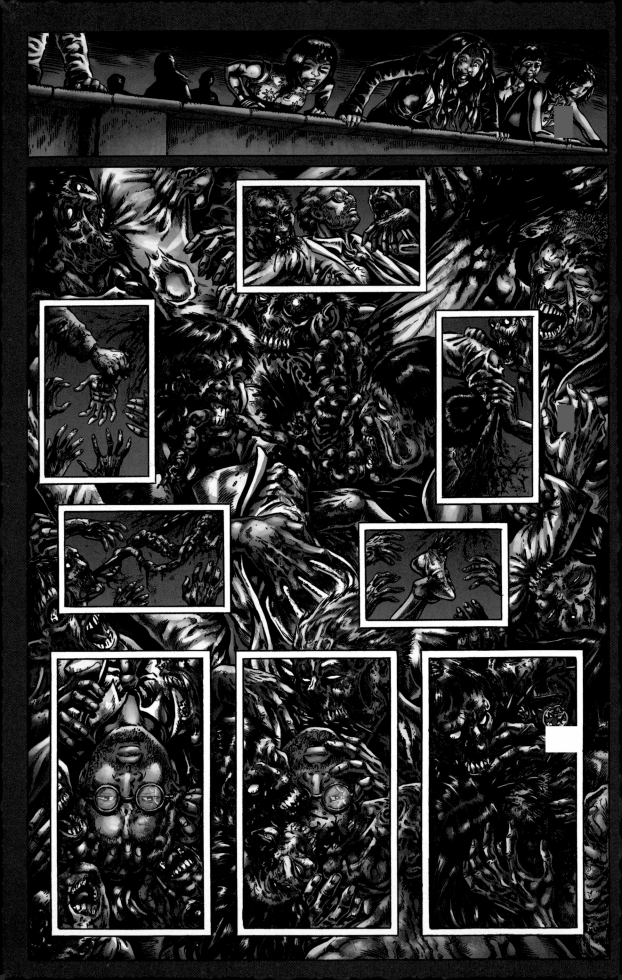

HE'S RIGHT.

ABOUT EVERYTHING ENDING.

I'VE DONE THE MATH.

HIS NAME WAS *NGUYEN* AND AMONG OUR KIND, HE WAS A GENUINE MISFIT.

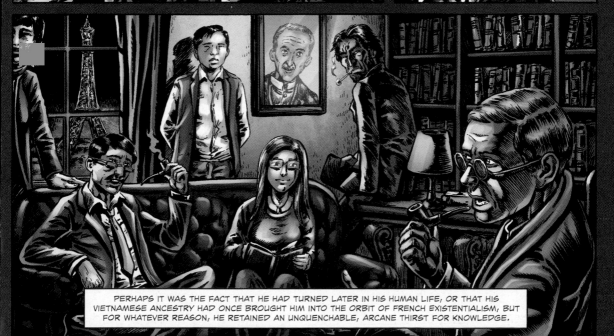

PERHAPS IT WAS THE FACT THAT HE HAD TURNED LATER IN HIS HUMAN LIFE, OR THAT HIS VIETNAMESE ANCESTRY HAD ONCE BROUGHT HIM INTO THE ORBIT OF FRENCH EXISTENTIALISM, BUT FOR WHATEVER REASON, HE RETAINED AN UNQUENCHABLE, ARCANE THIRST FOR KNOWLEDGE.

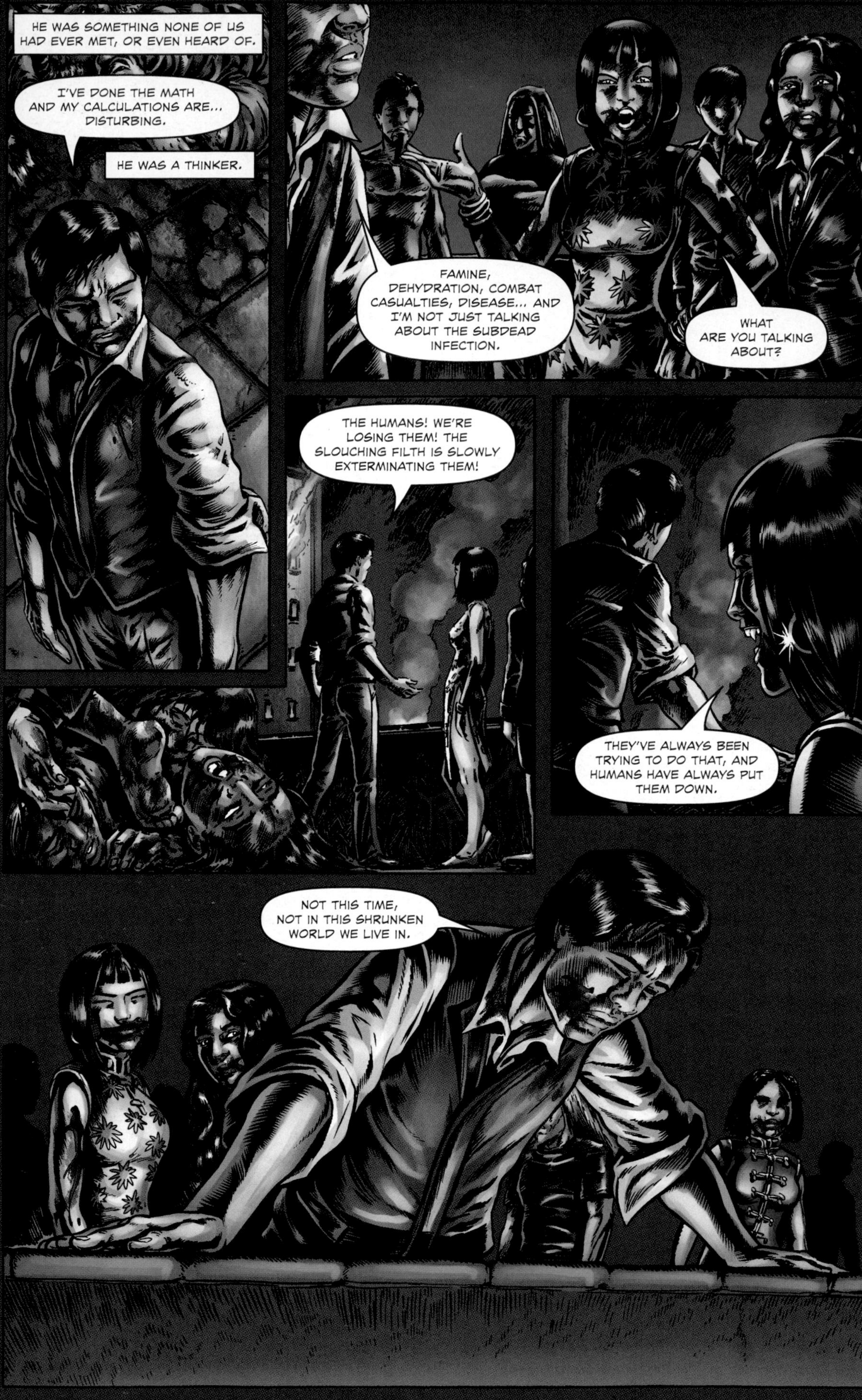
HE WAS SOMETHING NONE OF US HAD EVER MET, OR EVEN HEARD OF.
I'VE DONE THE MATH AND MY CALCULATIONS ARE... DISTURBING.
HE WAS A THINKER.
FAMINE, DEHYDRATION, COMBAT CASUALTIES, DISEASE... AND I'M NOT JUST TALKING ABOUT THE SUBDEAD INFECTION.
WHAT ARE YOU TALKING ABOUT?
THE HUMANS! WE'RE LOSING THEM! THE SLOUCHING FILTH IS SLOWLY EXTERMINATING THEM!
THEY'VE ALWAYS BEEN TRYING TO DO THAT, AND HUMANS HAVE ALWAYS PUT THEM DOWN.
NOT THIS TIME, NOT IN THIS SHRUNKEN WORLD WE LIVE IN.

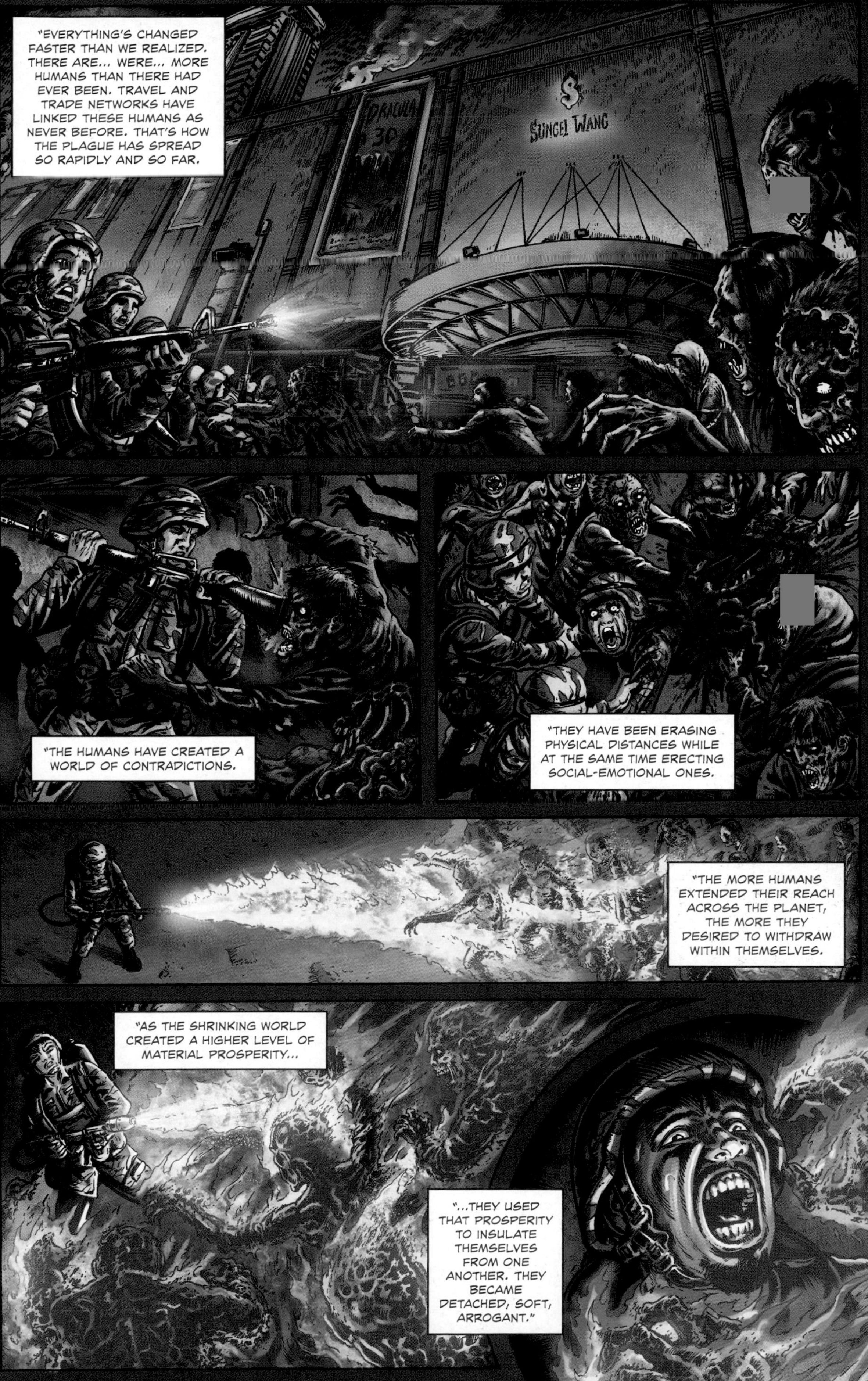
"EVERYTHING'S CHANGED FASTER THAN WE REALIZED. THERE ARE... WERE... MORE HUMANS THAN THERE HAD EVER BEEN. TRAVEL AND TRADE NETWORKS HAVE LINKED THESE HUMANS AS NEVER BEFORE. THAT'S HOW THE PLAGUE HAS SPREAD SO RAPIDLY AND SO FAR.
SUNGEI WANG
"THE HUMANS HAVE CREATED A WORLD OF CONTRADICTIONS.
"THEY HAVE BEEN ERASING PHYSICAL DISTANCES WHILE AT THE SAME TIME ERECTING SOCIAL-EMOTIONAL ONES.
"THE MORE HUMANS EXTENDED THEIR REACH ACROSS THE PLANET, THE MORE THEY DESIRED TO WITHDRAW WITHIN THEMSELVES.
"AS THE SHRINKING WORLD CREATED A HIGHER LEVEL OF MATERIAL PROSPERITY...
"...THEY USED THAT PROSPERITY TO INSULATE THEMSELVES FROM ONE ANOTHER. THEY BECAME DETACHED, SOFT, ARROGANT."

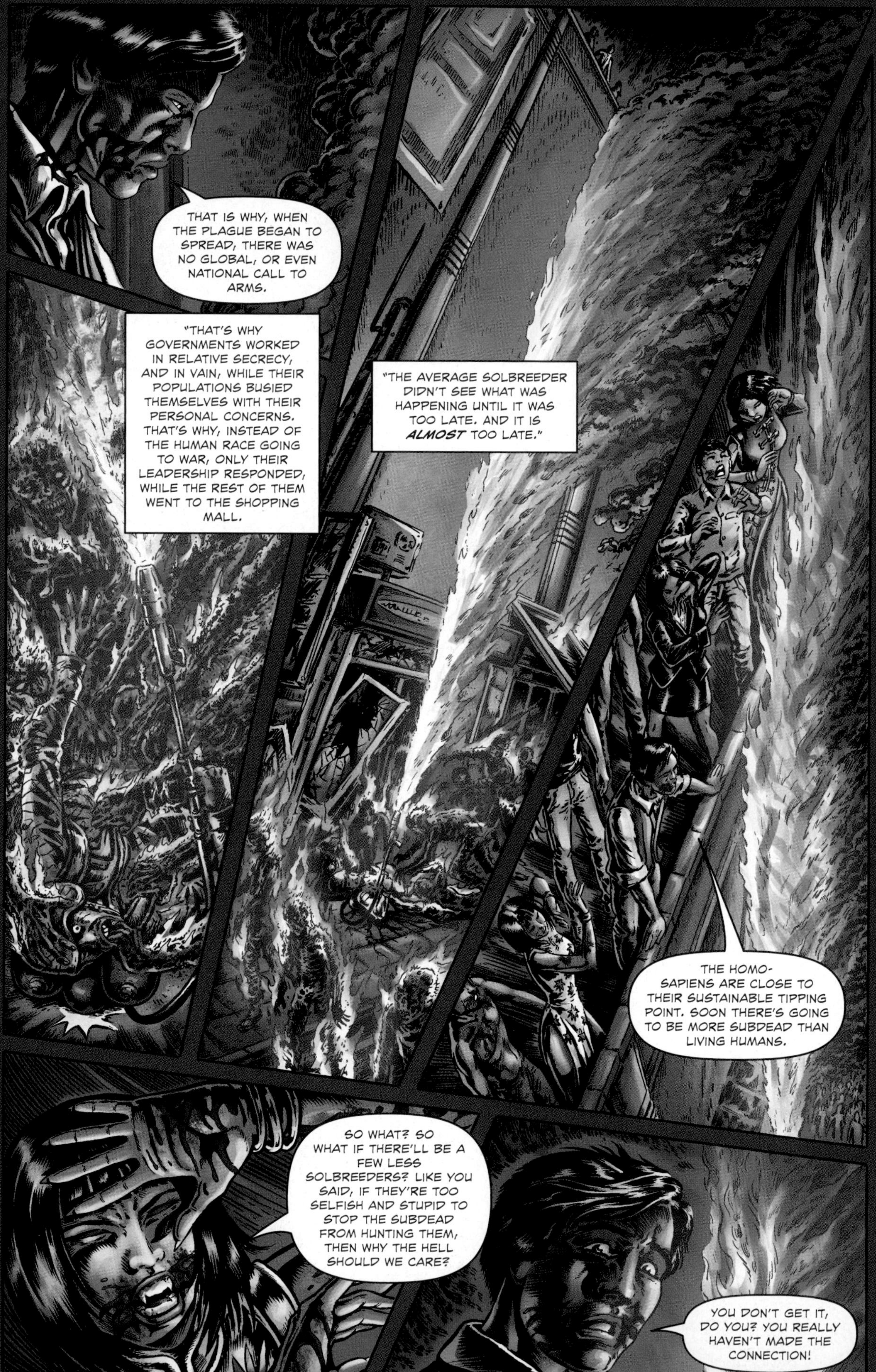
THAT IS WHY, WHEN THE PLAGUE BEGAN TO SPREAD, THERE WAS NO GLOBAL, OR EVEN NATIONAL CALL TO ARMS.
"THAT'S WHY GOVERNMENTS WORKED IN RELATIVE SECRECY, AND IN VAIN, WHILE THEIR POPULATIONS BUSIED THEMSELVES WITH THEIR PERSONAL CONCERNS. THAT'S WHY, INSTEAD OF THE HUMAN RACE GOING TO WAR, ONLY THEIR LEADERSHIP RESPONDED, WHILE THE REST OF THEM WENT TO THE SHOPPING MALL.
"THE AVERAGE SOLBREEDER DIDN'T SEE WHAT WAS HAPPENING UNTIL IT WAS TOO LATE. AND IT IS *ALMOST* TOO LATE."
THE HOMO-SAPIENS ARE CLOSE TO THEIR SUSTAINABLE TIPPING POINT. SOON THERE'S GOING TO BE MORE SUBDEAD THAN LIVING HUMANS.
SO WHAT? SO WHAT IF THERE'LL BE A FEW LESS SOLBREEDERS? LIKE YOU SAID, IF THEY'RE TOO SELFISH AND STUPID TO STOP THE SUBDEAD FROM HUNTING THEM, THEN WHY THE HELL SHOULD WE CARE?
YOU DON'T GET IT, DO YOU? YOU REALLY HAVEN'T MADE THE CONNECTION!

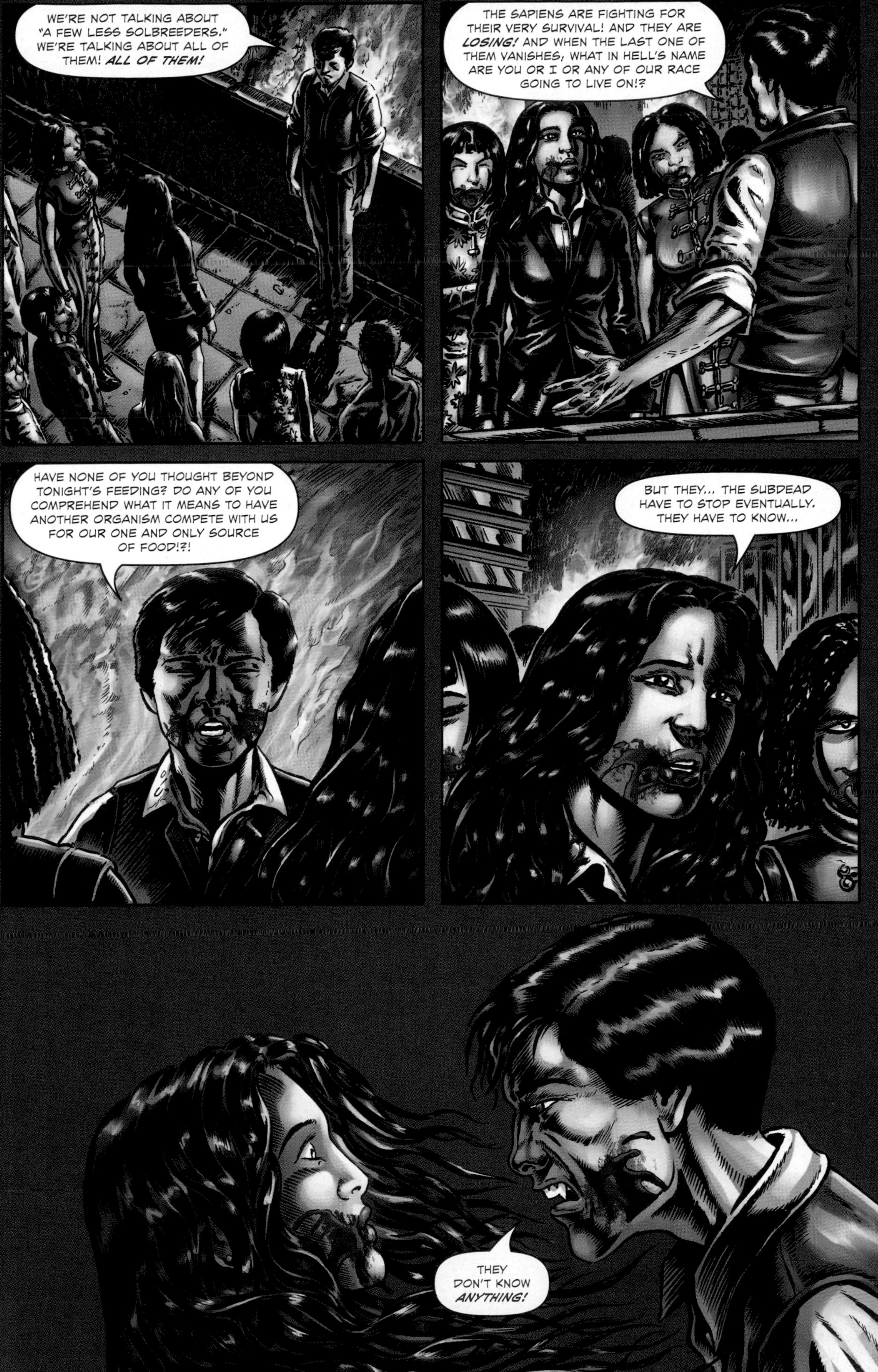
WE'RE NOT TALKING ABOUT "A FEW LESS SOLBREEDERS." WE'RE TALKING ABOUT ALL OF THEM! *ALL OF THEM!*
THE SAPIENS ARE FIGHTING FOR THEIR VERY SURVIVAL! AND THEY ARE *LOSING!* AND WHEN THE LAST ONE OF THEM VANISHES, WHAT IN HELL'S NAME ARE YOU OR I OR ANY OF OUR RACE GOING TO LIVE ON!?
HAVE NONE OF YOU THOUGHT BEYOND TONIGHT'S FEEDING? DO ANY OF YOU COMPREHEND WHAT IT MEANS TO HAVE ANOTHER ORGANISM COMPETE WITH US FOR OUR ONE AND ONLY SOURCE OF FOOD!?!
BUT THEY... THE SUBDEAD HAVE TO STOP EVENTUALLY. THEY HAVE TO KNOW...
THEY DON'T KNOW *ANYTHING!*

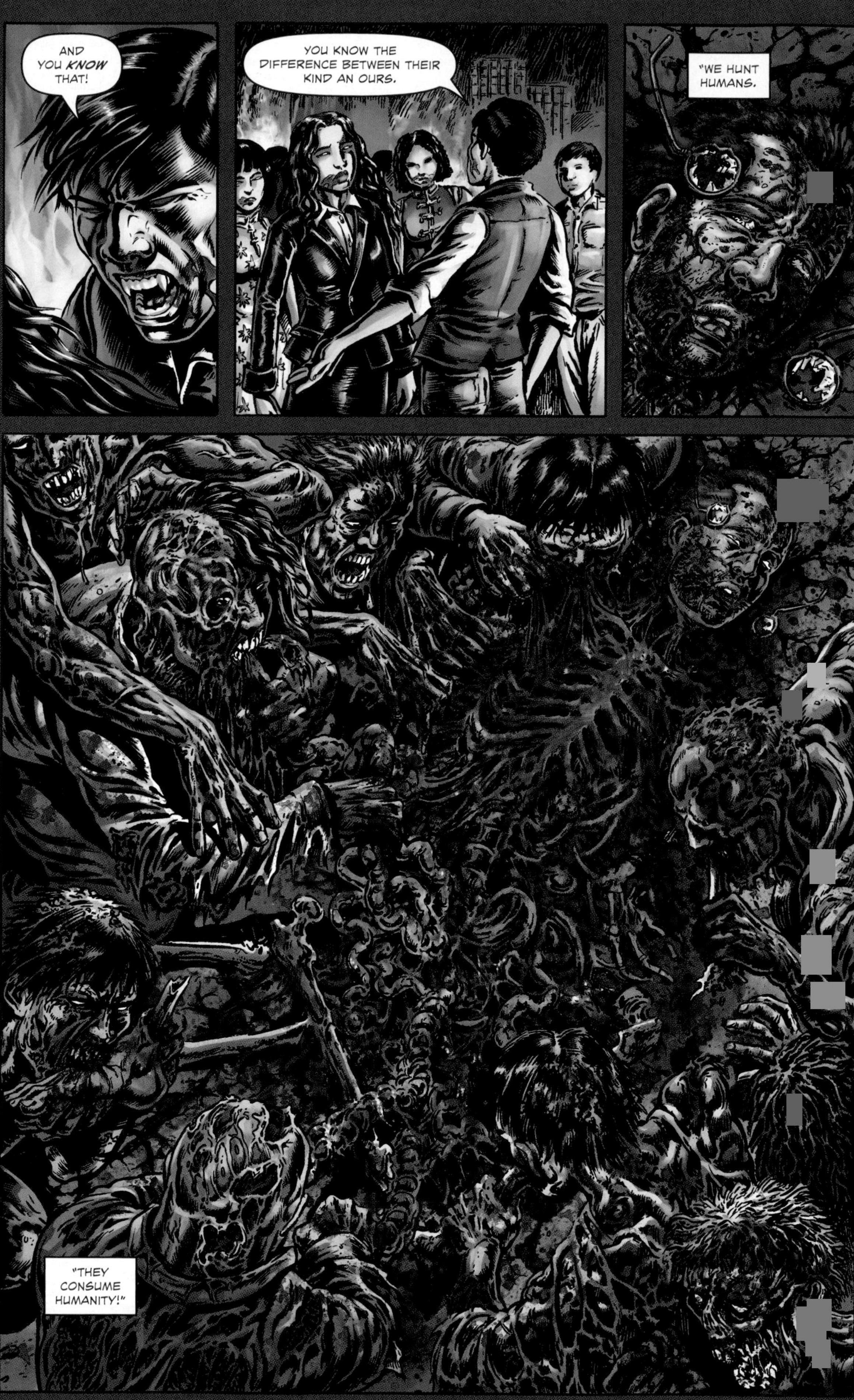
AND YOU *KNOW* THAT!
YOU KNOW THE DIFFERENCE BETWEEN THEIR KIND AN OURS.
"WE HUNT HUMANS.
"THEY CONSUME HUMANITY!"

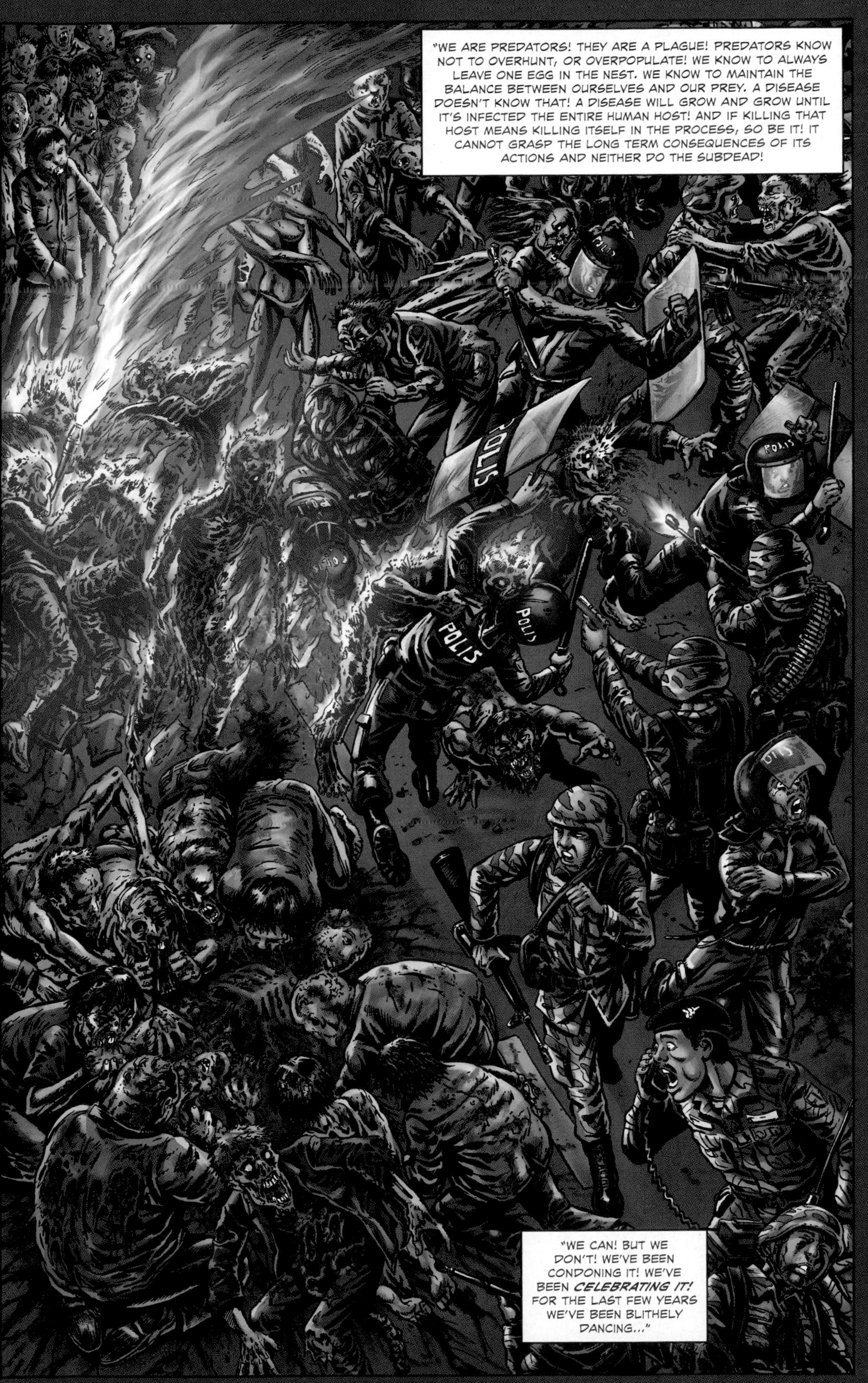
"WE ARE PREDATORS! THEY ARE A PLAGUE! PREDATORS KNOW NOT TO OVERHUNT, OR OVERPOPULATE! WE KNOW TO ALWAYS LEAVE ONE EGG IN THE NEST. WE KNOW TO MAINTAIN THE BALANCE BETWEEN OURSELVES AND OUR PREY. A DISEASE DOESN'T KNOW THAT! A DISEASE WILL GROW AND GROW UNTIL IT'S INFECTED THE ENTIRE HUMAN HOST! AND IF KILLING THAT HOST MEANS KILLING ITSELF IN THE PROCESS, SO BE IT! IT CANNOT GRASP THE LONG TERM CONSEQUENCES OF ITS ACTIONS AND NEITHER DO THE SUBDEAD!
POLIS
POLIS
POLIS
POLIS
POLIS
"WE CAN! BUT WE DON'T! WE'VE BEEN CONDONING IT! WE'VE BEEN *CELEBRATING IT!* FOR THE LAST FEW YEARS WE'VE BEEN BLITHELY DANCING..."

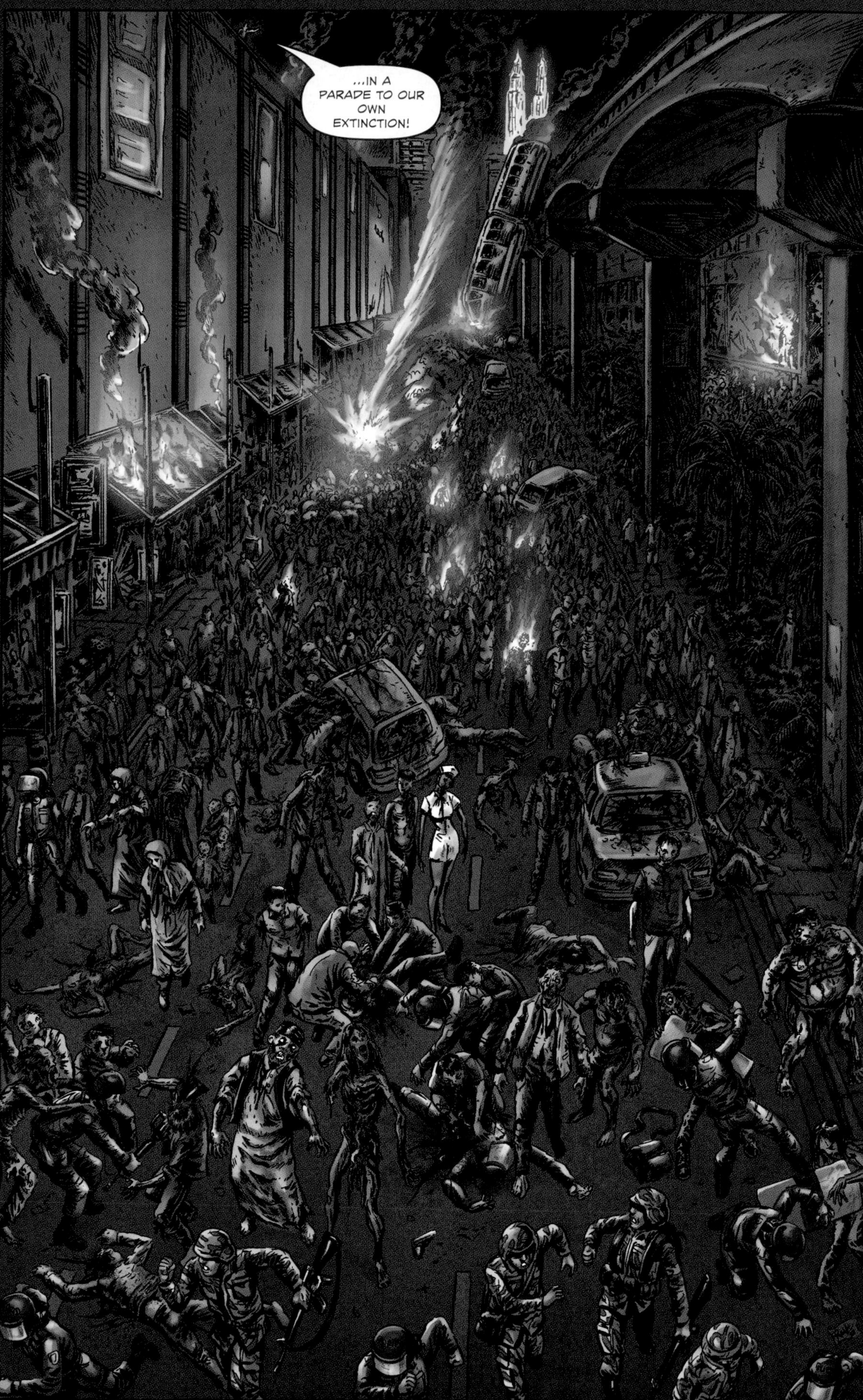
...IN A PARADE TO OUR OWN EXTINCTION!

Chapter 5

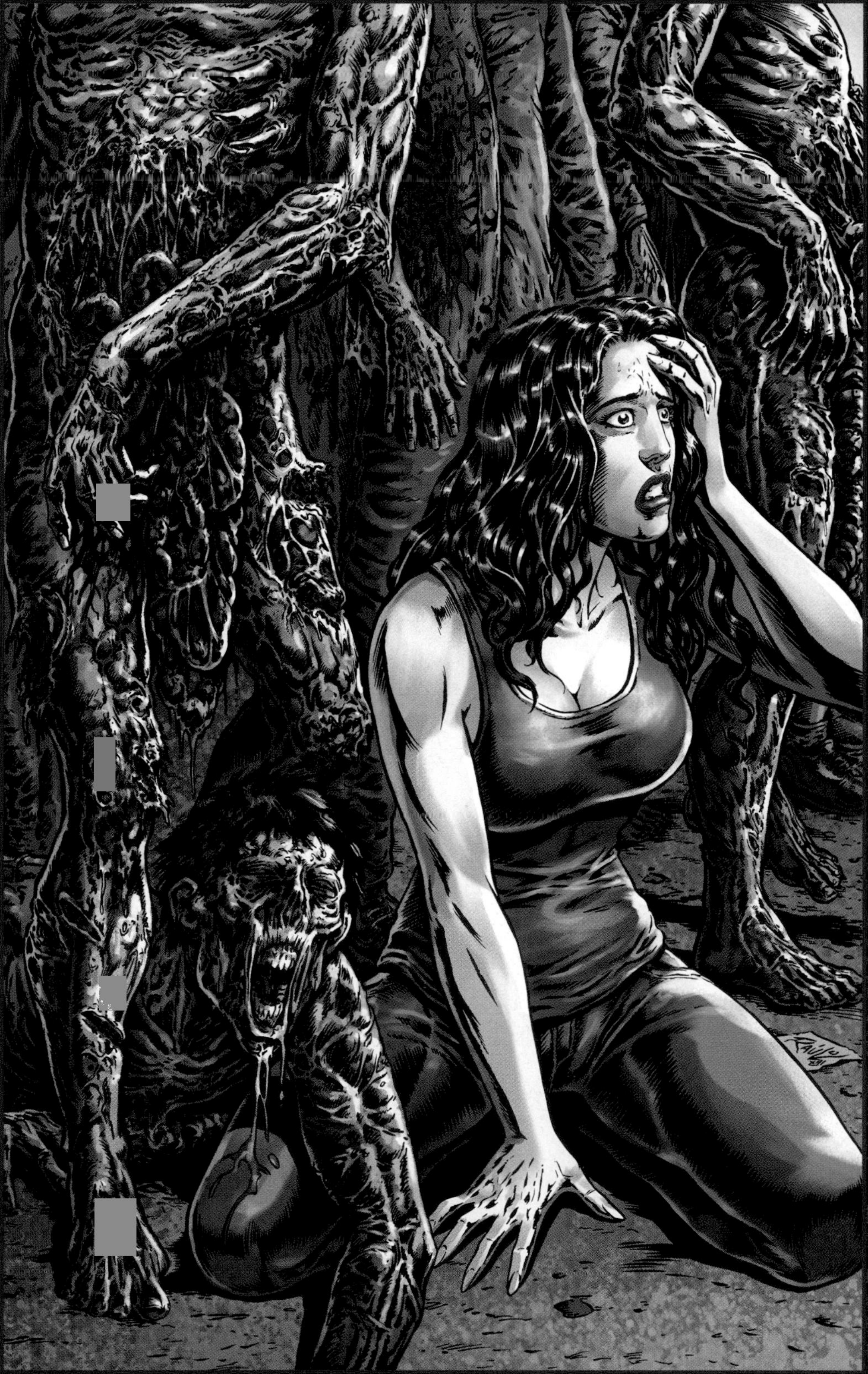

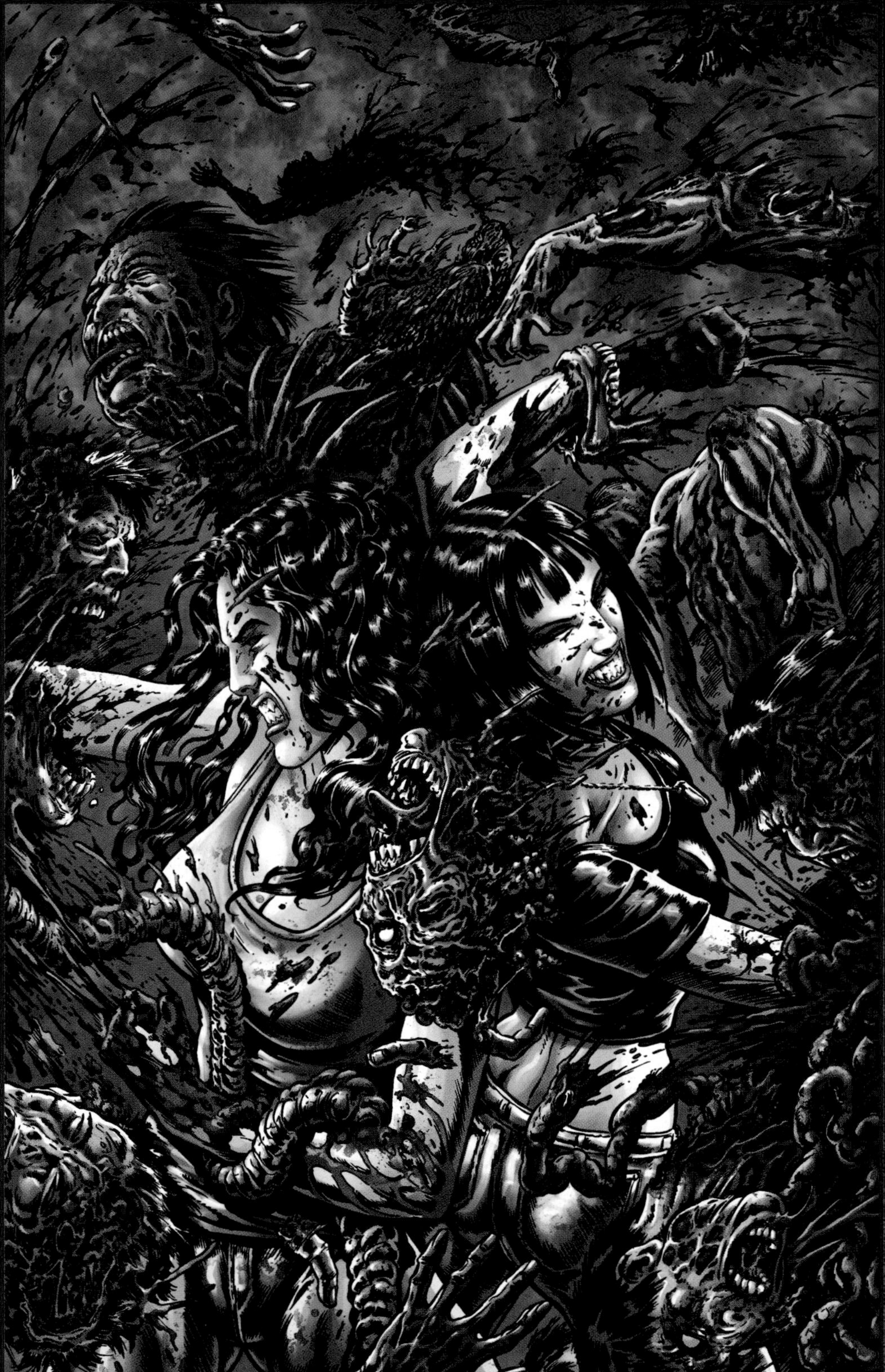

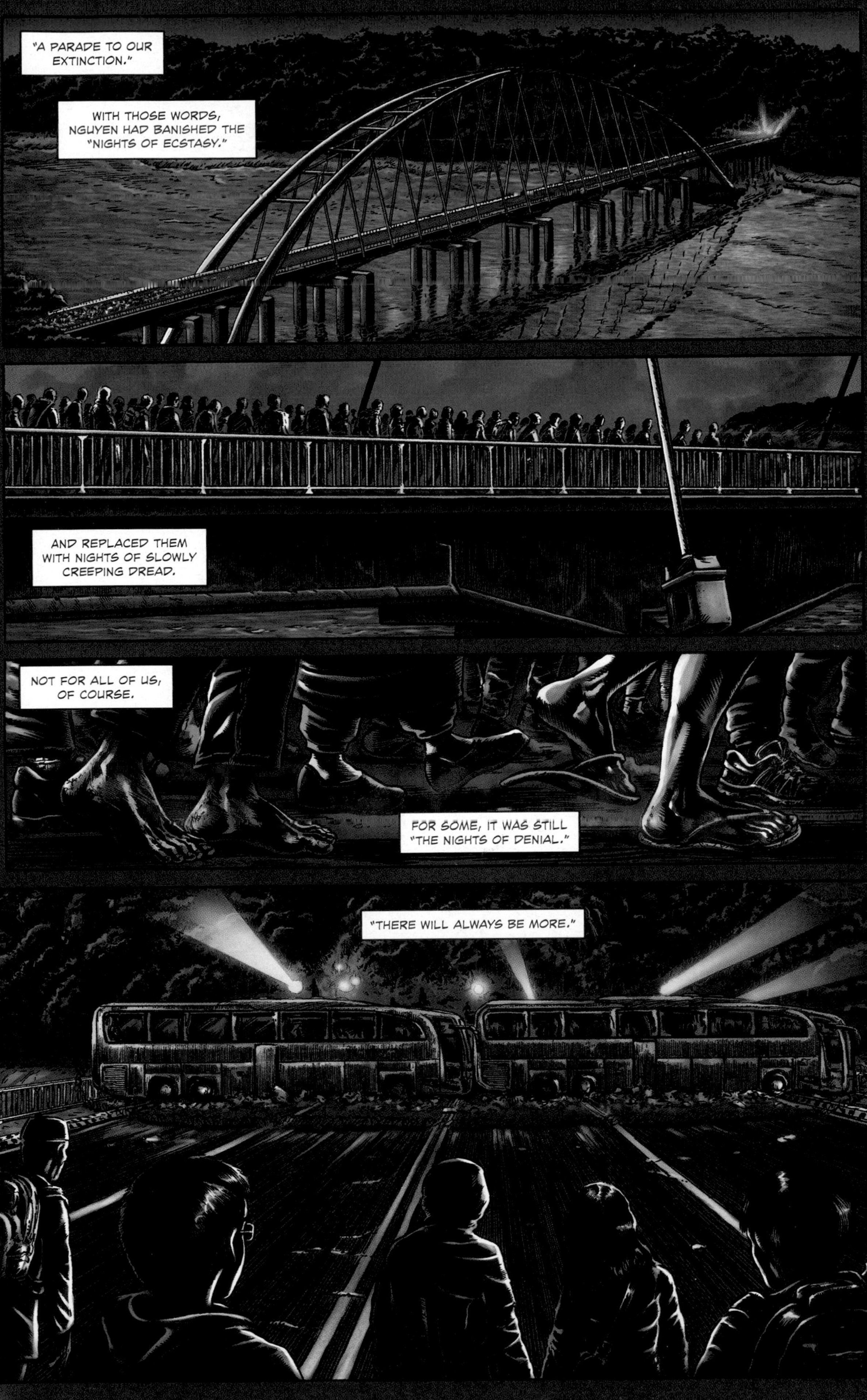
"A PARADE TO OUR EXTINCTION."
WITH THOSE WORDS, NGUYEN HAD BANISHED THE "NIGHTS OF ECSTASY."
AND REPLACED THEM WITH NIGHTS OF SLOWLY CREEPING DREAD.
NOT FOR ALL OF US, OF COURSE.
FOR SOME, IT WAS STILL "THE NIGHTS OF DENIAL."
"THERE WILL ALWAYS BE MORE."

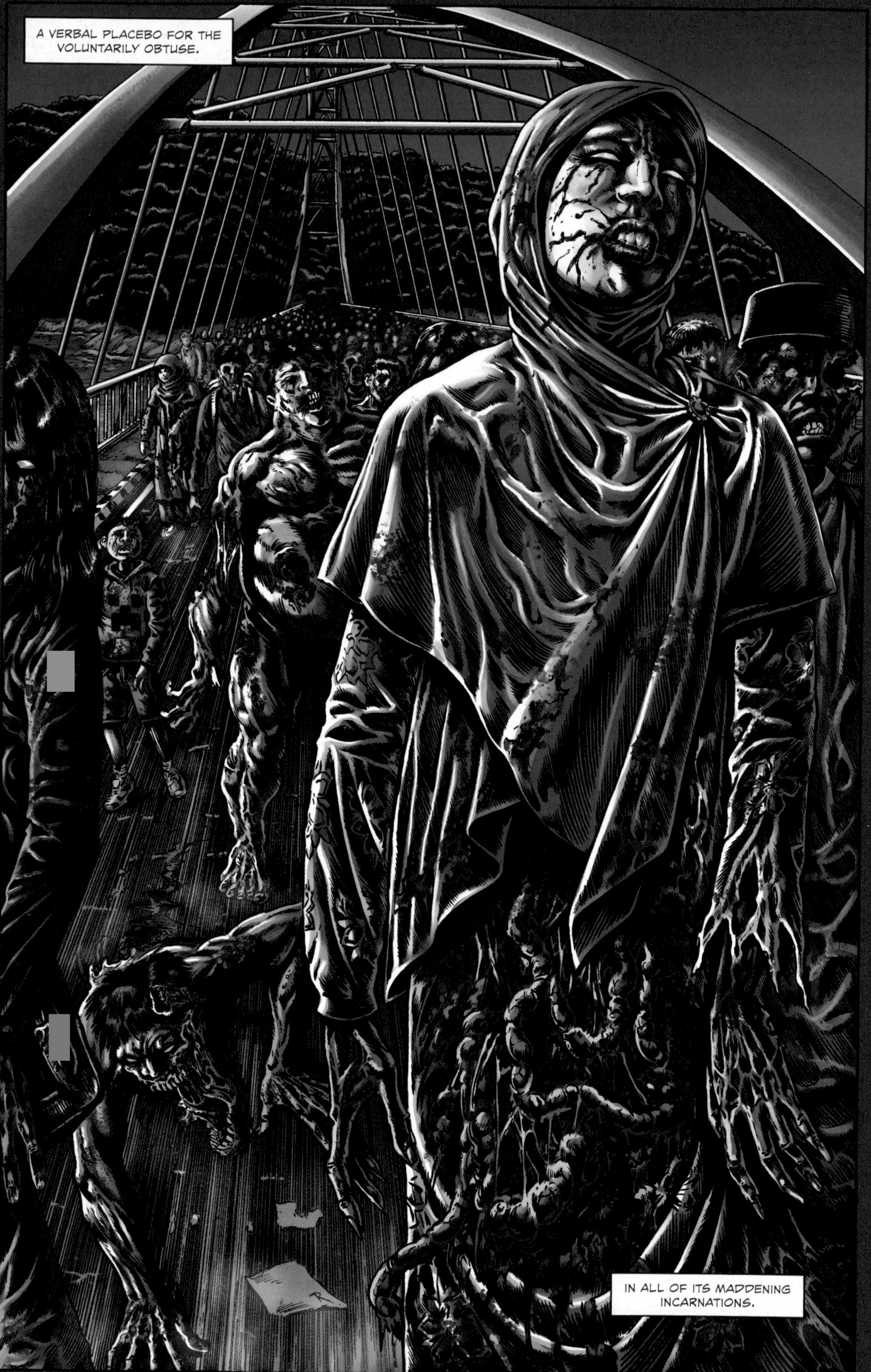
A VERBAL PLACEBO FOR THE VOLUNTARILY OBTUSE.
IN ALL OF ITS MADDENING INCARNATIONS.

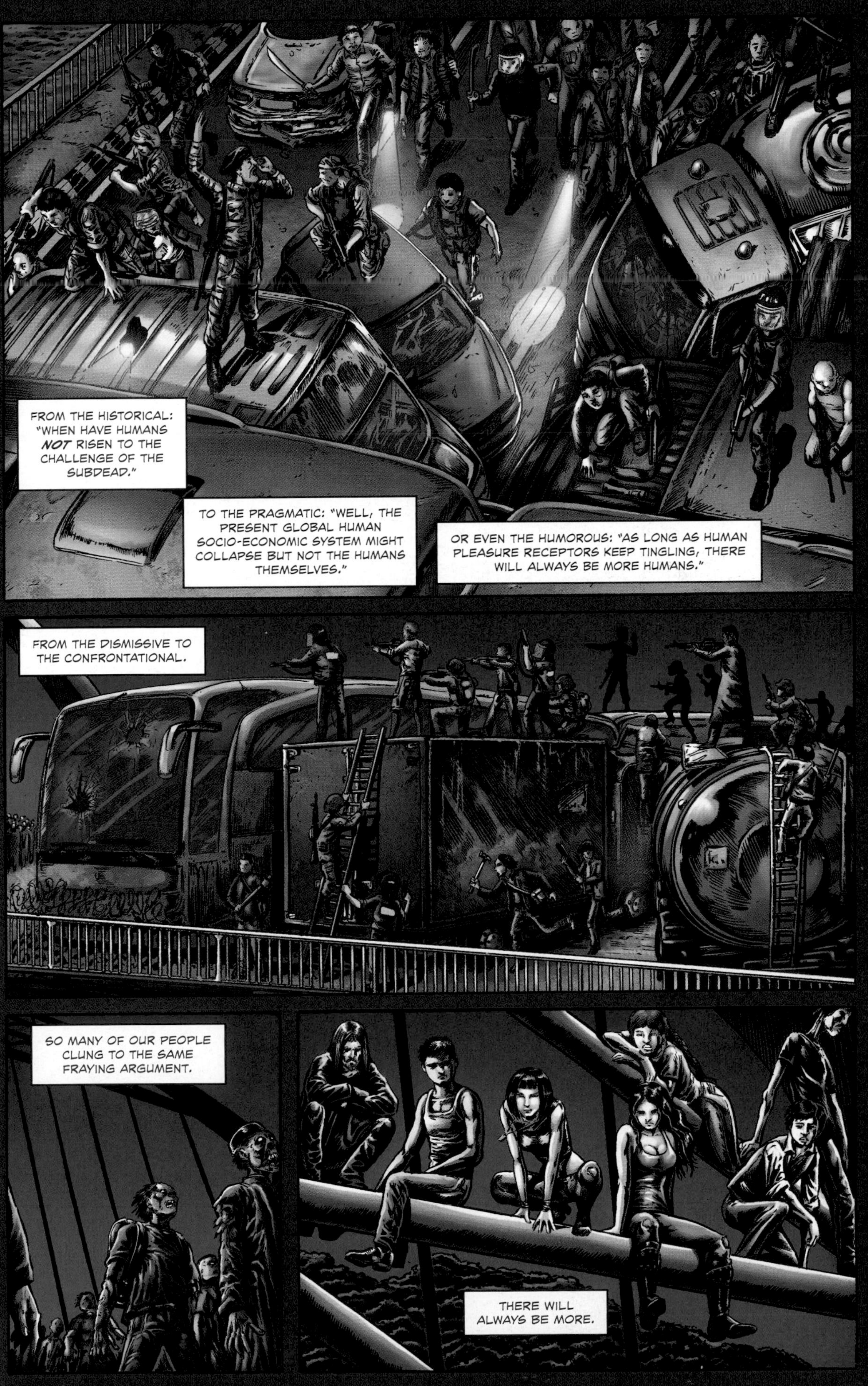
FROM THE HISTORICAL: "WHEN HAVE HUMANS *NOT* RISEN TO THE CHALLENGE OF THE SUBDEAD."
TO THE PRAGMATIC: "WELL, THE PRESENT GLOBAL HUMAN SOCIO-ECONOMIC SYSTEM MIGHT COLLAPSE BUT NOT THE HUMANS THEMSELVES."
OR EVEN THE HUMOROUS: "AS LONG AS HUMAN PLEASURE RECEPTORS KEEP TINGLING, THERE WILL ALWAYS BE MORE HUMANS."
FROM THE DISMISSIVE TO THE CONFRONTATIONAL.
SO MANY OF OUR PEOPLE CLUNG TO THE SAME FRAYING ARGUMENT.
THERE WILL ALWAYS BE MORE.

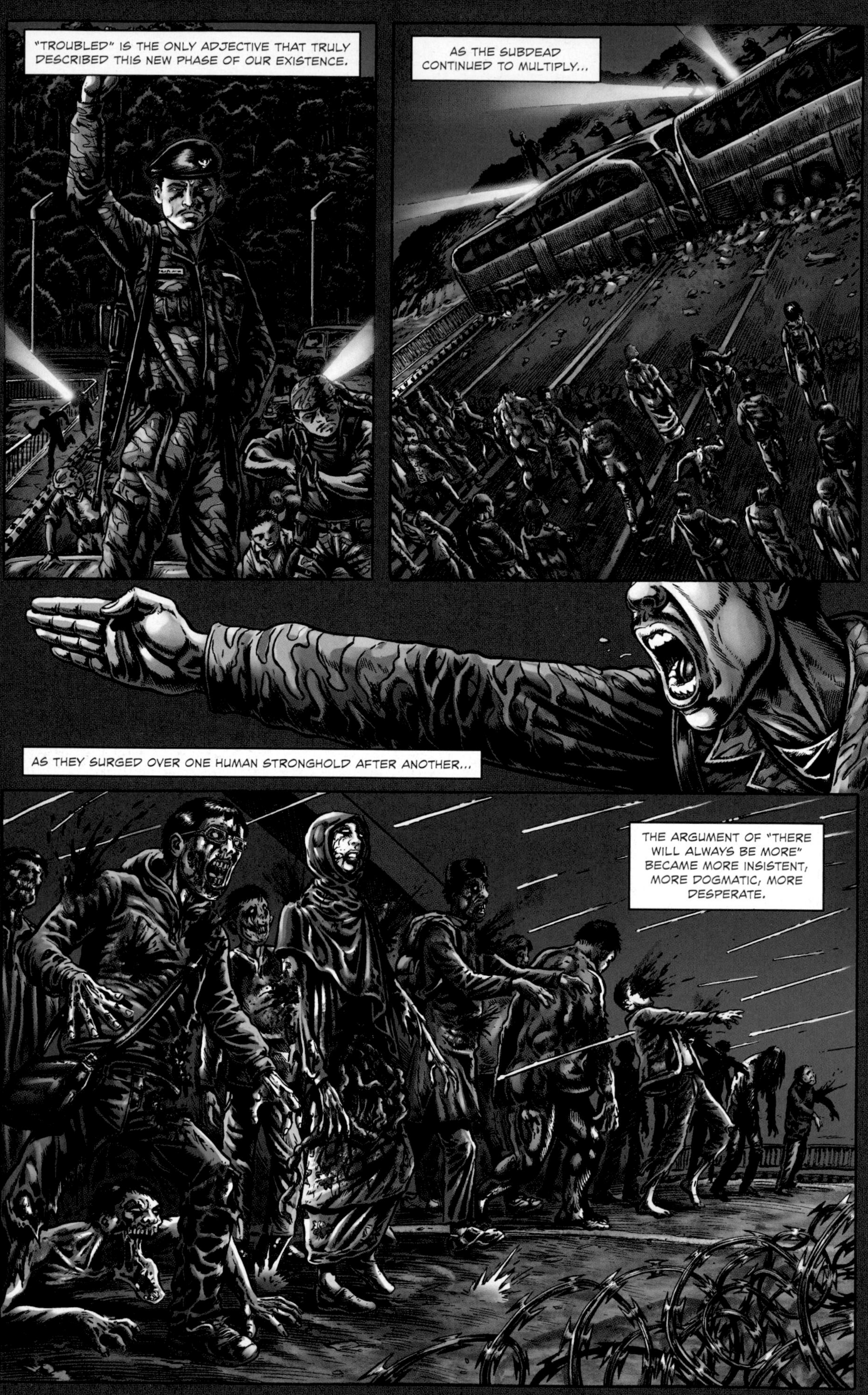
"TROUBLED" IS THE ONLY ADJECTIVE THAT TRULY DESCRIBED THIS NEW PHASE OF OUR EXISTENCE.
AS THE SUBDEAD CONTINUED TO MULTIPLY...
AS THEY SURGED OVER ONE HUMAN STRONGHOLD AFTER ANOTHER...
THE ARGUMENT OF "THERE WILL ALWAYS BE MORE" BECAME MORE INSISTENT, MORE DOGMATIC, MORE DESPERATE.

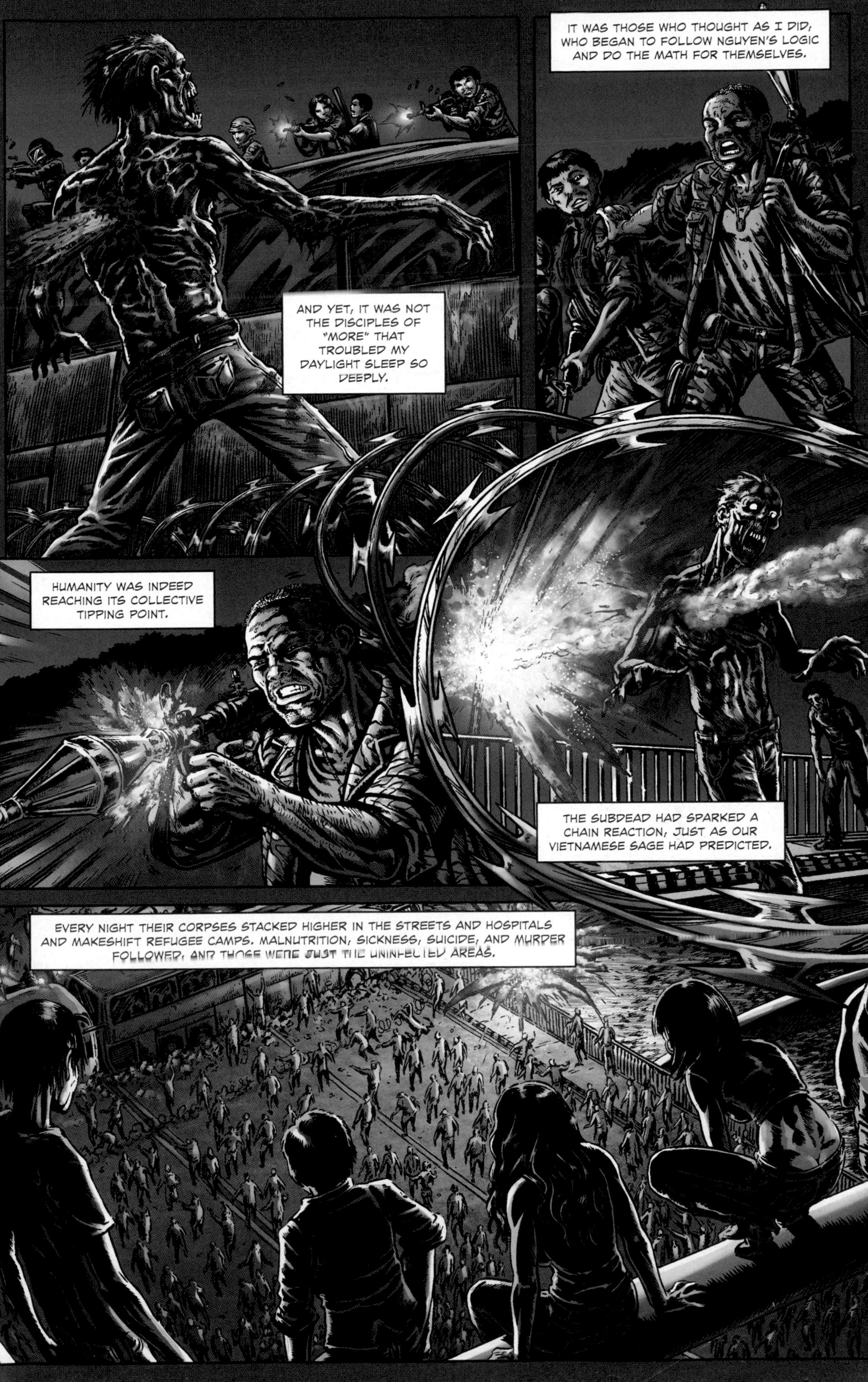
AND YET, IT WAS NOT THE DISCIPLES OF "MORE" THAT TROUBLED MY DAYLIGHT SLEEP SO DEEPLY.
IT WAS THOSE WHO THOUGHT AS I DID, WHO BEGAN TO FOLLOW NGUYEN'S LOGIC AND DO THE MATH FOR THEMSELVES.
HUMANITY WAS INDEED REACHING ITS COLLECTIVE TIPPING POINT.
THE SUBDEAD HAD SPARKED A CHAIN REACTION, JUST AS OUR VIETNAMESE SAGE HAD PREDICTED.
EVERY NIGHT THEIR CORPSES STACKED HIGHER IN THE STREETS AND HOSPITALS AND MAKESHIFT REFUGEE CAMPS. MALNUTRITION, SICKNESS, SUICIDE, AND MURDER FOLLOWED, AND THOSE WERE JUST THE UNINFECTED AREAS.

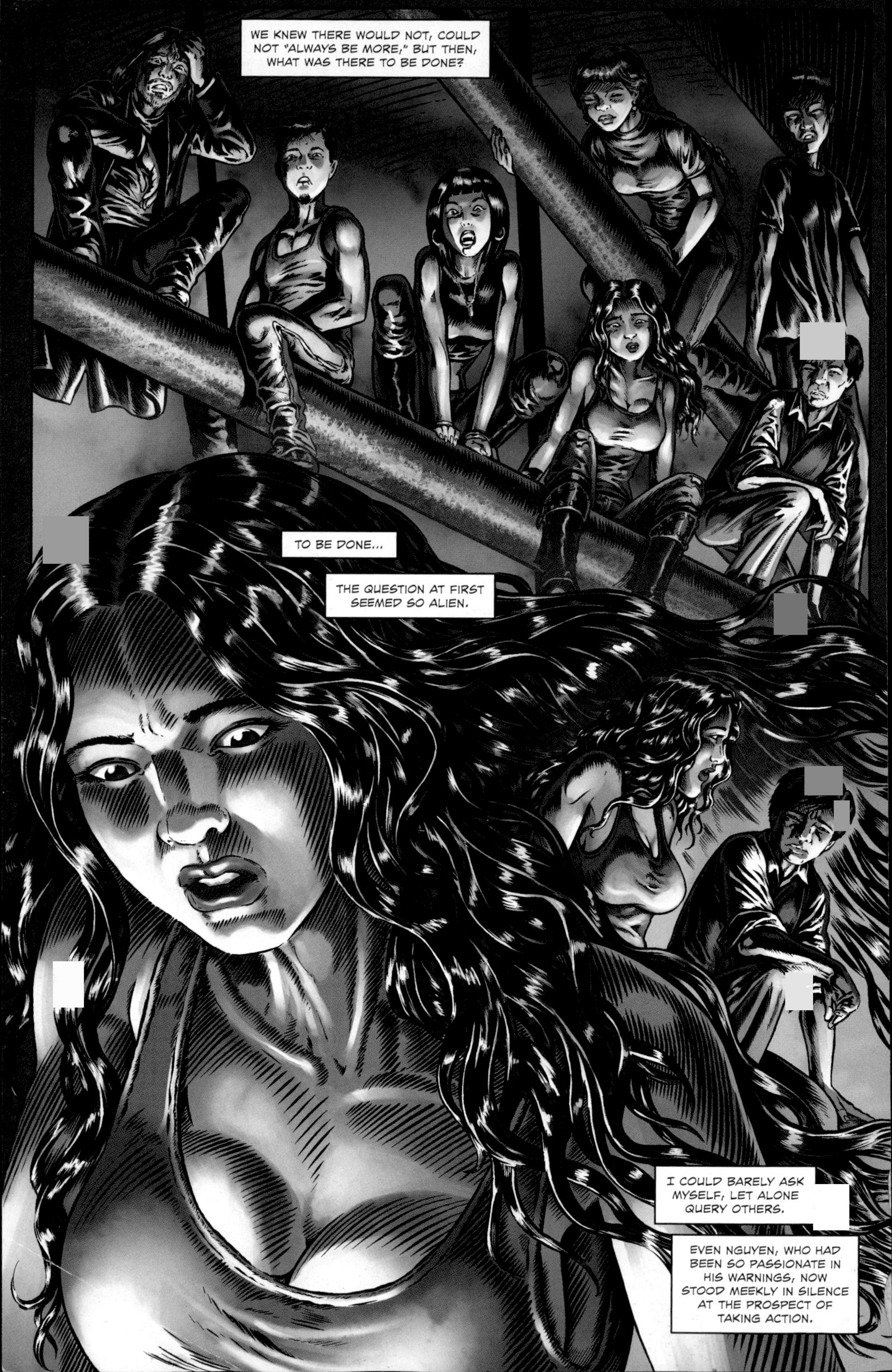
WE KNEW THERE WOULD NOT, COULD NOT "ALWAYS BE MORE," BUT THEN, WHAT WAS THERE TO BE DONE?
TO BE DONE...
THE QUESTION AT FIRST SEEMED SO ALIEN.
I COULD BARELY ASK MYSELF, LET ALONE QUERY OTHERS.
EVEN NGUYEN, WHO HAD BEEN SO PASSIONATE IN HIS WARNINGS, NOW STOOD MEEKLY IN SILENCE AT THE PROSPECT OF TAKING ACTION.

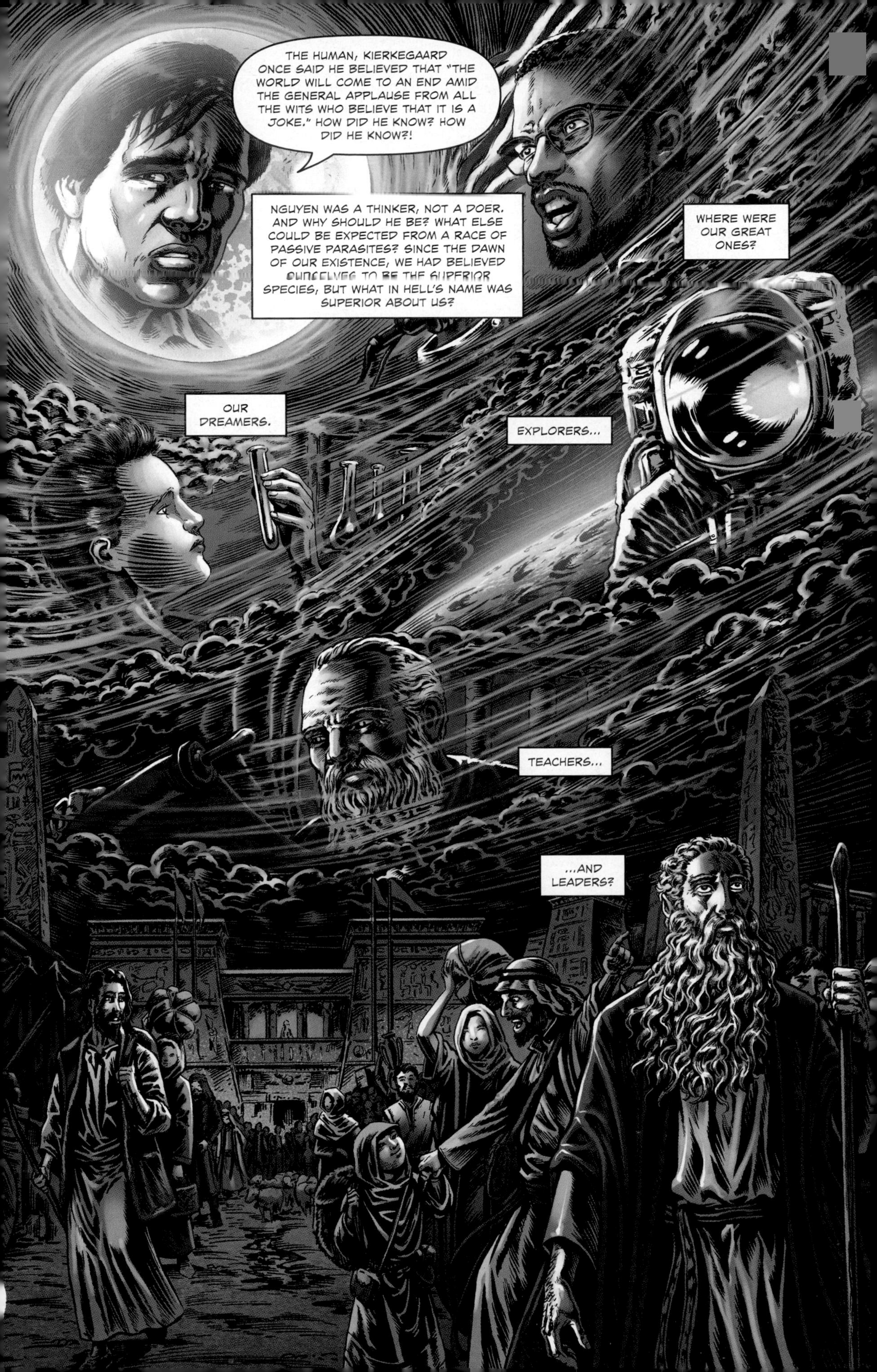
THE HUMAN, KIERKEGAARD ONCE SAID HE BELIEVED THAT "THE WORLD WILL COME TO AN END AMID THE GENERAL APPLAUSE FROM ALL THE WITS WHO BELIEVE THAT IT IS A JOKE." HOW DID HE KNOW? HOW DID HE KNOW?!
NGUYEN WAS A THINKER, NOT A DOER. AND WHY SHOULD HE BE? WHAT ELSE COULD BE EXPECTED FROM A RACE OF PASSIVE PARASITES? SINCE THE DAWN OF OUR EXISTENCE, WE HAD BELIEVED OURSELVES TO BE THE SUPERIOR SPECIES, BUT WHAT IN HELL'S NAME WAS SUPERIOR ABOUT US?
WHERE WERE OUR GREAT ONES?
OUR DREAMERS.
EXPLORERS...
TEACHERS...
...AND LEADERS?

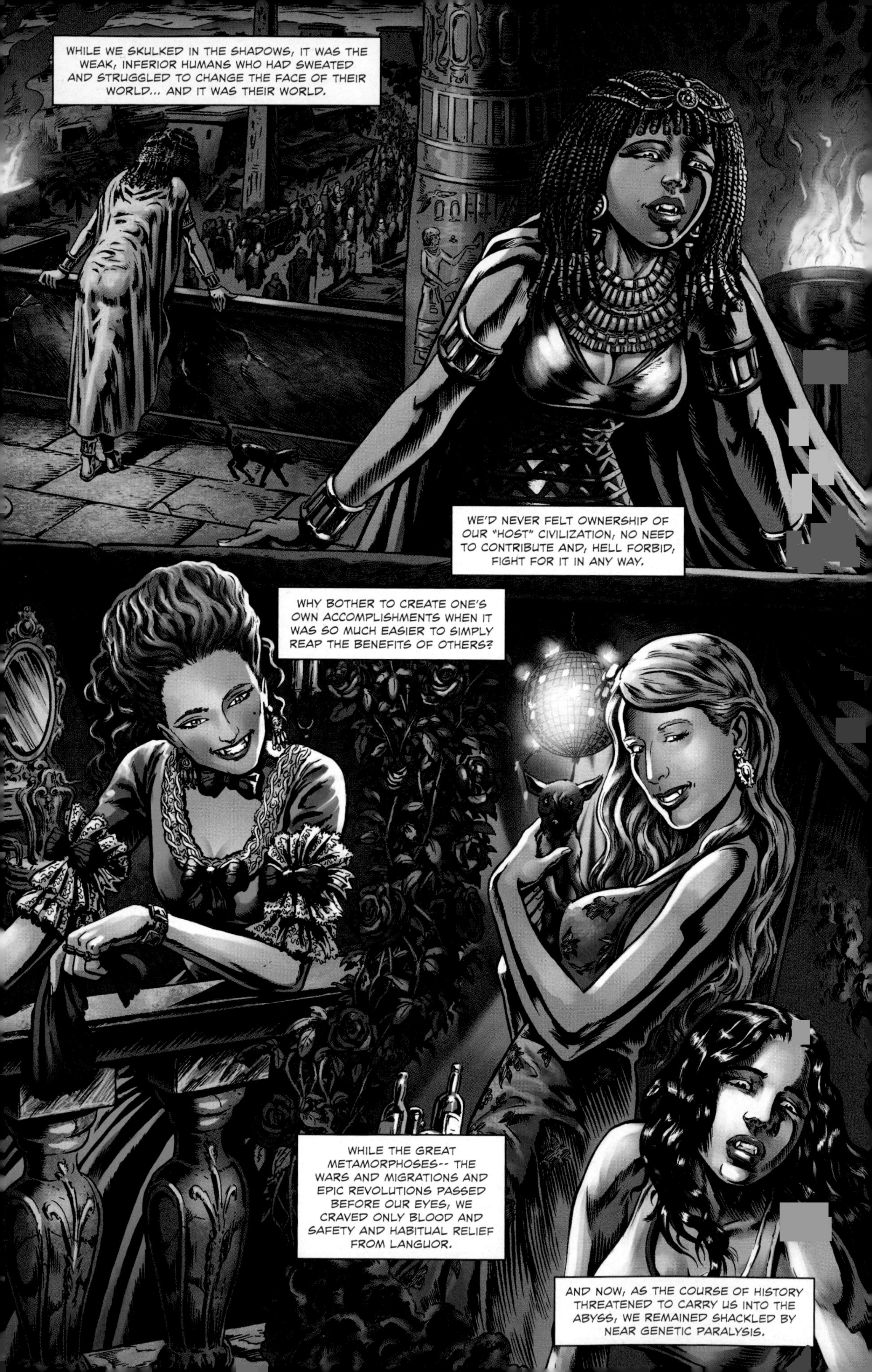
WHILE WE SKULKED IN THE SHADOWS, IT WAS THE WEAK, INFERIOR HUMANS WHO HAD SWEATED AND STRUGGLED TO CHANGE THE FACE OF THEIR WORLD... AND IT WAS THEIR WORLD.
WE'D NEVER FELT OWNERSHIP OF OUR "HOST" CIVILIZATION, NO NEED TO CONTRIBUTE AND, HELL FORBID, FIGHT FOR IT IN ANY WAY.
WHY BOTHER TO CREATE ONE'S OWN ACCOMPLISHMENTS WHEN IT WAS SO MUCH EASIER TO SIMPLY REAP THE BENEFITS OF OTHERS?
WHILE THE GREAT METAMORPHOSES-- THE WARS AND MIGRATIONS AND EPIC REVOLUTIONS PASSED BEFORE OUR EYES, WE CRAVED ONLY BLOOD AND SAFETY AND HABITUAL RELIEF FROM LANGUOR.
AND NOW, AS THE COURSE OF HISTORY THREATENED TO CARRY US INTO THE ABYSS, WE REMAINED SHACKLED BY NEAR GENETIC PARALYSIS.

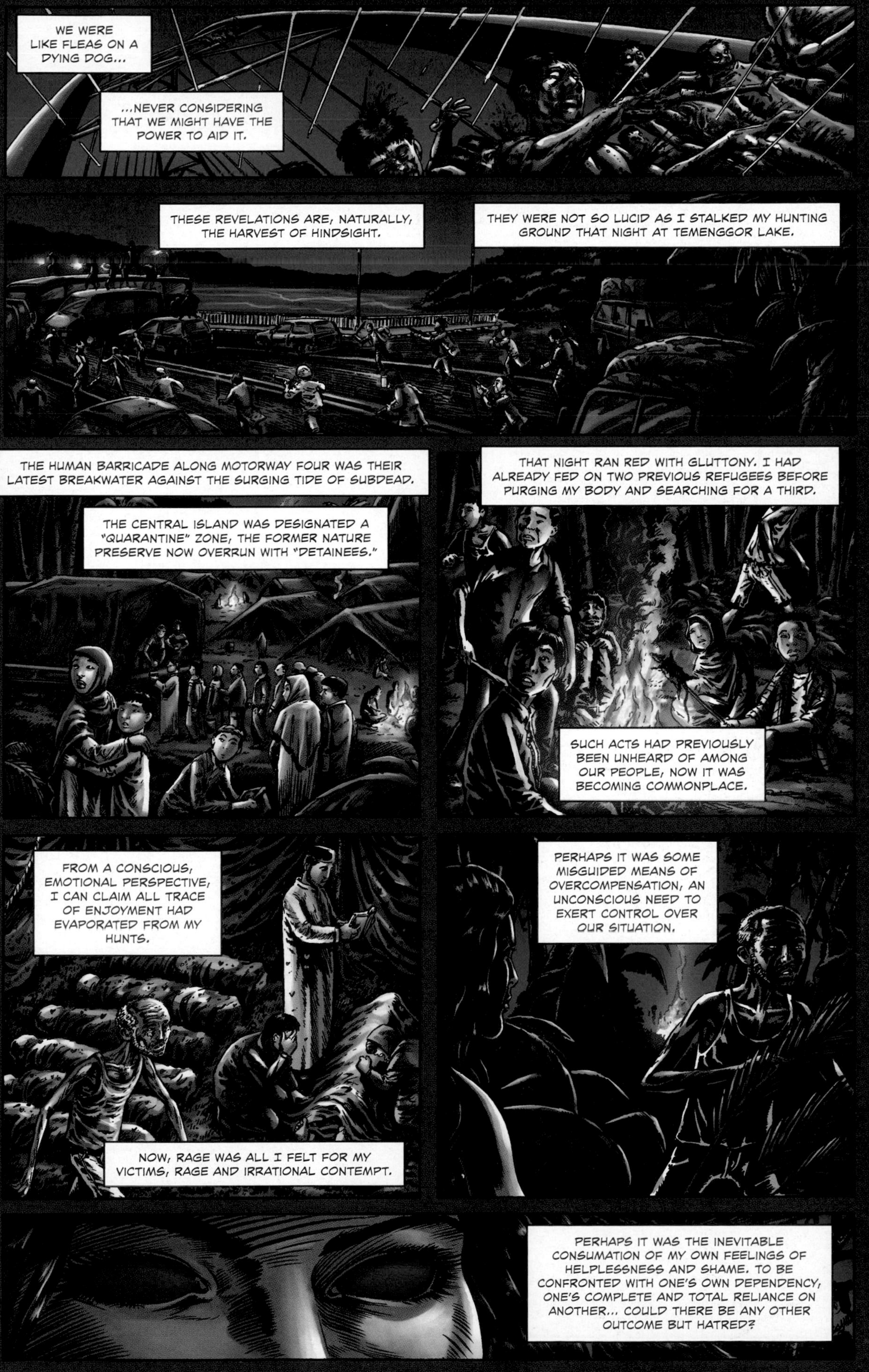
WE WERE LIKE FLEAS ON A DYING DOG...
...NEVER CONSIDERING THAT WE MIGHT HAVE THE POWER TO AID IT.
THESE REVELATIONS ARE, NATURALLY, THE HARVEST OF HINDSIGHT.
THEY WERE NOT SO LUCID AS I STALKED MY HUNTING GROUND THAT NIGHT AT TEMENGGOR LAKE.
THE HUMAN BARRICADE ALONG MOTORWAY FOUR WAS THEIR LATEST BREAKWATER AGAINST THE SURGING TIDE OF SUBDEAD.
THE CENTRAL ISLAND WAS DESIGNATED A "QUARANTINE" ZONE, THE FORMER NATURE PRESERVE NOW OVERRUN WITH "DETAINEES."
THAT NIGHT RAN RED WITH GLUTTONY. I HAD ALREADY FED ON TWO PREVIOUS REFUGEES BEFORE PURGING MY BODY AND SEARCHING FOR A THIRD.
SUCH ACTS HAD PREVIOUSLY BEEN UNHEARD OF AMONG OUR PEOPLE, NOW IT WAS BECOMING COMMONPLACE.
FROM A CONSCIOUS, EMOTIONAL PERSPECTIVE, I CAN CLAIM ALL TRACE OF ENJOYMENT HAD EVAPORATED FROM MY HUNTS.
NOW, RAGE WAS ALL I FELT FOR MY VICTIMS, RAGE AND IRRATIONAL CONTEMPT.
PERHAPS IT WAS SOME MISGUIDED MEANS OF OVERCOMPENSATION, AN UNCONSCIOUS NEED TO EXERT CONTROL OVER OUR SITUATION.
PERHAPS IT WAS THE INEVITABLE CONSUMATION OF MY OWN FEELINGS OF HELPLESSNESS AND SHAME. TO BE CONFRONTED WITH ONE'S OWN DEPENDENCY, ONE'S COMPLETE AND TOTAL RELIANCE ON ANOTHER... COULD THERE BE ANY OTHER OUTCOME BUT HATRED?

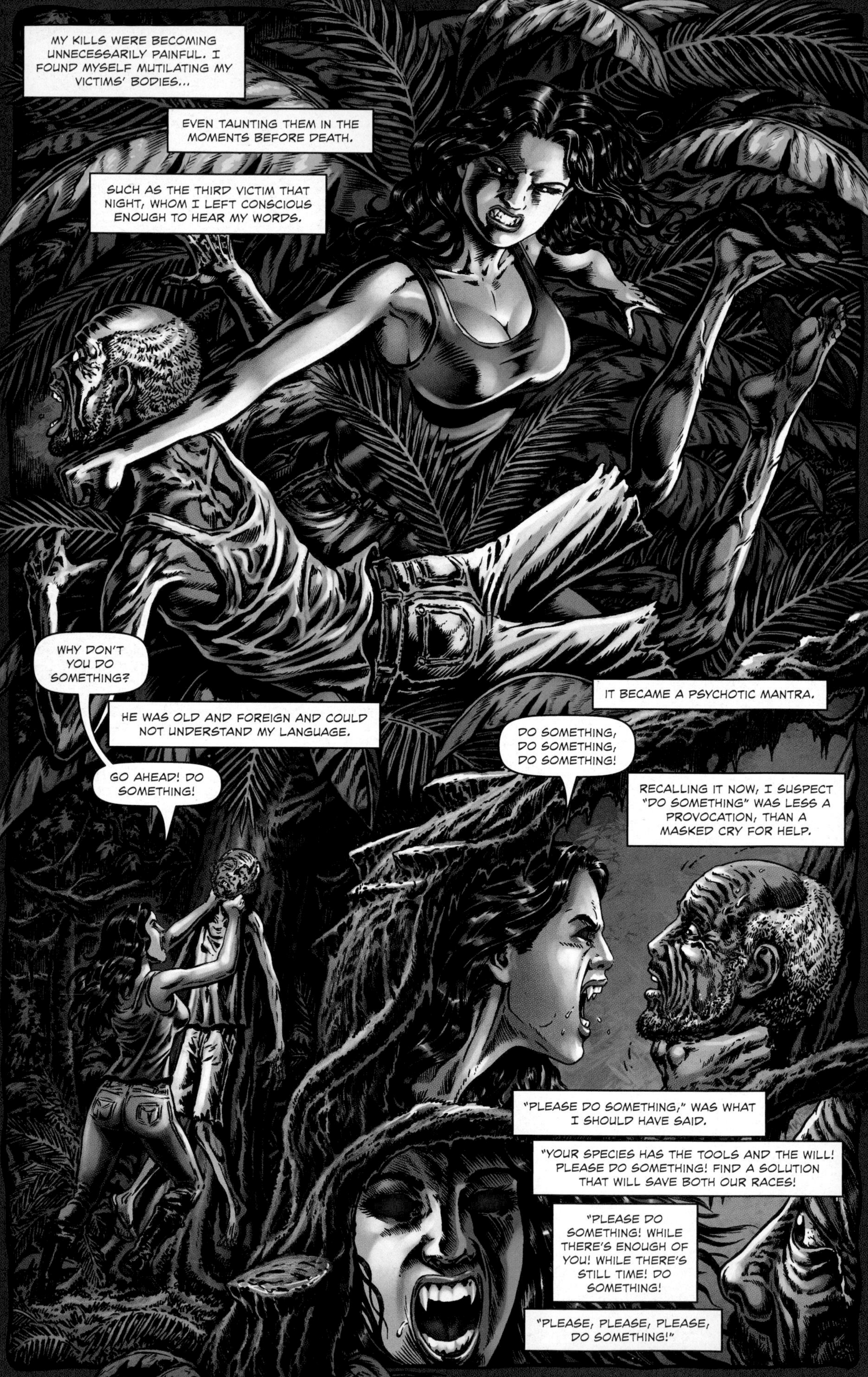
MY KILLS WERE BECOMING UNNECESSARILY PAINFUL. I FOUND MYSELF MUTILATING MY VICTIMS' BODIES...
EVEN TAUNTING THEM IN THE MOMENTS BEFORE DEATH.
SUCH AS THE THIRD VICTIM THAT NIGHT, WHOM I LEFT CONSCIOUS ENOUGH TO HEAR MY WORDS.
WHY DON'T YOU DO SOMETHING?
HE WAS OLD AND FOREIGN AND COULD NOT UNDERSTAND MY LANGUAGE.
GO AHEAD! DO SOMETHING!
IT BECAME A PSYCHOTIC MANTRA.
DO SOMETHING, DO SOMETHING, DO SOMETHING!
RECALLING IT NOW, I SUSPECT "DO SOMETHING" WAS LESS A PROVOCATION, THAN A MASKED CRY FOR HELP.
"PLEASE DO SOMETHING," WAS WHAT I SHOULD HAVE SAID.
"YOUR SPECIES HAS THE TOOLS AND THE WILL! PLEASE DO SOMETHING! FIND A SOLUTION THAT WILL SAVE BOTH OUR RACES!
"PLEASE DO SOMETHING! WHILE THERE'S ENOUGH OF YOU! WHILE THERE'S STILL TIME! DO SOMETHING!
"PLEASE, PLEASE, PLEASE, DO SOMETHING!"

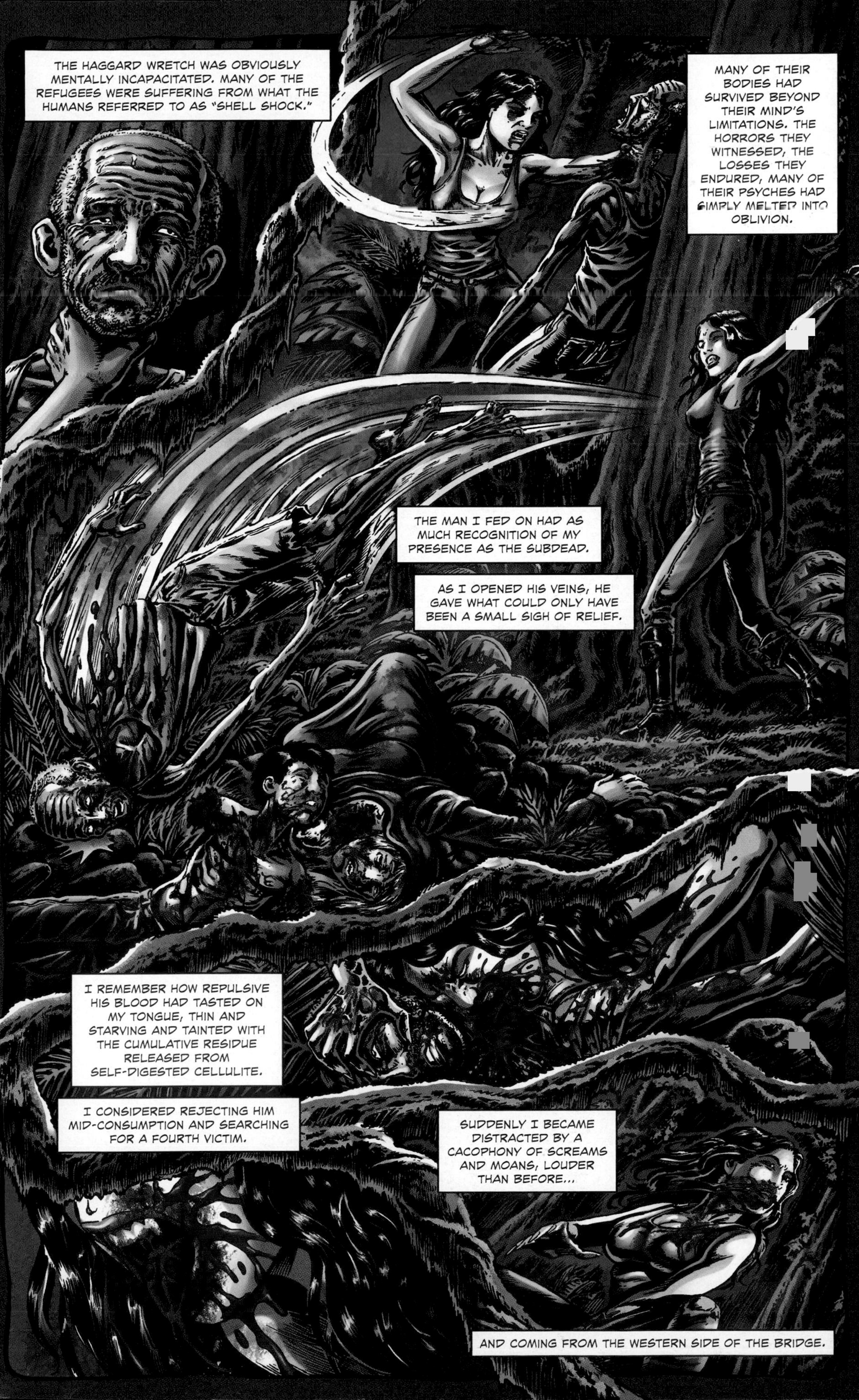
THE HAGGARD WRETCH WAS OBVIOUSLY MENTALLY INCAPACITATED. MANY OF THE REFUGEES WERE SUFFERING FROM WHAT THE HUMANS REFERRED TO AS "SHELL SHOCK."
MANY OF THEIR BODIES HAD SURVIVED BEYOND THEIR MIND'S LIMITATIONS. THE HORRORS THEY WITNESSED, THE LOSSES THEY ENDURED, MANY OF THEIR PSYCHES HAD SIMPLY MELTED INTO OBLIVION.
THE MAN I FED ON HAD AS MUCH RECOGNITION OF MY PRESENCE AS THE SUBDEAD.
AS I OPENED HIS VEINS, HE GAVE WHAT COULD ONLY HAVE BEEN A SMALL SIGH OF RELIEF.
I REMEMBER HOW REPULSIVE HIS BLOOD HAD TASTED ON MY TONGUE, THIN AND STARVING AND TAINTED WITH THE CUMULATIVE RESIDUE RELEASED FROM SELF-DIGESTED CELLULITE.
I CONSIDERED REJECTING HIM MID-CONSUMPTION AND SEARCHING FOR A FOURTH VICTIM.
SUDDENLY I BECAME DISTRACTED BY A CACOPHONY OF SCREAMS AND MOANS, LOUDER THAN BEFORE...
AND COMING FROM THE WESTERN SIDE OF THE BRIDGE.

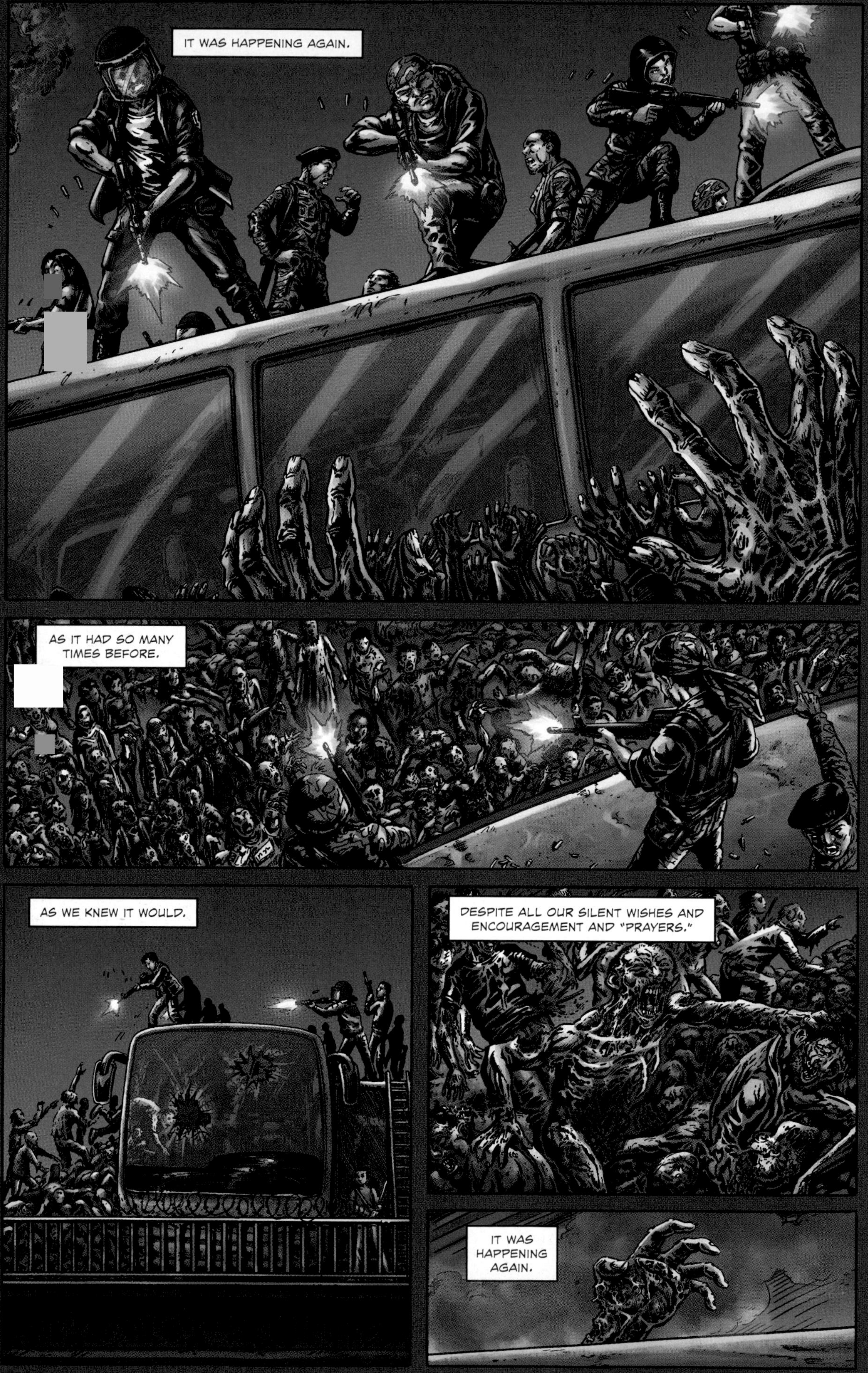
IT WAS HAPPENING AGAIN.
AS IT HAD SO MANY TIMES BEFORE.
AS WE KNEW IT WOULD.
DESPITE ALL OUR SILENT WISHES AND ENCOURAGEMENT AND "PRAYERS."
IT WAS HAPPENING AGAIN.

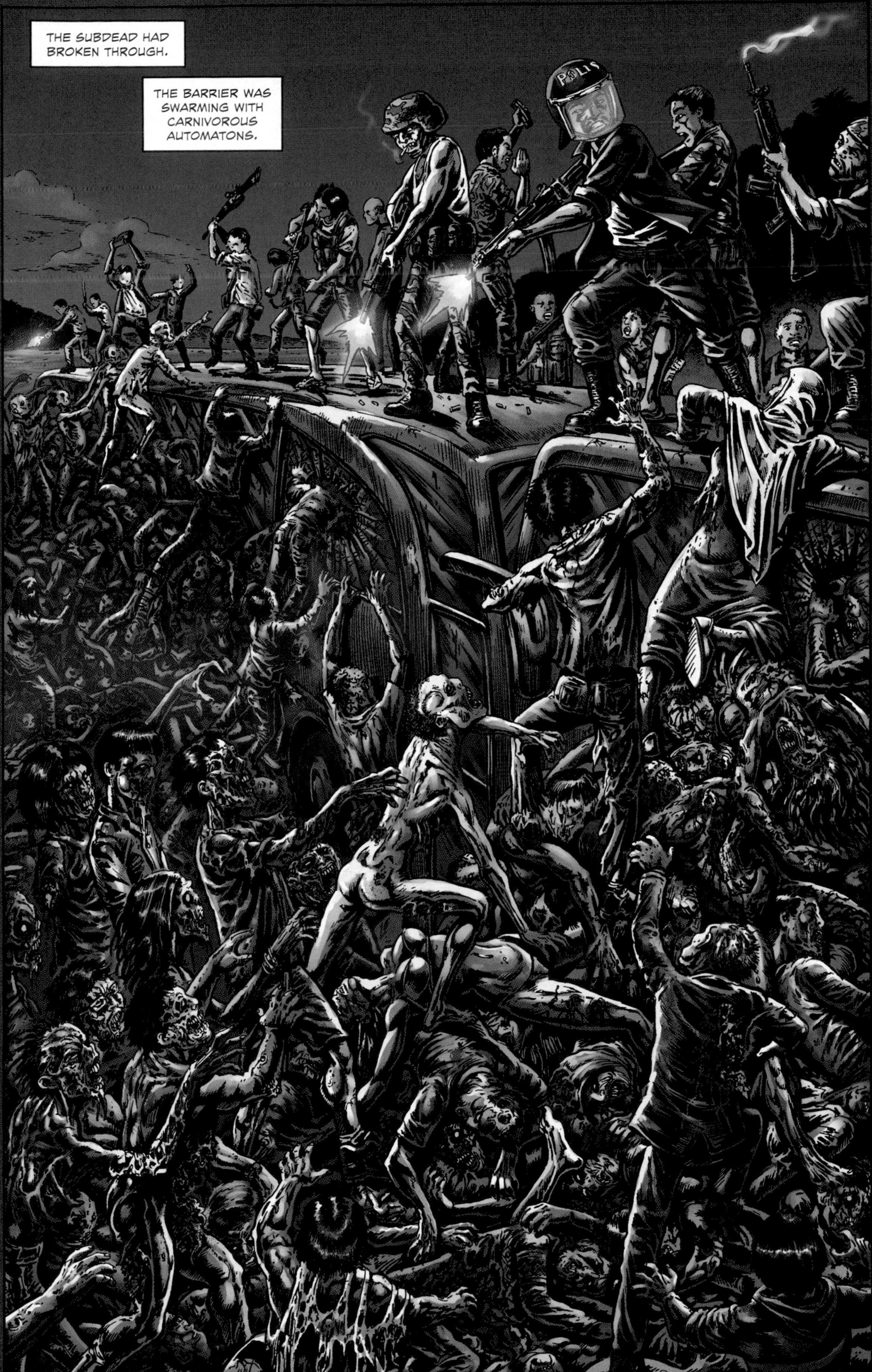
THE SUBDEAD HAD BROKEN THROUGH.
THE BARRIER WAS SWARMING WITH CARNIVOROUS AUTOMATONS.
POLIS

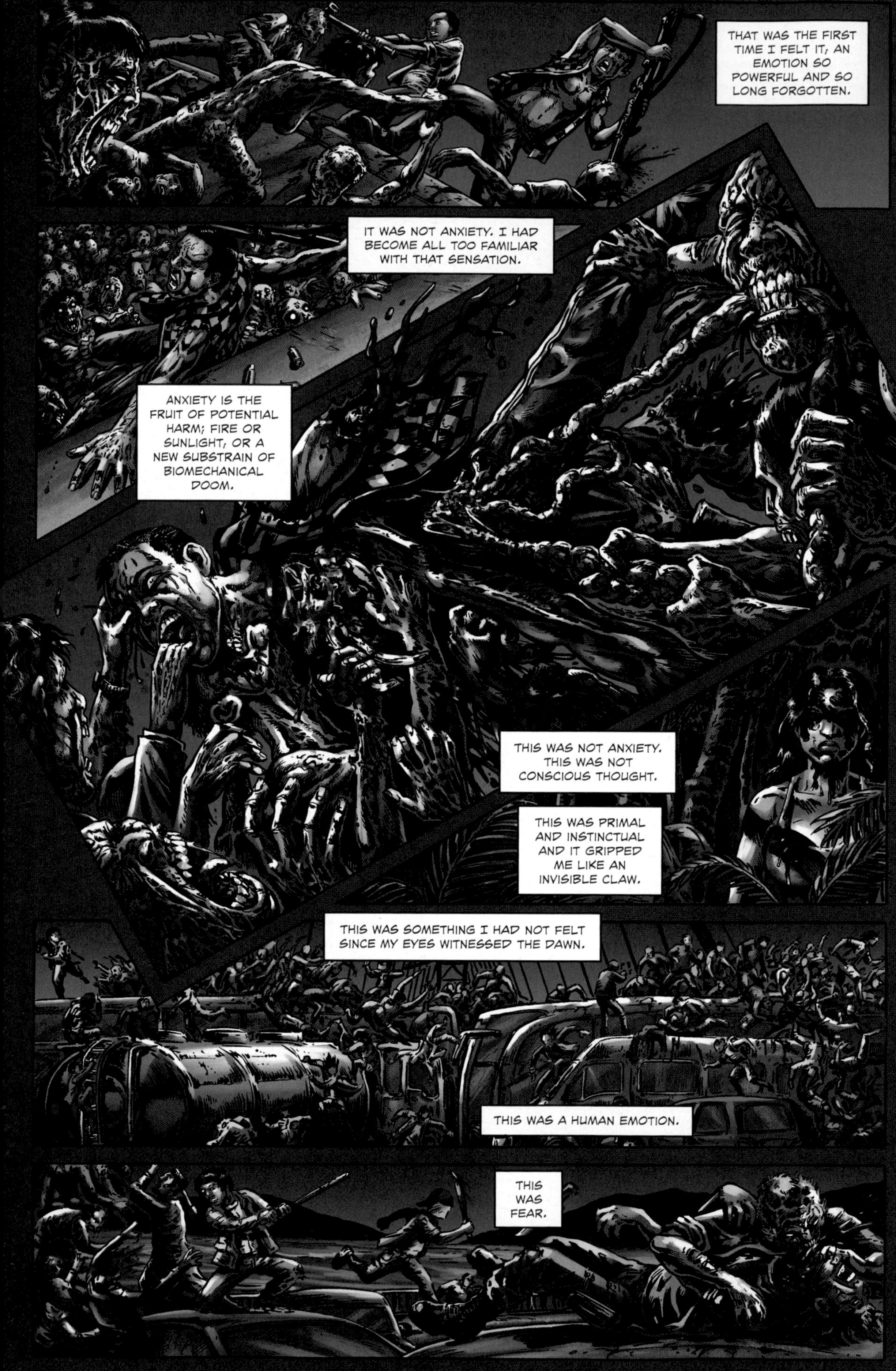
THAT WAS THE FIRST TIME I FELT IT, AN EMOTION SO POWERFUL AND SO LONG FORGOTTEN.
IT WAS NOT ANXIETY. I HAD BECOME ALL TOO FAMILIAR WITH THAT SENSATION.
ANXIETY IS THE FRUIT OF POTENTIAL HARM; FIRE OR SUNLIGHT, OR A NEW SUBSTRAIN OF BIOMECHANICAL DOOM.
THIS WAS NOT ANXIETY. THIS WAS NOT CONSCIOUS THOUGHT.
THIS WAS PRIMAL AND INSTINCTUAL AND IT GRIPPED ME LIKE AN INVISIBLE CLAW.
THIS WAS SOMETHING I HAD NOT FELT SINCE MY EYES WITNESSED THE DAWN.
THIS WAS A HUMAN EMOTION.
THIS WAS FEAR.

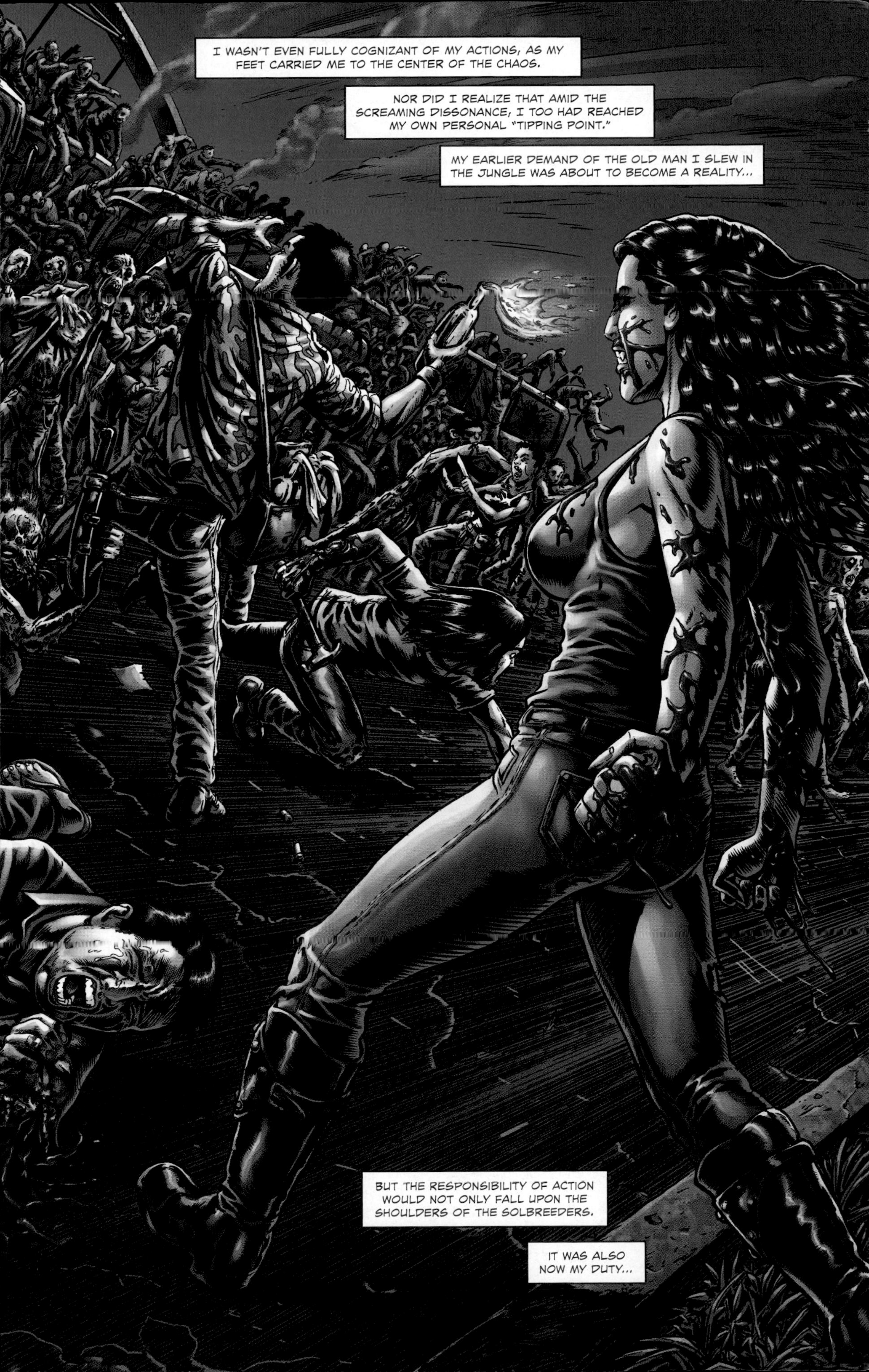
I WASN'T EVEN FULLY COGNIZANT OF MY ACTIONS, AS MY FEET CARRIED ME TO THE CENTER OF THE CHAOS.
NOR DID I REALIZE THAT AMID THE SCREAMING DISSONANCE, I TOO HAD REACHED MY OWN PERSONAL "TIPPING POINT."
MY EARLIER DEMAND OF THE OLD MAN I SLEW IN THE JUNGLE WAS ABOUT TO BECOME A REALITY...
BUT THE RESPONSIBILITY OF ACTION WOULD NOT ONLY FALL UPON THE SHOULDERS OF THE SOLBREEDERS.
IT WAS ALSO NOW MY DUTY...

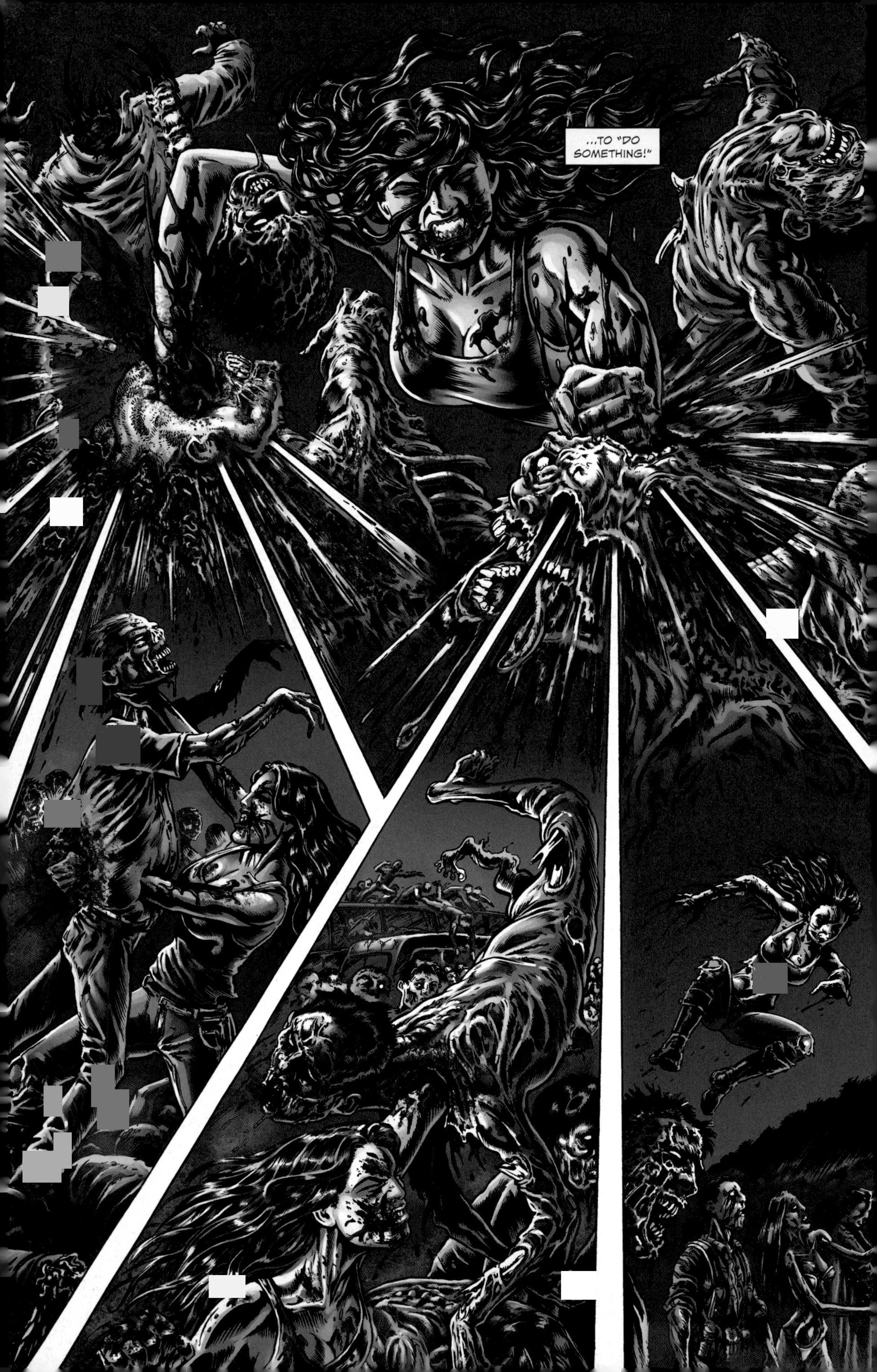
...TO "DO SOMETHING!"

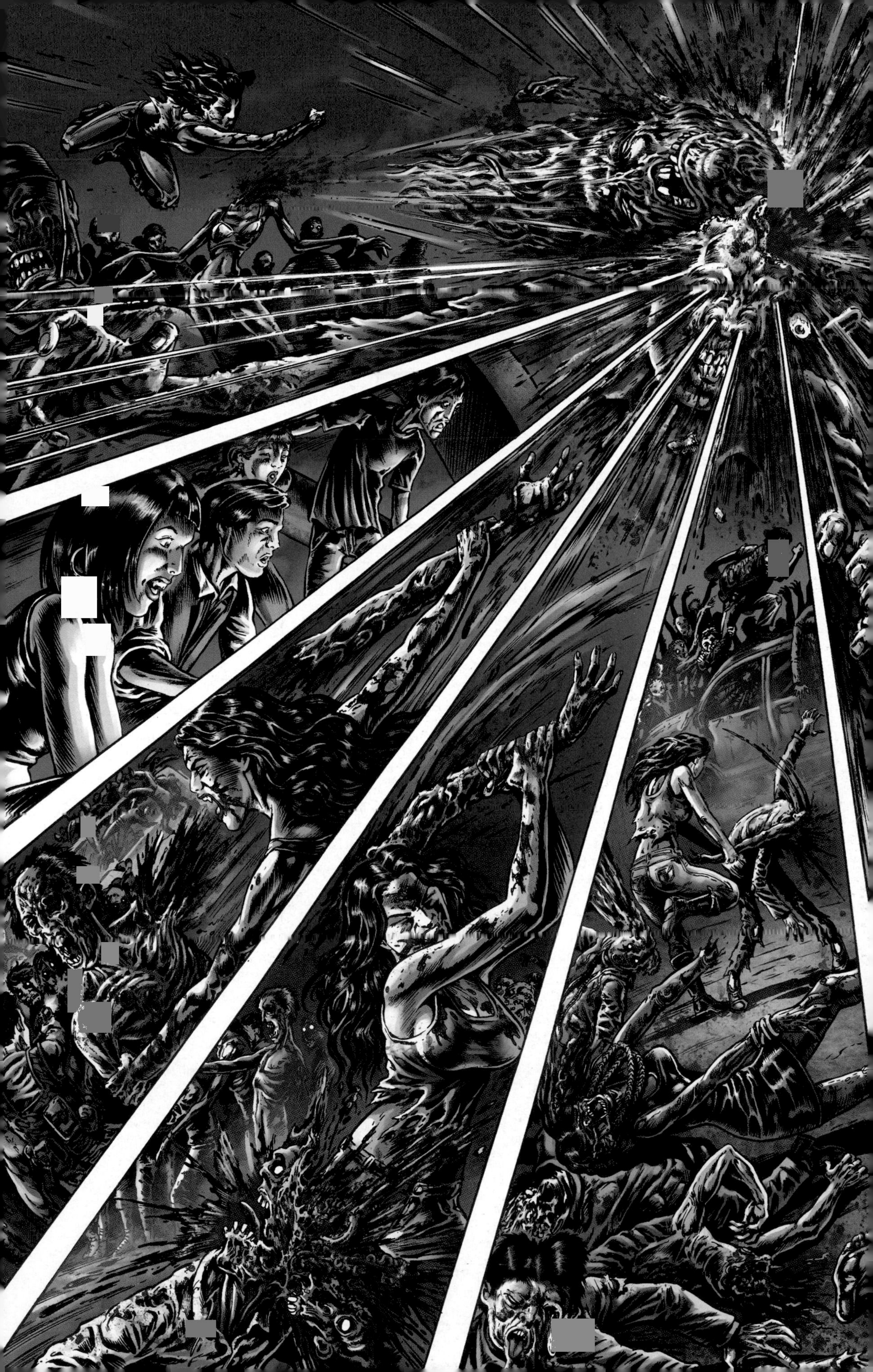

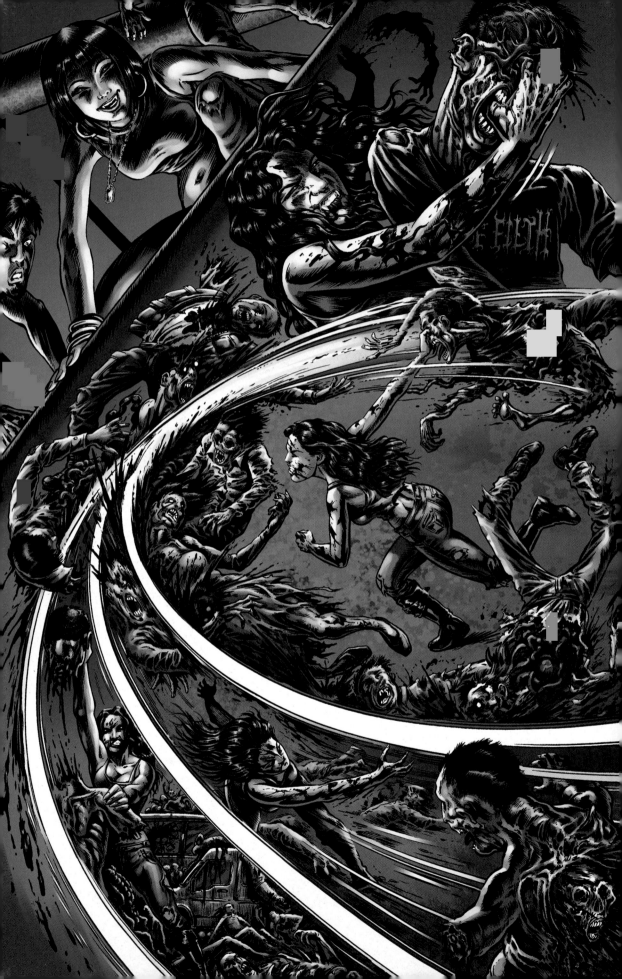

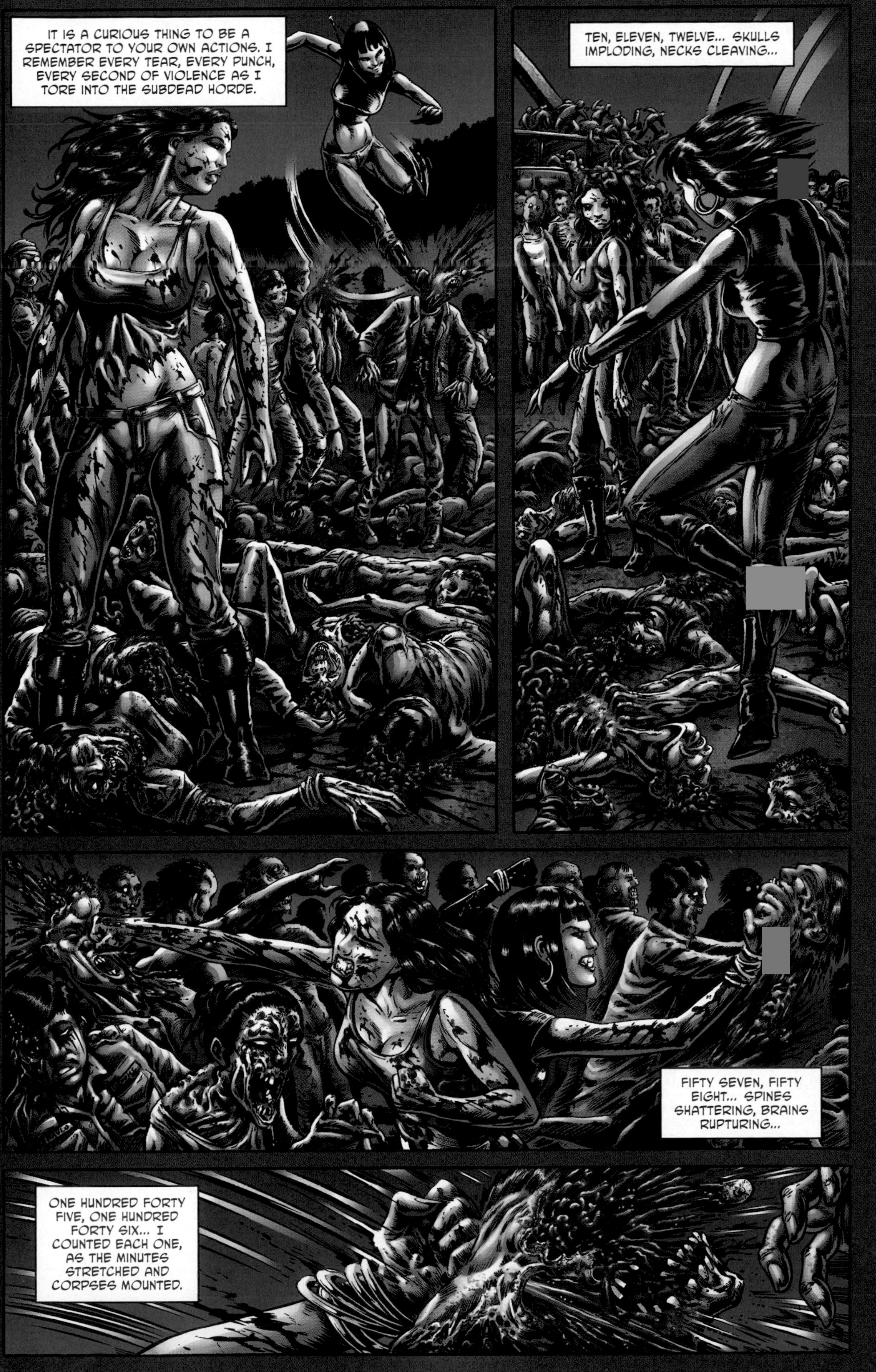
IT IS A CURIOUS THING TO BE A SPECTATOR TO YOUR OWN ACTIONS. I REMEMBER EVERY TEAR, EVERY PUNCH, EVERY SECOND OF VIOLENCE AS I TORE INTO THE SUBDEAD HORDE.
TEN, ELEVEN, TWELVE... SKULLS IMPLODING, NECKS CLEAVING...
FIFTY SEVEN, FIFTY EIGHT... SPINES SHATTERING, BRAINS RUPTURING...
ONE HUNDRED FORTY FIVE, ONE HUNDRED FORTY SIX... I COUNTED EACH ONE, AS THE MINUTES STRETCHED AND CORPSES MOUNTED.

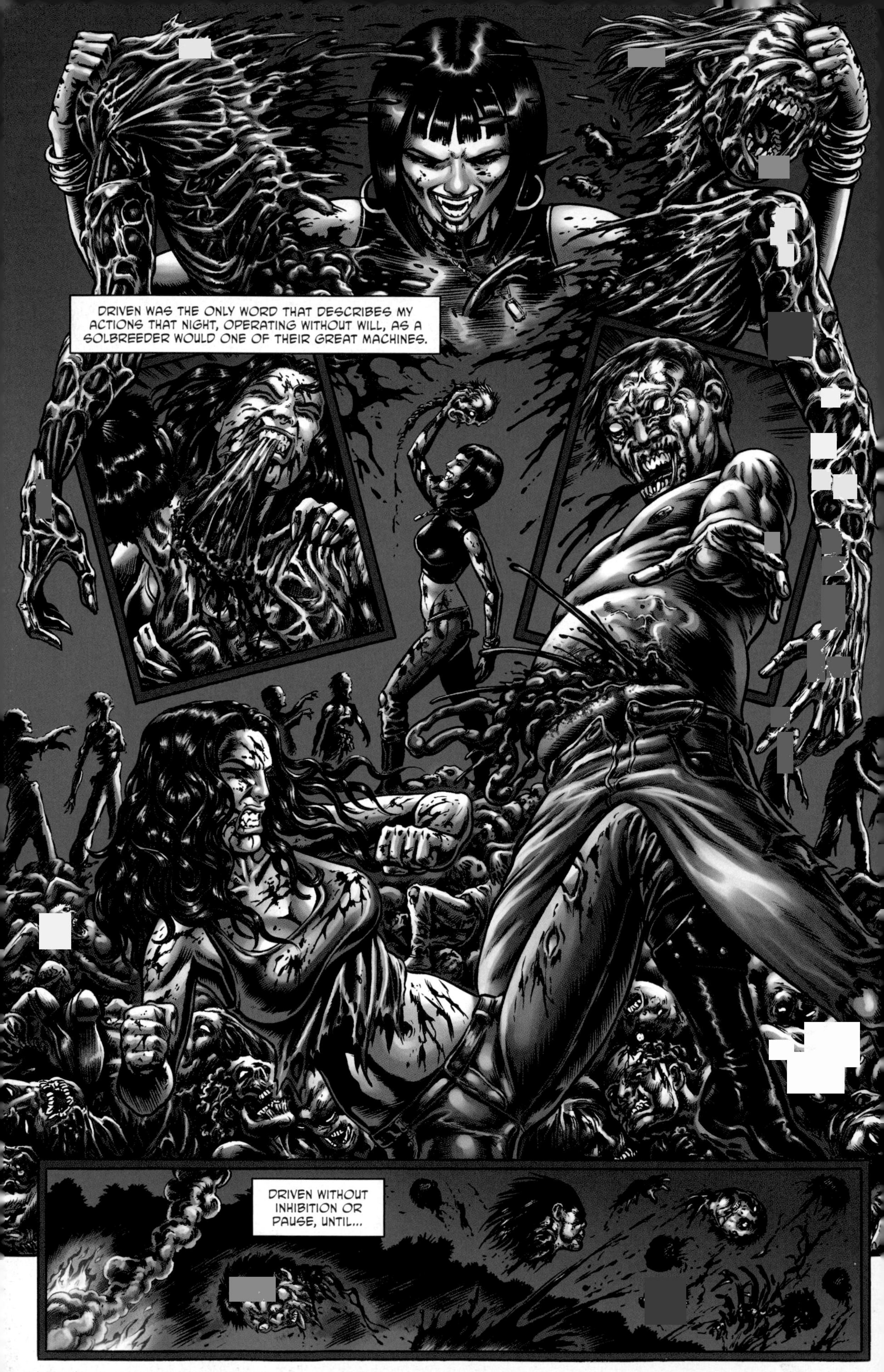
DRIVEN WAS THE ONLY WORD THAT DESCRIBES MY ACTIONS THAT NIGHT, OPERATING WITHOUT WILL, AS A SOLBREEDER WOULD ONE OF THEIR GREAT MACHINES.
DRIVEN WITHOUT INHIBITION OR PAUSE, UNTIL...

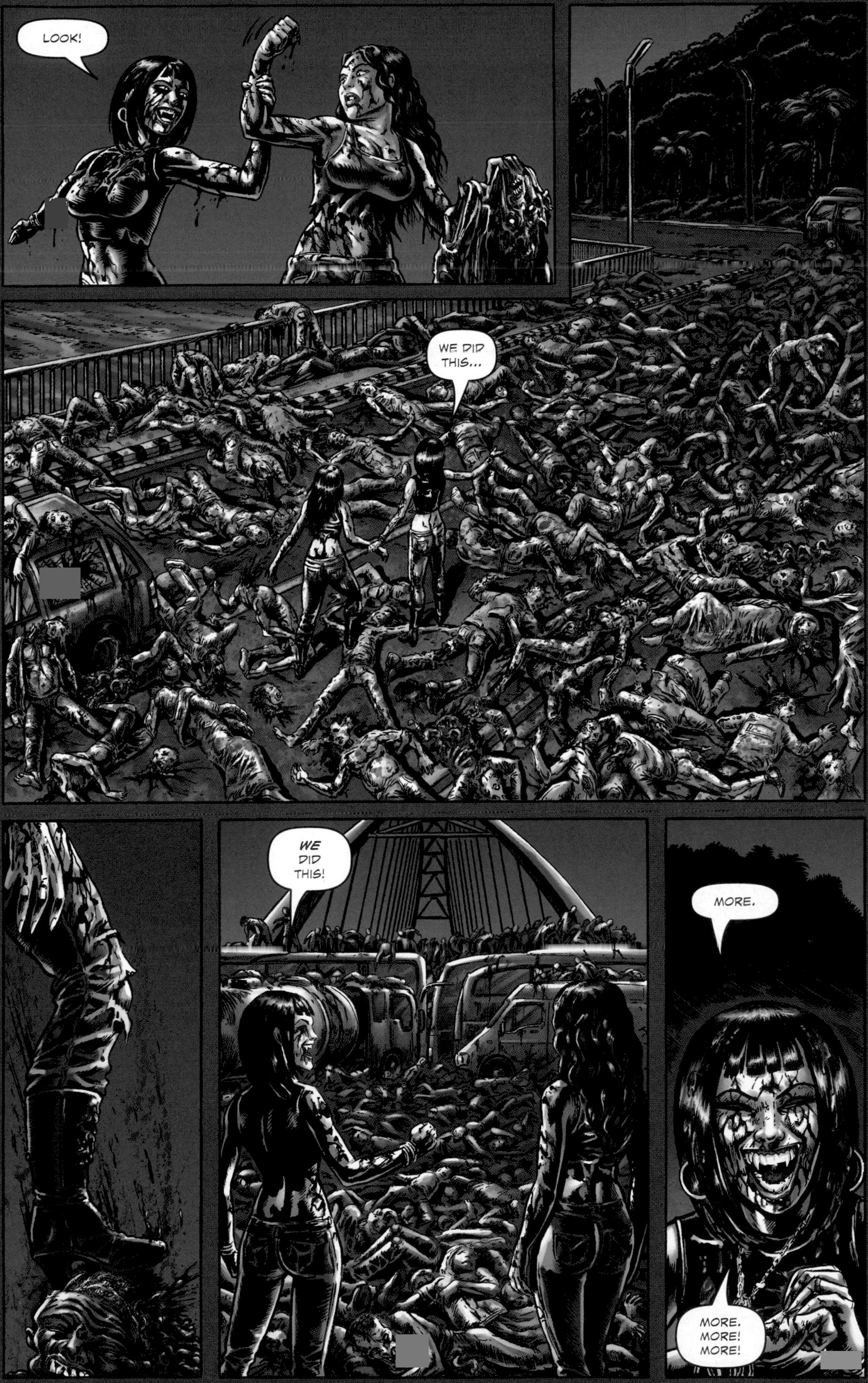
LOOK!
WE DID THIS...
WE DID THIS!
MORE.
MORE. MORE! MORE!

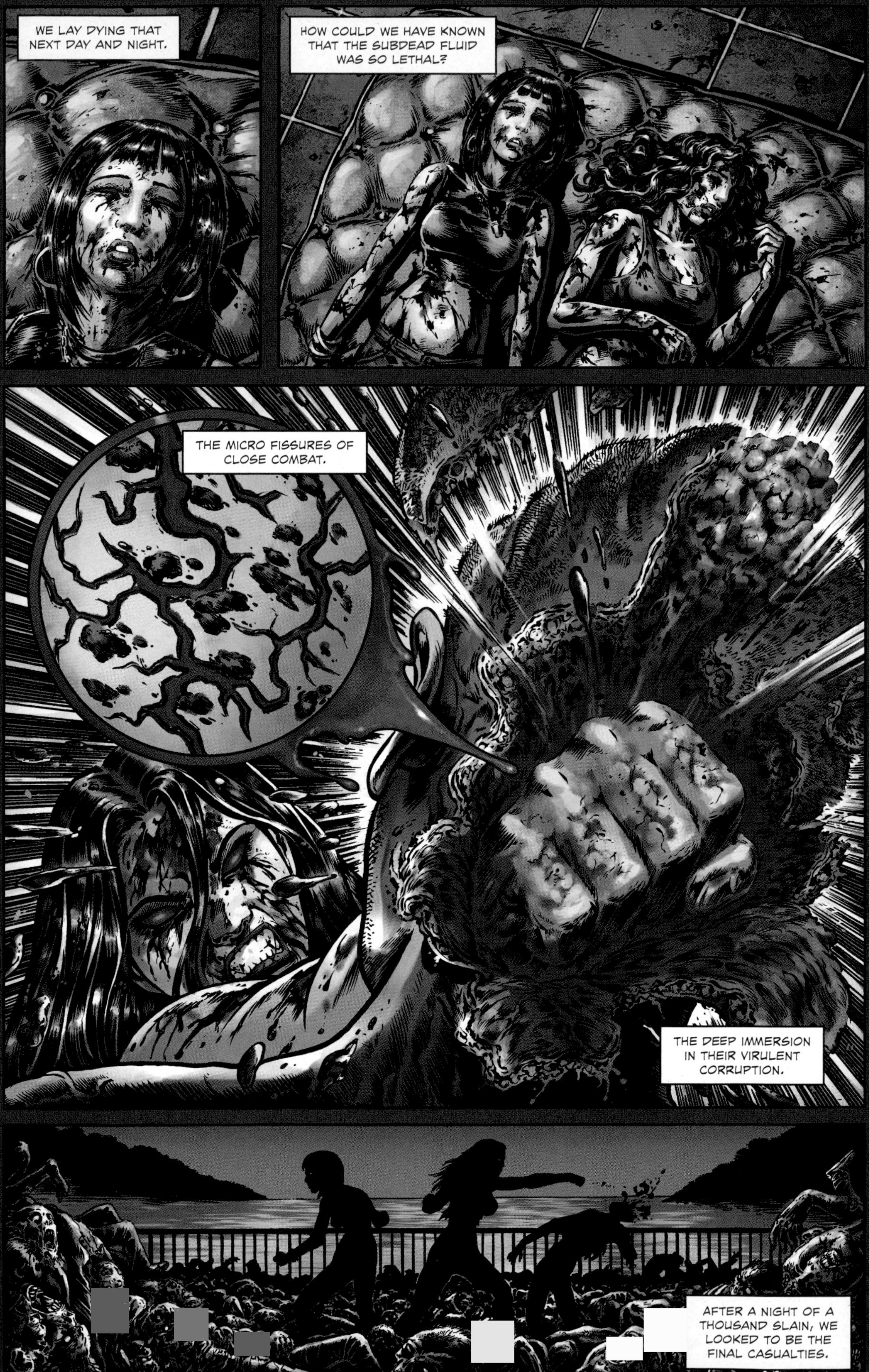
WE LAY DYING THAT NEXT DAY AND NIGHT.
HOW COULD WE HAVE KNOWN THAT THE SUBDEAD FLUID WAS SO LETHAL?
THE MICRO FISSURES OF CLOSE COMBAT.
THE DEEP IMMERSION IN THEIR VIRULENT CORRUPTION.
AFTER A NIGHT OF A THOUSAND SLAIN, WE LOOKED TO BE THE FINAL CASUALTIES.

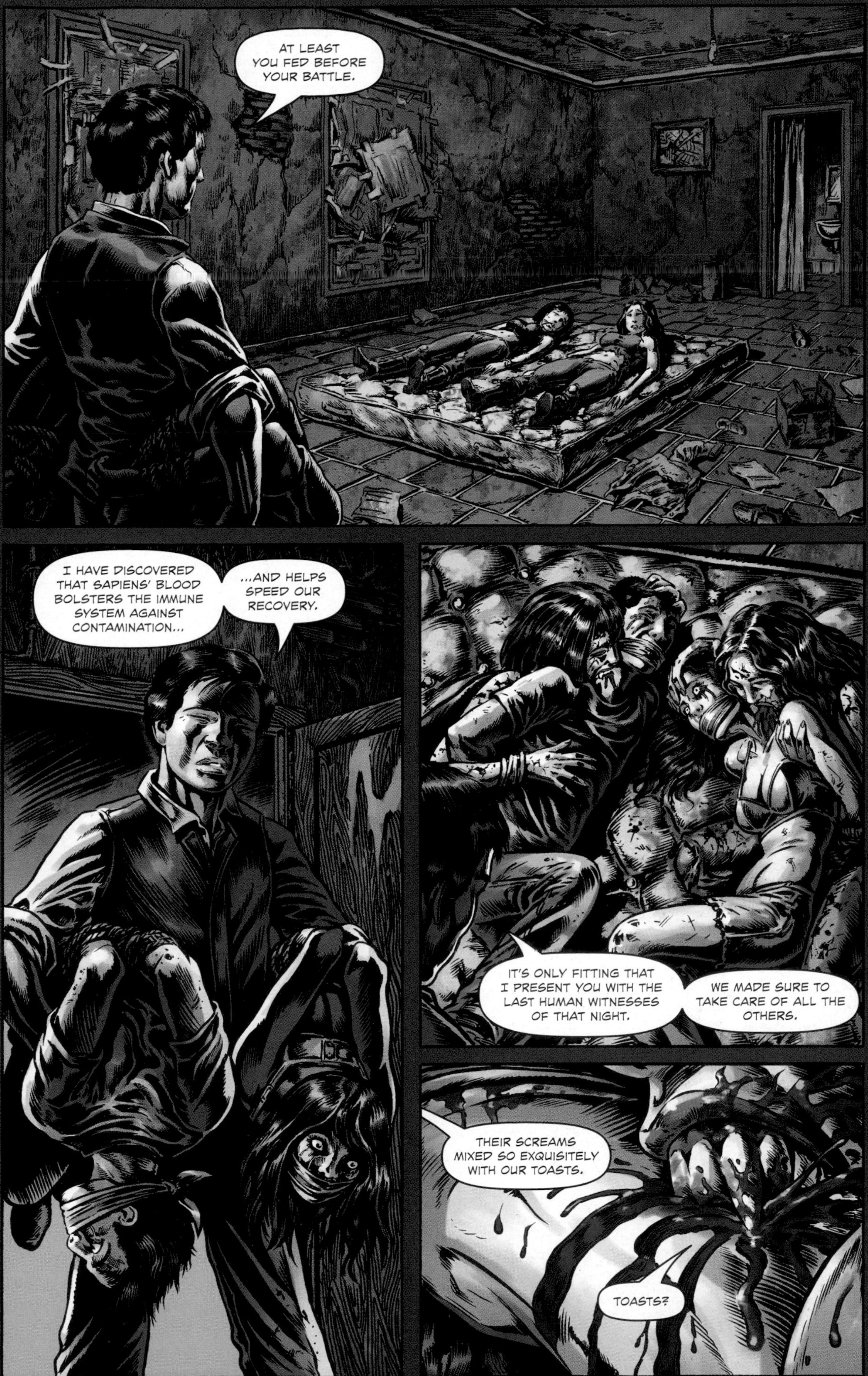
AT LEAST YOU FED BEFORE YOUR BATTLE.
I HAVE DISCOVERED THAT SAPIENS' BLOOD BOLSTERS THE IMMUNE SYSTEM AGAINST CONTAMINATION...
...AND HELPS SPEED OUR RECOVERY.
IT'S ONLY FITTING THAT I PRESENT YOU WITH THE LAST HUMAN WITNESSES OF THAT NIGHT.
WE MADE SURE TO TAKE CARE OF ALL THE OTHERS.
THEIR SCREAMS MIXED SO EXQUISITELY WITH OUR TOASTS.
TOASTS?

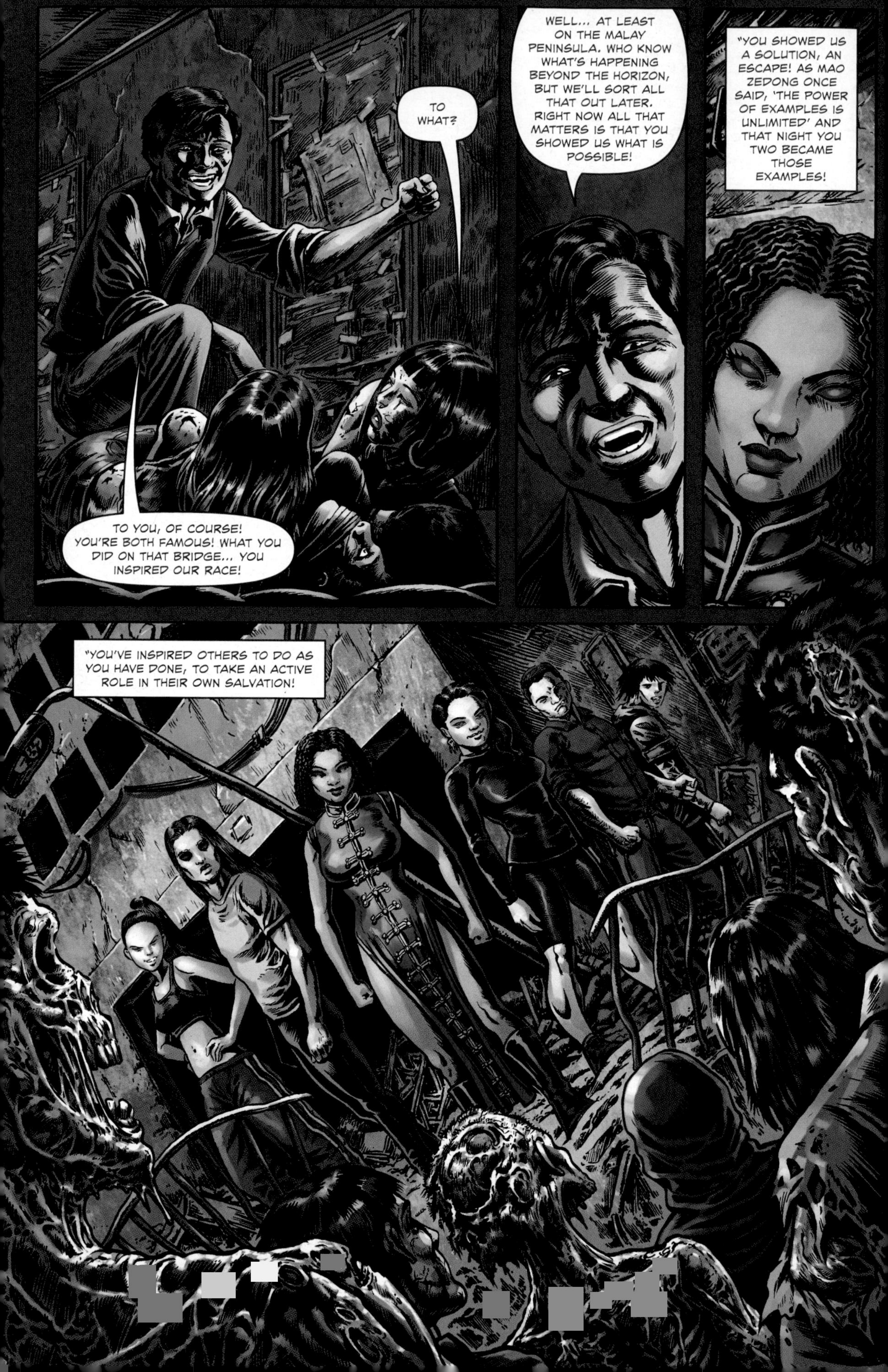
TO WHAT?
TO YOU, OF COURSE! YOU'RE BOTH FAMOUS! WHAT YOU DID ON THAT BRIDGE... YOU INSPIRED OUR RACE!
WELL... AT LEAST ON THE MALAY PENINSULA. WHO KNOW WHAT'S HAPPENING BEYOND THE HORIZON, BUT WE'LL SORT ALL THAT OUT LATER. RIGHT NOW ALL THAT MATTERS IS THAT YOU SHOWED US WHAT IS POSSIBLE!
"YOU SHOWED US A SOLUTION, AN ESCAPE! AS MAO ZEDONG ONCE SAID, 'THE POWER OF EXAMPLES IS UNLIMITED' AND THAT NIGHT YOU TWO BECAME THOSE EXAMPLES!
"YOU'VE INSPIRED OTHERS TO DO AS YOU HAVE DONE, TO TAKE AN ACTIVE ROLE IN THEIR OWN SALVATION!

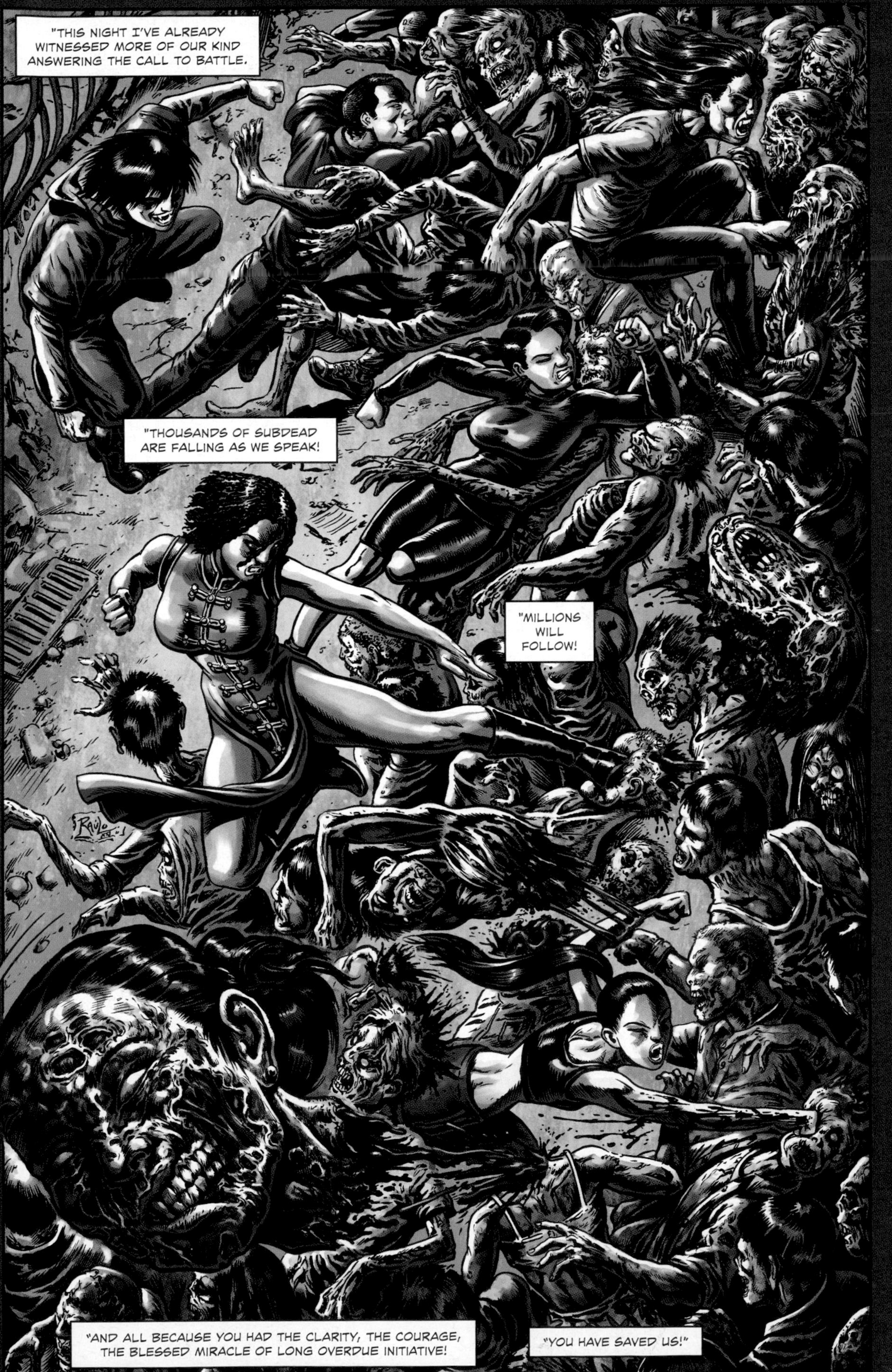
"THIS NIGHT I'VE ALREADY WITNESSED MORE OF OUR KIND ANSWERING THE CALL TO BATTLE.
"THOUSANDS OF SUBDEAD ARE FALLING AS WE SPEAK!
"MILLIONS WILL FOLLOW!
"AND ALL BECAUSE YOU HAD THE CLARITY, THE COURAGE, THE BLESSED MIRACLE OF LONG OVERDUE INITIATIVE!
"YOU HAVE SAVED US!"

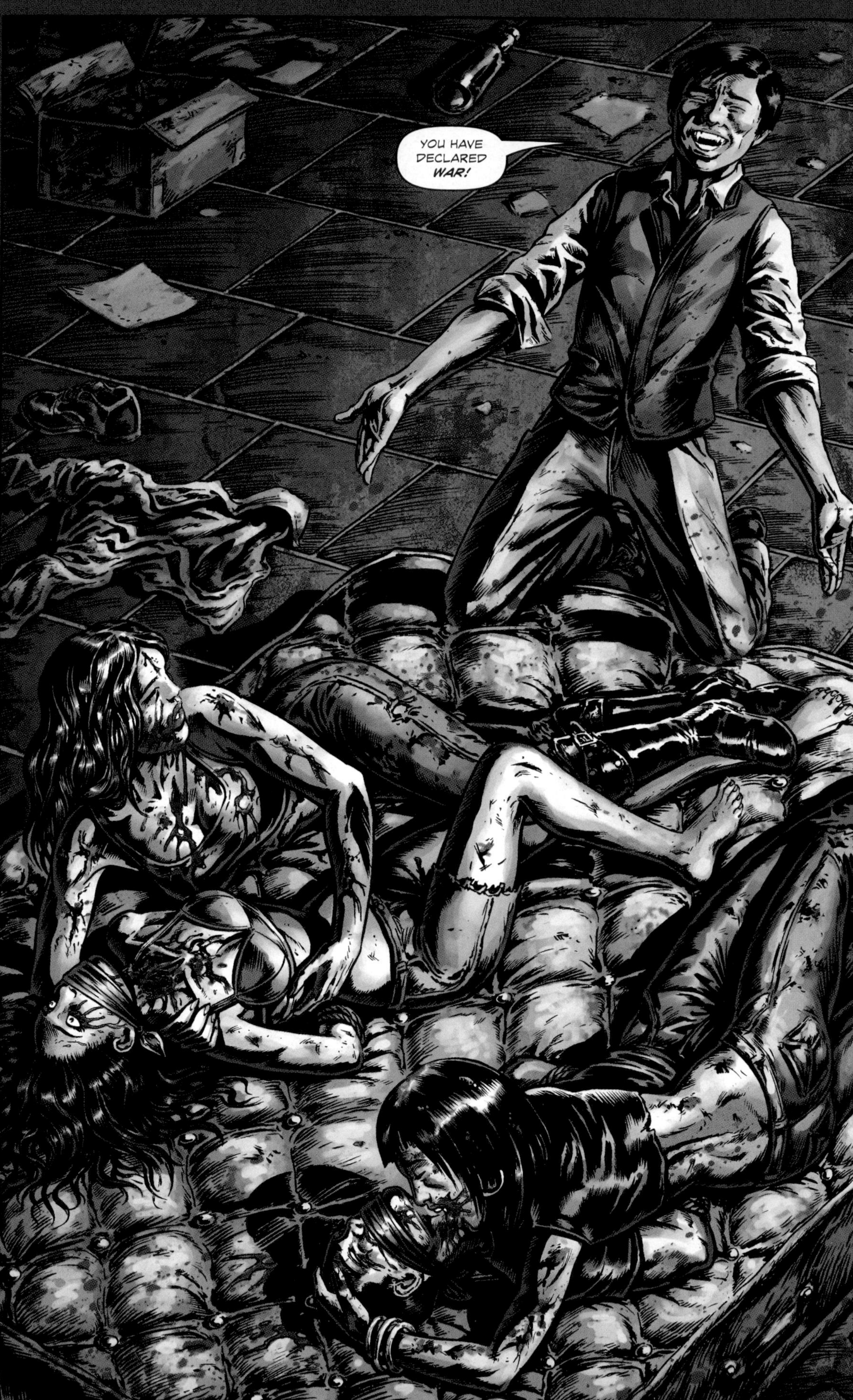
YOU HAVE DECLARED WAR!

Cover Gallery

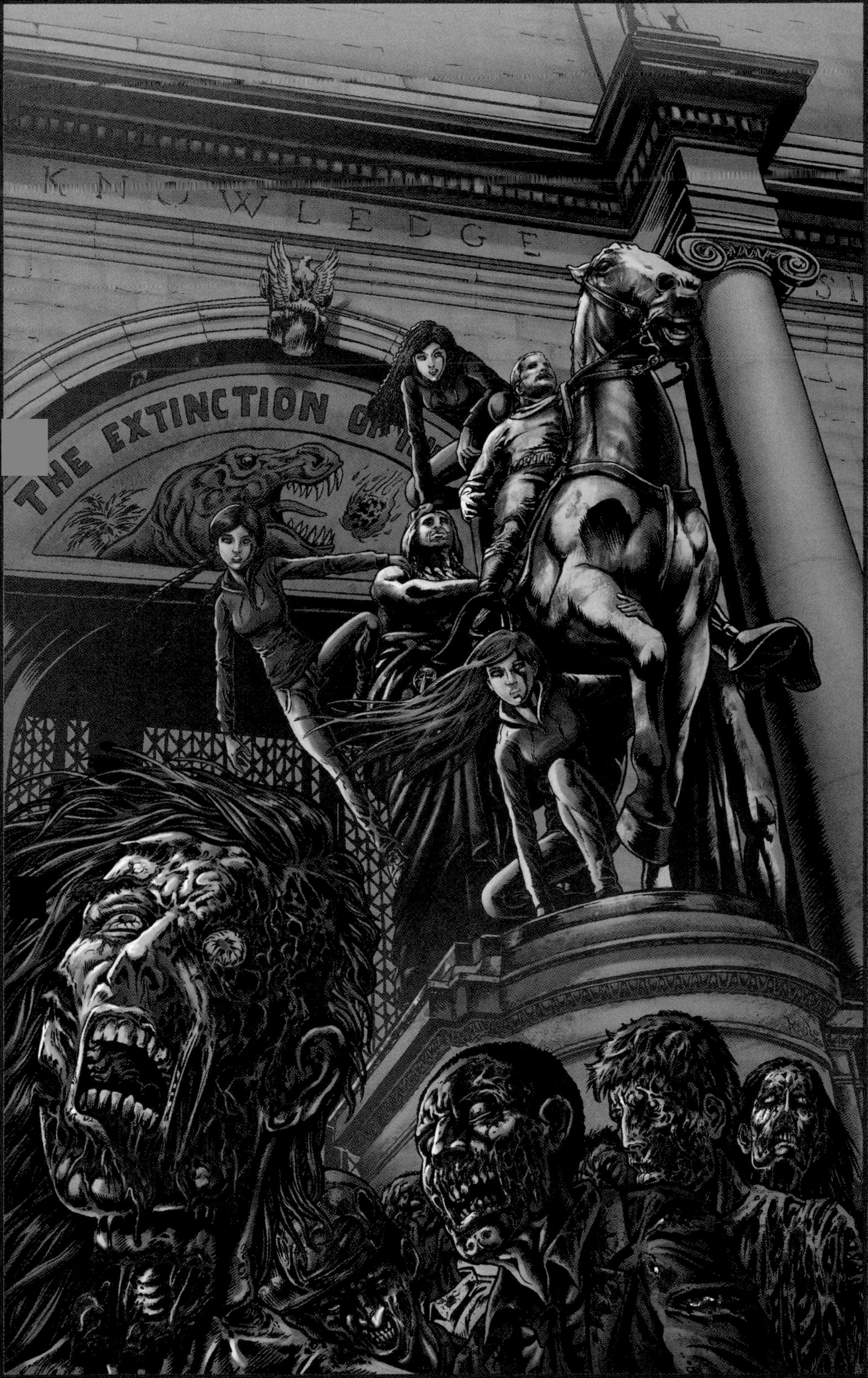
KNOWLEDGE
THE EXTINCTION

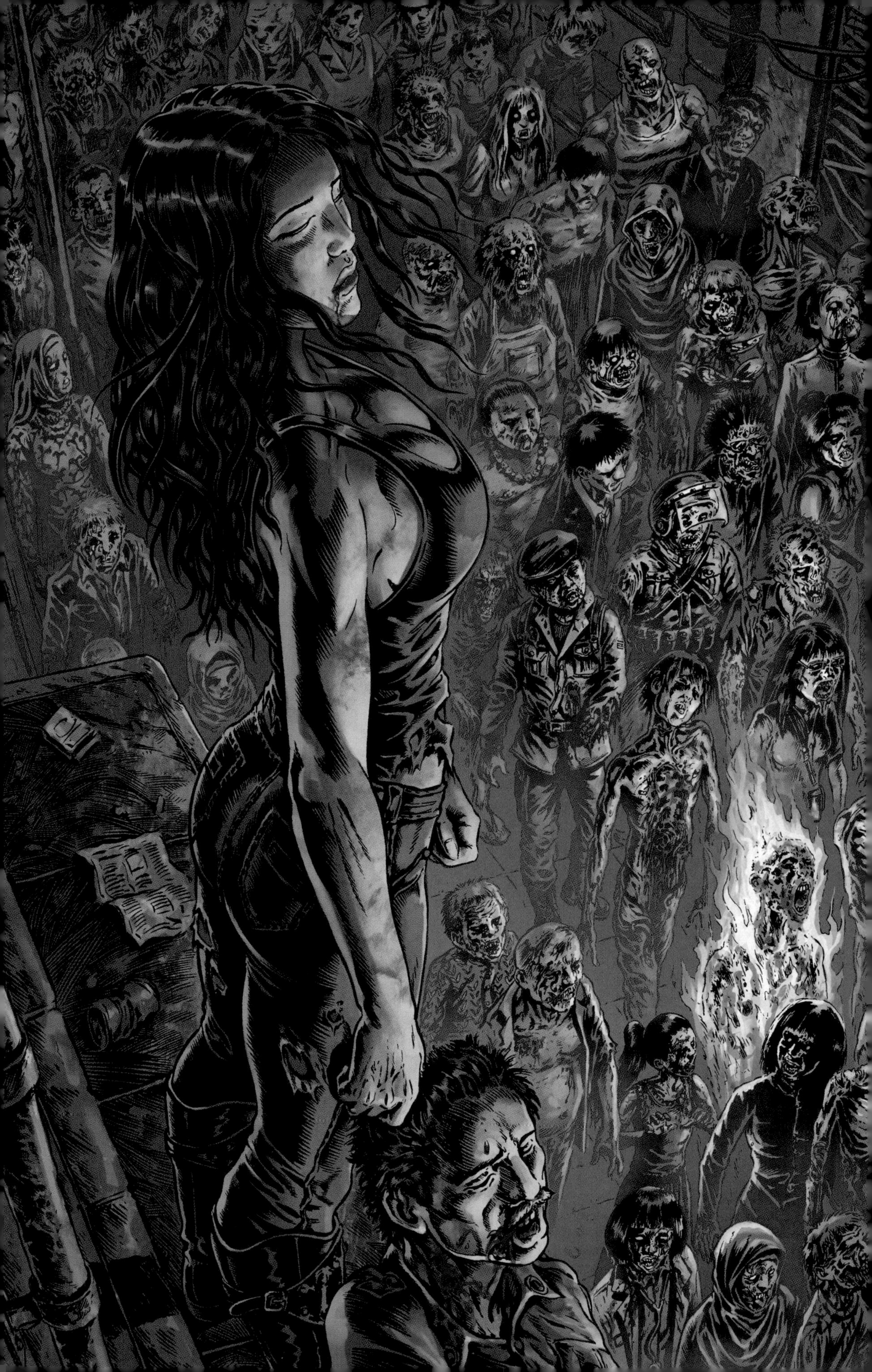

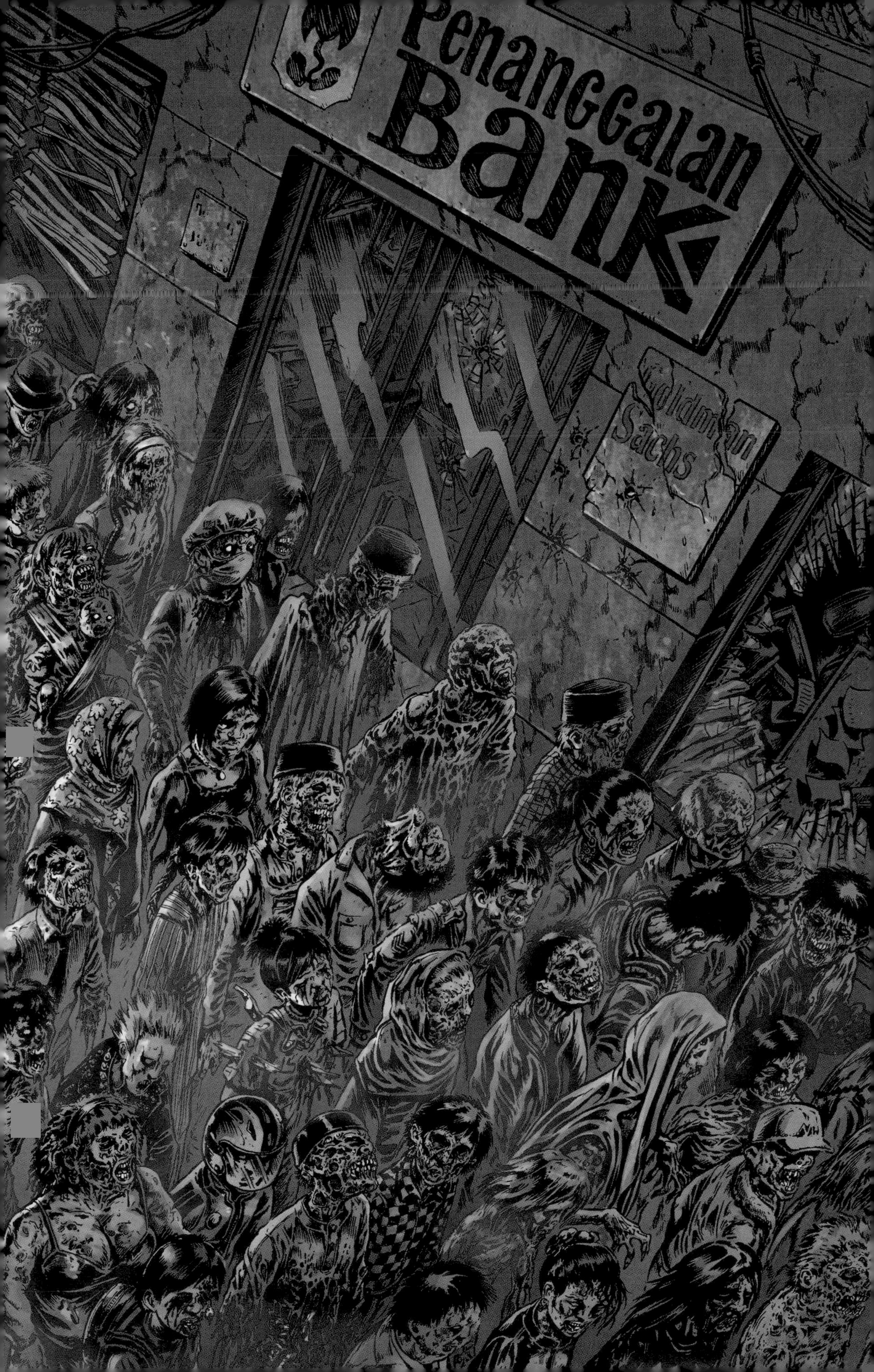
Penanggalan
Bank
oldman
Sachs

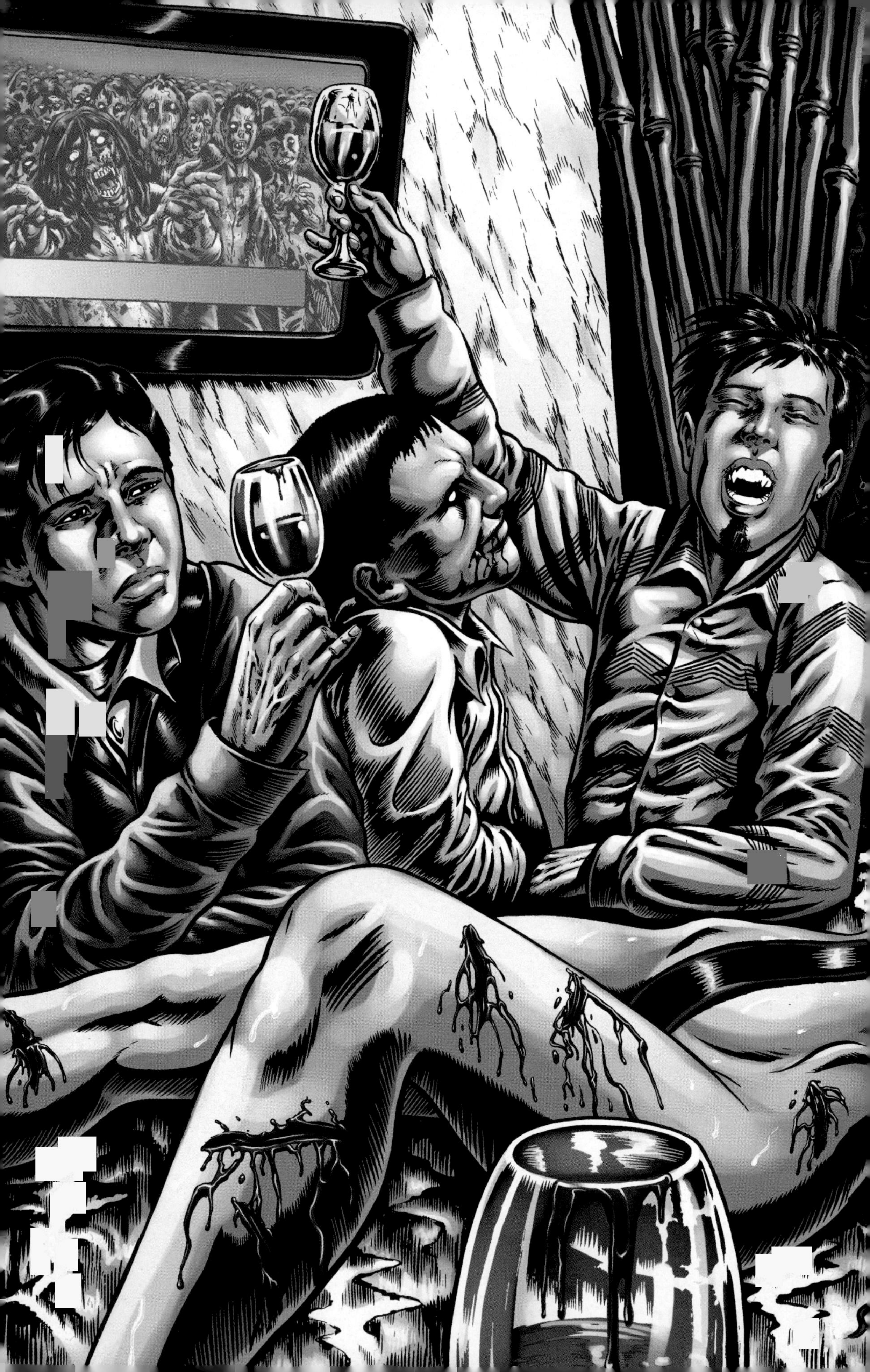

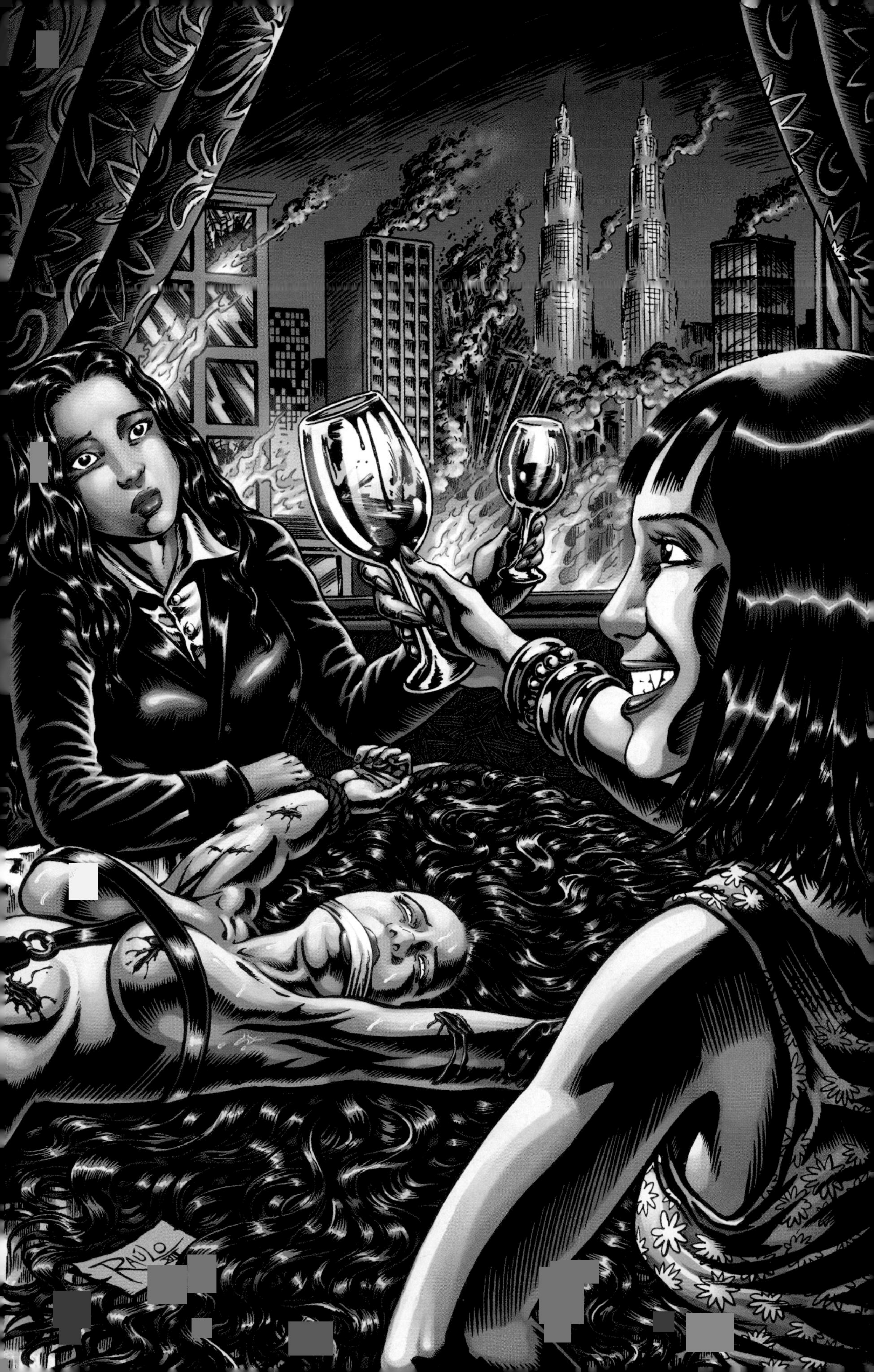

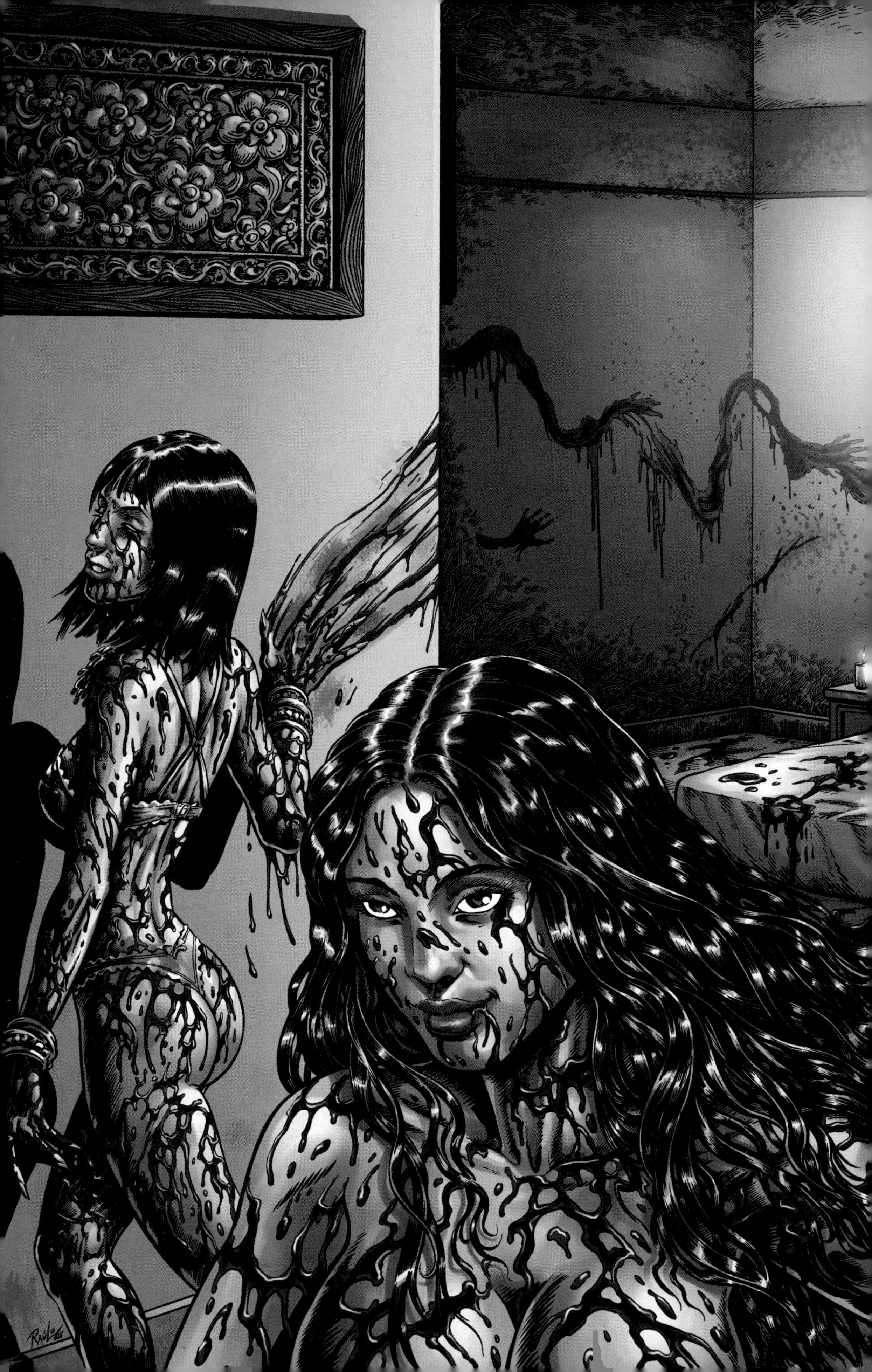

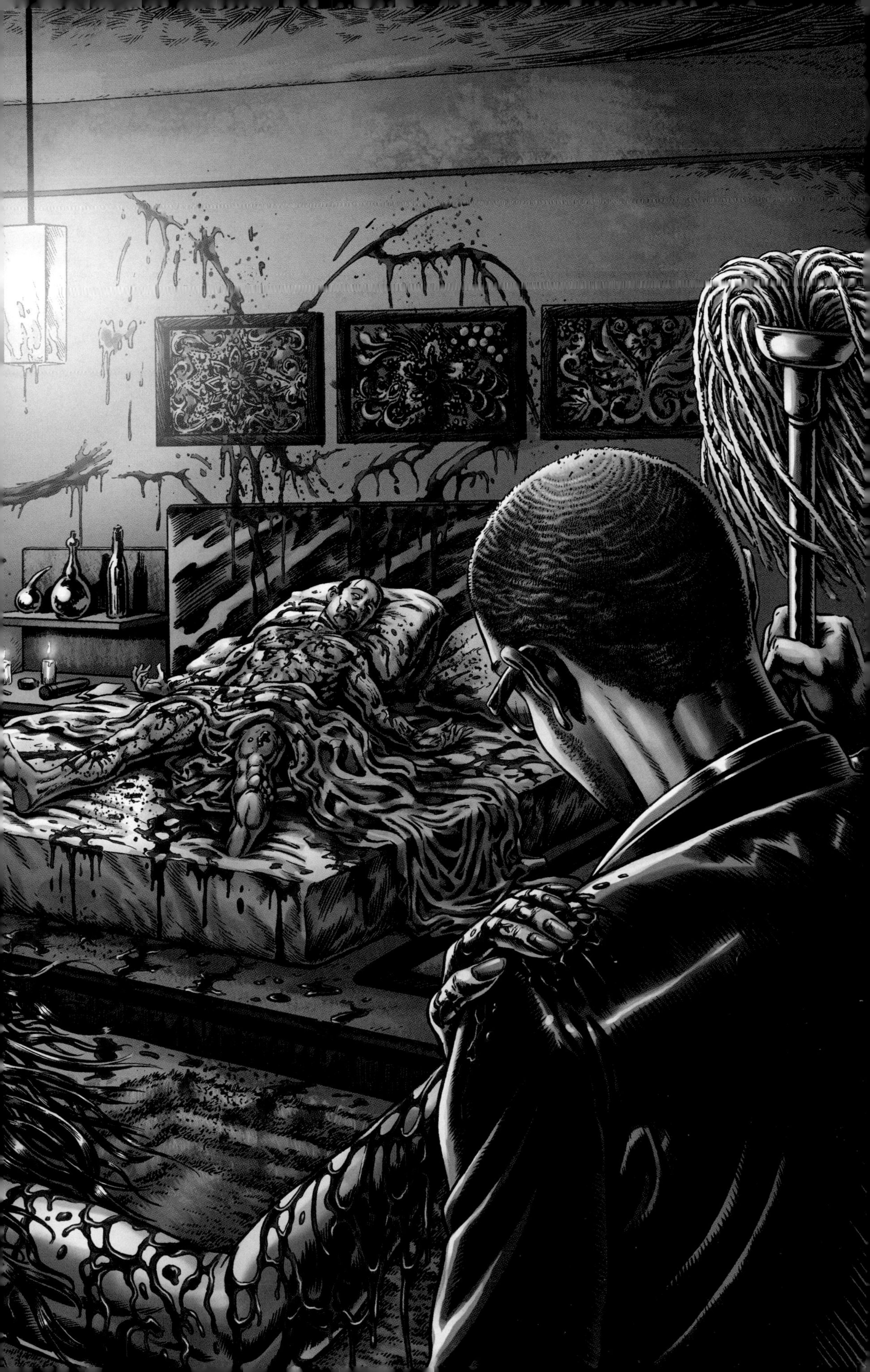

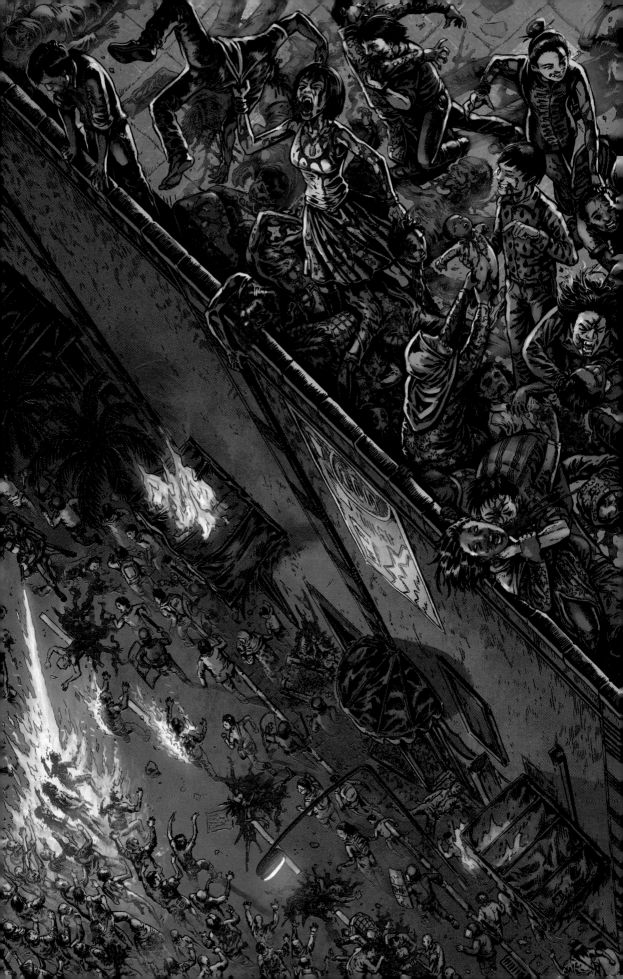

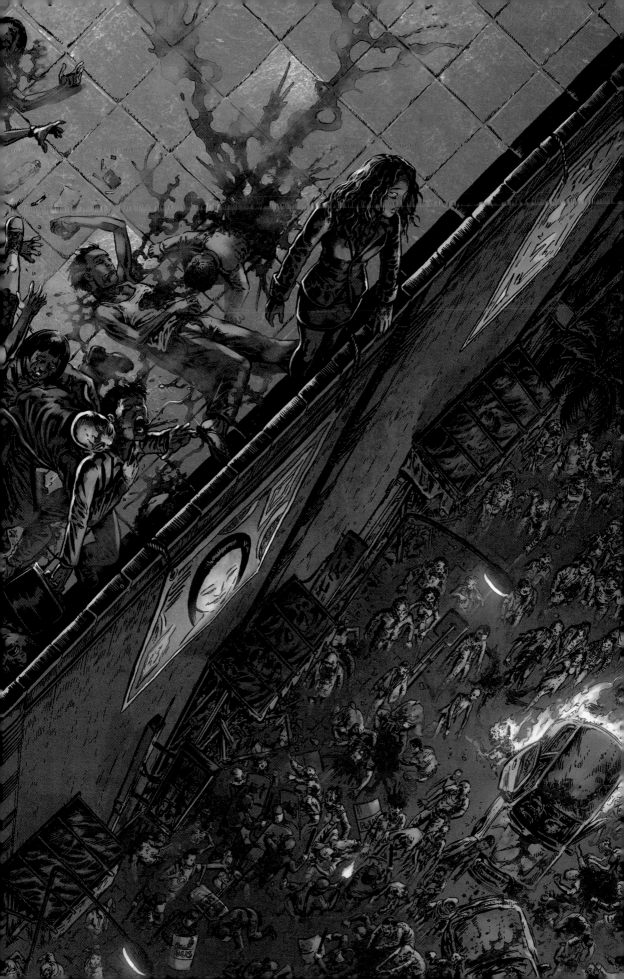

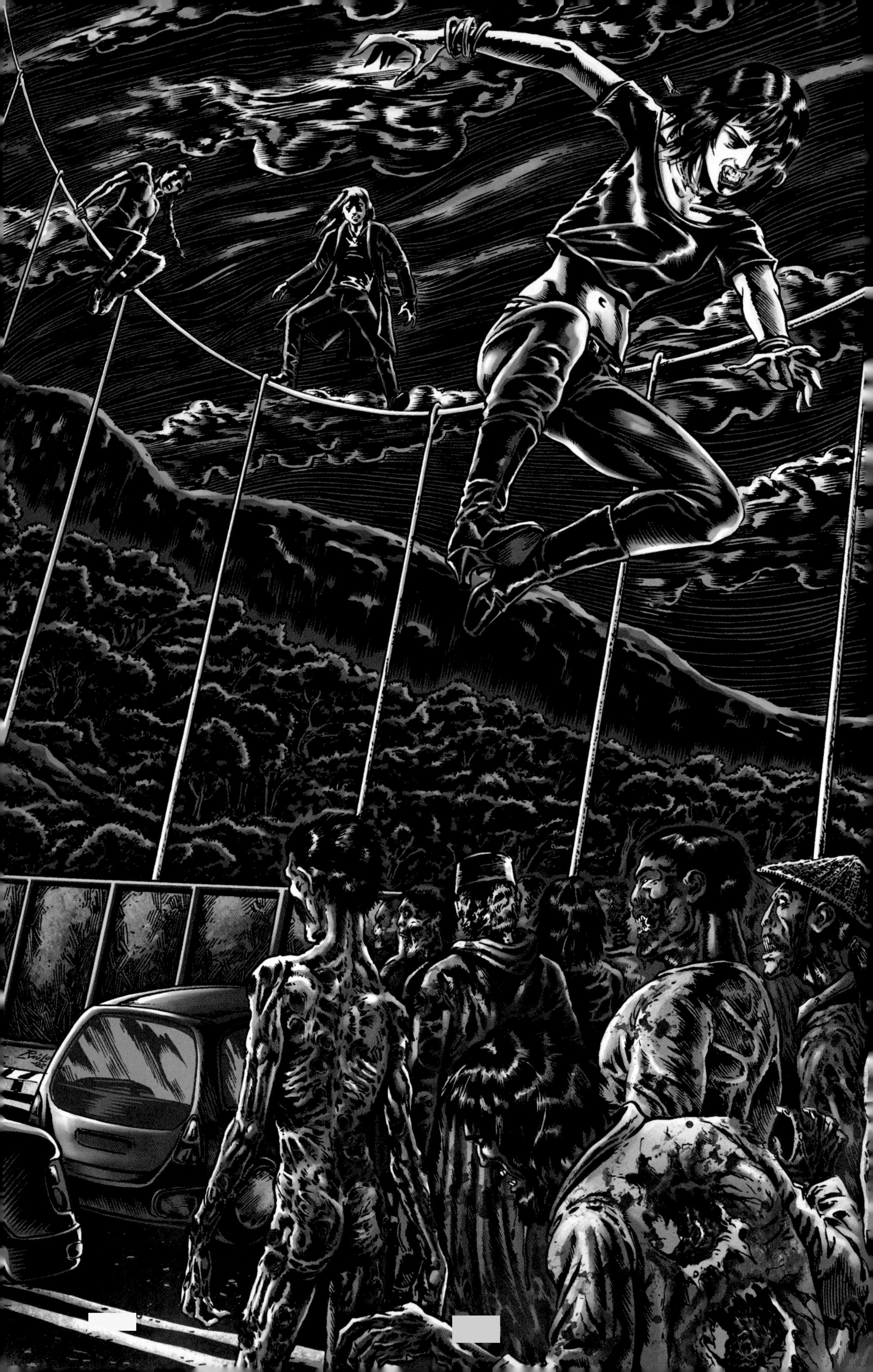

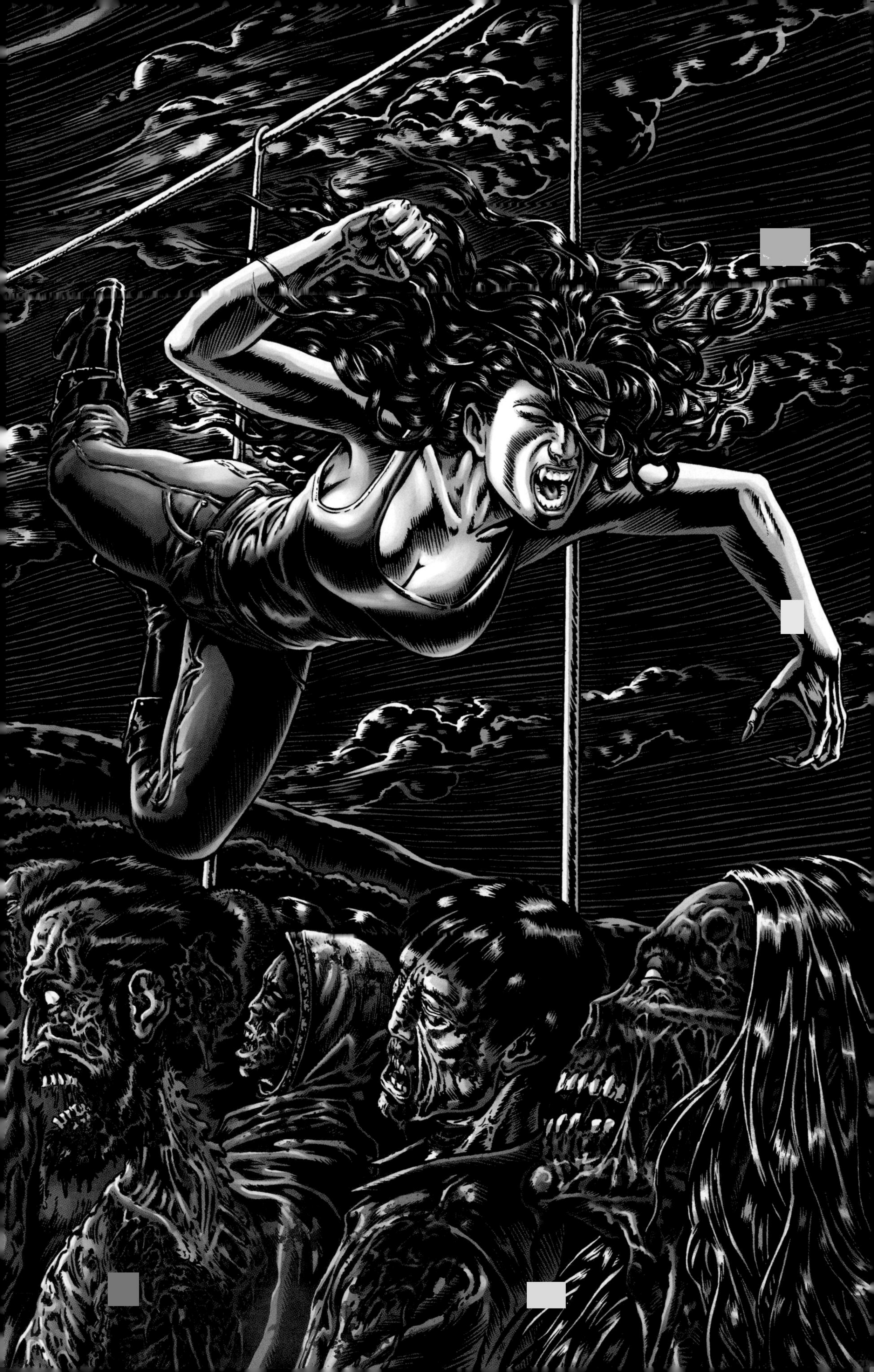

War Has Begun

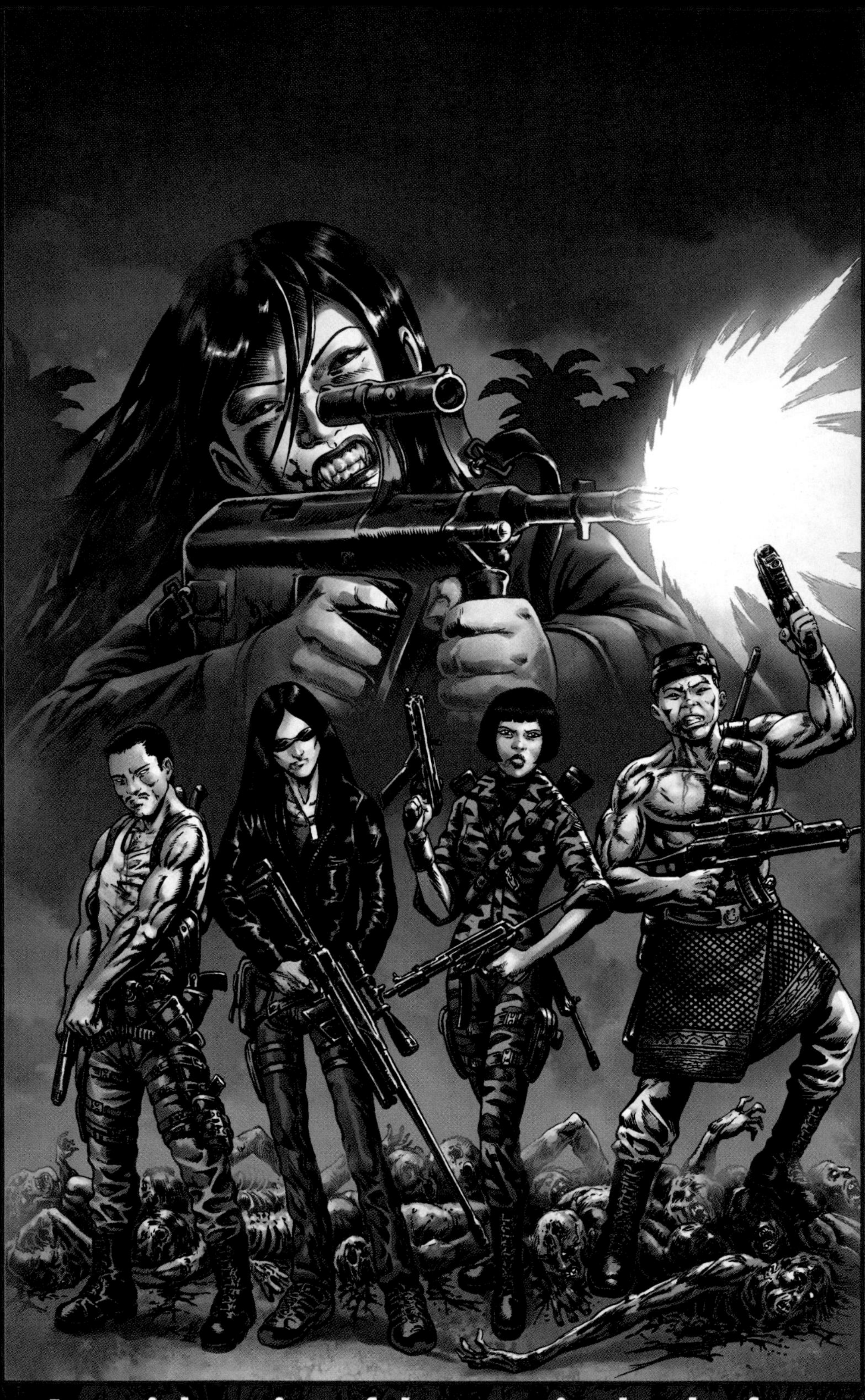

A special preview of the upcoming battles from Extinction Parade Vol 2: War

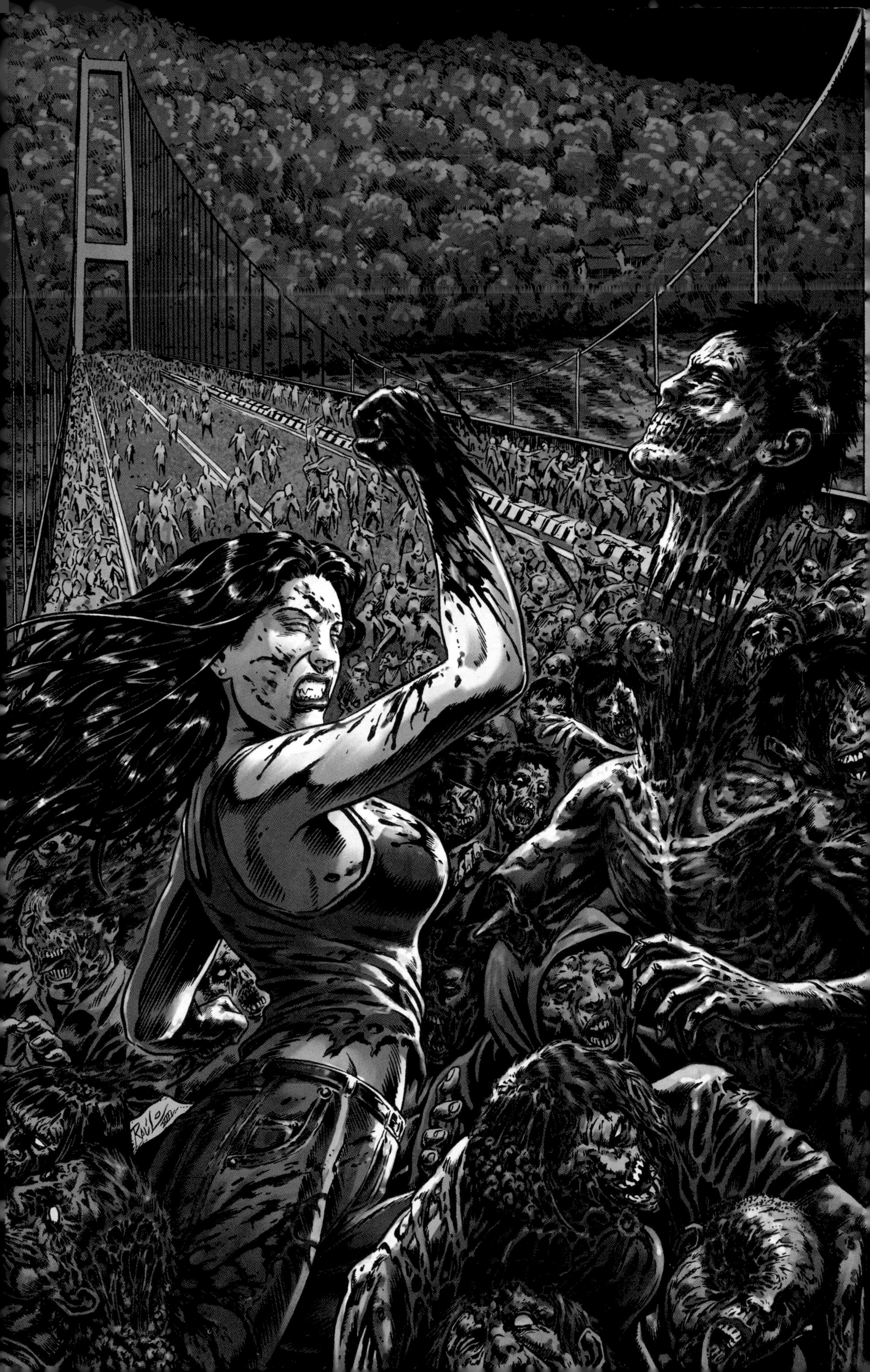

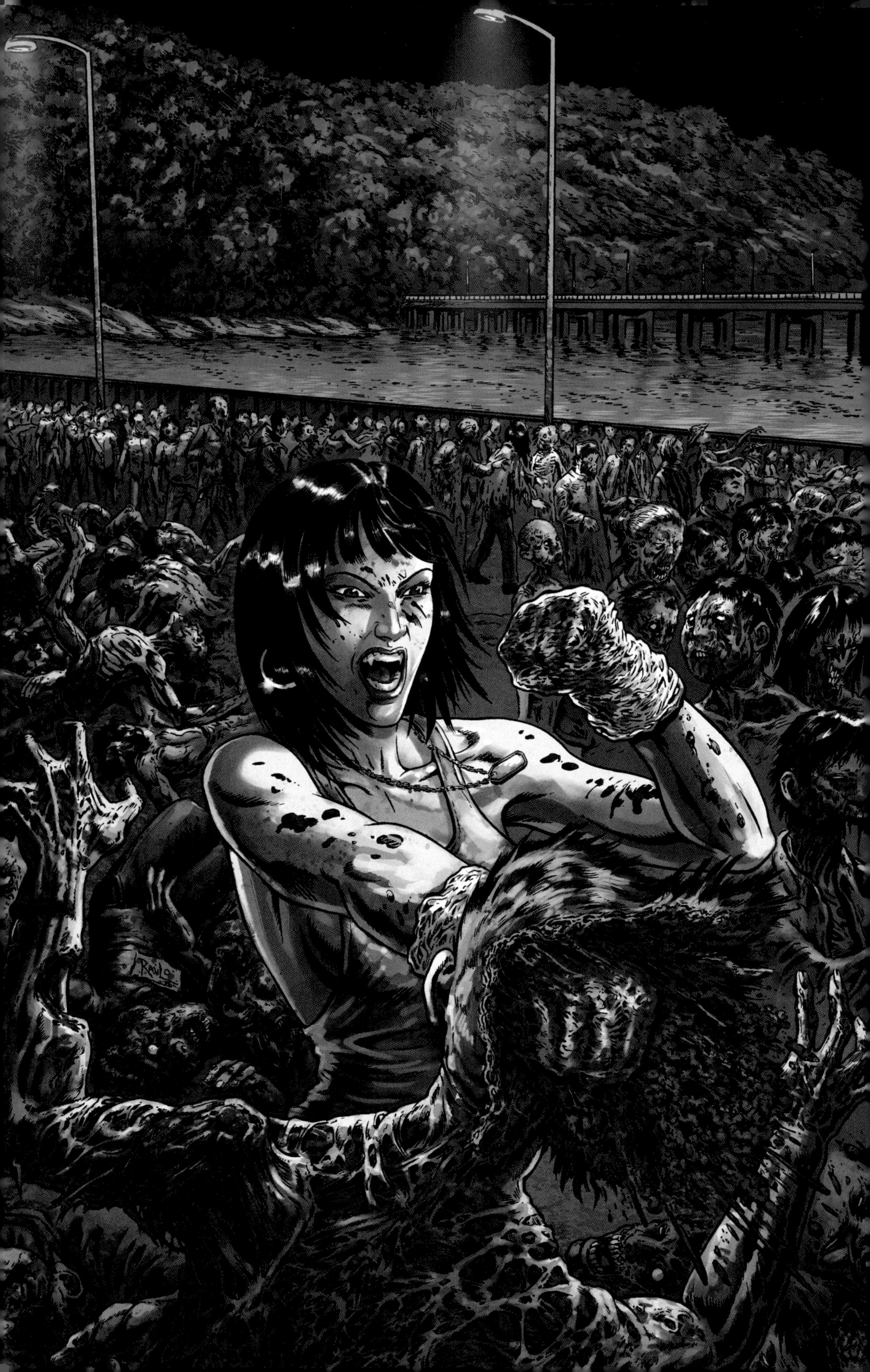

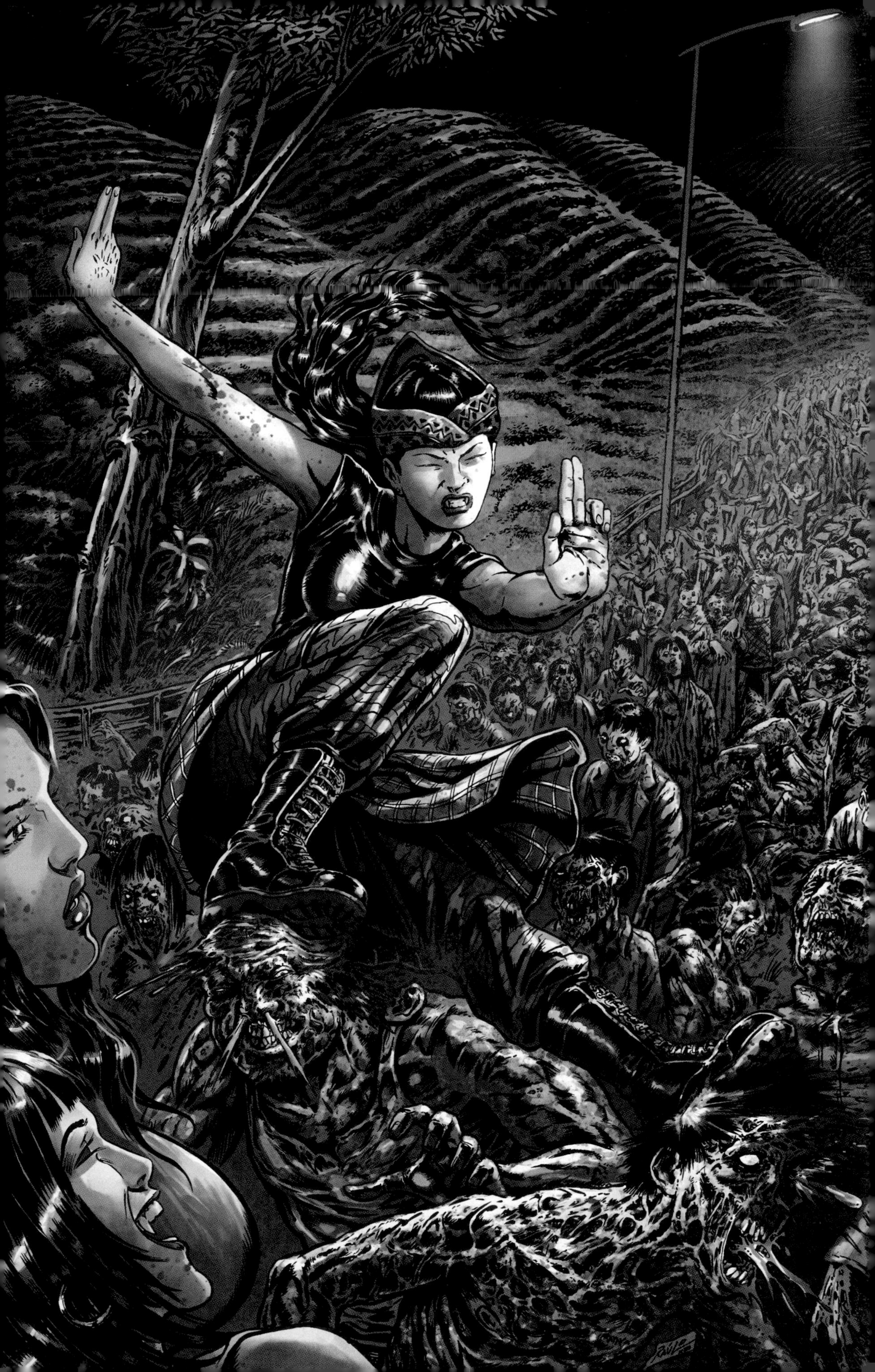

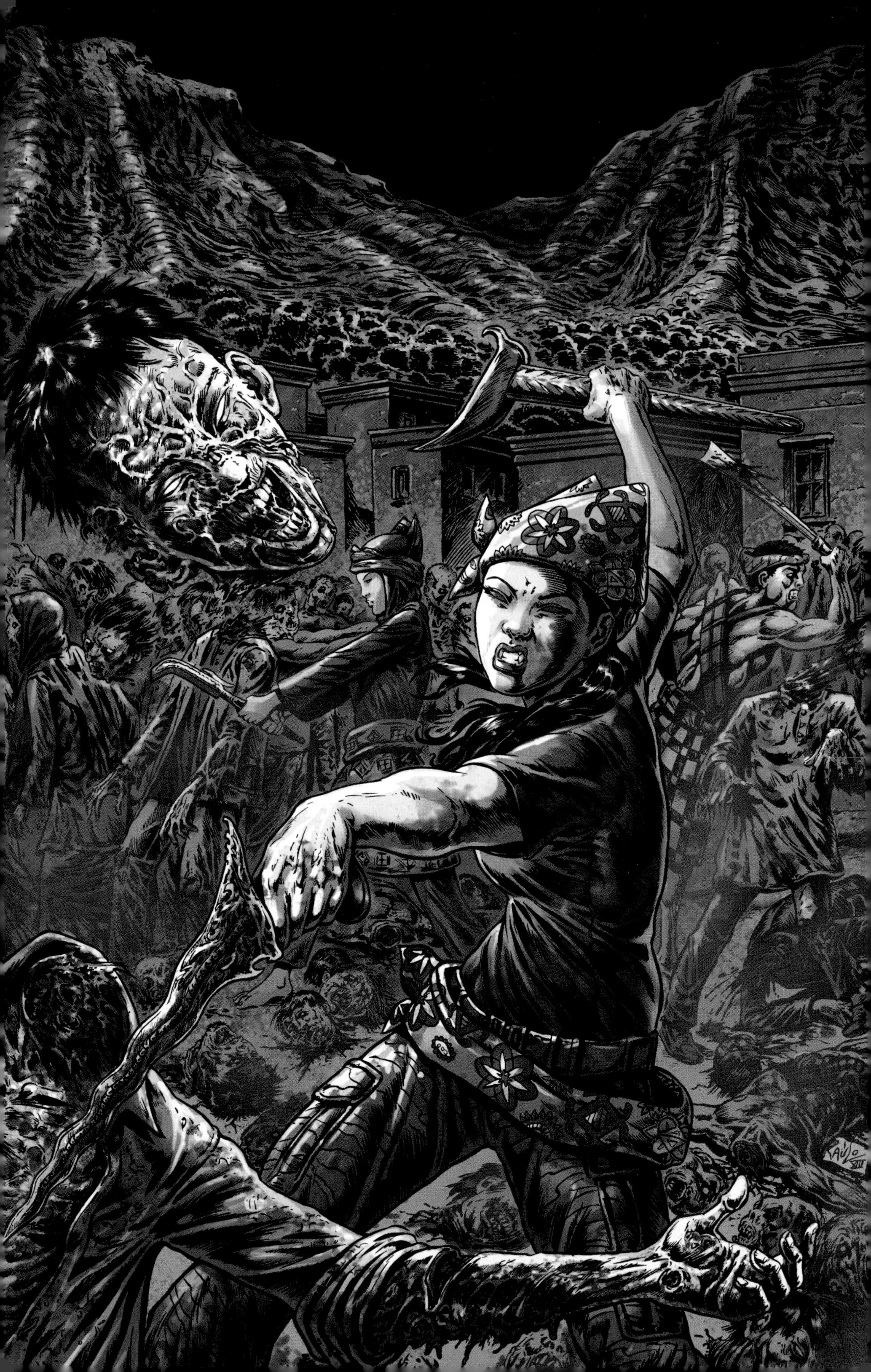

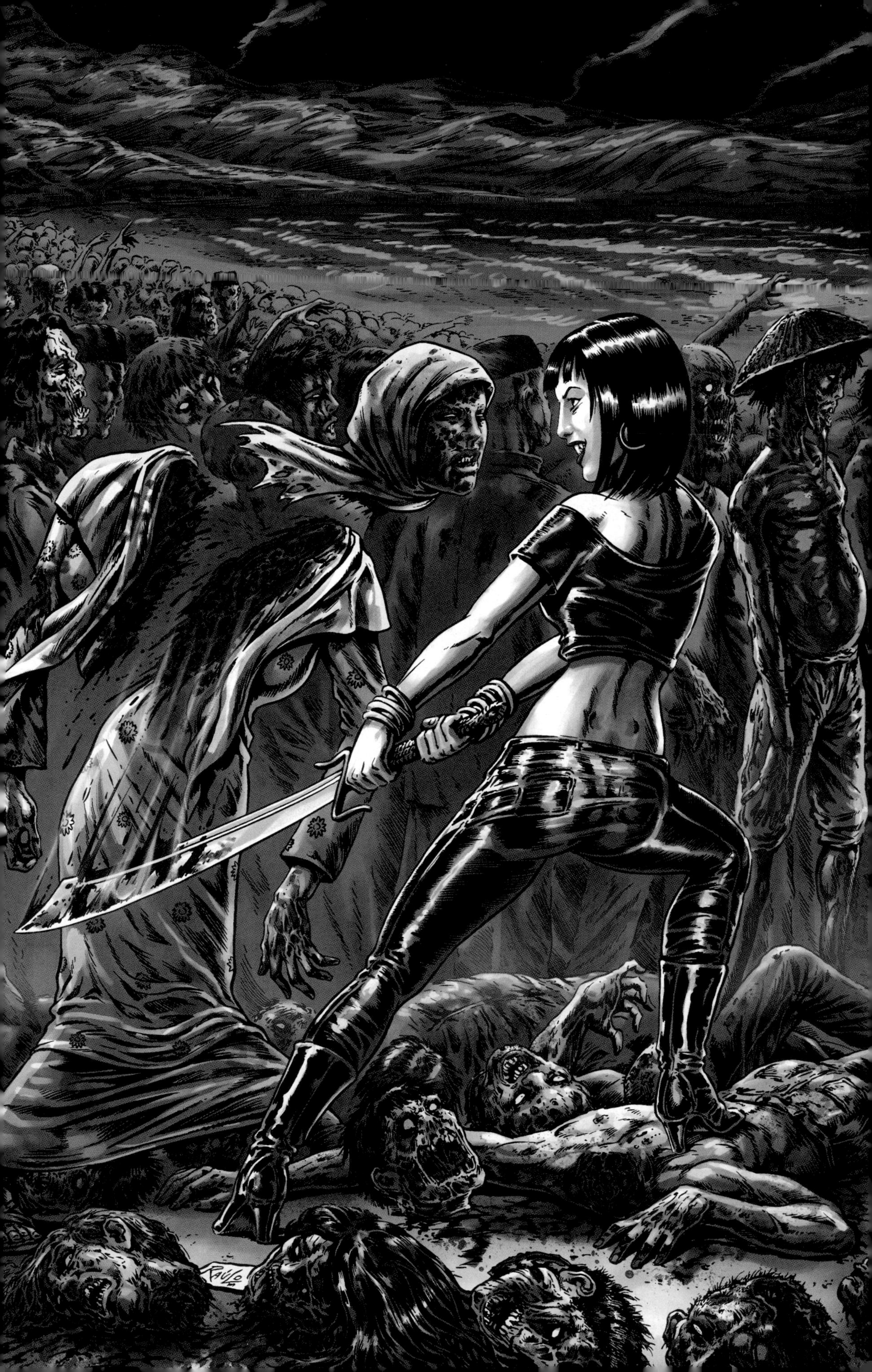

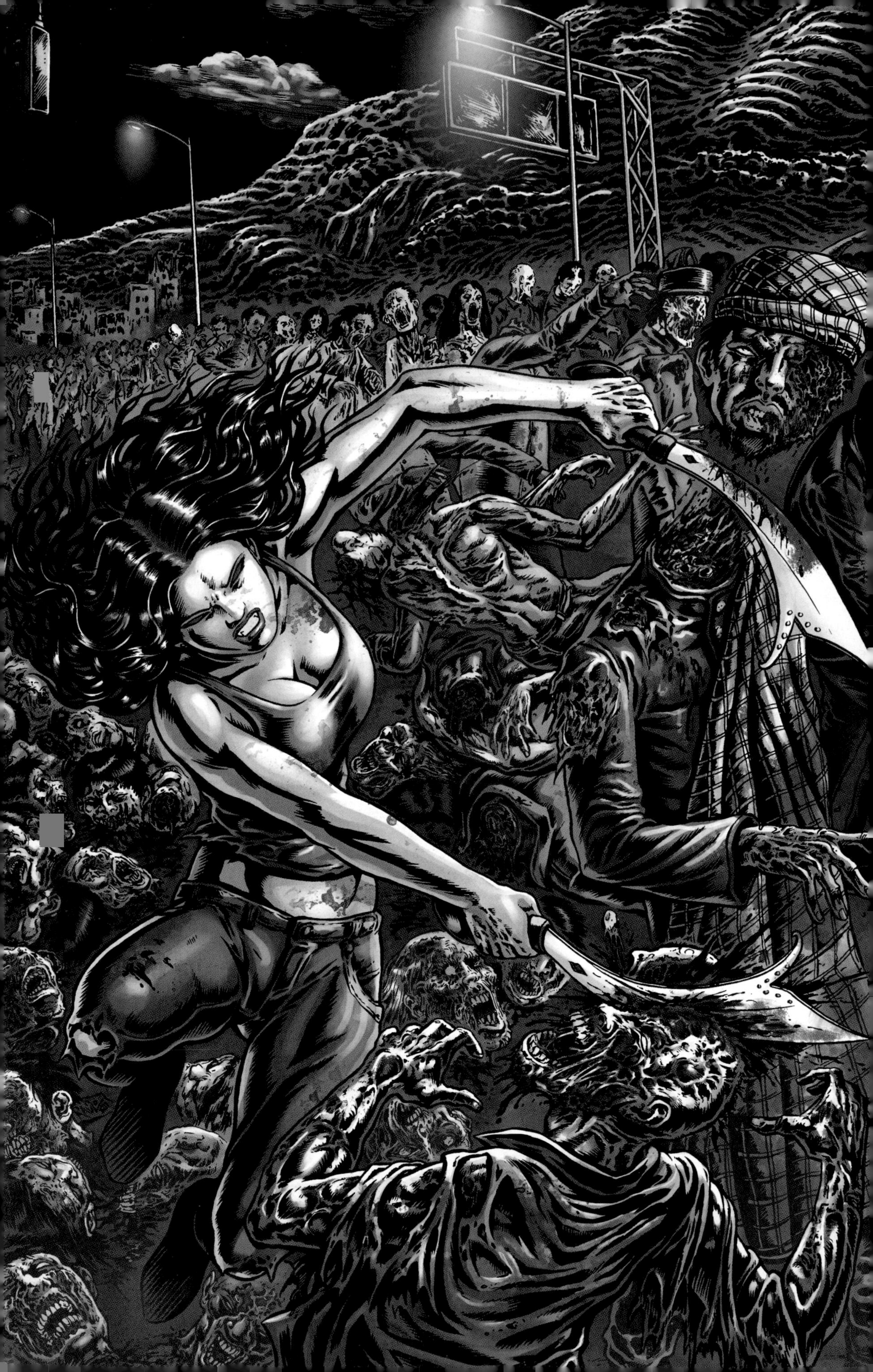

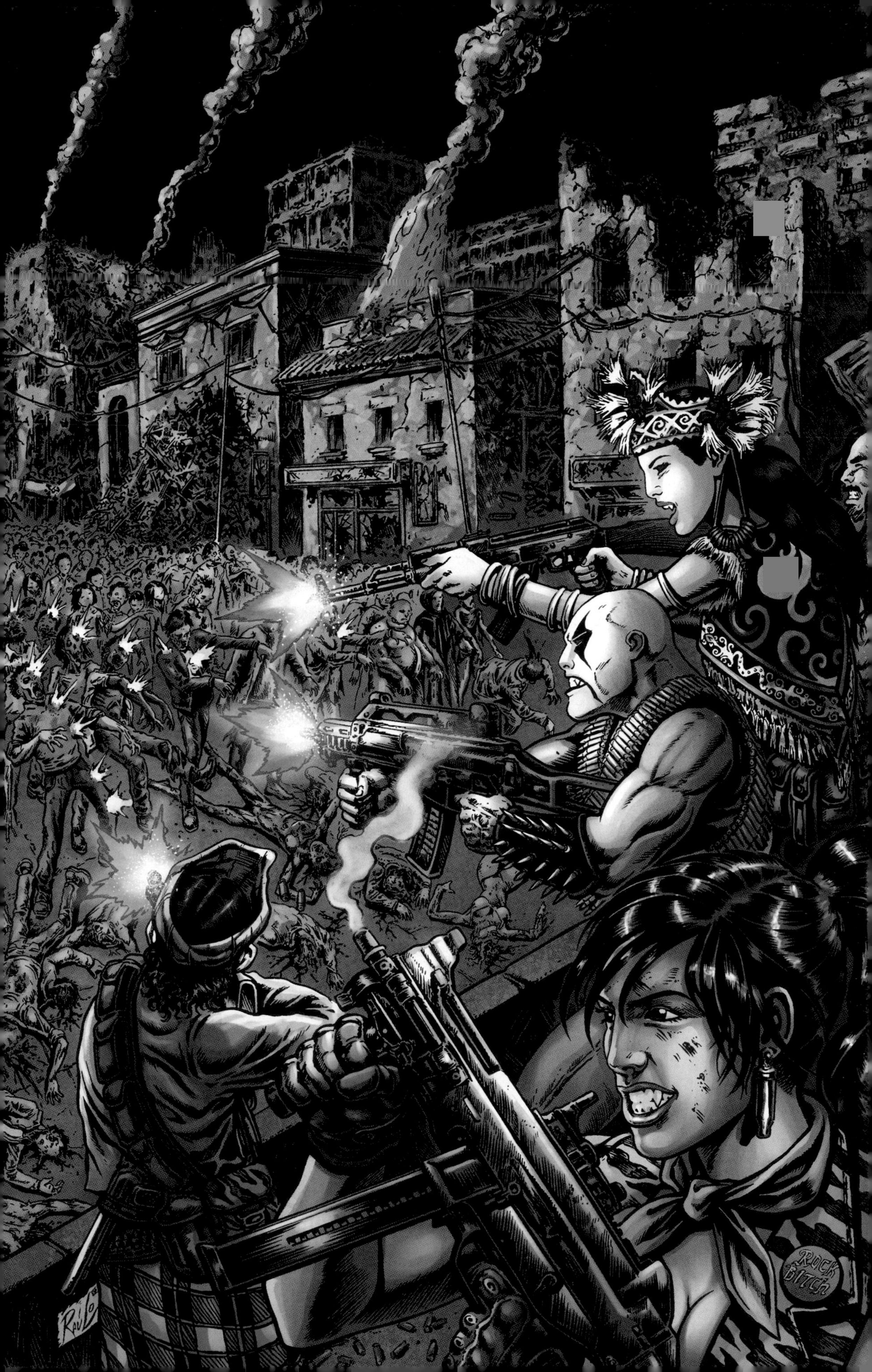
ROCK BITCh
RauLo

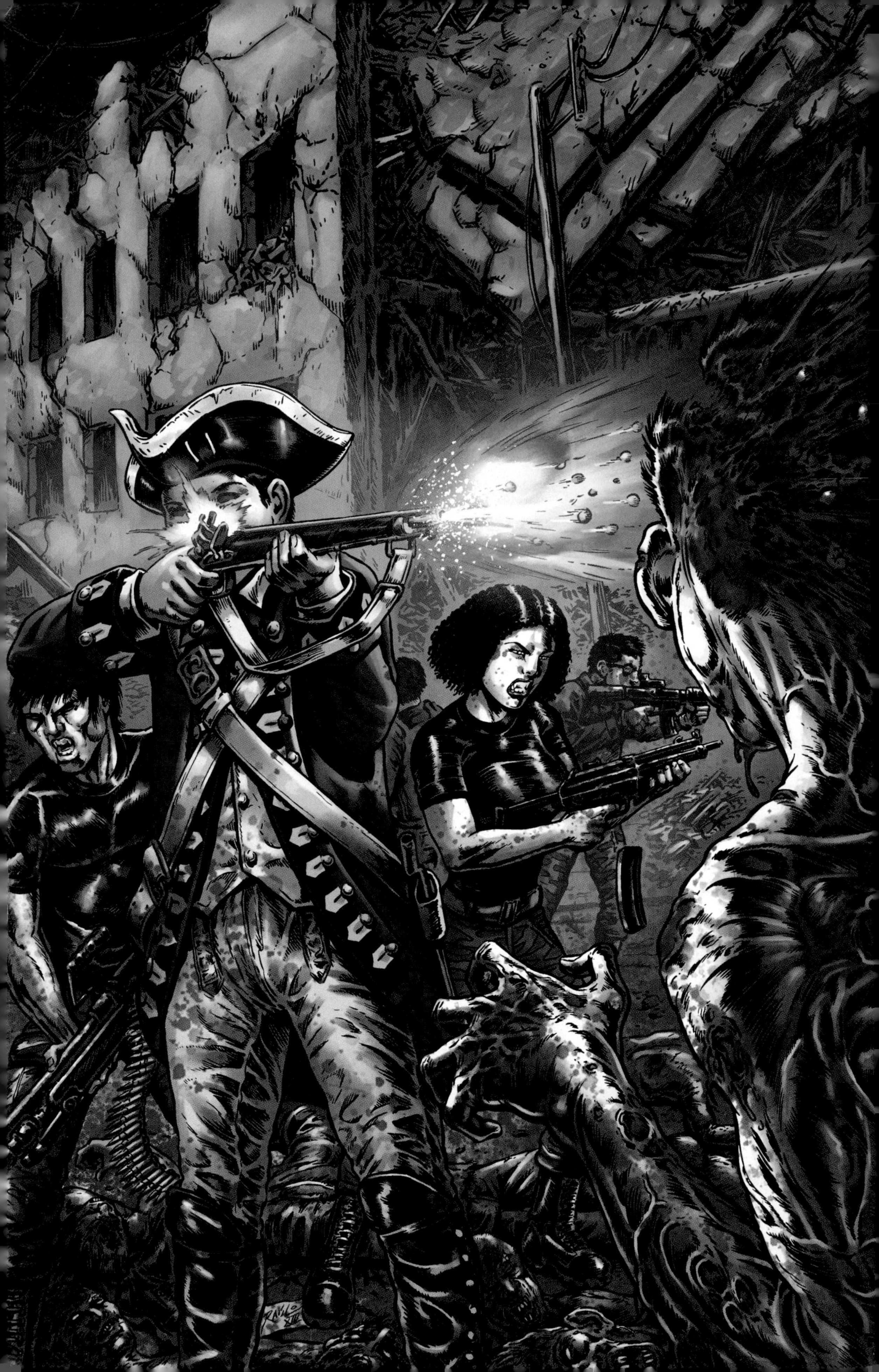

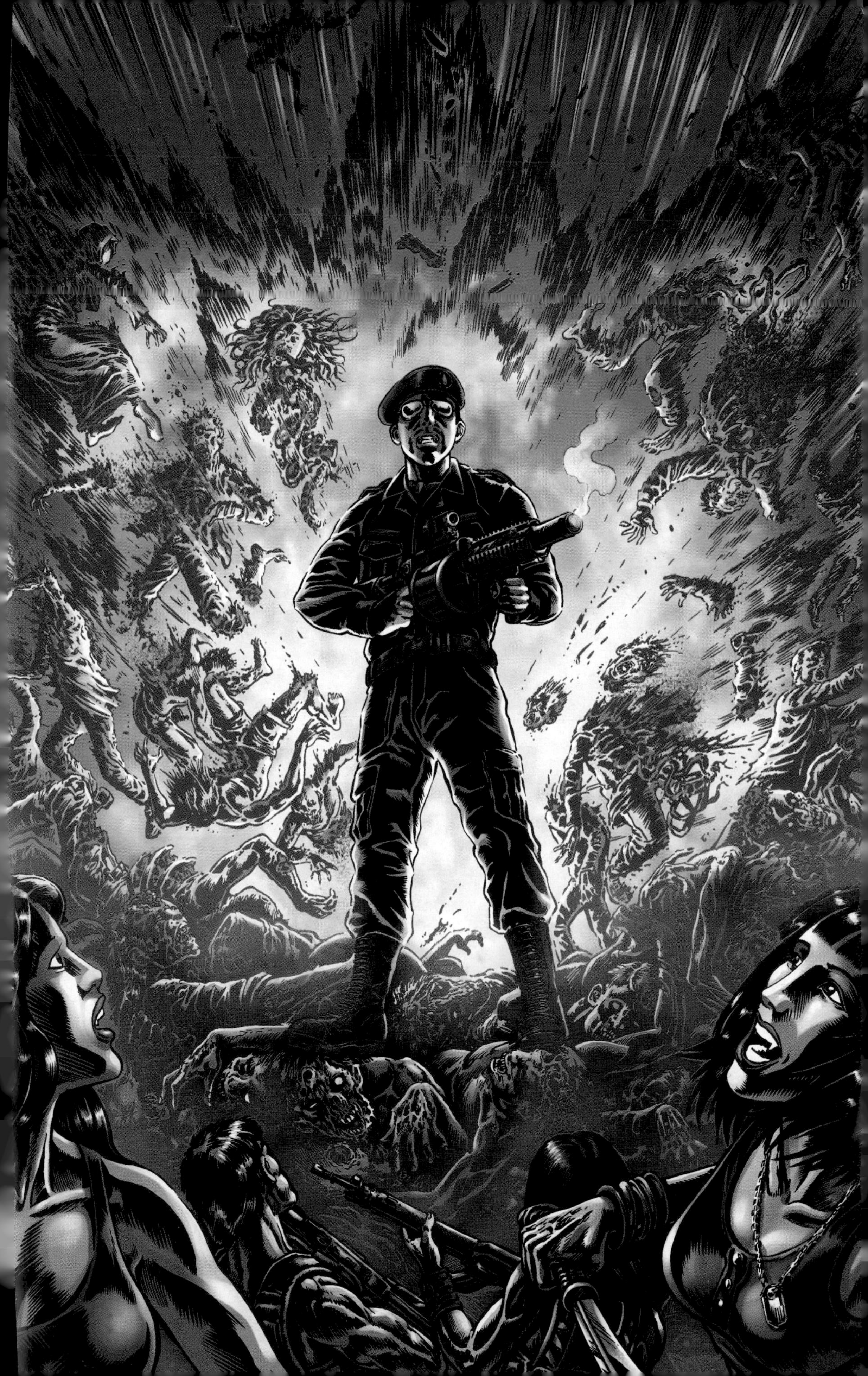

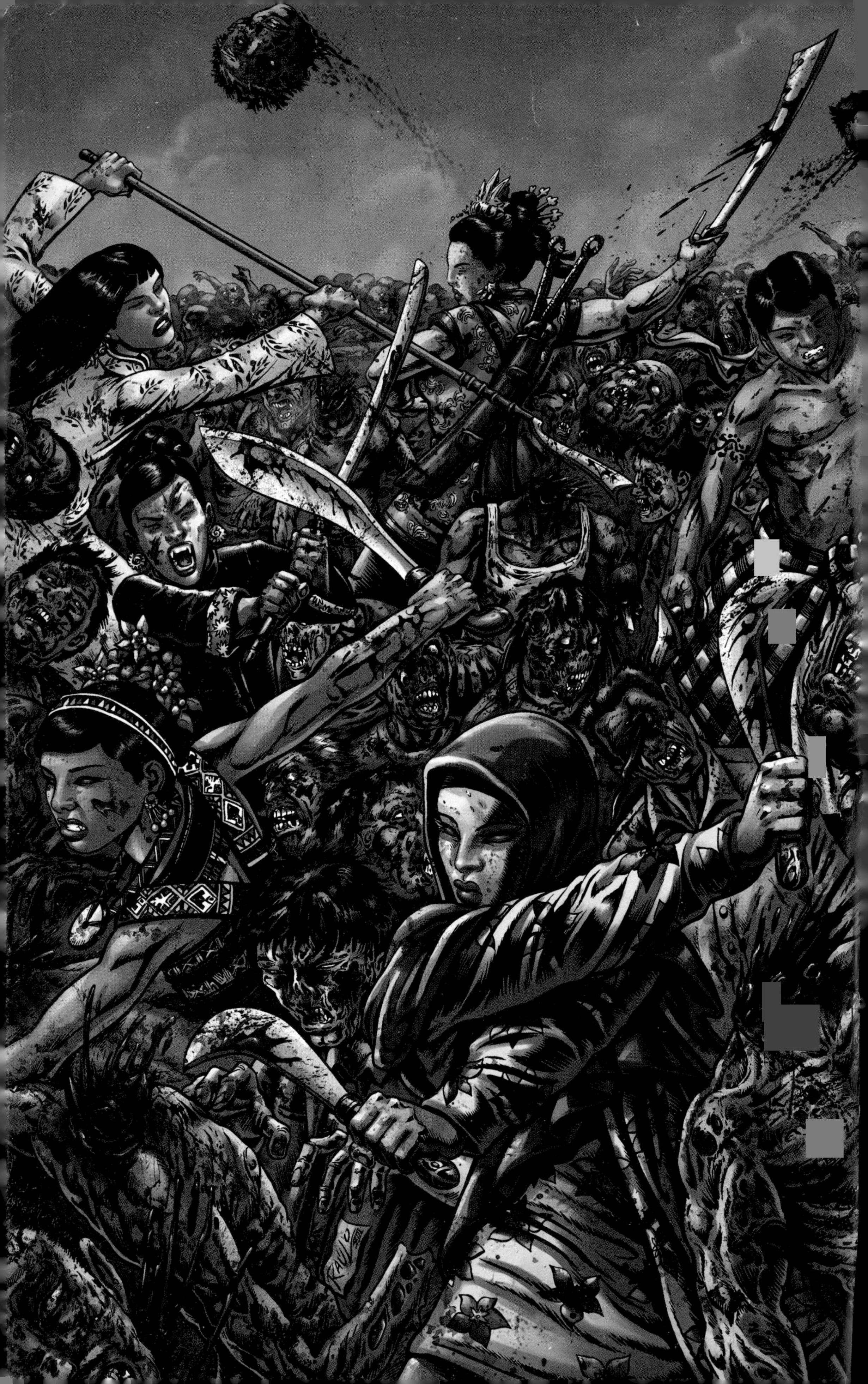